UNBENDING GENDER

UNBENDING GENDER

*Why Family and Work Conflict
and What to Do About It*

●

JOAN WILLIAMS

OXFORD
UNIVERSITY PRESS

OXFORD

UNIVERSITY PRESS

Oxford   New York
Athens   Auckland   Bangkok   Bogotá   Buenos Aires   Cape Town   Chennai
Dar es Salaam   Delhi   Florence   Hong Kong   Istanbul   Karachi   Kolkata   Kuala Lumpur
Madrid   Melbourne   Mexico City   Mumbai   Nairobi   Paris   São Paulo   Shanghai
Singapore   Taipei   Tokyo   Toronto   Warsaw

and associated companies in
Berlin   Ibadan

First published by Oxford University Press, Inc., 2000
198 Madison Avenue, New York, New York 10016

First issued as an Oxford University Press paperback, 2001

Oxford is a registered trademark of Oxford University Press

Library of Congress Cataloging-in-Publication Data
Williams, Joan, 1952–
   Unbending gender : why family and work conflict and what to do about it / Joan Williams.
   p.   cm.
Includes bibliographical references and index.
ISBN 0–19–509464–6 (Cloth)
ISBN 0-19-514714-6 (Pbk.)
   1. Work and family—United States.   2. Sexual division of labor—United States.
3. Mothers—employment—United States.   4. Family—Economic aspects—United States.
5. Work and family—United States—Forecasting.   I. Title.
HD4904.25.W55   1999
306.3'6—dc21   98–49089

Earlier versions of portions of this book have appeared in various journals: *Gender Wars:
Selfless Women in the Republic of Choice*, 66 N.Y.U. L. REV. 1559 (1991), reprinted with permission;
Is Coverture Dead? Beyond a New Theory of Alimony, 82 GEORGETOWN L. REV. 2227 (1994);
Implementing Antiessentialism: How Gender Wars Turn into Race and Class Conflict, 15 HARV.
BLACKLETTER L. J. (Spring 1999); *Do Wives Own Half? The Intersection of Property Law and
Family Law After Wendt*, 32 CONN. L. REV. (Fall 1999).

To two mothers who dedicated their lives to family work,
Jeanne Tedesche Williams and Ruth Fallon Dempsey

And to Jim, Rachel, and Nick, who taught me its true worth

Contents

•

What This Book Is About

Mary works as a secretary, from nine to six. She has been conflicted ever since her children were born. "Every day I leave my kids at child care, I think to myself: *What kind of a mother am I?* It's like I'm not raising my own kids." Today her kids are ten and sixteen. By the time she gets home, they have been at school and the after-school program for nearly ten hours. Because she is not around to drive them, her daughter cannot take ballet with her friends; her son is not in Boy Scouts. "If you can afford the cut in pay for the hours, the ideal situation would be to get home when they get home from school, 3 P.M., so you can take them to ballet and Boy Scouts." She asks her boss to cut down her hours. He won't hear of it.[1]

Susan worked hard in college and law school, and got a job doing work she loved. Then she had kids and cut back to a "part-time" forty-hour week. She became increasingly dissatisfied as she saw the best assignments going elsewhere and her own work becoming more and more routine. Meanwhile, her husband's high-pressure job kept him away from home much of the time. Ultimately they decided it would best for everyone if she quit. While she believes she made the right decision, she feels at a loss because she has to choose between work and family in a society that defines adulthood as having both. "There are so many hard questions. When there was no choice, maybe it was easier. Now there's a choice, which is good, but it's hard. . . . There are times when I'd really like to be out there in the career I more or less gave up. But I couldn't stand losing the time with my children."[2]

This book is about women like Mary and Susan, but it is not only about women. It is also about men like Doug, who works two jobs to support his family. Still, the bills mount up. He is more and more frustrated and depressed; finally he has to admit that his wife must go back to work. "I know she doesn't mind working, but it shouldn't have to be that way," he says morosely. "A guy should be able to support his wife and kids. But that's not the way it is these days, is it? Well, I guess those rich guys can, but not some ordinary Joe like me."[3]

It is also about men like Mark, an executive who regularly worked sixty or seventy hours a week while his wife stayed home with the kids. He missed his children's birthdays, their soccer games, the school play, and father-daughter banquets. When he died of a heart attack at fifty-seven, his widow invited no one from the company to speak at the funeral. "Why should I?" she asked a friend. "It was the *company* that killed him."[4]

This book is about how gender affects men as well as women; it is also about how gender affects children. Until their parents divorced a year ago, Sharon (age nine) and her brother, Chris (eighteen), lived in a single-family house in a solid middle-class neighborhood. Their mother, who had given up a career in broadcasting, earned $12,000 as a part-time drama teacher at the public school both children attended. Chris, an excellent student, hoped to go to a nearby Ivy League college. Today, after a bitter divorce in which their mother gave up all rights to alimony in exchange for uncontested custody, Sharon and Chris find themselves in straitened circumstances. Chris got into the high-prestige college he had hoped to attend, but could not go for lack of tuition money. At eighteen his child support stopped, so he is planning to work for a couple of years before attending the local state university. Sharon, Chris, and their mother live in a small apartment, far from Sharon's friends. The children's father retains $42,500 of his $50,000 salary.

Though each of these stories will resonate with many people, they do not seem intuitively linked. Works of social science and law as well as popular books have also failed to treat the phenomena they exemplify as being part of an overall pattern. This book provides a framework for understanding their commonality, for analyzing their causes and consequences, and for transforming the conditions that produce them. It links them all to our system of organizing market work and family work, which leads not only to work/family conflict, the time famine, working-class anger, and early death among successful men; it also leads to high rates of childhood poverty.

Feminists in recent years have focused on two major themes. One is the way women are disadvantaged by a particular type of sexuality: the eroticizing of dominance. The analysis of eroticized dominance has provided important insights into rape, domestic violence, and sexual harassment. Gay studies has explored the other major theme in contemporary gender studies: "gender-bending." An example of gender-bending is men in skirts.

While both these themes are important, neither captures the central dynamics underlying our gender arrangements with respect to market work and family work. In that context, the key fact is that gender has proved so *un*bending despite forty years of feminist challenge. To end the marginalization of mothers that persists up to the present day, we need to change not the ways we dress or who pierces their ears: We need to change the way we organize (market and family) work.

ACKNOWLEDGMENTS

I don't know if every book is the product of a community, but this one is. The book's frame was set at a lunch with Dorothy Ross and Linda Kerber, when they reassured me that there was enough there to write a book on ideal worker analysis. Dorothy also encouraged me to develop my analysis of domesticity as a strain of political rhetoric. Manuelita Ureta responded generously to my last-minute request for statistics on mothers' market work, generating new data despite her own busy schedule. Joan Retallack offered me a metaphor consult that led to my focus on the idea of gender as a force field. Sue Ross, Mike Selmi, Marley Weiss, Martha Chamallas, Marion Crain, and Amy Carpenter helped me work through Title VII and the Equal Pay Act, and helped formulate the potential lawsuits. The family law side of my argument became concrete only when Mitt Regan invited me to help organize and participate in a symposium on family law; Jana Singer, Naomi Cahn, and Karen Czapanskiy helped me work through my argument and saved me from my ignorance. The Interdisciplinary Reading Group on Gender helped me work through existing gender theory, including critical race theory, postcolonialism, and the analysis of gender as performance. Jim Kloppenberg kept insisting that I was a pragmatist, even during the era when I felt most estranged by neopragmatism, until I finally began to believe him. Randy Rabinowitz brought the *Trezza* case to my attention, and generally looked out for me on the labor side in a cordial and collegial way. Linda Chanow provided expertise with the work/life consulting community. Nancy Sachs contributed encouragement and vital on-the-ground expertise. Katherine Franke invited me to give an early version of Chapter 8 at her Feminist and Critical Race Theory Workshop. The Advisory and Leadership Committees of the Women's Rights Program at Harvard Divinity School provided interdisciplinary companionship and real-world feedback respectively; I thank Connie Buchanan for inviting my participation and Ann Braude for continuing it. Alda Facio, Lorena Fries, Lauren Gilbert, Marcela Huaita, Luz Rioseco, and Tammy Horn helped me immeasurably to reestablish my childhood ties with Latin America, which has greatly enriched my analysis; Marcella also tutored me in Peruvian family law and showed me the need for a cross-cultural analysis of family policy. Claudio Grossman has supported me in many ways, as a dean and as a friend.

Many friends and colleagues took time out of their pressured schedules to read drafts of individual chapters. These include: Kate Bartlett, Eileen Boris, Naomi Cahn, Martha Chamallas, Susan Connolly, Nancy Cott, Marion Crain, Adrienne Davis, Susan Eaton, Martha Ertman, Martha Fineman, Katherine Franke, Angela Harris, Linda Kerber, Andrew Marks, Martha Minow, Marcia Neave, Victoria Nourse, Joan Retallack, Jane Rice, Dorothy Roberts, Catherine Ross, Dorothy Ross, Nancy Sachs, Mike Selmi, Katharine Silbaugh, Jana Singer, Deborah Tannen, Chantal Thomas, Robin West, Lena Zezulin, and the Washington/Baltimore Feminist Law Professors' Reading Group.

I have also been lucky, thanks to the generous support of deans from American, University of Virginia, and Harvard Law Schools, to have had a wonderful group of research assistants, including Ashley Barr, Amy Carpenter, Linda Chanow, Britt Collins, Sue-Jean Kim, Aaron Minnis, Eleonora Somoza, and Wehtannah Tucker.

Many other people responded generously to my requests for help with various points of information despite other pressing demands on their time. These include Peter Cicchino, Egon Guttman, Mark Hager, Candy Kovacic-Fleischer, Binny Miller, Nell Jessup Newton, Diane Orentlicher, Andy Popper, and Suzanna Walters.

I want especially to thank those who provided crucial encouragement when I felt low, including Greg Alexander, Eileen Boris, Nancy Cott, Adrienne Davis, Terry Fisher, Jeffrey Goldberg, Jim Kloppenberg, Dorothy Ross, Sue Warga, Robin West, and Zipporah Wiseman.

For intellectual companionship on a day-to-day basis I thank Adrienne Davis, Co-Director of the Project on Gender, Work & Family. She has taught me more than I can repay, and has listened to me kvetch more than I care to remember. For administrative support that is as patient as it is intelligent and efficient, I thank Sharon Wolfe, without whom my productivity would be cut in half.

Very few authors indeed have the luck to have the kind of family support system I have relied on. Sarah Williams Ksiazek talked endlessly with me about the book, read many drafts, and offered excellent advice and support even when she was pressed for time and had enough worries of her own. Danny Goldhagen gave me the title and subtitle, and spent many hours working with me to make the book more readable; his generosity was particularly touching given his recent entry into our family. Roger Williams' vast knowledge of publishing and his unique generosity helped me in more ways than I can enumerate. Gina Cascone first got me thinking in concrete terms about writing for a nonacademic audience, read the entire manuscript, and was always ready to lend an ear. Norm Williams took my son for a crucial week when I had a deadline to meet. Jeanne Williams provided much of the inspiration for this book; she also offered good wishes, trips to Florida, and lovely grapefruits to sustain my momentum. Ruth Dempsey has long read and appreciated my law review articles, surely beyond the call of duty for a mother-in-law. Rachel and Nick have contributed by being such a gift in so many ways; as big kids they have been particularly generous and gracious in giving me the time necessary to get this book out the door.

My most profound and lasting debt is to Jim Dempsey. He has heard me develop the ideas in this book over a period of ten years, and has helped me formulate and reformulate them an almost infinite number of times. My most rigorous critic and most steadfast supporter, he has provided the kind of sustained assistance that makes a mother's career possible; often he has put his money where his mouth is despite societal pressures telling him he need not do so. Always interesting, secretly flexible, willing to get with the program, steady through the sturm und drang of life with Joan; choosing him remains the single best decision of my life.

UNBENDING GENDER

"I decided to quit my job and stay home. But it was my choice; I have no regrets. I am going to start a part-time quilt business."

"Wouldn't you really rather be able to continue in your career, earning at your current salary rate, while being able to give your children the time you feel they need?"

"Well, of course, that's what I really want."

The common assumption is that we are seeing the demise of domesticity in America. Domesticity is a gender system comprising most centrally of both the particular organization of market work and family work that arose around 1780, and the gender norms that justify, sustain, and reproduce that organization. Before then, market work and family work were not sharply separated in space or time. By the turn of the nineteenth century this way of life was changing, as domesticity set up the system of men working in factories and offices, while women (in theory) stayed behind to rear the children and tend the "home sweet home."

Domesticity remains the entrenched, almost unquestioned, American norm and practice.[1] As a gender system, it has two defining characteristics. The first is its organization of market work around the ideal of a worker who works full time and overtime and takes little or no time off for childbearing or child rearing. Though this ideal-worker norm does not define all jobs today, it defines the good ones: full-time blue-collar jobs in the working-class context, and high-level executive and professional jobs for the middle class and above. When work is structured in this way, caregivers often cannot perform as ideal workers. Their inability to do so gives rise to domesticity's second defining characteristic: its system of providing for caregiving by marginalizing the caregivers, thereby cutting them off from most of the social roles that offer responsibility and authority.

Domesticity introduced not only a new structuring of market work and family work but also a new description of men and women. The ideology of domesticity held that men "naturally" belong in the market because they are competitive and aggressive; women belong in the home because of their "natural" focus on relationships, children, and an ethic of care. In its original context, domesticity's descriptions of men and women served to justify and reproduce its breadwinner/housewife roles by establishing norms that identified successful gender performance with character traits suitable for those roles.[2]

Both the ideology and the practice of domesticity retain their hold. A recent survey found that fully two-thirds of Americans believe it would be best for women to stay home and care for family and children. Domesticity's descriptions of men and women persist in vernacular gender talk such as John Gray's *Men Are from Mars, Women Are from Venus*, as well as in the strain of feminist theory that associates women with an ethic of care.[3]

Even more important, market work continues to be structured in ways that perpetuate the economic vulnerability of caregivers. Their vulnerability stems from our definition of the ideal worker as someone who works at least forty hours a week year round. This ideal-worker norm, framed around the traditional life patterns of men, excludes most mothers of childbearing age.* Nearly *two-thirds* are not ideal workers even in the minimal sense of working forty hours a week all year. One-quarter still are homemakers, and many more work part time in an economy that rigorously marginalizes part-time workers.[4] Single as well as married mothers are affected: Never-married mothers are the group of women most likely to be at home.[5]

Moreover, full-time work is no guarantee of avoiding economic vulnerability. Even mothers who work full time often find themselves on the "mommy track." Full-time workers who cannot work overtime often suffer adverse job consequences because today many of the best jobs require substantial overtime. A rarely recognized but extraordinarily important fact is that jobs requiring extensive overtime exclude *virtually all mothers* (93 percent).[6]

Our economy is divided into mothers and others. Having children has a very strong negative effect on women's income, an effect that actually increased in the 1980s despite the fact that women have become better educated. The most dramatic figure is that mothers who work full time earn only sixty cents for every dollar earned by full-time fathers. Single mothers are most severely affected, earning the lowest percentage of men's average pay. Moreover, though the wage gap between men and women has fallen, the gap between the wages of mothers and others has widened in recent years. As a result, in an era when women's wages are catching up with men's, mothers lag behind. Given that nearly 90 percent of women become mothers during their working lives, this pattern is inconsistent with gender equality.[7]

If mothers have failed to achieve equality in market work, equality in the family has proved equally elusive. Buying and cooking food, doing dishes and laundry, caring for children—on average mothers spend thirty-one hours a week on these tasks. Many commentators have noted a striking contradiction: despite our self-image of gender equality, American women still do 80 percent of the child care and two-thirds of the housework.[8]

In short, the core elements of domesticity's organization of market work and family work remain intact, as indicated by the brief narratives with which this

---

* The data on this page are for mothers (of children under eighteen) who are twenty-five to forty-five years old—the key years both for child rearing and career development.

book begins. Women still specialize in family work. Men still specialize in market work. Market work continues to be framed around the assumption that ideal workers have access to a flow of family work few mothers enjoy. Social and cultural norms still sustain and reproduce this organization of (market and family) work.

Domesticity did not die; it mutated.[9] In the nineteenth century most married women were marginalized outside of the economy. Although women have re-entered market work, most remain marginalized today. This is not equality.

DOMESTICITY HURTS NOT ONLY WOMEN BUT ALSO MEN, CHILDREN, POLITICS, AND OUR EMOTIONAL LIFE

The commonplace observation is that women are hurt by the hard choices they face. Once the focus shifts away from women's choices to the gender system that sets the frame within which those choices occur, we can see that domesticity's peculiar structuring of market work and family work hurts not only women but also men, children, politics, and our emotional life.

Although the impoverishment of women upon divorce is a well-known phenomenon, commentators rarely link it with domesticity's system of providing for children's care by marginalizing their caregivers. Mothers marry, marginalize, and then divorce in a system that typically defines women's and children's postdivorce entitlements in terms of their basic "needs," while men's entitlements reflect the assumption (derived from domesticity) that they "own" their ideal-worker wage. This double application of the ideal-worker norm, first in market work, then in family entitlements, leaves roughly 40 percent of divorced mothers in poverty. Even in families that avoid impoverishment, the children of divorce often suffer downward mobility. A disproportionate number do not attain the educational level, or the class status, of their fathers.[10]

Domesticity takes a toll in a second way: by minimizing fathers' involvement. The current pattern of fathers largely exempted from child rearing is not eternal; it arose with domesticity. Before then, child rearing was considered too important to be left to women, and child-rearing manuals addressed fathers. Men were actively involved, in part because market work and family work were not yet geographically separated, so that fathers generally worked closer to home than most do today. Fathers' involvement also was considered necessary for orderly family governance. In a society that viewed women as the "weaker vessel," intellectually and morally inferior to men, it made no sense to delegate children's health, well-being, and eternal souls to the exclusive sphere of women. Domesticity changed parental roles. Child rearing came to be viewed as mothers' work, an allocation that persists up to the present day. One study estimated that an average American father spends twelve minutes a day in solo child care. Another reported that mothers spend about three times as much time as fathers in face-to-face interaction with their children.[11]

Domesticity also takes a toll on men by pressuring them to perform as ideal workers in an age when that often requires long hours of work; roughly one-third of fathers work forty-nine hours a week or more. The current fathers' rights and men's movements need to be seen not only as continued assertions of male privilege (which they are) but also as protests against the gender role domesticity assigns to men. That role includes both breadwinning and the narrow emotional range we associate with conventional masculinities: Men from Mars and women from Venus are by-products of domesticity.[12]

Domesticity also affects arenas of life we think of as unrelated to gender. It affects our politics in particularly destructive ways. Its relegation of child rearing to the private sphere intimates that the republic has no responsibility to play in raising its next generation of citizens. This is in sharp contrast to the understanding in France, for example, where child rearing is supported by generous leave policies and an extensive system of child-care centers, on the theory that the republic has an obvious interest in the health and development of its future citizens. At a more subtle level, as will be argued in chapter 6, the rise of domesticity accompanied an important change in the understanding of virtue. Whereas in classical republican thought virtue referred to the manly pursuit of the common good in the public sphere, under domesticity the preservation of the republic was thought to depend on the success of women in raising the next generation of citizens in the domestic sphere. Thus, with the rise of domesticity, virtues formerly thought to belong to civic life were relegated to private life. Communitarians who protest contemporary liberalism's neutral stance on issues of morality rarely recognize domesticity's role in redefining virtue as something that belonged in private as opposed to public life.[13]

Domesticity organizes our everyday tasks, our emotions, our politics. My goal is not to advocate sameness or androgyny, but to deconstruct domesticity and encourage the development of new ways of organizing work as well as family, emotional, and political life. The guiding principles are that society needs not only market work but also family work, and that adults who do family work should not be marginalized.

DECONSTRUCTING THE IDEAL-WORKER NORM IN MARKET WORK AND FAMILY ENTITLEMENTS: MESSAGES FOR LITIGATORS AND POLICY MAKERS

This book presents not only an analysis but a call to action. It proposes three shifts that point to a new paradigm I call "reconstructive feminism" (but could equally well be called "family humanism"). The first calls for eliminating the ideal-worker norm in market work; the second calls for eliminating the ideal-worker norm in family entitlements. The third calls for changing the ways we talk about gender.

Eliminating the ideal-worker norm in market work requires restructuring work around the values people hold in family life, in particular around the norm of parental care—the sense that children should be cared for (to a certain, undefined, extent) by their parents, not by "strangers." Work/family activists have tried for twenty years to persuade companies to offer part-time tracks and other flexible policies by showing the productivity and other benefits to be gained by doing so. The success of these efforts has been quite limited. Their primary result is a pyrrhic victory: a set of mommy-track policies that offer flexibility at the price of work success. What we need is not a mommy track, but market work restructured to reflect the legitimate claims of family life. This requires a new legal theory that defines the current structuring of market work as discrimination against women. Chapter 3 provides one.

It does so by showing how the current design of work discriminates against mothers. This analysis starts from the fact that the current ideal worker is someone who works full time (and often overtime) and who can move if the job "requires it." This way of defining the ideal worker is not ungendered. It links the ability to be an ideal worker with the flow of family work and other privileges typically available only to men.

Take elite jobs, in law firms or executive positions. To succeed in either context, workers typically not only must be able to do good work but also must be able to do it for fifty to seventy hours a week. Few mothers can do this because few women have spouses willing to raise their children while the women are at work. Another common job requirement in academics and management is the ability to relocate when opportunities arise, to advance in the profession or even to get a job. Few mothers can do this. As a consequence, women who are academics are more likely to drop out or to find themselves in adjunct or other non-tenure-track positions and are less likely to end up in tenure-track positions or in elite institutions. "Success" requires ideal-worker status. Few women have it.[14]

Requiring workers to have the social power of men excludes disproportionate numbers of women. Consequently, employers may be liable under federal antidiscrimination laws when they design workplaces in ways that require workers to have the flow of family work and other privileges available to few women. Companies will claim that their traditional practices are required by business necessity. But this is not so—for twenty years, studies have shown businesses that "family-friendly" policies are both feasible and cost-efficient.[15]

The second major shift required by reconstructive feminism is to eliminate the ideal-worker norm in family entitlements. Chapter 4 proposes that economic entitlements upon divorce should be redefined to eliminate the unstated principle that the ideal worker owns "his" wage: the he-who-earns-it-owns-it rule. This rule is inappropriate in a system in which the ideal worker's wage is the product of two adults: the ideal worker's market work and the marginalized caregiver's family work. When two family members work together to produce an asset, it makes no sense to award it unilaterally to one of them.

Each of these proposals will confront a basic challenge: Why change a system in which women often describe economic marginalization as their own choice? "My choice to stay at home is an expression of what is important to me," said the at-home mother celebrated in a recent *New York Times Magazine*.[16]

When mothers use choice rhetoric, they are being "realistic" in a society where the best jobs require ideal workers to have the ability to relocate and to command a flow of family work few mothers enjoy. Allowing women the "choice" to perform as ideal workers without the privileges that support male ideal workers is not equality. It is a system with "built-in headwinds" that discriminate against women (to quote a landmark employment discrimination case).[17]

If women are offered the option of keeping the jobs they want with the schedules they need, they stop describing marginalization as their choice. An example is the woman quoted at the start of this introduction, who readily agreed that what she really wanted was to stay in her original career, restructured to eliminate the current ideal-worker norm. To quote economist Ann Bookman, "What exactly are 'voluntary' part-time workers choosing? Are they choosing to work without health insurance or pensions? Are they choosing to have few opportunities for job advancement? . . . I don't think so."[18]

Women may choose not to perform as ideal workers, but they do not choose the marginalization that currently accompanies that decision. Chapter 1 examines the common claim that mothers' marginalization reflects their own choice. It explores how domesticity's ordering of family work and market work sets up force fields that frame women's choices, pulling men back into the ideal-worker role, and women into lives cut off from the social roles that offer authority and responsibility. This description shows our current gender arrangements as unyielding and unbending.

Chapter 2 examines the classic strategy feminists have proposed to change domesticity's ordering of (market and family) work. That strategy, which delegated child care to the market so that mothers could work full time, rested on assumptions that left intact too many of the structures of domesticity. Chapter 2 critiques those assumptions, and proposes a shift in feminist strategy designed to build a new feminist coalition. To create such a coalition requires new ways of talking that avoid old battles. These changes in gender talk, which are the third major shift advocated by reconstructive feminism, are the subject of the last four chapters of the book.

GENDER TALK: HOW TO BUILD
EFFECTIVE COALITIONS FOR GENDER CHANGE

We need to change the ways we talk about gender (including the ways feminists do so) in several different ways. The first requires a shift away from the current focus on sex and violence to a focus on the design of (market and family) work and the entitlements that flow from it. This is not to say that recent work on domestic violence, sexual harassment, and pornography is not important. It is, as is the insight that dominance is often eroticized. But the eroticizing of dominance is not the only gender dynamic at work in everyday life. The relationship of market work to family work, currently defined by domesticity, is another site for the production of gender that is equally important.

If the eroticizing of dominance helps us understand how men's sexual fantasies get translated into social power, a focus on work and family admits us to cherished dreams shared by men and women alike. If we woke up tomorrow and found a society where dominance was not eroticized, people still would be thwarted in the dreams they hold for their children and for themselves. Domesticity's warping of our social and family lives would still exist. As long as domesticity governs the organization of family work and market work, people's aspirations for family life will remain pitted against their aspirations for autonomy, self-sufficiency, and (if they are lucky) self-fulfillment through productive work.

Once domesticity takes center stage, we notice that—contrary to the assumption that women are united by gender—gender unites men but divides women. Chapter 5 argues that domesticity creates unnecessary gender wars between ideal-worker women and women whose lives are framed around caregiving. These often take on elements of race and class conflict, alienating working-class women and women of color from feminism. Chapter 5 explores in depth the differences in how domesticity is lived and imagined in different class and race contexts. It draws on the *antiessentialist* critique in feminist jurisprudence, which shows how traditional feminism represents the viewpoint of privileged white women. It turns antiessentialism from a critique of feminism into a way to design new strategies for building coalitions for gender change.

Chapters 6 and 7 explore the particularly bitter gender wars often called the "sameness/difference debate." This debate, which occurs both in feminist theory and in the popular arena over books such as Deborah Tannen's *You Just Don't Understand*, involves neither sameness nor difference; what it involves is women's relationships to domesticity. Chapter 6 examines how to defuse the debate over the ideology of domesticity, and its descriptions of women as "naturally" focused on relationships, children, and an ethic of care.

Chapters 7 and 8 are addressed to policy makers and to theorists. Chapter 7 discusses the gender wars that arise in policy debates over workplace benefits and family entitlements (the so-called "special treatment/equal treatment" debate). Its discussion develops a new model that melds equality analysis with an analysis of gender and power. The result is clear guidance for how to conform workplace leave and benefits policies, and rules concerning entitlements based on family work, to the mandates of equality. Chapter 7 also argues that equal treatment of men and women requires the elimination of masculine norms, which will sometimes require affirmative action.

Chapter 8 theorizes reconstructive feminism, which stems from John Dewey's vision of reconstruction in philosophy. Its goal is to turn feminists' attention outside the academy and toward the project of building wide popular coalitions that will create demand for fundamental social change. For this project, we need new ways of talking about social power. American feminists have often assumed that, if we need a language of gender and power, Catharine MacKinnon's dominance feminism is the one we need. Chapter 8 explores the limitations of dominance feminism and proposes a new way of talking about gender fundamentally different from MacKinnon's language of men's "feet on our neck." Given that domesticity organizes our aspirations as well as our everyday life, and given the ways domesticity shapes both our institutions and our identities, the most effective strategies for gender change use domesticity's own momentum to flip and bend it into new configurations, like a judo master flipping an opponent many times her weight. I call this strategy domesticity in drag; it separates the positive elements of domesticity from the destructive ones with which they are now so tightly intertwined. My insistent focus on strategic thinking raises important questions about how not to lose touch with authenticity when constructing coalitions in a world where gender means diverse things to different people. The book ends by examining where to draw the line in the interests of personal integrity, and how to justify that decision in a world without absolute truth.

SOME PROVISOS

Several provisos are in order. Much of the discussion in this book has focused on what is usually called the "traditional" family: a mother-caregiver, a father-breadwinner, and their children. Family studies stress an age of "postmodern" families with a wide variety of family structures.[19]

The focus on mother-caregiver, father-breadwinner families is appropriate for several reasons. First, recent data suggest that the decline in the number of married-couple families has slowed dramatically. More important is that even though the family as defined by domesticity has loosened its hold on social life, it retains a viselike grip on popular aspirations: the white picket fence in our heads is a central part of this narrative. Most important, however, is the fact that most postmodern families retain the mother-caregiver, father-breadwinner structure even if the parents are no longer married or never were. In virtually all families headed by never-married mothers, and in the nearly 90 percent of divorces where mothers retain custody, the father continues to be supported by a flow of family work from the mother of his children even if she is not his wife. In fact, domesticity's mandates affect divorced and never-married mothers even more harshly than married ones: While married mothers have access to an ideal worker's wage, many single mothers do not. This leads to poverty in single-parent families, as women marginalized by motherhood try to perform both as ideal workers and as caregivers in a system that assumes that all ideal workers are supported by a marginalized caregiver, and that all caregivers are linked with a breadwinner.[20] To the extent that certain racial and ethnic communities have a high percentage of single mothers, the current system penalizes them even more severely than it does the white community.

A second proviso concerns a lack of focus on gay families. This reflects the fact that the literature on the gendering of gay families is still young. From talking with divorce lawyers who specialize in gay partners, my sense is that many gay male couples often play quite traditional gender roles. In sharp contrast, the growing literature on lesbian parenting suggests that fewer lesbian couples track domesticity's gender roles than do other types of couples. The hold of domesticity's gender roles on couples that include a man reflects the powerful pull of the ideal-worker norm on men, whose self-image is so often linked with work success. It is important to remember that ideal workers and marginalized caregivers come in different body shapes; gender roles are logically independent of sexual orientation. Also, to the extent that lesbian relationships are egalitarian, they offer models of caregiving freed from the structures imposed by domesticity.

A third proviso is that although most of the discussion focuses on child rearing, it is only one type of caregiving. The focus on child rearing reflects in part its symbolic importance, for domesticity treats it as the paradigm case of caregiving. It reflects as well its practical importance: Roughly 90 percent of women will become mothers at some point during their work lives, and over 40 percent of workers are caring for children under eighteen. Nonetheless, a system that marginalizes caregivers hurts anyone with caregiving responsibilities: that includes not only parents but children. One recent survey found that more than one-quarter of workers over fifty have elder-care responsibilities, as do one-fifth of those over thirty.[21] These issues are further discussed in chapter 3.

A final proviso is that although this book concerns the settled household life, this focus is not meant to imply that is the only meaningful way to live. Alternatives have always existed, from monkhood to hippiedom, with many in between. Indeed, one prerequisite for healthy households is to provide alternatives for people not suited to household life. The central argument of this book is that conventional family life does not work well for those who live it. I cannot stress enough that this is not the same as saying that everyone should live conventionally.

PART I

•

Unbending Gender
in Social Life

CHAPTER ONE

•

Is Domesticity Dead?

"They have this arrangement. He earns the money and
she takes care of the house."

To the Editor:

As a full-time mother and "home manager," I greatly enjoyed Nina Barrett's
piece on motherhood [in the *Yale Alumni Magazine*]. Unfortunately, it took me
quite a while to get through it—my 14-month-old daughter pulled down the
contents of a shelf onto her head, wanted to hear *Hop on Pop* for the 15th time
that day, demanded a rice cake, requested assistance in dismantling the
stereo, and otherwise made claims on my expensively educated intellect.

I left a Yale doctoral program in 1988, disillusioned with academic life.
Since then, like Barrett, I have found my ambitions for a career—any career—

gradually being submerged by the desire to raise my children at home. I do work part-time, as a freelance copy editor. But working in sweat clothes at the dining room table, surrounded by toys and unfinished housework, is not exactly a fulfilling professional experience. Yet despite occasional longings for the world of "real" work, I am sure that I have made the right choice—for me.[1]

Women often use choice rhetoric to describe their decisions in favor of domesticity. So does everybody else. Economists have an entire "human capital" literature that attributes women's disadvantaged workforce position to the fact that they "self-select" into jobs that require less education and lower levels of skill. That literature has been extensively studied elsewhere, so I will give only one example from a paper filled with equations. Its conclusion pits choice against discrimination and concludes that "if women were to choose the same work patterns as men then they could and would enter more skilled occupations, and the male-female wage gap would be substantially reduced. To the extent that sex differences in labor force participation patterns are not themselves caused by discrimination, sex differences in occupations and wages are thus the result of free choices made by men and women."[2]

Courts use choice rhetoric, too. On the family side, a 1992 New York court refused to award a wife alimony on the grounds that she had chosen not to work for a year outside the home while her husband attended college. On the work side, the preeminent case is *Equal Employment Opportunity Commission (EEOC) v. Sears, Roebuck & Co.* In *Sears* the EEOC presented strong statistical evidence of discrimination, documenting that men predominated in high-paying commission sales jobs while women did lower-paying noncommission work, out of proportion to the presence of each sex in the qualified labor force. EEOC evidence also showed that the selection criteria for commission sales jobs were designed with men in mind: Illustrative questions asked if the applicant spoke in a low-pitched voice and participated in hunting, football, boxing, or wrestling. The *Sears* courts, however, heightened the standard to establish a prima facie case in sex discrimination. Under the new standard, the EEOC was required to show that the female employees at Sears were as interested in taking commission sales positions as their male counterparts. Both the trial and appeals courts accepted Sears' argument that women's lack of representation represented only their lack of interest in commission sales work.[3]

Yale law professor Vicki Schultz has documented that courts in sex discrimination cases often accept the argument that women "lack interest" in traditionally male positions. Schultz has argued persuasively that women's choices are framed by the actions of their employers, since most ordinary women do not spend time trying to get jobs for which women are never hired. In stressing employers' role, Schultz minimizes the role of women's "family responsibilities." Her point is apt for women in traditionally male blue-collar jobs, the focus of Schultz's study. But mothers' load of family work often does affect their workforce participation (as opposed to their job performance). A recent study by Jane Waldfogel, after controlling for potential work experience and for observable characteristics such as education, found that nearly half (45 percent) of the gender gap at age thirty is due to women's family status. Another 19 percent reflects women's lower levels of work experience. These data suggest that, very conservatively, at least two-thirds of the wage gap between men and women reflects women's load of family work. (This is not to deny that part of the remaining gap reflects old-fashioned sex discrimination.)[4]

In fact, if one reads studies by labor economists and lawyers, on one hand, and by family law scholars, on the other, a striking pattern emerges. The labor litera-ture often minimizes the impact of women's family work on their market work, while the family-related literature documents it in detail. Both use accurate data; they just focus on different groups. Labor economists focus on women who per-form as ideal workers, often in traditionally male jobs. These women's workforce participation often is not affected by their "second shift" of family work. The fam-ily literature focuses on homemakers and women who work part time, whose workforce participation clearly has been affected by the division of labor at home.[5]

The fear often expressed is that if feminists acknowledge the impact of women's load of family work, employers will say, "See, we told you so. That's why we don't want to hire women." Note, though, that the fact that *some* women's family work interferes with their workforce participation does not give employers an excuse to discriminate against *all* women. What the data show is that mothers often do not take jobs that require them to perform as ideal workers, not that women who do take such jobs perform worse than men. No one denies the fact that many women *do* perform as ideal workers. No one need deny that many do not.

Acknowledging the impact of the second shift makes women vulnerable only if one accepts the claim that women's "choice" to marginalize precludes discrimina-tion. That is the claim I challenge in this chapter. "Choice" is only a defense against discrimination if women's marginalization is freely chosen in the same sense that some people choose Mars Bars over Baby Ruths.

Mothers' choices to drop out or cut back on work are not like that; this chapter offers a close study of what they *are* like. The best text I have found for this purpose is a 1985 book by Deborah Fallows, entitled *A Mother's Work*. I will focus at length on Fallows' stunningly honest description of the process by which one woman aban-doned her career in linguistics in order to stay home with her children, because it allows us to examine the social dynamics that lead many women into domesticity's traditional "arrangement." Although Fallows' book has not often been discussed in feminist texts, it is important because she provides an articulate defense of a gen-der system we simultaneously live and deny. Fallows had the courage and the intel-lectual resources to defend that system in an articulate and principled way, and the ability to get her account published and publicized. (Her husband is James Fallows, one of the most successful journalists in Washington, D.C.)

Fallows' book does not provide a perfect text, for in some ways her experience is not representative. She clearly belongs to an inside-the-Beltway elite. Yet the viewpoint Fallows expresses represents what many Americans think; I hear it all the time, on the playground, in women's magazines, behind closed doors at work.

As will be discussed in chapter 5, Fallows expresses sentiments that are pervasive among working-class individuals as well as among more privileged people. If two-thirds of mothers of childbearing age do not perform as ideal workers, we need to know how they come to that decision.[6]

For the remainder of this chapter, I examine the constraints that frame women's choices. I do so by placing Fallows' story in two historical contexts. The first is the transition from status to affect, documented by legal historian Reva Siegel: a shift from a system where gender arrangements are described in the language of hierarchy to one in which they are described in the language of emotion. The second context is domesticity, the gender system that has already been introduced. A note of caution: My description will rely on the most developed literatures (on New England and the South). Regional differences and variations over time—so important for historians, whose goal is to capture the complexity of the past—are not as important here, where my goal is a snapshot designed to highlight the continuities between past and present. I will focus on the changes in domesticity over time only when I want to highlight specific shifts for specific reasons.[7]

FROM STATUS TO AFFECT

The first useful perspective is suggested by the work of legal historian Reva Siegel. Siegel points out an important shift in the way male entitlements are described. Originally they were described in the language of status or hierarchy. For example, under common law, a man was entitled to have his wife follow him wherever he wanted to live. Men no longer have that entitlement as a legal matter, but men as a group still enjoy it as a matter of social custom, as will be documented in chapter 4.[8]

Today working-class men often still use the language of status, defining the issue as one of whether the husband will "permit" the wife to work. But middle-class families are more likely to eschew the father-knows-best model in favor of a decision-making process that involves discussions in which the couple concludes that relocation "will make everybody happiest in the long run." This shift in justification is the transition from the language of status to that of emotion, from an open acknowledgment of male entitlements to one that justifies them as the optimal path to self-fulfillment for women as well as for men. With this as background, let us turn to Fallows' story.[9]

In a pattern typical of women of her class, Fallows trained for a high-status, traditionally male career. She liked her work, was good at it, and was offered good jobs and promotions. Yet after she had children she first cut back to part-time work and then quit. The very long hours required of professionals in her social context played a central role in her decision. "I now see women and men behaving the way those fathers of the 1950s did," she notes with disapproval. She did not want a family where children "say good-night to Mom and Dad on the phone instead of having books read and getting hugs," and eat dinner with their nanny instead of their parents.[10]

Fallows worked part time, though she was acutely conscious that she was not performing as an ideal worker. "The compromises I was making were professional, by being a part-time worker. My erratic work schedule worked well for me and my son, but it was hard on everyone else at my office. I missed meetings; I bowed out of last-minute crises; I wouldn't travel; I couldn't stay late. In short, I was not the kind of employee who could be counted on in a crunch. Dependable, yes, hardworking and competent, but highly restricted. I was passed over for projects I would have liked because they demanded the kind of performance and responsibility that didn't mesh with my private obligations as a mother."[11]

Part of the reason Fallows could not perform as an ideal worker was because of her husband's job. By her own account, it was all-consuming. He was rarely around during her pregnancy, and went to only two of eight Lamaze classes: "I persuaded friends to accompany me to the others or else I went alone." When they moved, her husband went on ahead while she stayed behind for three months to sell the house in Texas, pack up, and move into the new house in Washington "three weeks before our baby was due." He worked in a job that "required him to be at the office almost all the time." When Deborah went into labor, she trailed her husband Jim from office to office because she did not want to be alone. When she took nine-month-old Tommy visiting at Christmas, "Jim didn't come with us—even though we were going to visit his own parents." She held Tommy's first birthday party at Jim's office "because Jim couldn't get away."[12]

> Jim did what he could, pitching in when he was home. But the simple fact was that he wasn't able to be home very much. The tone was set by the workaholics . . . who made it seem wimpish to leave work before the dead of night. . . . We would all go in together on the weekends while Jim worked. Tommy would crawl around the floor of Jim's office, climb on the furniture, and then nap on the sofa—not so much to play as just to be in the presence of his dad.[13]

After two years Jim Fallows left his White House job. "His reasons were largely professional, but I know that he was also greatly concerned about the strain on our family life." He continued a successful and high-pressured career—eventually he became editor in chief of *U.S. News & World Report*. But he worked out of his house for a time, so he saw the boys at breakfast, after dinner (during dinner he often had press calls), and when they got home from school.

> All this has come, I can see, at a considerable cost to Jim's working life. I have heard him turn down breakfast, dinner, and evening meetings to be with the boys; I know he'll often rearrange appointments to take the boys to school. Every night, he works until 1 or 2 A.M., or later, to make up for the daytime interludes he's spent with the boys. Many of his friends and colleagues are single or childless. As he sees them sit down for an afternoon of uninterrupted work on a Saturday or Sunday, I can tell he's thinking how much more quickly he could finish an article or book if he were similarly

unencumbered. In short, he's made a trade: ambitious as he is, he has accepted less success—and money—than he might otherwise have. In exchange he has gotten to know his sons.[14]

He's made a trade; she's made a trade.

Is this equality? Look at the implicit entitlements at work. He is entitled to self-development by performing as an ideal worker, moving his family to take appealing jobs, and placing no limitations on the time demands his employer imposes as a cost of doing his work. To the extent he gives up the fastest track available, he has made a sacrifice. And employers are entitled to workers just like him. "I am not objecting to the fact that certain jobs require these extra sacrifices from their employees," says Fallows. "Work is sometimes like that, and the most responsible jobs often ask the most from the people who hold them." "If your [scientific] experiment bubbles at 1 A.M.," said another author, "you have to be there."[15]

Obviously, if one parent works these kind of hours, the child care and housework fall to the other. In a prior era, this distribution of entitlements would have been described in the language of status. A husband was entitled to the services of his wife, wrote William Blackstone in the eighteenth century, because "the inferior hath no kind of property in the company, care, or assistance of the superior, as the superior is held to have in those of the inferior." Early American courts used similar language. Here is an example from New York in 1897, holding that because a husband was entitled to his wife's services by means of the hierarchical relationship created by marriage, those services could not form the consideration for a contract between husband and wife.

> A man cannot be entitled to compensate his wife for services for nothing,
> by virtue of a uniform and a unchangeable marriage contract, and at the
> same time be under obligation to pay her for those services, by virtue of a
> contract made before marriage.

Men were entitled to their wives' services and to determine the family domicile; both persist to the present day, not as legal entitlements but as social customs, coded as choice or passed over in silence.[16]

The language of status gradually gave way to the language of affect. Reva Siegel traces this process in *Borelli v. Brusseau*, a 1993 California case striking down a marital contract in which the husband agreed to leave substantial amounts of property to his wife in exchange for her promise to provide twenty-four-hour nursing herself so that he would not have to go into a nursing home. The wife did so, but the husband did not change his will as promised. A court held that his estate need not deed her the property promised to her because the contract was invalid for lack of consideration: As a wife, she had a preexisting duty to provide "support," evidently including twenty-four-hour personal nursing care.[17] The court did not, of course, embrace the language of hierarchy; instead, it presented its decision as motivated by its desire to preserve marriage as a haven of caring protected from the values of the marketplace. Enforcing the contract, it said, would effect a transformation of "mores . . . to the point that spouses can be treated just like any other parties haggling at arm's length. . . . [E]ven if few things are left that cannot command a price, marital support remains one of them."[18]

Thirty years earlier Betty Friedan described the existing distribution of household work largely in the language of status. In the 1960s husbands were still entitled to wives' work, so wives could work outside the home only if husbands "let them." Today the result may well be the same, but the reasons offered are different. Thus Fallows presents her decision to stay home as a choice she made to improve her own emotional state. She was worried that Tommy's terrible twos were a protest against her absence; she quit to alleviate her worry. She quit both to avoid negative feelings and to experience positive ones, as leaving gave her more time "to partake of the pleasures of [Tommy's] company."[19]

This is the transition from status into affect. Fallows' sense that she stayed home to meet her own emotional needs cloaks her conviction that "as a parent I should have all the time . . . in the world to give." Though she states this in a gender-neutral way, she never applies this expectation to her husband. In fact, her ideal—"an insistence that the balance between parenthood and career be worked out by both parents"—receives virtually no attention. Instead she spends nine of the fourteen chapters of her book defending full-time motherhood by attacking day care.[20]

The odd thing is that Fallows' own experience with day care was a positive one. She describes Omeda, the middle-aged black child-care provider she used for her son during his first two years, this way:

> I remember many, many things about Omeda, but a few stick out in my mind: I would always see her dancing with the children when she played records; a briefly evident television set disappeared quickly, never to be seen again, when parents voiced concern; the children dressed up on every Halloween and were welcomed door to door in the neighborhood on Halloween morning. Tommy was very happy there.[21]

What's going on here? Why is Fallows so opposed to day care in principle despite the fact that it worked well for her in practice? Why does she insist on gender neutrality, only to apply such radically different standards to her husband and herself? Why does she pay so little attention to her ideal of equal parenting? To answer these questions, we must place her choices in the context of the gender system that has been shaping the lives of mothers for the last two centuries.

DOMESTICITY

In the following description, I stress the continuities in the gender system called domesticity. Yet obviously a social system that has persisted for two centuries has not remained unchanged. We have seen one important change already: the contemporary shift from the language of hierarchy to the language of affect. The following description will highlight continuities but will also include some discussion of changes over time.

In the contemporary version of domesticity, choice rhetoric serves to effect the translation from status to affect by focusing attention away from three constraints that form the backbone of domesticity's organization of work. The first is employers' entitlement to demand an ideal worker with immunity from family work. The second constraint is husbands' right, and their duty, to live up to this work ideal. The third involves the definition of the duties of a mother, as someone whose life should be framed around caregiving.[22]

Employers Are Entitled to Ideal Workers with Immunity from Family Work

Fallows' sense that employers are entitled to ideal workers with limited responsibility for family work played an important role in her decision to leave her career. As noted above, she felt uncomfortable working part time because she could not meet the work ideal. The widespread sense that employers are entitled to workers with limited caregiving responsibilities reflects the sharp split between work and family that is characteristic of domesticity. The classic expression of this split was the "arrangement" of the husband as breadwinner and the wife as homemaker.

We tend to think of this as the traditional family, but that is a misnomer. Before the nineteenth century, it would have made no sense to think of a breadwinner, with its connotation of someone who leaves the house to work for money. Inhabitants of small family farms throughout the country, and of the great plantations of the South, raised much of their own food. They produced not only their own bread but the yeast to raise it; made not only their own clothing but the thread to sew it; not only washed the clothes but produced soap and starch for laundering.[23]

In this context both parents "stayed home," but neither focused primarily on child care. To keep a household fed, shod, healthy, and housed required the full-time work of both parents—and of the children as well. Apart from a very small elite, men, women, children, apprentices, and servants worked side by side to produce much of what they needed to live.

This is not to say that men and women did identical work. Women did all the "indoors work," and were responsible for providing fruits, vegetables, dairy products, and fowl; for manufacturing goods needed by the family; for daily care of the house and lot; and for training and supervision of infants, older daughters, and female servants. Men were responsible for providing grain, fuel, and permanent structures such as houses, barns, and sheds; for making the equipment required both by themselves and their wives; and for supervising the work of older sons and male servants.[24]

Child care was not seen as a task requiring full-time attention. A biography of Harriet Beecher Stowe (1811–1891) notes that "[a]s long as [Harriet] was healthy, clothed, and fed, her caretakers assumed that all of her earthly wants were satisfied; listening to her questions, musing, and small childhood tragedies was a luxury for which they had no time. For sociability Harriet turned either to the books in her father's study or to the society of the kitchen help." Harriet was the seventh child in a large and complex household that included five older siblings, an orphan cousin, two bound servants, several students from the nearby Litchfield Law School, as many as eleven boarders from the Litchfield Female Academy, an aunt and uncle who often visited for lengthy periods, and often Grandma Beecher and her unmarried daughter. "To all of these full-time and part-time residents must be added the constant flow of visitors making themselves at home in the minister's house, and the high level of social activity that obtained in this sophisticated town. Who can blame five-year-old Harriet if she hardly noticed after her mother's death that she was gone?" [25]

Stowe's childhood represents the transition between domesticity and the system that preceded it. As of the early nineteenth century, many elements persisted of the gender system that preceded domesticity. For example, the key unit still was the household, not the biological family. Many households were composed not only of a mother, a father, and their children but of apprentices, bound servants (often children themselves), other relatives (aunts, orphans, grandmothers), boarders, and others as well. A significant portion of the population spent part of their lives in other families' households.[26] Many children were living in families other than their own by the time they were teenagers. Moreover, "the prevalent assumptions about family life made little distinction between a natural child and a servant of about the same age."[27] The views that the biological family needed its privacy and that minor children needed large amounts of parental attention were far in the future: these beliefs became prevalent only when the family was reconceptualized as primarily an emotional rather than economic unit. This reconceptualization was a central element of domesticity.

Though men and women typically did different work in the era before domesticity, women often did work associated with men. If the husband had a trade, the wife often worked with him, sewing the uppers on the shoes or tending the shop he owned. Throughout the eighteenth century, wives acted as "deputy husbands" when their husbands were away and often did work traditionally done by men in this capacity. We find reports of women as blacksmiths, wrights, printers, tinsmiths, beer makers, tavern keepers, shoemakers, shipwrights, barbers, grocers, butchers, and shopkeepers.[28] Women doing "men's work" did not jar contemporary sensibilities because men and women were not primarily defined by their separate spheres.

Women were defined, instead, by their inferiority. It was "an almost unquestioned premise that the father, as head of the household, had a right to expect respect and obedience from his wife and children. A father's authority over his family, servants, and apprentices was simply one link in what early commentators called the 'Great Chain of Being,' the line of authority descending from God."[29] Hierarchy was considered natural, inevitable, and desirable: humans above animals, the higher classes above the lower, God above the king, men above women. The only place that lacked hierarchy was the chaos of hell. "Differences in kinds of social being and the state of total subjection itself were part of the nature of things. Over the plantation was raised, not only its own proper patriarch, but also the imagery of a whole series of ruling fathers extended beyond the king to the Creator." The image of the stern father was "a pervasive mode of construing social authority in the North as well as in the South, on the eastern as well as the western side of the Atlantic."[30]

Gender hierarchy was an integral part of the Great Chain. "God's universal law gave to man despotic power / Over his female in due awe," said Milton. Family portraits prior to 1775 show the father on a higher plane than his wife and children. Not only was religious, political, and familial power concentrated in men; men also were associated with all good character traits. Women were the weaker vessel, "associated with deviousness, sexual voraciousness, emotional inconstancy, and physical and intellectual inferiority."[31] Witches provided a ready example of women's vulnerability to the devil. Sexually voracious and intellectually and morally inferior to men, women needed firm family governance. The father had rightful authority over all who "ate his meat." They were liable for "petit treason should they strike him down. ... The identification of both God and the king as fathers not only incorporated experience from everyday life into the highest levels of cosmology but also sanctified the authority of the head of each household."[32]

Religion, law, and custom all enforced the father's authority. Fathers, like all rulers, could mete out corporal punishment, limited only by the rule that a man could beat his wife only with a stick no thicker than his thumb.[33] Male power was reinforced by religion: The marriage ceremony required that women promise to obey their husbands. Men owned the labor of wives, children, servants, and apprentices. In the ordinary case, women never gained ownership of property, which was associated with masculinity. Children were the father's in more than name alone—he not only owned their labor but was entitled to their custody and was charged with their upbringing. Children's letters home typically were addressed to fathers, conveying respects to mothers in a postscript.[34] Puritan wives were expected to exhibit to their husbands an attitude of "reverence," defined as a mixture of fear and awe. The patriarch "had it in his power to punish or pardon and typically was less concerned with consistent performances than with the readiness of his dependents to adopt the submissive posture considered appropriate to a child confronted by a parent."[35]

So unquestioned was the father's power in the patriarchal household that political theorists in the seventeenth century justified monarchs' claims to absolute power by reference to it, with claims that the king was the father of his people. This was a natural step because the patriarchal family was viewed as an integral part of proper governance. Puritan selectmen often required convicts, children of the poor, single men and women, and recent immigrants to live in "well Governed families" so that "disorders may bee prevented and ill weeds nipt."[36]

Nor were family matters treated as private. For example, early divorce records in Puritan America showed that neighbors regularly entered into areas considered private in modern life. For example, when Mary Angel and Abigail Galloway looked through an open window and saw Adam Air and Pamela Brichford "in the

Act of Copulation," they walked into the house "and after observing them some time . . . asked him if he was not Ashamed to act so when he had a Wife at home."[37] This lack of privacy also occurred among the Virginia gentry of the eighteenth century. According to historian Rhys Isaac, "The ideal of the home as a center of private domesticity was not familiar to Anglo-Virginians in the mid-eighteenth century. They lived or aspired to live in the constant presence of servants or guests. Their houses were the sacrosanct setting for hospitality and for the open celebration of the major events of life and death. . . . Indeed, most of the dominant values of the culture were fused together in the display of hospitality, which was one of the supreme obligations that society laid upon the heads of households."[38]

This description of patriarchy highlights an important point: Domesticity was a great improvement over prior conditions. It represented an early attempt to conceptualize women as equal to men in a tradition that had defined them as men's inferiors. Despite this, domesticity neither promised nor delivered full equality.[39] For much of the nineteenth century, the ideal woman continued to be described as submissive; even in the 1950s, popular pictures still depicted the father on a higher plane than his family.[40] Fallows' description suggests that "ambitious" fathers remain the head of the household in important ways even today. "It seems odd that one person's job controls the household to this extent," the wife of a high-powered Washingtonian told me in 1995. But it did: His job determined where they lived, the family's social life, the allocation of household work, his wife's career plans.

Though paternal power persisted long after 1750, open hierarchy diminished. By 1776 all men had been declared equal. This had a profound influence on the development of domesticity. While the market economy reorganized work in ways that set the economic structure within which domesticity arose, the notion that men and women belonged in spheres that were separate but (in some sense) equal reflected the influence of Enlightenment ideals. Domesticity explained that women were not inferior; they were just different. In fact, they were equally important in their distinctive domestic sphere.

Domesticity not only bifurcated the work of adults into a women's sphere of the home and men's market work outside of it; it justified that reorganization through new descriptions of the "true natures" of men and women. To quote historian Christine Stansell:

> In eighteenth-century Europe and early nineteenth-century America, a striking rearrangement of gender identities and stereotypes occurred. To men were assigned all the character traits associated with competition: ambition, authority, power, vigor, calculation, instrumentalism, logic, and single-mindedness. To women were assigned all the traits associated with cooperation: gentleness, sensitivity, expressivism, altruism, empathy, personalism, and tenderness.[41]

Men belonged in the market because their natural competitiveness suited them for it. Women remained at home as "moral mothers" whose selflessness suited them to provide the moral uplift men needed when they staggered home to their haven from the heartless world.

Under domesticity, not only personality but also emotional expressiveness was gendered. "There is but little of genuine emotion in our [sex]," said an observer in 1839. Men were expected to be instrumental in their attitudes toward the world, to be doers. Self-control became closely identified with manhood.[42] A working-class man told Lillian Rubin in the 1970s, "Guys talk about things and girls talk about feelings." "After a lifetime of repressing his feelings," Rubin notes, "he often *is* a blank, unaware that he's thinking of or feeling anything."[43] Though Rubin links this phenomenon to class, Deborah Tannen found that it continued to characterize conventional masculinity in the 1980s. Men, she found, often assume that the purpose of conversation is problem solving, an approach not shared by women.[44] Our particular gender arrangements, which associate conventional masculinity with tight self-control and a narrow emotional range, make men from Mars and women from Venus.

Domesticity gendered not only personality and emotional expressiveness but also market work, which was designed for workers without household responsibilities. In addition, business and the professions as well as "male" working-class jobs were associated with male personality traits and male access to family work. More recent versions of domesticity sometimes mute the explicit gendering of jobs but continue to define the ideal worker in terms that reflect assumptions drawn from domesticity. Most notable is the construction of the ideal worker, without significant responsibilities for child rearing or housework. Also important is the tradition of underpaying women working in traditional women's jobs on the grounds that they are working just for "pin money." In the nineteenth century, women's salaries were so small that they did not provide sufficient funds to buy the food, lodging, and clothing they needed to survive, pressuring even working women into sexual/economic relationships with men. Even today, salaries in traditionally female jobs still are half to one-third those in traditionally male working-class jobs; for in many white-collar jobs the fraction is even smaller. Moreover, employers of predominantly female workforces often do not provide health insurance, on the assumption that their employees are married to breadwinners with family health benefits.[45]

When feminists began to challenge domesticity in the 1960s, they focused on gaining access to market work; soon they added the demand that men share equally at home. Fewer focused on the way the ideal worker is defined as someone with immunity from family work. In an era when many "good" blue- as well as white-collar jobs require substantial overtime and one-third of fathers work forty-nine or more hours a week, the time has come to challenge the employer's right to define the ideal worker as someone who is supported by a flow of family work most men enjoy but most women do not. This way of organizing (market and family) work is the first important element Fallows, and other contemporary women, carry over from domesticity.[46]

Men Are Entitled (and Required) to Be Ideal Workers

Masculinity is measured by the size of a paycheck.[47]

The birthright of every American male is a chronic sense of personal inadequacy.[48]

Under patriarchy, men's authority was based on their role in the structure of governance: "Household authority was the basis of the political order."[49] To achieve the ideals of masculinity, a man had only to use the weapons placed at his disposal (violence, property, and threat of damnation) to "govern" his household and other social inferiors. This changed under domesticity. The association of masculinity with breadwinning, so that manhood became contingent on success in market work, was a sharp shift whose significance is often underestimated.

When historian Arthur Cole examined the lives of eighteenth-century merchants, he found that their relationship with market work differed from that of men who lived after them: "[B]usiness had not become so much an end in itself and success in business did not become so adequately a basis for self-satisfaction, as was to become the case in the next centuries."[50] Before the nineteenth century, men's sense of themselves was linked as much to religious, political, and social roles as to economic ones.

With the shift from patriarchy to domesticity, "a man's work t[ook] on a separate meaning and provide[d] the chief substance of his social identity," according to historian E. Anthony Rotundo. According to historian Robert Griswold, "Despite men's differences, breadwinning has remained the great unifying element in fathers' lives. Its obligations bind men across the boundaries of color and class, and shape their sense of self, manhood, and gender." A law student in 1820 noted that business engages a man's "mind and occupies his thoughts so frequently as to engross them almost entirely and then it is upon his employment that he depends almost entirely for his happiness of life." "I often think it is so different for men from what it is with us women," a woman told her suitor in 1868; "[l]ove is our life, our reality, business yours." "If a man was without 'business,'" writes Rotundo, "he was less than a man." Said a New York college student in 1844, "It is so unmanly so unnatural to spend a lifetime in the pursuit of nothing"; for him, the alternative to "nothing" was "suitable employment." Unemployment quickly brought on feelings of worthlessness. Lucien Boynton in 1839 reported "the 'Blues'" and "a painful vacancy in my mind" after a week of unemployment: "My soul feels as tho it has been feeding on wind and vapor."[51]

The term *breadwinner* was coined between 1810 and 1820. The rise in importance of men's success at work was tied to the decline of the traditions of deference that had accompanied the Great Chain, whereby each member of the hierarchy was expected to give "due deference" to those above him, and expected to receive due deference from those below. Even into the nineteenth century, the Great Chain lived on unexamined in many areas of life and, in many contexts, elites still enjoyed the deference of their social inferiors. Yet in the course of the nineteenth century, traditional norms of deference gave way to the "self-made man," a term that entered the language in the 1840s. For the first time in history, a man's social position (in theory, anyway) was determined by his own success. And the key to success was work. In this context, dedication to work could become obsessive. One commentator wrote in 1836 that an American man "is never . . . so uneasy as when seated by his own fireside; for he feels, while conversing with his kindred, that he is making no money. And as for fireside reading . . . 'he reads no book but his ledger.'" Another warned in 1903 against the "masculine disease": "the habit and fury of work, unreasoning, illogical. quite unrelated to any [economic] need." These patterns persisted throughout the twentieth century. Said one feminist man in the late 1970s, "Work is the institution that most defines the majority of adult males. Many of us look to work for our most basic sense of worth."[52]

If the new focus on work presented opportunities, they were accompanied by risk. As men's breadwinner status came to underlie their claims to familial and social dominance, anxiety became a permanent feature of masculinity: "Sons had to compete for manhood in the market rather than grow into secure manhood by replicating fathers," one commentator noted as early as 1920. Not much had changed by 1990, when another commentator noted, "Success must be earned, manhood must be proved—and proved constantly." Many men found the market a "site of humiliation," to quote Thoreau. Daniel Webster made a similar point much earlier: "How entirely sure we are and easy about everybody's fortune but our own." These feelings were echoed by Morton S. Bailey, a lawyer just starting out, in 1880: "I am in continual doubt and full of misgivings lest the future be darker than the past, and with this feeling of dread do you wonder that I hesitate to make the advancing steps or that I would almost rather not take them at all." For if the nineteenth century brought an economy wide open with the chance to make money, it also saw persistent cycles of boom and bust; for both wage laborers and businessmen, the nineteenth-century economy was volatile in the extreme. Grueling hours and abrupt dismissals were common for workers; bankruptcy was commonplace for businessmen large and small. Mark Twain became a rich man but died a pauper, a pattern repeated many times in both directions. During this period many states passed Homestead Acts to protect the family home from seizure for the husband's business debts.[53]

Men were well aware that not only their own fortunes but those of their entire families depended on their success as breadwinners. In 1844 Alexander Rice reminded his fiancée that he was the person "upon whose arm you are to lean thro' life, upon whose reputation your own will rest and upon whose effects your happiness as well as his own will mainly depend." The tenuousness of masculinity was bad enough for middle-class men struggling to get established in business or the professions. It was worse for working-class men, who typically had no control over the success of the businesses that hired and fired them.[54]

The close linkage of masculinity with breadwinning has proved remarkably resilient despite the shift of women into the labor force. "Women just aren't raised with the idea of being the primary wage earner," said a woman in 1998 who had found herself thrust into that role. "I mean, think about it, most women work, but their husbands usually make more money. Usually way more money. I didn't want that level of responsibility." A recent literature review concluded "[v]irtually all men believe that being a good father means first and foremost being a good provider." Jean L. Potuchek's 1997 study of dual-earner families found that "both men and women attach different meanings to the employment of wives than to the employment of husbands. Reports from men indicated that, even when their wives were employed, they still felt a special obligation to provide."[55]

Potuchek found that the most common approach among employed wives was the *employed homemaker,* who does not see her job as occupying a central role in the lives of her family and sees her husband as the breadwinner. In only 20 percent of the dual-earner couples studied did the women consider themselves co-breadwinners or committed workers; these women were also less likely to have children at home. Apart from this group, most women (83 percent of women and even a higher percentage of child-rearing mothers) felt their husbands should be the primary providers (even when economic circumstances made this impossible) or had husbands who were primary providers (even when they regretted this). In other words, even among women who work, few are breadwinners. The data linking men with breadwinning are even more dramatic. Roughly three-fourths of men in dual-earner families either performed as breadwinners or wished they could. Those who didn't included few fathers. Potuchek's research can be summarized by this insight: "[B]readwinners who build model airplanes differ fundamentally from fathers who co-parent. This basic distinction is often misunderstood."[56]

The shift of women into the workforce has undermined neither domesticity's linkage of women with caregiving nor its association of men with breadwinning. Domesticity's patterns of market work and family work continue to describe a broad range of Americans. Households of rich men are most likely to conform to the housewife/breadwinner model.[57] Susan Ostrander's study reports that very successful men tend to be so tied up with their work that they play little role in their own households. Often highly successful men are physically absent for long periods of time: "He worked abroad for months. He expects there will be peace at home when he returns. I don't bother him with petty domestic details. He doesn't have time for that." Says Ostrander of upper-class women: "They not only run the house, they do so in a way that shields their husbands from any concern over what goes on there; they do so even when he is away from home for extended periods of time." Lorna Wendt, whose divorce from the CEO of a major division of General Electric has been widely publicized, has drawn the public eye to the lifestyle of the rich and famous men who do not even pack their own suitcases.[58]

The gender patterns in the families of highly successful men emerge clearly in Arlie Hochschild's study of a large American corporation she calls Amerco. Said one executive:

We made a bargain. If I was going to be as successful as we both wanted, I was going to have to spend tremendous amounts of time at work. Her end of the bargain was that she wouldn't go out to work. So I was able to take the good stuff and she did the hard work—the car pools, dinner, gymnastic lessons.

Hochschild points out that fatherhood, to one of these men, brought forth the image of a performance—school plays, ballet recitals, soccer games. "[H]e knew little about those times when his children were offstage, unable to get started on something, discouraged, or confused." While most managers looked back on their fathering years with "a kind of mild regret that they had spent so little time with their children," the most telling reaction was a woman whose husband ultimately was fired. She exploded:

My husband missed our children's *birthdays!* He missed their *games!* He missed the father-daughter *banquets!* Didn't the company get *enough* of his time? Because we saw *nothing* of him!

When another executive died of a heart attack, his widow invited no one from the company to speak at the funeral. "Why should I?" she asked a friend. "It was the *company* that killed him!" This story reminds us that highly successful men experience not only the benefits but also the "lethal aspects of the male role."[59]

The linkage of masculinity with work success is inscribed onto men's literal bodies not only in heart attacks but also in higher rates of impotence among unemployed men.[60] Different groups of men experience this linkage in different ways. Studies of men in poor urban neighborhoods suggest that, lacking access to the breadwinner role, these men often define masculinity more in terms of sexual performance and displays of toughness rather than in terms of work success.[61] Working-class men have often stressed sexuality as well—think of the sexual posturings of Elvis Presley, Marlon Brando, James Dean. But even among disenfranchised men, breadwinning retains an imaginative hold. One reason drug dealing is such a booming business is that it offers underclass men virtually their only opportunity to work hard and get ahead.

For working-class men today, the breadwinner role is often a source of particular pain. Ellen Israel Rosen's 1987 study of blue-collar women found that "[r]egardless of a woman's real contribution to the family, the husband is defined as the main breadwinner." Rosen reported that the women she studied realized that "their husbands' sense of manhood is contingent on the shared belief that his paycheck is 'supporting the family,'" so women define their work as "helping their husbands." "I feel that when I'm working I bring home a good pay. It helps out. I wouldn't say I'm working just to spend. Today you need to work. A woman needs to help out her husband."[62] These women saw their work as "help" to their husbands as a way of preserving the sense that their husbands were the breadwinners in the family.

Roberta Sigel's 1996 study of gender in New Jersey confirmed that blue-collar men today often feel significant anxiety over their work roles. The men in her blue-collar focus group expressed anxiety that women were taking over men's jobs, as well as the conviction that women were inherently unsuited for blue-collar work, which they described in highly gendered terms as heavy and tiring. Men in the focus group felt "intense fear" of unemployment and "justly aggrieved" by what they perceived to be the invasion of unqualified women into their turf. The middle-class men Sigel interviewed did not feel similarly embattled; Sigel attributes the difference to the fact that middle-class men are less likely to face female competition.[63]

But this is untrue. In fact, women have flooded into white-collar jobs but made very little headway into blue-collar ones. The high levels of anxiety among blue-collar men reflect not actual competition from women but the fact that such men feel their provider status slipping away, whereas middle-class men do not. Blue-collar males have seen their hourly wages shrink since 1978. Nearly 15 percent of the men Lillian Rubin talked to in the nineties were jobless. Even when employed, working-class men today often earn less than their fathers; salaries of high-school-educated men have fallen since 1974, and they have lost ground relative to same-class women and to college-educated men.[64] Today's working-class men were born a generation too late. Their fathers could, with luck, deliver the basic accouterments of middle-class life—the house, the car, the washing machine. Today they can't. Economists Frank Levy and Robert Michel note that "back in the 1970s, the average guy with a high school diploma was making $24,000 in today's dollars. Today a similar guy is making about $18,000."[65] Many have suffered permanent lay-offs, or have had their wages cut, or have seen their wives' incomes rise faster than their own; 80 percent of the decrease in the wage gap in recent years is due to decreases in men's wages.[66] In a culture that ties masculinity to the size of a paycheck, working-class status today is often accompanied by a sense of threatened masculinity. "In the span of a few decades, foreign investment, corporate flight, downsizing, and automation have suddenly left members of the working class without a steady family wage, which compounded with the decrease in strength of labor unions, has left many white working-class men feeling emasculated and angry. It seems that overnight, the ability to work hard and provide disappeared."[67]

As if that weren't enough, working-class men's loss of the family wage has led to a loss of deference within the family. "It's my house; you'll do what I say" remains a favorite saying of working-class fathers. In 1976 Lillian Rubin noted the high level of deference paid to working-class men. By the nineties, many looked back on those days with nostalgia. "Thirty years ago," said one young man, "if the man said: 'This is what we're going to do and that's it,' the woman would say 'okay.' Nowadays, boy, you've got to argue up and down, to get the point across, to get your way, or try and get half your point across." Asked by the focus group moderator why this was so, he answered, "They're allowed to give their opinion more." Sigel takes special note of the word *allowed*. Lillian Rubin quotes thirty-one-year-old Joe Acosta describing his wife in 1991: "She's different since she went back to work, more independent, you could say. We fight a lot more than we used to." Rubin notes that working-class women's demands for equal participation in family work has become "a wrenching source of conflict" in many households. She concludes that working-class men, "battered by economic uncertainty and by the escalating demands of their wives, feel embattled and victimized on two fronts—one outside the home, the other inside."[68]

As long as masculinity is linked with breadwinning, working-class men will feel embattled. This is true of all races, but men of color face particular problems, because racial prejudice also interferes with their ability to play the breadwinner role. The situation is particularly acute for African-American men. From emancipation on, a key way of effecting white supremacy has been to cut black men off from steady work.[69] This pattern continues up to the present: The earnings of black men are only two-thirds those of white men, and the gap between black and white men's earnings has widened significantly since 1979.[70] Black men's relative inability to get good, steady jobs often bars them from the provider role that provides the conventional basis for male dignity.[71] To the (significant) extent that racial prejudice cuts men of color off from good jobs, they experience the hidden injuries of class in ways that are linked with race and ethnicity. "Since whites defined 'achieving manhood' as the ability of a man to be a sole economic provider in a family," notes bell hooks, black men are often viewed as "failed men."[72] The same may be true of other men of color.

Most men feel they have little choice but to perform as ideal workers, regardless of how exploitative the conditions of work and regardless of women's demands for equality. And most women will not question their husbands' right to perform as ideal workers any more than Fallows did. A recent study of New York law firms found that women did not urge their husbands to cut back their hours despite the burden this placed on them as wives. A study of divorced couples found that men who fail "to accomplish ascendant masculinity via a successful career" can be rewarded with divorce even if they are family-involved men who contribute much more to family work than most other men.[73]

When the opera singer Beverly Sills left New York to follow her husband to Cleveland, she felt that "[m]y only alternative was to ask Peter to scuttle the goal he'd been working toward for almost 25 years. If I did that, I didn't deserve to be his wife."[74] No "good" wife would want to rob her husband of full masculinity—this is why researchers find such unquestioned support for men's careers. This is the second constraint Fallows and other contemporary women carry over from domesticity.

Mothers Should Have "All the Time and Love in the World to Give"

The final set of constraints that frame contemporary women's "choice" stem from assumptions about motherhood and children's needs. Fallows states her ideal ("as a parent I should have all the time and love in the world to give") as an ungendered norm. Yet, as noted above, she never applies this standard to her husband, and her book's title shows that she is talking about a *mother's* work, not a *parent's*. Her message is that mothers, not both parents, should have "all the time in the world" to give. Most contemporary women agree. A 1995 study found that 88 percent of the women surveyed believed it was their primary responsibility to take care of the family.[75]

The notion that mothers should have all the time in the world to give embeds three defining elements of domesticity: domesticity's symbolic separation of home and work, the material conditions of motherhood, and the linkage of class formation and gender roles.

The Symbolic Separation of Home and Work

Domesticity's separation of home and work is the conceptual framework that underlies two powerful forces that feed mothers' sense that they should have all the time in the world to give. The first is anxiety over the prospect of leaving child care to the market ("commodifying" it); the second is the erasure of household work.

The separation of home and work is a central tenet of domesticity. The physical separation of work life from home life was effected in the nineteenth-century commercial and industrial economy by separating market work from family work both geographically (into factories) and temporally (into a preset "workday," in sharp contrast to earlier patterns, which interspersed work and family life).

The separation of home and work was symbolic as well. Nancy Cott has argued that the new role domesticity assigned to women was a way of coming to terms with the moral shock felt during the transition to capitalism. Whereas self-interest traditionally had been decried both in religion and in political theory, in the nineteenth century it became enshrined as the key to social improvement.[76] People dealt with their profound discomfort with the emerging capitalist order by preserving the older virtues and associating them with women. Said one New England pastor in 1827:

> It is at home, where man . . . seeks a refuge from the vexations and embarrassments of business, an enchanting repose from exertion, a relaxation from care by the interchange of affection; where some of his finest sympathies, tastes, and moral and religious feelings are formed and nourished;— where is the treasury of pure disinterested love, such as is seldom found in the busy walks of a selfish and calculating world.[77]

In the home and in women rested the antidote for the "selfish and calculating" world of the market. "Our men are sufficiently money-making," said an influential editor in 1830. "Let us keep our women and children from the contagion as long as possible." She wished "to remind the dwellers in this 'bank-note world' that there are objects more elevated, more worthy than pursuit of wealth."[78]

Domesticity created a symbolic world that divided into a private sphere of selfless women and a public sphere of market actors pursuing their own self-interest. Shifting child care to the market from the "home sweet home" disrupts this tidy dichotomy. It raises the frightening specter of children relegated to a callous and self-seeking market realm, a fear of commodification we can call commodification anxiety.

Commodification anxiety fuels the sense that mothers should have all the time in the world to give. For example, at a recent conference, a young officer raised her hand to say she was rising fast in the military. People kept telling her she could be a general. "But I'm going to quit. I'm getting married, we want to have children, and I can't take the lifestyle. And then people say, 'Why would you want to be a general? None of them has a life. They just work all the time.'" She was confused and conflicted. "I don't want my children raised by strangers."[79]

Note the language. Why are child-care providers "strangers"? When you leave a child at school, no one ever thinks of asking, "How does it feel to leave your child with strangers?" If teachers are not strangers, why are caregivers?

This language reflects domesticity's central defining split between men's commercial interactions with strangers in the market and the intimate family atmosphere of home. If child care is in the market, then it is consigned to the market realm, where strangers pursue their own self-interest. As is so often the case, the metaphor proves stronger than the reality that one's child-care provider is hardly a stranger, and probably has complex motivations, of which self-interest is only one. For example, Fallows' actual experience with child care contradicted the sobering imagery of market care: Recall her baby-sitter, Omeda, dancing with the children and going door to door at Halloween. These images do not fit with the disturbing imagery that predominates in Fallows' description of child care in America: of a bleeding child left uncomforted, of children crying unattended, of caretakers paying little attention to the children, of peeling paint and inadequate supplies and children literally tied into their places at the table, waiting for long periods for food.[80]

These images are shocking, without a doubt. But they are mostly of day care for the poor—who indeed often face care that is shockingly bad. But that is not the kind of day care the Fallows family ever had, or would have. It is hard to see why the low quality of child care for the poor explains Fallows' decision to stay home.[81]

The callous imagery of the market as a cold and uncaring place is not an accurate description of many child-care situations. Yet the commodification anxiety derived from domesticity forms an unspoken, and often unconscious, cultural background for many mothers' sense that they should not have their children raised by "strangers," but instead should frame their own lives around caregiving. The sentiment that mothers should have "all the time in the world to give" also reflects a second dynamic that stems from domesticity's separation of home and work: the erasure of household work. To sketch its contours it is useful to begin with the phrase "time to give."

Note that the issue is who will "give time," not who will do laundry, child care, dishes, shopping, and other household work. Historian Jeanne Boydston has tracked the role of domesticity in erasing the existence of women's household work. Before the nineteenth century, women's work was acknowledged as *work* owned by the husband, just as he owned the labor of his children and servants. With the shift away from open hierarchy to the new imagery of men and women sovereign in their separate spheres, the fact that men still owned the right to their wives' services became a fact that needed to be explained. The solution, Boydston argues, was the "pastoralization" of women's work, its depiction as the "effortless emanations of women's very being." The notion that women's spinning, weaving, sewing, soap and candle making, laundering, gardening, livestock tending, cooking, canning, and child rearing were not really work eliminated the need to explain why men still owned the right to such services. "[O]ne cannot confiscate," Boydston notes tartly, "what does not exist." In other words, the erasure of household work served to defuse the tension between the ideology of equality and the persistence of male entitlements originally described in the language of gender hierarchy.[82]

Given the persistence of both the aspiration to gender equality and men's traditional entitlement to household work, it should not surprise us that the erasure of household work persists up to the present. Said one irate mother,

> I get so sick of people asking me, "Do you work?" Of course I work! I've got five children under ten—I work twenty-four hours a day! But of course they mean, "Do you work for pay, outside your home?" Sometimes I hear myself say, "No, I don't work," and I think, "That's a complete lie!"

It is a complete lie. The notion that mothers' family work is not "work" serves to gloss over the fact that mothers at home not only care for the kids but clean the shirts. When a wife stays home full or even part time, her husband's contributions to family work typically decrease. As a result, husbands of homemakers earn more and get higher raises than similarly educated men whose wives do no market work. But women at home typically insist that they are there to pay "rich attention" to their children (to quote a woman from the 1970s), not to do the housework.[83]

I have found that when mothers quit, they often say that it was because "it just wasn't working": everyone was grumpy and rushed, there never seemed to be anything clean to wear or anything for dinner, every childhood illness created a family crisis of who would miss work. Note that many of these things relate to family work. When a mother stays home "because it just wasn't working," she avoids the increased level of conflict often found in households where men are required to do significant amounts of domestic work. Instead, her husband receives the clean clothes, meals, and child care required to support his ability to perform as an ideal worker. This is the contemporary version of domesticity's erasure of household work. It is a strong influence on many women who stay home "to take more responsibility for raising my children."[84]

Changes in the Material Conditions of Motherhood

This sense that mothers should have all the time in the world to give also reflects the material conditions of motherhood under domesticity, notably men's withdrawal from family work and a delivery system for child services premised in significant part on mothers being at home. As noted above, with the rise of the market economy men gradually withdrew from the family work they had performed before it. After 1800 fathers lost their earlier role as the primary instructors of children; as early as 1842, a commentator lamented that fathers are "eager in the pursuit of business, toiling early and late, and find no time to fulfill ... duties" to their children. Whereas men in the eighteenth century had done much of the shopping, in the nineteenth century that too became women's work; by the twentieth century, shopping was a defining feature of femininity ("I live to shop"). By then, according to historian Ruth Schwartz Cowan, "[v]irtually all the stereotypically male household occupations were eliminated by technological and economic innovations."[85]

The withdrawal of men from family work meant that women had two choices: They could either do it themselves or leave it undone. The sense that mothers should have "all the time in the world to give" often reflects the very practical point that many opportunities (notably lessons) and necessities (notably medical appointments) still assume a level of parental availability inconsistent with ideal-worker status. So do "volunteer" activities in children's schools, which parents often feel are mandatory to establish goodwill—indeed, a correlation exists between parental involvement and children's school success.[86] After-school programs represent a countertrend to this system of delivery of child services through mothers, but in a society where two-thirds of mothers of childbearing age still do not work full time full year, this unofficial system is unlikely to change soon. One upper-middle-class child in Washington, D.C., awarded the Nobel Prize to:

> My Mom Mary
> Nobel Prize
> For driving
> Me in Circles
> Again and again

Many families affluent enough to do so will continue to dedicate their resources to gaining access to the system of child services now delivered mostly by mothers. This system places a significant burden on less affluent families. Said the secretary quoted in the preface, the mother of children ages ten and sixteen, "If you can afford the cut in pay for the hours, the ideal situation would be to get home when they get home from school, 3 P.M., so you can take them to ballet and Boy Scouts."[87] The alternative was for her children to miss Scouts and dance class. The sense that child rearing demands a mother's presence reflects, in part, the very practical point that children can miss out on important learning and social opportunities if their mothers as well as their fathers perform as ideal workers.

Domesticity's Linkage of Gender, Class, and Children's Needs
Domesticity not only makes mothers the primary delivery system for services to children; it also links access to middle-class status with conventional gender roles. Domesticity from the beginning has been linked with class—it emerged in the nineteenth century as a strategy by which the middle class differentiated itself from the working class.[88] Keeping an "Angel in the Home" cost money: what made it possible was a middle-class salary. According to historian Christine Stansell:

> The middle class . . . was only emerging, an economically ill-defined group, neither rich nor poor, just beginning in the antebellum years to assert a distinct cultural identity. Central to its self-conception was the ideology of domesticity, a set of sharp ideas and pronounced opinions about the nature of a moral family life.[89]

Mothers stayed home both to signal class directly, for "ladies" did not work, and to transmit middle-class status to their children. This was part of an important shift in the organization of class. Before the nineteenth century, class typically was inherited. So long as this remained true, upper-class parents felt they could rely on servants to raise their young, because the crucial education consisted of class-appropriate decorum. That, and money, ensured that children would step into their parents' social position. With the rise of the middle class, in sharp contrast, class status depended on parents' ability to transmit skills, because each generation had to earn its living on its own. This engendered the "fear of falling": the fear among middle-class families that their children would not develop the self-discipline and skills needed to gain personal access to middle-class life. Once parents felt it their duty not only to train offspring in class-appropriate decorum but to pass on the specific skills and attitudes necessary for middle-class life, they became more reluctant to delegate child care to lower-status people who might not share their values.[90]

Thus arose the sense that mothers should care for their own children. Prescriptive writers in the nineteenth century reconceptualized child rearing as something requiring close attention; "the ability to attend personally to one's children was one of the marks of a good mother." Child care became "the central and most time-consuming family labor for most middle-class women." Prescriptive writers warned that constant vigilance was necessary against potential physical dangers and argued that mothers should be freed from other demands in order to pay close attention to their children's education and character development. By 1842 one French visitor found that Americans gave children an importance he found "almost idolatrous."[91]

Underlying domesticity's romantic description of mothers selflessly devoted to children's needs are class aspirations acknowledged today only in accepted codes (parents want their children to be "successful" and "productive"). To quote Lillian Rubin, "professional middle-class parents . . . assum[e] that their children are destined to do work like theirs—work that calls for innovation, initiative, flexibility, creativity, sensitivity to others, and a well-developed set of interpersonal skills." Mothers stay home to develop these skills in their children. Barbara Ehrenreich is one of the few writers who recognize the link between gender roles and class formation:

> The concern was expressed in various ways. "I don't want to miss the early years"; or "I don't want to leave my children with just *anyone*." But the real issue was the old middle-class dilemma of whether "anyone" such as a Jamaican housekeeper or a Hispanic day-care worker was equipped to instill such middle-class virtues as concentration and intellectual disci-

pline. For many young middle-class couples the choice was stark: Have the mother work and risk retarding the child's intellectual development, or have the mother stay home, build up the child's I.Q., and risk being unable to pay for a pricey nursery school or, later, private college.

"It is one thing to have children," Ehrenreich notes, "and another thing . . . to have children who will be disciplined enough to devote the first twenty or thirty years of their lives to scaling the educational obstacles to a middle-class career." Much of what mothers do is designed to preserve and pass on what has been called the family's social capital: their style of life, religious and ethnic rituals, and social position.[92]

Today the need for parental care is closely linked with the sense that children need to "keep up" in an era of economic anxiety. This has produced shifts in child-rearing norms that have rarely been noted. A sharp shift occurred between the generations of my mother (b. 1918) and mother-in-law (b. 1923) and my own (b. 1952). Both my mothers—one affluent, one working-class—think my generation is truly odd because we focus so much attention on our children.[93] If one rereads the Mrs. Piggle-Wiggle books, published in the late 1940s and early 1950s, one finds their attitude fleshed out. These charming children's books tell the story of Mrs. Piggle-Wiggle, an expert at curing children of misbehavior. In the books, mothers focus on getting invited to Mrs. Workbasket's Earnest Workers Club and having the boss to dinner in order to help their husband's careers; serving meals to husbands who are cross if they are late; appeasing husbands to avoid having them spank some sense into the children; making brownies, cocoa, a coconut cake, a chocolate cake, an applesauce cake, gingerbread; setting out petunias and zinnias, nursing cottage tulips and phlox. No mother is ever shown playing with her children. Nor do children expect to be entertained. They do an endless stream of errands and chores for the adults and they entertain themselves. They go down to the basement and build a workbench, build a tool bench, ride bikes, repaint and repair them, tinker with machines, make caramel apples, establish a Neighborhood Children's Club and a Picnic Club. Only one child ever takes a lesson.[94]

In the 1930s and 1940s domestic workers were rarely hired for full-time child care: "Generally, domestics 'looked out' for children during the day's work," but the focus was on housework, not child care. This is in sharp contrast to current conditions, when child care workers typically are hired with the understanding that they will fit in what housework they can after they play with and generally attend to the children. "These kids," said one acquaintance of the old school, "it's incredible. They have a real 'peel me a grape' attitude." In the fifties and sixties, stay-at-home mothers thought their job was to make a "nice home." The notion that mothers' role was to "entertain" children (as they would describe it) would have seemed as bizarre as the contemporary notion of "floor time."

> What [Stanley] Greenspan [a renowned child psychiatrist who teaches at George Washington Medical School] is saying is this: Spend at least thirty minutes a day focusing exclusively on your child, and let her take the lead.

Tune in to her interests and feelings, and march to her drummer. If she wants you to get down on all fours and bark like a dog, do it. Participate in the action, but don't control it—she's the director, and you're the assistant director.... Floor time, writes Greenspan, "creates the whole basis for security, trust, and self-worth that a child will need from here on."

Greenspan's recommendation is for half an hour of floor time per child per day. Yet he admits that floor time was not part of his own childhood. "In fact, Greenspan's mother used to tell him that he was such an easy, independent baby that she would leave him outside the house in a crib while she was inside doing chores. In retrospect ... Greenspan suspects that he actually 'wasn't so tickled at being left alone.'"[95]

While domesticity has long linked gender and class with children's needs, this discussion demonstrates important shifts over time. Harriet Beecher Stowe's household predated the conviction that children's future is in peril unless they have the full-time attention of their mother. Even in the era of Mrs. Piggle-Wiggle, mothers' focus still was more on "making a nice home" than on floor time. Yet if the expectation that mothers will "keep children challenged and stimulated" is relatively recent, the linkage of mothercare with the fear of falling socially and economically is nearly two centuries old. Greenspan's "floor time" represents the end point of a process whose early stages are documented by historian Mary Ryan in early nineteenth-century Utica, New York, where mothers stayed home to ensure that their sons had the resources to "get ahead." We have not come so far from the nineteenth-century sense that mothercare is vital to the process of transmitting middle-class status.[96]

CHOICE OR DISCRIMINATION?
GENDER AS A FORCE FIELD

I didn't make the world.[97]

The past is never dead. It's not even past.[98]

As Lillian Rubin has noted, only "a tiny minority of us ever are involved in inventing our present, let alone our future." Most of us "struggle along with received truths as well as received ways of being and doing."[99] Indeed, if every single person protested each and every constraint handed down to us, our society would be rapidly immobilized. Hence it is not surprising that women facing the constraints handed down by domesticity speak of having made a "choice." But the fact that women have internalized these constraints does not mean that they are consistent with our commitment to gender equality.

A central message of this book is that mothers' marginalization reflects not mere choice; it also reflects discrimination. Note that choice and discrimination are not mutually exclusive. Choice concerns the everyday process of making decisions within constraints. Discrimination involves a value judgment that the constraints society imposes are inconsistent with its commitment to equality.

Current discussions often confuse the relationship between choice and discrimination by setting up a dichotomy between agency and constraint. Those who stress constraint almost to the exclusion of agency (notably Catharine MacKinnon) are pitted against those who stress agency while glossing over the existence of powerful constraints (notably Katie Roiphe). Clearing up this confusion requires a language that captures both the social constraints within which people operate and the scope of agency they exercise within those constraints.[100]

The most common existing language speaks of individuals making bad choices due to false consciousness. The drawbacks of this approach include its judgmental tone and the implication that some of us escape the social structures that, to a greater or lesser extent, create all of us. The stark reality is that we all have to function within society as we find it. Though we didn't make the world, we have to make do with it.

What we need to do to function in the world as we know it is very different from what we need to do to change it. Social critique requires a language that keeps choice and constraint simultaneously in focus, and highlights the way social structures help create the lives they shape. One helpful model is Pierre Bourdieu's notion of "*habitus*—embodied history, internalized as second nature and so forgotten as history." My analysis of *A Mother's Work* is meant to highlight "the active presence of the whole past" in structuring our sense of what is desirable and feasible in the present. Bourdieu offers a language that avoids the condescension of the false-consciousness formulation while capturing "the coincidence of the objective structures and the internalized structures." A subjective sense of authenticity and repose about one's "choices" may reflect no more than a decision to bring one's life into alignment with the expectations and institutions of domesticity.[101]

"It just wasn't working"—this formulation encodes as choice an economy with work schedules and career tracks that assume one adult in charge of caregiving and one ideal worker, men's felt entitlement to work "success," and a sense that children need close parental attention. It encodes a habitus structured by domesticity, with default modes that set up powerful force fields pulling women back toward traditional gender roles. Women's sense of relief when they give up trying to perform as ideal workers reflects the fact that they no longer have to fight the stiff headwinds from domesticity: they can go with the flow of domesticity's ideal-worker/marginalized-caregiver patterning. The force field imagery also explains why battles women win over the politics of housework have to be refought over and over again: Without constant vigilance, people tend to get sucked back into the default mode. "An institution, even an economy, is complete and fully viable only if it is durably objectified not only in things, that is, in the logic . . . of a particular field, but also in bodies, in durable dispositions to recognize and comply with the demands immanent in the field."[102] Many women find that ceding to the demands of domesticity is the only way to have their lives make sense. This explains their sense of "choice." It also shows that choice rhetoric is not evidence that the ideal-worker norm is consistent with equality for women.

Domesticity's organization of market and family work leaves women with two alternatives. They can perform as ideal workers without the flow of family work and other privileges male ideal workers enjoy. That is not equality. Or they can take dead-end mommy-track jobs or "women's work." That is not equality either. A system that allows only these two alternatives is one that discriminates against women.

CONCLUSION

This chapter has sketched the contours of the gender system I have called domesticity. We can see that some of the basic tenets of domesticity persist, namely three sets of entitlements: the entitlement of employers to hire ideal workers, for men to be ideal workers, and for children to have mothers whose lives are framed around caregiving. Together, these three entitlements set up a powerful force field that pulls fathers into the ideal-worker role and mothers into lives framed around caregiving. Choice rhetoric serves to veil the powerful mandates of domesticity in the language of self-fulfillment. In chapter 2 we turn from why domesticity has proved so unbending to examine the chief strategy feminists have used to challenge it, to analyze how that strategy defined the problem and why it failed.

•

CHAPTER TWO

From Full Commodification to Reconstructive Feminism

"Some kids at school called you a feminist, Mom, but I punched them out."

The traditional feminist strategy for women's equality is for women to work full time, with child care delegated to the market. Economist Barbara Bergmann has christened this the "full-commodification strategy." Its most influential exposition was in Betty Friedan's 1962 *The Feminine Mystique.*[1]

This strategy proved extraordinarily effective in starting what Friedan called a "sex-role revolution": Whereas few mothers of young children were in the labor force in the 1960s, most are today. But what is required to start a revolution is often different from what is required to complete it. This chapter critiques the full-commodification strategy from the standpoint of another strain in feminist thought, which focuses on the devaluation of work traditionally associated with women.[2]

Friedan defended the full-commodification model by depicting housewifery as virtually a human rights violation, culminating in her famous analogy to a concentration camp.[3] In the popular imagination, feminism still is linked with the glorification of market work and the devaluation of family work. This leaves many women confused once they have children. When they feel the lure and importance of family work, they are left with the sense that feminism has abandoned them.[4] Mothers who frame their lives around caregiving may feel that feminism contributes to their defensiveness at being a part-time real estate agent or "just a housewife."

Another challenge for feminism is the sense that "all feminism ever got us was more work."[5] This reflects the situation that has resulted because the full-commodification model did not go far enough in deconstructing domesticity. This model glossed over the fact that men's market work always has been, and still is, supported by a flow of family work from women. Because women do not enjoy the same flow of family work from men, allowing women to perform as ideal workers means that most must do so without the flow of family work that permits men to be ideal workers. The result is that most women go off to work only to return home to the second shift, leaving many feeling distinctly overburdened and skeptical of feminism.

These forces have exacerbated the unpopularity of feminism among many Americans. "Don't use the word," warned a publisher, "you'll lose half your audience." A 1998 *Time*/CNN survey found that only about one-quarter of U.S. women self-identify as feminists, down from one-third in 1989; just 28 percent of those surveyed saw feminism as relevant to them personally. A common rejoinder is that a "feminist majority" supports programs such as equal pay for equal work. But the sharp disparity between support for feminist programs and support for "feminism" reinforces the sense that feminism is not a beckoning rhetoric.[6]

In part feminism's unpopularity reflects only that it is, inevitably and appropriately, inconsistent with femininity's demands for compliant and reassuring women rather than "strident" and "ball-busting" ones. But the high levels of unpopularity are tied as well to the specific inheritance of the full-commodification model. This chapter explains how and argues for a mid-course correction. Feminists need to abandon the full-commodification model in favor of a reconstructive feminism that pins hopes for women's equality on a restructuring of market work and family entitlements. Instead of defining equality as allowing women into market work on the terms traditionally available to men, we need to redefine equality as changing the relationship of market and family work so that all adults—men as well as women—can meet both family and work ideals. This new strategy holds far greater potential for raising support for feminism by building effective coalitions between women and men, as well as with unions, the "time movement," and children's rights advocates.

THE ORIGIN OF THE FULL-COMMODIFICATION STRATEGY: WHY ACCESS TO MARKET WORK SEEMED SO IMPORTANT

> We have so arranged life, that a man may have a home and family, love, companionship, domesticity, and fatherhood, yet remain an active citizen of age and country. We have so arranged life, on the other hand, that a woman must "choose"; must either live alone, unloved, uncompanioned, uncared for, homeless, childless, with her work for sole consolation; or give up all world-service for the joys of love, motherhood, and domestic service.[7]

> She does not have to choose between marriage and career; that was the mistaken choice of the feminine mystique.[8]

In this chapter my first task is to examine the full-commodification model in its initial context in order to appreciate why it made sense to Friedan in 1962. Access to market work was not a key agenda for women's rights advocates in the first half of the nineteenth century. They focused instead on gaining entitlements for women based on their family roles.[9] It was only after the Civil War that feminists began to focus on equal access to market work as the key to women's equality. Indeed, feminists from other countries often have a hard time understanding U.S. feminists' obsession with market work.[10] Why did it take on such profound importance?

Feminists' emphasis on market work reflects the freighted quality of work roles in the twentieth century. In prior eras, privileged women did not need market work to maintain their social position. In the eighteenth century status was tied not to work roles but to class: Privileged women enjoyed high levels of deference and respected social roles by virtue of their membership in the elite. This tradition of social deference gradually ended in the nineteenth century, but by then privileged women had begun to transform their accepted role as the moral beacons of the home into leadership roles within their communities. Women joined clubs, societies, and associations that took active leadership roles in many communities, and engaged in activities that subsequently have turned into consumer, welfare, and environmental activism and social work. Through the female moral reform and temperance movements, women began to challenge traditional male privileges, notably the sexual double standard and the traditional right of a man to "correct" his wife. The "age of association" offered huge numbers of women interesting work and a respected role in their communities.[11]

As the twentieth century progressed, the work formerly performed by married women in associations gradually was professionalized and taken over by men, and the Woman's Christian Temperance Union and like organizations ceased to be sources of status and became objects of derision. People began to place in work the hopes for vocation and self-fulfillment that earlier eras had reserved for religion. With increases in mobility and new patterns of social isolation, work often represented people's chief social role and the center of social life. By midcentury, for all but a tiny group of the very rich, social status was determined by work roles. Arlie Hochschild argues in her most recent book, *The Time Bind*, that today work has become the center of workers' social and emotional as well as their economic lives.[12] Work also provides the key to most social roles involving authority and responsibility even when those roles do not stem directly from the market.

Friedan's emphasis on market work reflects not only the end of the era of women's associations but also the withering of respect for women's domestic role. *The Feminine Mystique* reflects housewives' lack of status by the 1960s. "What do I do? ... Why nothing. I'm just a housewife," quotes Friedan. In a world where adult "success" was defined by work, housewives lost a sense of self. "I begin to feel I have no personality. I'm a server of food and a putter-on of pants and a bedmaker, somebody who can be called on when you want something. But who am I?" said one. And another: "I just don't feel alive." Friedan concludes: "A woman who has no purpose of her own in society, a woman who cannot let herself think about the future because she is doing nothing to give herself a real identity in it, will continue to feel a desperation in the present. . . . You can't just deny your intelligent mind; you need to be part of the social scheme." To a nineteenth-century "moral mother," the notion that she played no part in the social scheme would have seemed bizarre.[13]

Meanwhile, increasingly misogynist attacks on housewives at midcentury were linked with the anxiety produced by the changing roles of men. Books such as David Reisman's 1950 *The Lonely Crowd* and William Whyte's 1956 *The Organization Man* reflected widespread fears that men, formerly manly and inner-directed, were becoming feminized and outer-directed by the lockstep of corporate life. Said Reisman, "Some of the occupational and cultural boundaries have broken down which help men rest assured that they are men." Whyte and Reisman painted a picture of "outer-directed" men eager for approval. They reflected men's sense of an imagined past where they had independence and autonomy. Men's sense of loss was exacerbated by their loss of patriarchal authority over children, as a result of the growing importance of peer influence attributable to the rise of mass consumer culture and the spread of secondary schools. Cartoons, films, and studies abounded with imagery of henpecked men unable to stand up to domineering wives.[14] The "moral mother" had become the domineering housewife.

Friedan's belittlement of housewives was an ingenious use of misogynist stereotyping in the cause of women's liberation. She deployed misogynist images of women as evidence that the breadwinner/housewife model hurt not only women but their families as well. She skillfully turned the literature attacking housewives into evidence in favor of the need to eliminate the housewife role. She argued, first, that housewifery frustrated women so much that they made their husbands' lives a misery. To these arguments Friedan added a deadpan public health perspective: "The problem that has no name . . . is taking a far greater toll on the physical and mental health of our country than any known disease."[15]

In summary, the full-commodification strategy arose in a social context where work roles determined social status and personal fulfillment to an extent they never had before. Access to market work seemed particularly important because the only accepted alternative, the housewife role, had lost the cultural power it had enjoyed during the nineteenth century, and had become the object of misogynist attack. Ironically, the cultural devaluation of housewives ultimately came to be associated not with misogyny but with feminism. As we will see later, this stemmed in part from events that occurred after Friedan had ceased to dominate the feminist scene.

Friedan Strategically Downplayed the Changes Necessary to Incorporate Mothers into the Workforce

Friedan's goal was to start a "sex-role revolution." To accomplish this, she had to downplay the changes necessary to incorporate mothers into market work. First, she minimized the difficulty of finding a responsible job after a period out of the workforce. She pointed to the suburban housewife who found "an excellent job in her old field after only two trips to the city." "In Westchester, on Long Island, in the Philadelphia suburbs," she continued breezily, "women have started mental-health clinics, art centers, day camps. In big cities and small towns, women all the way from New England to California have pioneered new movements in politics and education. Even if this work was not thought of as a 'job' or 'career,' it was often so important that professionals are now being paid for doing it." "Over and over," she continued, "women told me that the crucial step for them was simply to take the first trip to the alumnae employment agency, or to send for the application for teacher certification, or to make appointments with former job contacts in the city." The only thing women had to fear, Friedan implied, was fear itself.[16]

She also minimized the question of who would take care of the children. "There are, of course, a number of practical problems involved in making a serious career commitment. But somehow those problems only seem insurmountable when a woman is still half-submerged in the false dilemmas and guilts of the feminine mystique." Friedan criticized one woman willing to accept only volunteer jobs without deadlines "because she could not count on a cleaning woman. Actually," Friedan tells us, "if she had hired a cleaning woman, which many of her neighbors were doing for much less reason, she would have had to commit herself to the kind of assignments that would have been a real test of her ability." Would a "cleaning woman" really have solved this family's child care problems? Typically they come only once a week.[17]

This was one of the rare moments where Friedan mentioned household help. Her erasure of women's household work was strategic, for she knew full well what was required for a wife and mother to go back to work. When she returned to work in 1955, she hired "a really good mother-substitute—a housekeeper-nurse." But she carefully evaded this threatening issue in *The Feminine Mystique*. It soon returned to haunt women.[18]

Friedan's evasion of these difficult issues was understandable, and probably necessary, at the time she wrote *The Feminine Mystique*. If she had demanded that husbands give up their traditional entitlement to their wives' services, husbands simply would have forbidden their wives to work. If she had admitted the difficult obstacles mothers would face in a work world designed for men, her revolution never would have gotten off the ground. To give Friedan her due, she did reopen each of these questions as soon as she felt she could. By 1973 she was demanding that men share equally in family work, a theme she had mentioned but downplayed eleven years earlier. She also argued that it was "necessary to change the rules of the game to restructure professions, marriage, the family, the home." Finally, in 1981, Friedan picked up a theme she had not stressed twenty years before: that our society devalues work traditionally associated with women. In her controversial *The Second Stage*, Friedan bent over backward to send the message that she was no longer belittling family work, and demanded that work be restructured around its requirements.[19]

But by this time Friedan was no longer in control of the conversation she had helped create. Popular feminism fossilized into the full-commodification strategy and stayed there. Some feminists engaged in frontal attacks on homemaking, as in Jessie Bernard's statement that "being a housewife makes women sick." That statement was repeated almost verbatim a quarter century later in Rosalind C. Barnett and Caryl Rivers' *She Works/He Works*, which asserted in 1996 that "[t]he mommy track can be bad for your health." *She Works/He Works* dramatizes the extent to which popular feminism remains stuck in the full-commodification model. It reports that women are now happy and healthy in the workforce, men are helping at home, and children are better off than ever in day care. It glosses over the pervasive marginalization of mothers, the widespread sense of strain among parents of both sexes, and the central fact that mothers' entrance into the labor force has not been accompanied by fathers' equal participation in family work.[20]

In fact, the drawbacks of the full-commodification model became evident as early as the 1970s. Some drawbacks concern its hidden racial and class dynamics; these are so complex and important they are discussed in detail in chapter 5. Other dynamics became apparent much earlier. One way to trace the dawning recognition of these drawbacks is through stories in women's magazines in the 1970s through the 1990s. *Glamour* and *McCall's* are most useful for this purpose.

Articles in the 1970s showed great excitement about the prospect of going to work and remind us what a big step it was to take even a part-time job for little money. "I got the check from *GLAMOUR* and bought some schoolmarm clothes. For the first time since we'd been married, I didn't feel guilty spending money on myself," recounted one woman. Another article on the same topic commented, "A very striking conclusion to come out of the questionnaire is that six out of ten women who work believe that what suffers most . . . is the quality of their housekeeping, but their letters are eloquent testimony that their most frequent reaction is, 'So what!'" This article discussed the excitement of market work and the challenges of combining this new role with their existing workload: "I don't think you have to make a choice. I never felt I had to compromise my femininity to continue to work. . . . It makes perfect sense to me to move from one area to another (i.e. home to office). In one day, I pick a fabric for a chair, arrange a party, sign a business deal, pay bills and give rich attention to my husband and children." Other articles are more realistic but still upbeat: "There is a whole generation of liberated young women who are quietly putting the ideals of revolution into practice, combining marriage, motherhood, and a master's degree, cooking and career. . . . Combining the two is far from an easy task. It is not an impossible dream but it takes hard work. The trick is in learning how; the art is in doing it well." This was the era of the Enjoli perfume ad: "I can bring home the bacon, fry it up in a pan. And never, never, never let you forget you're a man." A TV jingle declared:

> I can put the wash on the line,
> feed the kids, get dressed, pass out the kisses
> And get to work by five to nine
> 'Cause I'm a woman.[21]

By 1975 one begins to hear of "casualties." "For more than two years, Ms. Chechik ran her own interior design boutique. Being mother, wife, homemaker and career woman had . . . exhausted her physically and mentally. . . . She explained that by the time she finished all her housework, it was one or two in the morning 'and I was so hyper I couldn't sleep.' When she began breaking out in hives, [she] decided that something had to go: it was the boutique." Men also awoke to the implications of the new trends: "My husband doesn't *mind* my working, but he won't help me. He says when I can't do my own work then I'll have to quit. So naturally I don't ask him to do anything for me." Said one husband, "Now it's all very fine to agree that today's women should have more rights, but whom do they think they are going to get them from? From me, that's who. Well, I don't have enough rights as it is."[22]

Articles in the 1980s show the dawning recognition that entering the workforce without changing the conditions of work resulted in longer working hours for women. The term superwoman was coined in the early 1980s, implicitly blaming the situation on women themselves. The term deflected attention away from the fact that women were forced to do it all because men would not give up their traditional entitlement to women's household work.

Many older women's attitudes toward feminism still stem from this period. My son's nursery school principal reflected this image when she asked, with some satisfaction, as I struggled with car pools and logistics, "It's not so easy to combine being a mother with a full-time career, is it?" I replied, "It's not so easy being 'just' a mother either. It involves important work, and a lot of it." This reply blunted her implied criticism that feminism devalues women's family work. "Yes," she said, "when the women's lib people came along, those of us who had stayed home realized we had a lot of skills."

Note how she moved from an attack on feminism to an acknowledgment of feminists' role in revaluing domestic work—but only under prodding. Her first response had been to associate feminism with the belittlement of family work. The same instinct persists in the popular press. The following is from Anne Roiphe, whose daughter Katie later made her name as a writer by attacking the notion of date rape.

> In the early days of the [feminist] movement we thought we could do without [families]. Then we created a model of equality that left children waiting at the window for someone to come home. Then we floundered and demanded day care and deprived women who wanted to watch their two-year-olds pound pegs into holes of their earnest desire. We woke up to discover that our goal of equality had created a generation of gray flannel suits who played tennis to win and could tell you all about IRAs and CDs and nothing about Wynken, Blynken, and Nod.[23]

In the popular imagination, feminism came to be associated with careerists whose model of equality married them to money rather than to caregiving. Thus, to Deborah Fallows, "the feminist movement seemed mainly to celebrate those heroines who had made their mark in business, politics, or the arts; and magazines like *Working Mother* tried to say it was all pointless anyway, since working makes for better mothers and stronger children." Fallows bristled when she heard Gloria Steinem on the radio decrying the "narrow and stifled" lives of women at home. "The feminists may officially say that 'choice' is at the top of their agenda for women. But there are too many hints and innuendos that suggest that this talk comes fairly cheap."[24]

If the first liability of the full-commodification model is its devaluation of family work, the second is its denial that structural changes are necessary in order for women to reach equality. Women's entrance into the workforce without changes to either the structure of market work or the gendered allocation of family work means that women with full-time jobs work much longer hours than women at home. Although it made perfect sense for Friedan to argue in 1962 that women should join the workforce without waiting for changes from their husbands, their employers, or the government, it quickly became apparent that "having it all" under these circumstances often leads to exhausted women doing it all.[25]

"Feminists have long fought for day-care and family-leave programs, but they still tend to be blamed for the work-family conundrum," observed feminist writer Wendy Kaminer. A *Redbook* survey in the mid-1990s found that nearly 40 percent of women polled said that feminism had made work/family conflict worse, while another 32 percent felt it made no difference. Said a trade unionist writing in *The Nation* in 1996, "By the mid- to late eighties, younger women no longer praised the [feminist] movement for giving them access to jobs, but blamed 'feminists' for longer hours and job insecurity. As one tired machinist put it, 'Before the women's movement we did the housework and the men took out the trash. But since we were liberated they don't take out the trash anymore.'" When women were asked to select the most important goal for the women's movement in 1989, a *Time*/CNN poll rated "helping women balance work and family" at the top of their list; the second was "getting government funding for programs such as child care and maternity leave." One stressed-out mother of two asked Gloria Steinem, "Why didn't you tell us that it was going to be like this?" Steinem replied: "Well, we didn't know."[26]

In "The Superwoman Squeeze" in 1980, *Newsweek* spotted the syndrome Arlie

Hochschild named the "second shift" nine years later.[27] That article painted a picture of "an eighteen-hour mother" who works incessantly from sunup to midnight, while her husband "occasionally helps clean up or puts the boys to bed. But for the most part, Jim reads in the living room while Sue vacuums, does late-night grocery shopping, grades papers from 9 P.M. to 11 P.M. and collapses." *Newsweek* documents the "guilt, the goals, and the go-it-alone grind [that] have become achingly familiar to millions of American women." "Now we get the jobs all right," said one woman, "all the jobs: at home, with the kids, and at work."[28]

In her brilliant 1989 book *The Second Shift*, Arlie Hochschild sought to transform work/family conflict from being evidence against feminism into proof of the need for more of it. She argued that men were enjoying the benefits of wives' salaries but refused to share equally in household work. Through carefully constructed narratives, she communicated the message that women's failure to perform as ideal workers was attributable in significant part to their husbands' failure to shoulder their fair share of family work.[29]

Hochschild crystallized an important change. Once husbands lost their felt entitlement to have women do all the housework, the revised standard version of the full-commodification model stressed the need to reallocate household work. This was a shift in focus away from early feminists' reliance on the government, as they envisioned day care centers as being as common, and as free, as public libraries. Thus the solution Hochschild highlighted in the first edition of her bestseller was a redistribution of family work between fathers and mothers (a shift from her path-breaking call nearly twenty years earlier for restructuring of "the clockwork of male careers").[30]

Another element of the full-commodification model was its focus on relatively privileged women. This emphasis was reflected both in the assumption that market work meant high-status, high-paying careers, and in the assumption that child care should be delegated to the market, often without much consideration of what this would mean for women who cannot afford quality child care.[31]

The final assumption of full-commodification feminism was that women should be ready, willing, and able to delegate child care to the same extent male ideal workers do. This proved the most problematic assumption of all.

THE NORM OF PARENTAL CARE

Every day I leave my kids at day care, I think to myself: *What kind of a mother am I?* It's like I'm not raising my own children.[32]

The biggest problem as I see it for both men and women [lawyers] is how to balance children in a large-firm environment. I plan to go part-time when I have a child, and I *hate* the idea. If the firm had a 24-hour day care or nursery, I would not work part-time—I would stay full-time. Obviously, even this is no solution: kids can't grow up in a day care center.[33]

A central assumption of the full-commodification model was that women would feel comfortable delegating family work to the market to the same extent traditional fathers had. Many don't. Recall the young officer, discussed in chapter 1, who didn't want her children "raised by strangers."

Lillian Rubin comments, "The notion that mom should be there for the children always and without fail, that her primary job is to tend and nurture them, that without her constant ministrations their future is in jeopardy, is deeply embedded in our national psyche." Mothers who do not stay home often find themselves wondering, as did the woman quoted earlier, "What kind of a mother am I?" Sometimes this manifests as explicit gender policing; an extreme example is the hate mail received by the Boston family whose nanny killed their son. "It seems the parents didn't really want a kid," said one caller to a talk show host. "Now they don't have one." Note that the mother "at fault" worked only part time.[34]

As noted in the introduction, two-thirds of Americans believe it would be best for women to stay home and care for family and children. In significant part, this reflects the paucity of attractive alternatives.[35] In European countries, the shift of mothers into the workforce was supported through government benefits. In Russia and Eastern Europe, programs included maternity leave with guaranteed reemployment, sick leave, and paid time off for child care and housework. In Western Europe, high-quality child care is provided or subsidized by the government. In France, an extensive system of neighborhood child-care centers exists throughout the country, staffed by trained teachers and psychologists, with ready access to medical personnel, so that children's illnesses are both spotted and treated at the center. Parents fight to get their children in, with the sense that being in child care helps children develop social skills. In Belgium and France an estimated 95 percent of nursery-school-age children are in publicly funded child care. Sweden also has a comprehensive system of quality child care.[36]

In the United States, feminists' dream that day care facilities would be as common as public libraries never came true. In 1971, when Congress passed the Comprehensive Child Development Act, President Nixon vetoed it under pressure from an intense lobbying campaign that decried the proposal as "a radical piece of social legislation" designed to deliver children to "communal approaches to child-rearing over and against the family-centered approach." A 1975 proposal was also defeated, decried as an effort to "sovietize the family." As a result, the United States offers less governmental support for child care than does any other industrialized nation. The successful efforts to defeat the kinds of proposals implemented in Europe dramatizes how profoundly U.S. women have been affected by Americans' distinctive lack of solidarity.[37]

As a result, the imagery and the reality of day care are different here than elsewhere. Where child care is prevalent and government-sponsored, it is seen as an expression of social solidarity and national investment in the next generation. In sharp contrast, in the United States, day care is seen as an expression of the market. These perceptions are accurate in part. In countries with significant government support for child care, notably France, child-care workers are well-paid civil servants with steady and respected employment. Child care in the United States, in sharp contrast, suffers from very low wages and very high turnover. One child-care worker of my acquaintance works for Head Start; after fourteen years and several promotions, she now earns about $14,000 a year. At these pay rates, high rates of turnover are not surprising. Nor is it surprising that many Americans have a negative image of day care centers. While many centers are excellent, market realities militate against quality child care.[38]

Day care in the United States also suffers from imagery and symbolism derived from domesticity. Recall the insistent split between home and market. As discussed in chapter 1, domesticity from the beginning provided very negative images of the market. If economics encapsulates our positive imagery of the market as the benign deliverer of quality goods to satisfied customers, domesticity embeds very different imagery of the market as a selfish and calculating world out of touch with people's needs for genuine intimacy. Throwing child care into this metaphoric maelstrom in a society without a third realm of social solidarity results in a predictable revulsion against market solutions. Some people preserve the negative market imagery for day care centers and contrast it with their chosen form of care. Despite the shift of child care into the market, today most Americans choose child care that is as homelike as they can manage. Keep in mind that one-third of married mothers, and a slightly higher percentage of single ones, are home full-time. Most children not cared for by their mothers are cared for by another relative—care by relatives (typically fathers or grandmothers) accounts for nearly 50 percent of all children in child care. Another 22 percent are cared for by nannies in their own homes, or in the homes of their sitters. All in all, in one-half to one-third of families, mothers are at home. In the remaining families, about 70 percent of children are in care associated with home or family. Only about 30 percent of children in child care are in day care centers.[39]

As always, the material and the metaphoric feed off each other. When mothers quit market work for lack of suitable child care, the paucity of good alternatives gets encoded as mothers' "preference" to care for children at home. As discussed in chapter 1, the material conditions of motherhood in a society that delivers child services primarily through mothers become evidence of mothers' choice to stay home. This in turns gets encoded in negative market imagery of day care—as in Fallows' book—and is not counterbalanced by alternative imagery of day care as a place where children receive professional services and develop social skills in ways they cannot in an isolated home setting.[40]

A second major force feeding the resistance to day care as a solution is the sharp increase in the number of hours in the workweek. Juliet Schor, in *The Overworked American*, documented that Americans' average workweek has lengthened in recent years. Increases are concentrated in "good" jobs with a high benefits "load," which include high-paying blue-collar jobs as well as many high-status white-collar jobs. Factory workers in 1994 put in the highest levels of overtime ever registered. Nearly one-fourth of office workers now work forty-nine or more hours a week. A survey of Fortune 500 corporations in the 1970s found that many managers worked sixty hours a week or more, excluding business travel: "They'd leave home at 7:30 A.M. and return home about the same time that evening. They'd also bring home a few hours of work each day." This has not changed much. As noted in the introduction, one-third of fathers work forty-nine or more hours a week; in high-status white-collar jobs it is closer to 50 percent. Said one forty-one-year-old public relations officer in a major corporation: "I can't imagine having a baby, which I want to do, and still keeping this job. All corporate jobs are like this—you're valued according to the long hours you are willing to put in, and the schedule is so rigid that anyone who wants to do it differently has to leave." Schor notes, "The 5:00 Dads of the 1950s and 1960s (those who were home for dinner and an evening with the family) are becoming an endangered species." The increase in hours means that an ideal worker with a half-hour commute to a "good" job often will be away from home from 8:00 A.M. to 7 P.M. Very few people would consider this an ideal schedule for both parents in a family with children. The result is often that, among people with access to "good" jobs, fathers work overtime while mothers work part-time or on the no-overtime mommy track. Families see little choice.[41]

The forces named thus far—the lack of social solidarity and the sharp increase in working hours—are peculiar to the United States. However, data from Sweden raise intriguing questions about whether the full-commodification model is viable even where these peculiarly American conditions do not exist.

Sweden has implemented the full-commodification model with a level of commitment higher than anyplace else in the world. As a result of a severe labor shortage in a country with no self-consciousness about crafting governmental solutions to social problems, Sweden encouraged workforce participation by mothers by providing child care as well as generous parental leaves available to either parent, accompanied by government efforts to increase men's participation in family work.

The result has not been equality for women. Swedish mothers still suffer marginalization in order to care for children. As of 1986, 43 percent of working women were employed part time. Women continued to do a disproportionate share of family work and took fifty-two days of leave for every day taken by a man. Industrial workers were much less likely to take parental leave than were professional and public employees. Sweden's level of sex segregation is *higher* than even our own very high level: One study concluded that 70 percent of all women would have to change occupations for women to achieve the same occupational distribution as men. Swedish women earn only 37 percent of the country's total wages.[42]

These findings place the full-commodification strategy in a somber light. The Swedish example suggests that many people in advanced industrialized countries feel that having both parents working the ideal-worker schedule is inconsistent with the level and type of parental attention children need. This reflects the fact that children's success in these middle-class societies depends in part on parents' ability to instill the discipline, motivation, and independence necessary to do well in middle-class life.

To say this in a less clinical way, one key to success in life is having your children turn out well: healthy, well-adjusted, secure, successful (in widely varying senses of the word). We are willing to give up a lot to achieve this; often we do. In the face of our dreams for our children, marginalization at work often seems a price worth paying even if it may lead to disappointments or to economic vulnerability later on in life.

All this suggests that it is time to acknowledge the *norm of parental care*. Let me say loud and clear that this is not the same as saying that children need full-time mothercare. Domesticity's mother-as-sole-source ideal is not ideal at all. Its most important drawback is that it links caregiving with disempowerment. Not only does this make children vulnerable to impoverishment if their parents divorce; it also means that the adults who know our children best and are most invested in meeting their needs have relatively little power within the household and outside of it. Sociological studies since the 1960s have documented that power within the family generally tracks power outside it.[43]

Its second drawback is that where the mother's personality is not an easy fit with that of a particular child, that child is offered very little opportunity to develop relationships with other adults with whom s/he may have more natural rapport. Childhood expert T. Berry Brazleton suggests this is a common occurrence. He describes the difficulties of one mother in relating to her quiet and somewhat inexpressive child, noting that the father had better rapport. "Laura's quietness continues to be a drain on Mrs. King.... Mr. King sees this quietness for what it is, a gentle personality who looks and listens rather than using activity as a communication system." Laura brightened at the sound of her father's voice when she was less than a month old. But Mrs. King—"daunted," "in tears," "embarrassed" by Laura's inexpressiveness—did most of the caregiving. When she became pregnant again, "she hoped sincerely for an active boy."[44]

A third drawback of the mother-as-sole-source model is that the tasks required to make a household run today may not mix well with quality child care. Deborah Fallows provides an example:

> I had packed up both children and was headed out the door when my husband, who by then had left the government and was working at home, asked, "Where are you going?" "To Sears, to get some hooks for the closet...." We went out prepared for everything—back-up clothes for the baby, cookies for the three-year-old, extra diapers, extra wipes, strollers, umbrellas, damp cloths, plastic bags. When we got to the parking lot, I nursed Tad in the car to stop his crying while Tommy ate cookies. Tad had a bout of diarrhea, and I changed him from top to toe. By then, the wet summer heat was building. We were all sticky and irritable. I was sweating, feeling nauseated. Before we could make it out of the car, a thunderstorm let loose and we were trapped. More nursing, more cookies, more changing. The storm tapered off to a gentle rain, which we finally braved to get into the store. Of course they didn't even have the hooks I was looking for.

Any parent who has struggled with a cranky baby in the supermarket or has woken a sick or sleepy child to drive an older sibling to a lesson knows that children are not always well served by the mother-as-sole-source supplier model.[45]

While Friedan was right to reject that model, the time has come to abandon the fiction that both mothers and fathers can perform as ideal workers in a system designed for men supported by a flow of family work from women. We need to open a debate on how much parental care children truly need given the trade-offs between providing money and providing care. A good place to start is with the consensus that children are not best served if both parents are away from home eleven hours a day. This means that the jobs that require fifty-hour workweeks are designed in a way that conflicts with the norm of parental care.

Beyond the fifty-hour week, little consensus exists about how much child care is delegable. However, once feminists name and acknowledge the norm of parental care, discussions of how much delegation is too much will replace conversations in which mothers protest that they "chose" to cut back or quit when further investigation reveals that they did so because they could not find quality child care, or because the father works such long hours that without a marginalized mother the children would rarely see a parent awake.

A formal acknowledgment of the norm of parental care will serve a second important purpose as well: to empower mothers in situations where their partners meet demands for equal contributions to family work by claiming that virtually all child care is delegable. This dynamic does not emerge when mothers marginalize without a fuss; in such cases the conclusion that not all child care is delegable typically is treated as a matter of consensus. But when mothers refuse to follow docilely in domesticity's caregiver role, a game of chicken emerges in which fathers advocate higher levels of delegation than mothers consider appropriate. The classic example is of the high-status father who advocates hiring two sets of nannies to give sixteen hours of coverage so that no one's career is hurt. Or the father who suggested that his wife hire a babysitter to care for the children during a weekend when he had promised to be available so that she could take a long-planned trip. One ambitious father expressed it this way: "Over-involvement with children may operate to discourage many fathers from fully sharing because they do not accept the ideology of close attention to children."[46] Until this "ideology" is formally stated and publicly defended, mothers will have their decision to marginalize cited as evidence of their own personal priorities (for which they should naturally be willing to make trade-offs) rather than as an expression of a societal ideal (for which parents share equal responsibility).

Naming and acknowledging the norm of parental care can help poor women as well as more privileged ones. One central difficulty in the welfare reform debate is the lack of a language in which to defend the right of poor women to stay home with their children, in a society where the child care available to them is often not only unstimulating but downright unsafe. As will be discussed at greater length in chapter 6, it is hard to defend poor women's right to stay home in a society where a much higher percentage of poor women than of working-class women are homemakers: about 33 percent of poor women are at home, but only about 20 percent of working-class ones. This situation is bound to generate working-class anger. Naming the norm of parental care is not enough to change the dynamics of the welfare debate; that will require a social system where working-class as well as poor children are seen as being entitled to a certain amount of parental care. But acknowledging the existence of a norm of parental care is an important first step.[47]

Defining the norm of parental care starts from an assessment of children's needs, and then splits the resulting responsibilities down the middle. In such a world, mothers' work patterns would look much more similar to fathers.' Consider the following example. Say the parents of elementary-school children decide that one parent needs to be home two days a week, to drive the children to doctor and dentist appointments, to enable them to take lessons not available in the after-school program, to help with homework, to allow for play dates. Then the father and the mother would both work four days each week, and half a day or not at all the fifth. This would be much easier for an employer to accommodate than if the mother comes in alone demanding a three-day week. "They are so unreasonable," a top manager complained to me recently. "A woman came in demanding a three-day schedule. We told her she could either work four days a week and keep her [middle-level] management position, or three days a week in which case she would have to give it up, because things around here just won't run with a three-day-a-week manager. She got angry and quit." If fathers were truly sharing in family work, mothers' demands would be much easier to accommodate. This would end the situation where the only viable alternative a family sees is to have the mother quit or go part-time (making, on average, 40 percent less per hour than a full-time worker), in which case the father has to work overtime to make up for the loss in income. A more equal sharing of market and family work would also avoid the situation where, if the parents divorce, the children are impoverished along with their marginalized mother. We have much to gain from shifting to a strategy of reconstructing both the ideal-worker and marginalized-caregiver roles we have inherited from domesticity. The time has come to abandon the full-commodification strategy in favor of ending the system of providing for children's care by marginalizing their caregivers. This is the agenda of reconstructive feminism.

RECONSTRUCTIVE FEMINISM

In my view feminism has never been anti-family, but the time has come to point out that feminism is pro-family, in that it advocates changes that will help children as well as women. The system of providing care by marginalizing the caregivers hurts not only children but also the sick and the elderly. The current system rests on the assumption that all people at all times are the full-grown, healthy adults of liberal theory, making the social compact and pursuing citizenship and self-interest within it. This is a very unrealistic view of human life. The time has come to recognize that humanity does not consist only of healthy adults. We have changed from a society that formally delegates to women the care of children, the sick, and the elderly to a society that pretends those groups do not exist. The result, to women's credit, is that women still do the caregiving. But they pay a stiff price for doing so.

Law professor Martha Fineman has argued that the remedy is to recognize dependence as a fact of life and to spread its costs by providing income supports for dependent caregivers. This would mean sharing the burden of child rearing and illness as we have shared the burden of old age, by publicly financing a system like Social Security. The alternative to an embrace of dependence is to change work structures that penalize caregiving, such as the severe wage penalty currently associated with part-time work.[48] The third alternative is what we have today: In one of the richest countries in the world, nearly 80 percent of the poor are women and children.[49]

We need to end the marginalization of caregivers by changing the definition of the ideal worker so that it reflects the norm of parental care. Instead of simply allowing women to work on the same terms traditionally available to men, we need to change the conditions under which both men and women work. The Swedish example suggests that men will not participate equally in family work so long as they have to marginalize to do so. When asked why they do not take parental leave and work part time, Swedish men say they do not want to be passed over at work. Not surprisingly, working-class men feel even less free to risk marginalization at work than do middle-class ones.[50]

Polls show that strong support exists for the strategy of redesigning work. A 1989 survey found that nearly eight out of ten people preferred a career path that would offer slower advancement in return for being able to schedule their own full-time hours and give more attention to their families, in contrast to a fast track that allowed less time for family life. Fifty-four percent of those surveyed in a Gallup poll—men as well as women—identified flexible work hours as their highest priority. A number of recent polls of employees and college students identified policies such as flextime and family-oriented sick leave as the most preferred benefits, more popular than on-site child care. By a three-to-one margin, Americans surveyed in a 1998 survey for the National Partnership for Women and Families said that "time pressures on working families" are getting worse, not better; nearly 60 percent said that "finding time for both work and family responsibilities had gotten harder rather than easier" for families like theirs in the last five years. A 1998 poll found that 80 percent of both men and women felt that the shift of women into the workforce is making it harder to raise children. Seventy percent said they worry very often or somewhat often about shortchanging their family, their jobs, or themselves because there is not time to do everything they need to do. Polling also documents that Americans are concerned about obtaining leaves from work. Over two-thirds of Americans under forty say they will need family leave in the next ten years; nearly two-thirds under sixty say they will have responsibility for elder care.[51]

The original full-commodification model did not go far enough. It shifted women into the workforce without changing the rules of the game, namely, that employers were entitled to ideal workers and that men were entitled to be them. Reconstructive feminism aims to go much further, deconstructing domesticity by eliminating the ideal-worker norm. Chapter 3 argues that the ideal-worker norm in market work constitutes discrimination against mothers, and therefore against women. Chapter 4 challenges the ideal-worker norm in the divorce courts. These two proposals would substantially shift the force fields that pull women into marginalization and mothers and children into poverty.

In contrast to many earlier feminist strategies that focused on eliminating entitlements for caregivers, the focus of reconstructive feminism is on eliminating the carrots, and the sticks, that keep men in the ideal-worker role. Chapter 3's proposal eliminates the stick that keeps men performing as ideal workers: the threat of marginalization at work. Chapter 4's proposal eliminates the carrot that keeps men in the ideal-worker role: their current entitlement to walk with their wallets upon divorce, carrying with them the chief family asset—the ideal worker's wage.

What a Shift in Strategy Offers Women—and Their Children

A shift away from the full-commodification model offers the opportunity for new alliances within and outside of feminism. For a decade, feminist jurisprudence has focused largely on sexual harassment, domestic violence, and pornography. While these issues are important, so are work/family issues. As noted above, a 1989 poll showed that many U.S. women feel that balancing work and family should be the top priority of the women's movement. Recent union polling found that the most frequently expressed problem—rated higher even than concerns for job security— was that both parents must work: "When you come home at seven or eight o'clock, you don't have quality time. And your children are left alone and raised by someone else. I think this is a tremendous problem," said one focus group member.[52]

Feminists have tended to shy away from work and family issues in part because they have proved very divisive in the past. The full-commodification model—by enshrining ideal-worker women as models of what women should strive for— alienates many women whose lives are framed around caregiving. The problem is an important one because so many women's lives are framed by caregiving, as documented in the introduction.

The proposal to restructure market work, in sharp contrast, does not favor ideal workers over caregivers or vice versa. Instead, it brings the two groups together by allowing ideal workers more time for caregiving, while valuing caregivers' work and protecting them and their children from economic vulnerability. Reconstructive feminism replaces the traditional focus on market work with a more balanced focus on market work *and* family work. This will help end the association of feminism with the devaluation of family work. Language here is very important. I have found that replacing the common phrase "resolving the work/family conflict" with "restructuring market and family work" commonly brings a shock of recognition to caregivers that feminists are on their side, not aligned with the array of social forces that belittle them.

The second major proposal of reconstructive feminism is to deconstruct the ideal-worker norm in family entitlements. Here the focus is on gaining entitlements for women whose lives are framed around caregiving, not because they have "special needs" but on the grounds that the current system awards to divorcing men an asset that reflects not only the value of men's market work but also the value of women's domestic labor. Linking a proposal concerning market work with one concerning family work reinforces the message that these two kinds of work are equally important to the feminist imagination.

Reconstructive feminism takes very seriously the common assertion that feminism hurts children. The analysis thus far shows that, far from protecting children, domesticity's organization of market and family work hurts them in two major ways. The first is economic: Children are impoverished by a system that marginalizes their mothers. This is particularly true in the United States, which provides few social supports for caregivers, and where children's claim on an ideal-worker father often proves illusory. The result is a system that impoverishes mothers and children. Some are impoverished when they first marginalize for the good of their children and then, upon divorce, find themselves and their children cut off from the bulk of the ideal worker's wage. (This is the topic of chapter 4.) Others are never-married mothers, many of whom got pregnant young and subsequently found their job and school prospects hampered by the assumption that students and workers have no child-care responsibilities. In an era when well over half of children will spend some time living in a single-parent household, overwhelmingly with single mothers, the assumption that all children will have steady access to an ideal worker's wage leads to widespread childhood poverty.[53]

Domesticity's particular organization of market and family work disadvantages children in a second way as well. As noted above, forty years of sociological studies document that power within the family generally tracks market power outside of it. More recently, this literature has been complemented by economic analyses pointing out that parties' negotiating power within a unit depends on which party has the best alternative outside it. In an ideal-worker/marginalized-caregiver household, men have the bargaining advantage because they can always walk away with the chief asset of the family—their ideal-worker wage.[54]

Lillian Rubin details this dynamic in her description of Phyllis Kilson, a forty-six-year-old mother who went back to work after her children were grown: "Gary always made all the big decisions, and I never felt like I had a right to my say. I mean, I tried sometimes, but if he said no, I figured I didn't have a right to contradict him. Now I make money, too, so it's different. I go out and buy something for the grandchildren, or even for me, without asking him, and he can't say anything." Children suffer in a system that first allocates children's care to women and then marginalizes the women who do it, thereby undercutting their power to stand up for children's needs. The most dramatic example is when a mother suffering from domestic abuse feels she cannot leave the abuser because she has no other way to support herself. The domestic-violence literature suggests this situation is not uncommon. In the words of one expert in the field, "The domestication of women [in the home] is a precondition for the crime we define as domestic violence."[55]

In a recent radio interview, Patricia Hersh, the author of a book that argues that adolescents need more time and attention from their parents than they currently receive, was faced by an interviewer who kept asking whether Hersh really meant that mothers should stay home. Reconstructive feminism provides a ready response. Children *do* need substantial amounts of parental attention, but this does not mean that mothers are duty-bound to quit. If a widespread agreement exists that children need more parental attention, society should make parents free to give it without incurring the risk of marginalization at work. A society that takes the norm of parental care seriously would not marginalize those who live by it.[56]

In summary, reconstructive feminism solves several problems inherited from the full-commodification model. In addition, it helps defuse the conflicts between ideal-worker women and women whose lives are framed by caregiving; the emotional energy that now goes into this debate could more profitably be used to bring about gender change. The key message is that child rearing is too important to be done under the current conditions of marginalization and disempowerment.

What a New Strategy Offers to Men

> I look at the grief and anxiety my father had by being a sole provider, and I would like to change that definition of being a man.[57]

A shift to reconstructive feminism not only holds the potential for uniting diverse groups of women; it also opens an increased possibility of building coalitions with men. The full-commodification model pins women's hopes for equality on a redistribution of gendered work within the household; in doing so, it pits mothers against fathers in a zero-sum game where someone has to marginalize. Under these conditions, few men envision equal sharing: one study estimated that only 13 percent do. In sharp contrast, the proposal to restructure work offers the chance to build a coalition of all concerned parents. The goal is to allow fathers as well as mothers the opportunity to perform simultaneously both as ideal workers (under a redefined ideal) and as adults responsible for caregiving.[58]

"Women may change all they want; unless men undergo corresponding transformations, change will grind to a halt." Feminists have ignored this maxim at their peril. Forming a coalition with men should be possible because the current gender system consigns men to a role that hurts them. Chapter 1 explored the linkage of masculinity and anxiety; books ranging from *The Organization Man* to *Death of a Salesman* and *Mr. Popper's Penguins* document the oppressiveness of the ideal-worker role. Gore Vidal summed it up:

> The thing that makes an economic system like ours work is to maintain control over people and make them do jobs they hate. To do this, you fill their heads with biblical nonsense about fornication of every variety. Make sure they marry young. . . . Once a man has a wife and two young children, he will do what you tell him to. He will obey you. And that is the aim of the entire masculine role.[59]

The pressures of the ideal-worker role have increased in recent decades. The overworked American run to the ground by *market* work is the American father. Thirty percent of fathers with children under fourteen now report working fifty or more hours a week. The same percentage works weekends at their regular job; many others work a second job. Long hours have become intertwined with masculinity. Arlie Hochschild quotes one worker: "Here in the plant, we have a macho thing about hours. Guys say, 'I'm an eighty-hour man!' as if describing their hairy chests." She describes a factory worker who could not assert his masculinity by being the only wage earner; instead he did so by working many more hours than his wife. One law student protested that "large firms . . . make it a policy to steal people's youth with the promise of future largess. . . . [L]aw school is a perfectly appropriate time to consider whether the death of the body is a fair price for the life of the mind."[60]

If the ideal-worker norm delivers a gray "life at hard labor" for men who fulfill it, it also disadvantages those who don't. According to Arlie Hochschild, the term "'family man' has taken on negative overtones, designating a worker who isn't a serious player. The term now tacitly but powerfully calls into question a worker's masculinity. It was precisely to avoid being classified as a 'family man' that the majority of men . . . stayed clear of the [family-friendly] policies that one might have expected a 'family man' to embrace." One management consultant recalled a client reluctant to promote an employee who frequently left the office at 5 P.M. "I don't think we can promote Bill," the client said at first. "He's got a wife who is a lawyer, and he is responsible for a lot of the child care. We're not convinced that he is serious about his career."[61]

The ideal-worker norm produces a wage gap not only between mothers and others but also between men whose wives do market work and men whose wives don't. This gap reflects the fact that although men with working wives do not share equally in family work, they do considerably more than men whose wives stay home. This leaves the husbands of housewives free to "go the extra mile" at work. Said one attorney:

> Law firms, consciously or unconsciously, discriminate against women when they require their attorneys to work long hours. . . . Of course, we men who like our kids get penalized, too. I came to the conclusion even before graduation that working in a law firm was inconsistent with my notions of being a good father.[62]

Surveys confirm men's dissatisfaction with the ideal-worker role. One study found that nearly three-quarters of the men surveyed said they would prefer the "daddy track" to the fast track. More than half of men surveyed in a 1990 poll said they were willing to have their salaries cut by 25 percent if they could have more personal or family time. In another, nearly 40 percent of fathers said they would quit their jobs if they could in order to spend more time with their children. *Time* reported that nearly half of men between eighteen and twenty-four surveyed expressed interest in staying home with their children. And some did. Said Peter Lynch, one of the most successful mutual fund managers in the country, explaining why he left his job to spend more time with his family: "Children are a great investment. They beat the hell out of stocks."[63]

If men are so eager to spend more time with their families, why don't they just do it? First, they can't afford to be marginalized economically. Many families are too dependent upon men's wages for them to refuse to perform as ideal workers: In the average white middle-class family, the husband earns roughly 70 percent of the income. Men of color tend to earn a lower proportion of the family income, but average family income tends to be lower, too, making it equally impractical for most to accept marginalization. In short, most men feel there is little choice but to perform as ideal workers to the extent class, race, and talent allow them to do so.[64]

Men often feel they must perform as ideal workers for a second reason, explored above: Work success is so tied up with most men's sense of self that they feel little choice but to try to fulfill the ideal-worker role. Men's sense of themselves as potent beings is connected with their work performance in very literal ways. Nothing ruins most men's self-esteem, a recent study found, like being married to a woman who earns more. Rates of impotence soar in unemployed men, as do rates of divorce, domestic violence, and suicide. "[E]mployment is a central part of the personal identity of most men. Therefore, when a man is not employed, he and his family are likely to have problems."[65]

Once feminists stop focusing exclusively on redistribution of work within the household, they can ally with men who find the ideal-worker role oppressive and/or inconsistent with their notions of responsible fatherhood. Feminists need to send the message that their proposals would free men from the sole-provider role that many men have always found oppressive and which many more today cannot fulfill. Reconstructive feminism holds the promise of liberation for men as well as women.

What's in It for Nonparents?

A central message of reconstructive feminism is that raising children is not a private frolic of one's own. Raising the next generation is important work that needs to be acknowledged and supported. Yet this does not mean that the proposal to reconstruct market work around caregiving holds advantages only for parents. The graying of America means that increasing numbers of people will be responsible for aging parents. One study found that 10 to 34 percent of workers have responsibility for an aging relative. About 8 percent provide some major care for aging parents. A national study found that 29 percent of all caregivers had rearranged their schedules to accommodate elder-care demands. Twenty-nine percent of all caregivers had considered quitting; 9 percent actually did. The Family and Medical Leave Act gives employees time off to care for one's own parents only, which may change the traditional pattern that women do a disproportionate amount of elder care. Many Americans also need time off to care for seriously ill partners. This includes partners with AIDS as well as people with a wide range of diseases that fifteen years ago would have led to death, but today require a significant period of caregiving followed by partial or total recovery.[66]

Workers without caregiving responsibilities would also benefit in a number of ways from the proposal to restructure work. The existing management literature (examined in depth in chapter 3) suggests that the most effective and practical way to offer flexibility is for managers to ask not "Why do you need it?" but "Will it work?" Once managers begin asking only whether a proposal for flexibility works, nonparents will be offered flexibility for any of a wide range of life goals other than caregiving. Many adults without caregiving responsibilities nonetheless want balanced lives, but are currently barred from attaining them for fear that work/life balance will bar them permanently from the fast track. What most people want are the benefits of the fast track—interesting work, personal development, success —not the speed. The speed is the price they pay to get ahead and to get access to interesting work. What would they do if they did not need to spend all their time at the office? Like two Amerco executives in Arlie Hochschild's book, some might take a trip around the world. Others would use the time for community service, as was suggested by one highly placed insurance executive when I gave a presentation on reconstructive feminism. As communitarians have noted, the people who used to provide the bulk of community service were mothers at home. Now that most mothers work at least part time, community service needs to be seen as part of every adult's life work. We need to create time for it.[67]

New Alliances with the "Time Movement," Unions, and Children's Rights and Welfare Groups

Reconstructive feminism also opens up alliances with three other types of groups: the "time movement," unions, and welfare and children's rights advocates. The growing time movement protests the increase in working hours. It has wide appeal: Jeremiads such as Joe Dominguez and Vicky Robin's *Your Money or Your Life*, Juliet Schor's *The Overworked American*, and Arlie Hochschild's *The Time Bind* all were influential. Dominguez and Robin argue that "we are working more, but enjoying it less (and possibly enjoying less life as well)." They link overwork with increased stress and mortality rates. They present a detailed program for how to cut back on expenditures so as to cut down the amount of income one needs and (as a result) the amount one has to work. "Our jobs have replaced *family*, neighborhood, civic affairs, church and even mates as our primary allegiance, our primary source of love and site of self-expression" (emphasis added, but note that family comes first).[68]

Schor's book argues that Americans are trapped in a "work-and-spend" cycle that requires them to work ever longer hours to support a level of consumption dramatically higher than that of previous generations. "We could now reproduce our 1948 standard of living (measured in terms of marketed goods and services) in less than half the time it took in 1948." Instead, middle-class Americans buy bigger, more luxurious houses and "shop til we drop." She argues that we need to challenge capitalism's incentive structure, which has led to longer and longer hours. "Half the population now says they have too little time for their families. . . . [B]etween 1960 and 1986, the time parents actually had available to be with children fell ten hours a week for whites and twelve for blacks." One Harris poll quoted by Schor reported a decline of nearly 40 percent in free time since 1973. She also reports increasing levels of stress. Thirty percent of all adults now report experiencing high stress every day; even more report experiencing it every week. One-third of all Americans say they feel rushed to do the things they have to do, up from a quarter in 1965. During the first half of the 1980s, workers' compensation claims related to stress tripled.[69]

"So long as there is one who seeks work and cannot find it, the hours of work are too long." The time movement is often linked with proposals to shorten the workweek in order to decrease unemployment. Schor makes a series of proposals, including requiring that each job have a standard schedule (set by the employer) that allows the employee (at his/her sole option) to take overtime pay in terms of "comp time" rather than in money. She also proposes prohibiting mandatory overtime, ending the discriminatory treatment of part-time work, and allowing people to take pay increases in time off rather than in money.[70]

A shift in strategy, away from having women perform as ideal workers and toward a challenge to the conditions of work, holds the promise to tap the strong feelings awakened by the time movement. Although the time movement in the United States often speaks in the language of therapeutic self-improvement, at issue are questions that can also be framed in terms of class (as Schor makes clear). Workers' right to protect their family life against employers' overweening demands has long been an important issue. In the nineteenth century the solution advocated was a "family wage" that would allow workers to keep their wives at home. Today unions need to join with other forces to protect family life in two basic ways. The first is to limit the amount of overtime workers can be required to put in; this has already been an issue in some strikes, notably at auto plants. The second is to require that part-time workers be paid at the same rate as full-time workers, ending the long-established system of paying part-time workers depressed wages based on a highly gendered sense that they are not ideal workers. During the 1997 UPS strike, the Teamsters retained unions' traditional focus on turning "bad" part-time jobs into "good" full-time ones. The union did not protest the company's practice of paying part-time workers at roughly half the rate received by full-time employees. In a recent and laudable shift of policy, the AFL-CIO finally is beginning to demand equal pay rates for equal part-time work.[71]

Unions are beginning to take work/family issues more seriously in other ways. A ten-union coalition in New York City has begun lobbying New York State for child-care benefits as generous as those in Europe, and has begun its own multi-union child-care fund as well. As unions come to realize that their future depends on their ability to organize and represent a workforce that is increasingly female and nonwhite, they can be expected to become more receptive to work/family issues than they were in the past.[72]

Union polling confirms these issues' importance. In one 1996 poll, both men and women said that the best way to strengthen values is for parents to spend more time with their children. Another poll, quoted above, found that the most frequently expressed problem was that both parents must work. One focus group member from St. Louis said, "It is hard to bring home a decent paycheck, to have a family and spend enough time with your family." When asked how best to improve the economic situation of people like themselves, 72 percent said that "reducing stress on working families with policies like flexible hours and affordable day care" would be very effective. The same poll also found that those interviewed considered "combining work and family" to be the biggest problem facing women today (34 percent), considerably higher than the problem of equal pay for equal work.[73]

Reconstructive feminism would also be attractive to groups concerned with children's rights and poverty, who sometimes do not see feminists as sharing their basic concerns. A key liability of the full-commodification model, discussed above, is the sense that women's liberation comes at the expense of children. In fact, as discussed above, domesticity's ordering of family and market work impoverishes children by impoverishing their caregivers by means of two distinct dynamics: by structuring work around a male norm most mothers cannot meet, and through divorce awards that typically assign ownership of the ideal worker's wage to the father and sharply limit claims by his children and their caregiver. The conjunction of these two dynamics is predictable: One-fifth of all American children are poor, and (as noted above) women and children represent nearly 80 percent of those in poverty.[74] As will become clearer in chapters 3 and 4, the strategy of deconstructing the ideal-worker norm will help children by ending the association of poverty and caregiving.

CONCLUSION: FROM THE FULL-COMMODIFICATION MODEL TO RECONSTRUCTIVE FEMINISM

The early feminist vision of two parents working forty-hour weeks did not come to pass; neither did the vision of child-care centers being as common and as respected as public libraries. What we have instead, as documented in the introduction, is an economy of mothers and others, where many fathers work overtime and a majority of mothers are not ideal workers. This chapter proposes that we abandon the full-commodification strategy in favor of transforming domesticity's norm of mothercare into a template for restructuring the relationship of market work and family work.

If we as a society take seriously children's need for parental care, it is time to stop marginalizing the adults who provide it. The current structure of work is not immutable: it was invented at a particular point in time to suit particular circumstances. Those circumstances have changed. Chapter 3 examines in depth the proposal to restructure work around a particular set of family values: those represented by the norm of parental care.

•

CHAPTER THREE

Deconstructing the Ideal-Worker Norm in Market Work

For thirty years feminists have focused on defending the rights of women who experience discrimination despite their ability to perform as ideal workers. *Price Waterhouse v. Hopkins* shows the continuing importance of such work. Ann Hopkins worked for six years at Price Waterhouse and "was generally viewed as a highly competent project leader who worked long hours [and] pushed vigorously to meet deadlines." None of the other candidates in her year "had a comparable record in terms of successfully securing major contracts for the partnership"; one contract alone was worth $25 million. The only woman among the eighty-eight candidates for partnership the first year she was considered, ultimately she was denied partnership. The record showed that one partner had advised her to take "a course in charm school"; another had advised her to "walk more femininely, talk more femininely, dress more femininely, wear make-up, have her hair styled, and wear jewelry."[1]

As long as women such as Ann Hopkins remain targets of discrimination, the defense of ideal-worker women needs to remain part of the feminist agenda—part, but not all. Most mothers, we have seen, do not perform as ideal workers. Only about a third of mothers of childbearing age do, even in the minimal sense of working full time full year. Antidiscrimination law needs to help not only the women who can perform as ideal workers but also the majority who can't.[2]

A closer analysis shows that the ideal-worker schedule is only one type of masculine norm at work in today's economy. The *Hopkins* case involves another: the definition of jobs in terms of what theorists call "masculine gender display"— walking, talking, and dressing in masculine ways. In jobs involving physical (as opposed to mental) work, a third type of masculine norm emerges, as when facilities, equipment, or job requirements are designed to accommodate most men but not most women.[3]

This chapter first documents the intense sex segregation in the economy and points out the role played by masculine norms in maintaining it. Yet such norms have been defined as discrimination only in two narrow contexts: where they take the form of sexual harassment or of stereotyping. This chapter argues that jobs designed around masculine norms discriminate against women in other contexts as well. Designing jobs around men's bodies obviously excludes the large majority of women, who are smaller and lighter than most men. Jobs designed around an ideal-worker schedule discriminate against women on the basis of their inability to command the flow of family work that supports most male ideal workers. Requiring workers, if they want to achieve equality, to exercise the social power typically available only to men— to command a flow of family work, to have the kind of body machines are designed around, to relate to others in masculine terms— constitutes discrimination against women.

This chapter first documents the paucity of women in the best blue- and white-collar jobs held by men. The analysis of the economy in the first half of this chapter also documents the role of masculine norms in excluding women. It then shows how traditionally female jobs allow women to avoid the kinds of norms that make life difficult for them in the higher-paying positions traditionally held by men.

This proposal to eliminate masculine norms in market work raises immediate questions of feasibility. How is it possible to replace or modify costly facilities and equipment designed around masculine norms without bankrupting the economy? Perhaps it would be nice to redesign job schedules to make all jobs more accessible to those without the breadwinner's traditional access to family work, but wouldn't this be prohibitively expensive in an era of intense competition? As it turns out, consultants have been working with businesses for twenty years and have shown that a redesign of work often makes workplaces *more* productive, rather than less so.

If the goal of eliminating masculine norms is feasible, the next question is how to achieve it. This chapter articulates a legal strategy and a series of public policy proposals designed to reconstruct the market world to eliminate the economic marginalization of women. Not only do we need to fight for equality in the workplace as it is today; we also need to deconstruct masculine norms in market work. Women will gain equality only when ideal workers no longer have to drop the baby.

WHY WOMEN REMAIN IN WOMEN'S WORK

> Like machine and tool specifications based on the dimensions of the average
> male body, no-leave and other personnel policies that fail to take account of
> child-bearing and child-rearing needs also reflect the assumption that only
> men, indeed only men in traditional families, belong in the workplace.[4]

Most women work with other women. Three-fourths of all working women still
work in predominantly female occupations. Relatively few women gain access to
the best jobs society has to offer: upper-level management and professional positions for college-educated workers, blue-collar work for workers with only a high-
school education.[5]

Most women remain in "women's work," in substantial part, because masculine
norms exclude them from jobs traditionally held by men. Such norms operate differently in the white- and blue-collar contexts. Whereas women typically have little trouble stepping onto the bottom rungs of job ladders that lead to high-level
managerial and professional jobs, they are blocked from promotion by job requirements that require workers to have gender privileges few women enjoy: access to a
flow of family work from a spouse, and the kind of mentoring and social contacts
that still follow the social patterns of masculinity.

In traditionally male blue-collar work, women often don't even get in the door.
Women have trouble getting hired because of intensely gendered job descriptions
that send the message that women need not apply; because equipment designed
around men's bodies excludes disproportionate numbers of women; and because the
scheduling of such jobs requires access to spousal work at a level available to most
men but few women. Finally, severe sexual harassment plagues the few hearty souls
who take traditionally male blue-collar jobs despite the clear signals that these are
jobs designed for men. Promotion tracks also present a problem for women aspiring
to blue-collar positions in a number of ways that will be discussed below.

Only some of these dynamics have been viewed as discriminatory. Sexual harassment has, along with the treatment experienced by Ann Hopkins. But designing
production processes around male bodies has not, nor has scheduling market work
around the flow of family work men enjoy but women do not. These have been considered, respectively, women's lack of qualifications for the job and mothers' choice.
This chapter argues that both constitute discrimination against women.

Of Mommy Tracks and Basketball Hoops: Masculine Norms in the Best White-Collar Jobs

> When people are thinking of who they'll promote, whether consciously or
> subconsciously, a picture of a white male pops into their minds and that's
> their definition of what a manager should look like.

> I'd win lots of awards when I'd win contests and they'd give me money
> clips and tie tacks. And I'd say, What I am supposed to do with these
> things? I don't need a money clip. I don't need a tie tack.[6]

In the white-collar context, the problem is not access but advancement. "[A] virtual closing of the gap in education and skills between men and women during the 1970s and 1980s" has not led to proportional representation of women in high-level white-collar jobs. "Female workers have moved into male-dominated professions, but . . . they are still dramatically underrepresented at the highest levels of occupational status and financial reward. . . . [T]hey hold about thirteen percent of tenured academic posts, six percent of the partnerships of the large law firms, five percent of federal elective offices, and three percent of the executive positions at publicly traded corporations." Although women represent about 46 percent of the U.S. workforce, they hold only about 5 percent of the top-level jobs. Their representation in senior management positions has risen at a glacial rate, from 3 percent in 1980 to 7 percent today. They probably hold no more than 20 percent of the jobs in the uppermost four levels of corporate hierarchies.[7]

Studies by national and local bar associations document these patterns in law firms. By the 1990s women were nearly half of the new recruits of top law firms in New York City, but 89 percent of the partners still were men. An American Bar Association (ABA) study found that men still were 87 percent of the partners of all law firms with two or more lawyers. ABA surveys found that men were more than twice as likely to be partners when compared to women of similar backgrounds. In the fifteen years after 1970, twice as many men as women hired by large New York law firms were promoted to partner.[8]

Pay differentials also persist. One study found that the median income of women ten years out of law school is 40 percent lower than men's. Research reviewed by the ABA Commission on the Status of Women in the Profession found pay gaps of 10 to 35 percent between male and female general counsels. A survey of firms in the San Francisco area found that male partners are more likely than females to be higher-paid equity partners.[9]

"Throughout the '80s we were told it was simply a matter of time," said Patricia Wald, now a judge on the United States Court of Appeals for the District of Columbia Circuit. "But now . . . we know better. There are indeed more women in big firms, there are more women partners (about eleven percent), but nowhere near the level one would expect from the number of entry-level associates (about fifty percent)." Moreover, the situation may well be deteriorating rather than improving. *Glass Ceilings and Open Doors*, a study by sociologist Cynthia Epstein commissioned by the Bar Association of the City of New York, found a sharp decrease in the numbers of women being made partner after 1990.[10]

Law is not the only high-status white-collar profession still dominated by men. As of 1990, the top-ranking partners in Wall Street were still 99 percent male; in accounting, women were only 5.6 percent of the partners at national firms in 1988. In business, virtually all upper-level management positions still are held by white men. The Federal Glass Ceiling Commission reports that 95 to 97 percent of senior managers of Fortune 1500 companies are men; little change has occurred since 1979. Only two women were CEOs of Fortune 1000 companies by 1994.[11]

Women professionals typically are given far fewer chances for advancement than male ones. A 1990 study found that a woman with an MBA from one of the top twenty business schools earned an average of 12 percent less than a comparable man the year after graduation, a pay gap that increases with age. The median annual income of members of the Stanford Business School class of 1982 who were employed full time ten years later was nearly 40 percent higher for men than women—and this, of course, does not count the women no longer in the workforce. In 1992 compensation for women executives was still less than two-thirds that of male executives. "Twenty years ago, the question of why no women headed large corporations had a standard answer: Too few in the pipeline." The same answer is not so readily accepted today.[12]

Men still dominate the upper levels of academic posts as well. "In 1920, when women won the right to vote, twenty-six percent of the full-time faculty in American higher education were women. In 1995, thirty-one percent of full-time faculty in American higher education are women—an increase of five percent over seventy-five years!" Women enter many graduate programs in roughly equal proportions with men, but they hold fewer than 15 percent of tenured academic posts. Women are also much more likely to drop out of academics and to teach at community colleges or nonelite colleges and universities. They are also much less likely than men to get tenure: women's rate of tenure (46 percent) was the same in 1992 as it was in 1975, though men's tenure rate rose sharply, to 72 percent in 1994–1995. The gap between the wages of male and female academics also persists, with no noticeable improvement since 1982. In legal academics, men still comprise 81 percent of tenured law school faculty and 92 percent of law school deans.[13]

Why do women reach the best white-collar jobs in such tiny numbers? The time is past for arguing that no women are in the pipeline. The chief reasons for women's lack of representation are the glass ceiling and the maternal wall.

The Glass Ceiling

One day I noticed a toy basketball hoop on the wall of a colleague's office. When I remarked on it, he explained that it was meant to make people feel more comfortable.

I'm sure it does make some people feel more comfortable; I suspect those people are predominantly male. To men, the hoop signaled his good intentions by recalling the pattern of male bonding through sports. To many women, it may signal they do not belong in a profession where comfort levels often depend on competence in masculine gender performance. I myself decided to quit law firm practice during a lunch when it became clear I was odd (wo)man out because I knew nothing about football. I had no desire to learn, and realized in a flash I would never make partner.

The patterns of social bonding in high-status jobs remain distinctly masculine. This means that professional success often requires being "one of the boys," an effort more likely to be successful in men than in women. Studies of the glass ceiling stress the ways mentoring and other opportunities are linked with what theorists call masculine gender performance—behaving in the ways traditionally expected of men. "Today, the prevailing culture of many businesses is a white male culture," said a Labor Department report. It quotes the CEO of a major national retailer: "The old-line companies are run by the white '46-long' guys who practice inappropriate male rituals [such as] male bonding through hunting, fishing, and sports talk. . . . Too much so-called 'strategic planning' takes place after the bars close—that kind of male friendship ritual is irrelevant to business."[14]

Common glass-ceiling practices include different treatment of men and women with respect to job assignments that lead to advancement, initial placement in relatively dead-end jobs, and lack of mentoring for women. *Glass Ceiling* found many instances of differing treatment. "It's always going to be tough to figure out how to treat the women, but now it's worse and I'd rather not be in a mentoring relationship with them," one manager told a researcher. Women also lack access to informal networks; in focus groups they spoke of men going out for beers or to the gym with the boss, occasions when women were not invited. Almost 93 percent of senior women executives in a 1992 survey felt a glass ceiling exists. One-quarter felt that "being a woman/sexism" was the biggest obstacle they have had to overcome in their careers.[15]

The practices that add up to the glass ceiling are often unconscious, as when women's work is scrutinized more closely than men's. Plum assignments and promotions are rewards given to workers who seem able, committed, and serious; in the eyes of some beholders, men fit these images more often than do women.

The Maternal Wall

"Since I came back from maternity leave, I get the work of a paralegal," protested one Boston lawyer. "I want to say, look, I had a baby, not a lobotomy." Prominent sex discrimination attorney Judith Vladek replied, "Women should be told the truth. Having a baby is used as an excuse not to give women opportunities. The assumption is that they have made a choice, that having children ends their commitment to their career." Vladek added that many women postpone having children "only to learn that putting off motherhood doesn't help. Even if they take just six weeks of maternity leave, they come back and find out that they've been passed over for a promotion or that their job was eliminated during their leave. I've seen it in every kind of workplace." At the hearing of the ABA's Commission on Women, Barbara P. Billauer, president of the Women's Trial Board, testified:

> Every single woman that I have spoken to without exception, partner or associate, has experienced rampant hostility and prejudice upon her return [from maternity leave]. There is a sentiment that pregnancy and motherhood has softened her, that she is not going to work as hard.

One top performer in a business setting described her nationally known employer as "racing into the 1950s. . . . I was the only female in the sales force, and they had no maternity policy. My boss had the attitude that if you want to play in a man's world you have to bear the consequences. He was of the mind set that women with kids should be at home."[16]

Reports are widespread that women experience a maternal wall. New York and Harvard researchers repeatedly heard reports of mothers receiving less desirable assignments than they had received BC (before children). *Glass Ceilings* reports that women who returned to work after the birth of children not only experienced less desirable assignments but also had the sense that if they were ideal workers, that proved they were irresponsible mothers. "Comments made by various lawyers often reflected the belief that a woman's first priority should be her children."[17]

Such comments place mothers in the catch-22 situation the U.S. Supreme Court decried in *Price Waterhouse v. Hopkins*. In that case, Ann Hopkins was faulted for being too aggressive in a context where aggressiveness was part of the job description. She was between Scylla and Charybdis: She could be aggressive but unqualified because she was insufficiently feminine, or she could be feminine but unqualified because she was insufficiently aggressive. The situation is similar when women find that if they perform as ideal workers, they are condemned as bad mothers; if they observe the norm of parental care, they are condemned as bad workers. Mothers can't win. This emerges clearly in the practice of asking female job candidates what their plans are for marriage and a family. I myself faced such questions in 1980; they remain common today. In one law firm interview in 1998, a partner advised a woman law student to take off her wedding ring.[18]

The maternal wall is not limited to the law. In her in-depth study of a large corporation, Arlie Hochschild reports on one woman's return from maternity leave. The woman recalled:

> Men in my office were putting money on the table that I would never show up at work again when the baby was born. I had to prove that when I came back, I was as good as I was when I left. Men were waiting to say, "I *told* you so."

She received the message that if she did perform as an ideal worker, it would prove her a bad mother. "One man commented pointedly to another man in my presence, 'It takes a lot more than paying the *mortgage* to make a house a home.'"[19]

The assumption that motherhood does, and should, preclude women from performing as ideal workers affects all women, not just mothers, as employers become wary of hiring women on the grounds that women have "disappointed them in the past." Said a senior editor at *Working Mother* magazine, "[T]he impact of motherhood shadows every woman, narrowing her options. Even those without children may be harmed; the mere fact that they are of childbearing age may compromise their career prospects."[20]

The maternal wall is composed partly of old-fashioned stereotyping of women who are capable of performing as ideal workers along with the men. But it is also composed of three practices that drive mothers out of the workforce of their "own choice": the executive schedule, the marginalization of part-time workers, and the expectation that workers who are "executive material" will relocate their families to take a better job.

The Executive Schedule. As noted in the introduction, virtually no mothers work substantial amounts of overtime. This presents a problem for women in the best white-collar jobs because the executive schedule typically stretches from fifty to eighty hours a week. A Canadian survey of American and foreign executives found that nearly 56 percent worked between forty-six and sixty hours a week, an average of 20 percent longer than twenty years ago. A study of DuPont managers found they averaged fifty-five hours a week. The percentages are much higher at the top levels. Gone are "bankers' hours," from nine to three. The great American speed-up affects all economic levels: Americans now work more overtime than at any point since World War II.[21]

The overwork requirement is particularly well documented among lawyers. An ABA survey found that at least 55 percent of all lawyers worked over 2,400 hours per year, which averages out to 45 hours a week. At least 13 percent of lawyers worked even more, billing 2,880 hours a year, or nearly 60 hours a week. The average large firm in New York City requires associates to bill up to 2,500 hours annually; some require billings of 3,000 hours, which requires an average of 80 hours in the office a week. One influential report concludes that "the legal work makes dramatic demands on the practitioner's time and makes it difficult or nearly impossible to have a life in which family obligations or other non-work activity may be experienced in a conventional way." Said one New York lawyer:

> I couldn't come home at nine three nights a week after my kids have gone to bed. . . . It's not something I could have done in their infancies, and it would be even harder now with my daughter in first grade, having homework, to say "See you tomorrow; see you in the morning, if I happen to be around when you're up."[22]

The executive schedule drives many women off the promotion track. In a recent survey of executive women, "most of the women said they forsook the goal of top-ranking management at a big public firm because the grueling work hours expected of executives made it difficult to meet family obligations." A survey of women graduates of Harvard's business, law, and medical schools found that most (70 percent) worked shorter hours after having children, though most (85 percent) believed that this would hurt their careers. They were right. Catalyst, an organization that has long worked to increase opportunities for women, concluded that "the reality is, if a woman wants to obtain a top management position, [she] cannot be the primary caretaker of [her] child."[23]

In jobs structured around a flow of family work men have but women don't, women must choose between work and family while men can have both. Nine out of ten men in upper-level corporate management have children and a nonworking spouse. As Deborah Rhode has pointed out, most female executives have neither. Almost one-third of women in senior positions, but only 6 to 8 percent of men, never marry. Only about 30 percent of women in senior positions have children, as compared to 90 percent of the men. Ninety-three percent of married women lawyers have spouses who work full time, a disproportionate number of them as high-level professionals; these husbands do not provide their wives with the flow of family work avail-able to the nearly half of married male attorneys who are married to housewives. Fe-male executives also tend to be married to same-class males who work full time, but the men are often married to homemakers. A recent DuPont study found that its male executives are now *more* likely to have an at-home wife than they were ten years ago.[24]

These patterns mean that the cost to families of mothers' and fathers' success is very different: Where the father is the executive, the family can live up to the norm of parental care, but where the mother is the executive, it can't. No wonder far fewer mothers "succeed."[25]

Instead, many marginalize. The term "mommy track" was first used in a *New York Times* article about lawyers. It reported, "Women who choose to put in fewer hours and spend more time with their families say they are considered less serious by male colleagues." One big-firm associate told the reporter there was "no chance" she would make partner despite the fact she worked twelve-hour days, employing two shifts of baby-sitters. "You accept it," she said, "because your kids are worth it." Note her unquestioning assumption that her employer is entitled to marginalize her because she did not keep an executive schedule.[26]

In a social context where full-time work often precludes a normal family life, part-time work would seem a logical alternative. The following section explains why it is not.

The Marginalization of Part-Time Work. The decision to work part time generally means restricted prospects for advancement and lower pay, despite comparable qualifica-tions. "[W]hen you work part-time or temporary, they treat you differently, they don't take you serious," said one secretary. The same pattern persists as the job sta-tus rises. Even women in "retention"—part-time jobs designed to retain valued employees—typically suffer in terms of advancement. *Glass Ceilings* found that part-timers—almost exclusively women—generally are taken off the partnership track either as a matter of official policy or as a matter of practice. Another recent study found that virtually the only profession in which part-time work did not hurt women's careers was nursing. Outside of nursing, most employers see part-time workers as "putting up a sign: 'Don't consider me for promotions now.'"[27]

"Part-time work is still widely viewed as an occupational dead end," said one influential commentator. According to another, "Women who take part-time work are often so grateful for the option that they do not mind facing dimmer prospects. For law firms, part-time work means retaining talented workers while paying them less and not worrying about making the[m] partner." A part-time lawyer quoted in one news story earned 69 percent of what full-time lawyers earned for each hour she worked, somewhat higher than the average figure of 60 percent. In addition, in many professional contexts, part-time workers receive the paradoxical message that the only responsible way to work part time is to work full time. "People who work part-time and who are seriously committed to their practice don't really work part time," said one law firm partner. Another part-time lawyer noted that her firm had given her a bonus because they acknowledged that she had worked full time. But they still calculated her salary as if she had worked 80 percent, rather than 100 percent, of the firm's established schedule.[28]

Many women who work part time do so for only a limited period; then they return to full-time work. However, not only are part-timers penalized during the period they work part-time, but they suffer long-term consequences for having done part-time work. Even if someone who has been working part time later takes a full-time job, she (or he) is likely to earn far less than someone who always worked full time.[29]

Part-timers also generally get less interesting work and less respect. *Glass Ceilings* found that part-time associates believe they get low-profile assignments that hurt their chances of success. According to Fern Sussman, executive director of the Association of the Bar in New York, "The top tier is the full-time partnership track lawyer who has all the perks and prestige, and the bottom tier is the part-time track, made up largely of women." Some firms have made the mommy track a formal option, instituting a "permanent associate" track. One commentator raised the "frightening possibility" that law firms will evolve into institutions "top-heavy with men and childless women, supported by a pink-collar ghetto of mommy lawyers," often with permanent-associate status.[30]

Part-time work is also penalized in many other types of businesses. In a recent study of a large corporation she calls Amerco, Arlie Hochschild found that although many corporations offer part-time work and other "family-friendly" policies, very few parents took advantage of them. Instead, parents at the large corporation Hochschild studied were working longer and longer hours. She asks why workers aren't choosing to participate in family-friendly programs, and concludes that workers prefer to be at work rather than at home.[31]

While this may be true in some cases, in her many conversations with the employees at Amerco, Hochschild uncovered another reason why many workers eschew family friendly policies: any worker who so much as expressed interest in part-time work was immediately and permanently barred from advancement. Hochschild cites the example of Eileen Watson, a thirty-year-old ceramics engineer who worked sixty to seventy hours a week. After the birth of her first child, she asked to cut back to 60 percent for a few years, to gain something closer to a forty-hour workweek. She presented the idea to her boss, suggesting that a young, newly hired engineer could take over three to four hours of her daily work at a lower rate than she was paid. She would take a 40 percent pay cut, and the company would come out ahead financially. Her manager agreed, but Eileen found herself working more than the agreed number of hours. Though she continued to excel at her work, her boss resisted the arrangement.[32]

> He said to me, "Eileen, I don't know how to do part-time. My experience is that people who put in the hours are the ones who succeed." I said, "Measure me on my results." He replied, "No. It doesn't work that way. What matters is how much time you put into the job, the volume of the work.... That's all I know how to understand as a basis for getting ahead."

Indeed, like most successful managers at the company, her boss worked extremely long hours; most managers could do so because their wives were homemakers. Said one successful manager in response to a survey by a junior (male) manager reporting that company employees wanted a better balance between work and family:

> Dave blew up at me: "Don't *ever* bring up 'balance' again! I don't want to hear about it! Period! Everyone in this company has to work hard. *We* work hard. *They* have to work hard. That's the way it is. Just because a few women are concerned about balance doesn't mean we change the rules. If they chose this career, they're going to have to pay for it in hours, like the rest of us."

"The way they managed their lives and the way they were brought up is being challenged," observed the junior manager. A DuPont vice president was more tactful: "Managers like me who have had the comfort of relying on our spouses to handle most family issues often fail to understand how critical [work/family] programs are to our employees who need them, and, therefore, to business success." The National Study of the Changing Workforce found that supervisors with employed spouses provide more job-related and family support than those married to homemakers. Meanwhile, a study by the Families and Work Institute found that the bosses women found most difficult to deal with have wives who do not work outside the home.[33]

Hochschild's data suggest that parents' reluctance to take advantage of family-friendly policies reflects their desire and their need to avoid marginalization at work. Eileen's part-time schedule helped get her fired, a pattern documented elsewhere. Lora Ilhardt was laid off from her part-time job in the legal department of Sara Lee in a context where circumstances strongly suggested that she would not have been fired had she worked full time. Another part-time worker was among the first released during a layoff because of her "unusual work arrangement." A recent study suggests this is not uncommon.[34]

When Eileen lost her job at Amerco, she was given two months to find a new job within the company. Two years later, Hochschild found her working full time. Eileen's story suggests that parents eschew part-time and other flexible policies not because they prefer work to home, but because the alternative is rigorous marginalization that ultimately can get you fired. What workers like Eileen want is "an array of possible timetables that allows women and men alike to combine ambition and the family."[35]

Hochschild's study also shows why companies often implement their policies in a punitive way even after management consultants have documented that flexibility would save money. The key is in who is implementing the policies. Said one top-level manager with a workaholic schedule and a wife at home:

> Time has a way of sorting out people at this company. A lot of people that don't make it to the top work long hours. But all the people I know who *do* make it work long hours. . . . The members of the Management Committee of this company aren't the smartest people in this company, we're the hardest working. We work like dogs.

This is a singularly open statement about how to succeed in business: The crucial factor is not competence but a flow of family work from a wife at home. Of the twelve top managers Hochschild interviewed, all worked fifty- to seventy-hour weeks and most had homemaker wives. Most had never experienced the tug of family needs because their wives generally took care of all domestic matters. As discussed in chapter 1, successful men tend to have marriages with gender patterns that disappeared a generation ago in the bulk of the population, with wives operating virtually as single parents and not "bothering" their husbands with domestic "details." "The higher up you go, the likelier it is that you will have a traditional marriage," noted one commentator. This describes the executives who implement family-friendly policies.[36]

Middle management often actively opposes flexible policies as well. The head of a large engineering division told Hochschild in a "pleasant, matter-of-fact" way, "My policy on flextime is that there is no flextime." Middle managers, with direct control over workers' evaluations and the authority to grant flexibility or deny it, often felt that flexible schedules were "one more headache."[37]

"Family-friendly" policies often create a mommy track that most men and ambitious women want nothing to do with. Hochschild tells the story of Denise, assistant marketing director for one of Amerco's most successful product lines. When she was pregnant, she reported of her co-workers, "They *corner* you with questions. . . . 'What are you going to do when both you and Daniel have emergencies at work?'" Hochschild explained, "In this atmosphere, Denise wanted absolutely nothing to do with flexible or shorter hours. With a gender war on, shorter hours meant surrender." No wonder mommy-track policies have had limited success.[38]

Relocation. In addition to scheduling issues, a major issue in business and academics is that relocation often is required for advancement. In this society, families often move to advance men's careers but rarely do so to advance women's. As noted before, while fewer men can count on a family willing to move to advance their careers than was the case a generation ago, in most families that do move to advance a spouse's career, that spouse is the husband. This pattern presents two types of problems for women. First, it requires women to turn down promotions they otherwise would accept. This means that men can succeed simply by "making the right moves," whereas many women can succeed only if they are so stellar that they survive even though they did not make the right moves (literally and figuratively).[39]

Second, women's careers are disrupted when they leave good jobs to follow their husbands, often taking less good jobs or dropping out of the workforce altogether as a result. A 1985 poll found that 71 percent of women thought they should relocate if their husband received a very good job offer in a different city; another study found that half of women, and two-thirds of men, put the husband's career first. Men's preferential access to relocation is a survival of the notion that the man is the "head of the family": recall that under common law, a married woman was legally required to follow wherever the husband chose to live. In a system where women managers typically have to sacrifice family life to "succeed" and where many women lack the ability to relocate, huge numbers of women trained for management positions drop out. One study found that one-fourth of all women MBAs had dropped out of the labor force.[40]

The relocation issue also plays an important role in academics. Due to the scarcity of academic jobs, relocation is often required to get a job or to move up in the profession. Academics also imposes a rigid tenure clock that requires a period of intense effort at precisely the period when most families have young children. These job structures tend to keep women out of academics and to land them in less elite institutions if they stay.

In conclusion, although women enter the promotion tracks that lead to the best (and traditionally male) white-collar jobs, their careers often stall because those jobs are structured to require not only excellent work but access to gender privileges most women lack. These include the ability to fit into social patterns designed around masculinity, to move their families to take a new job or a promotion, to have a spouse willing to raise the professional's children according to the norm of parental care. Employers discriminate against women when they structure work to require employees not only to be competent but also to have gender privileges typically available only to men.

Cockpits, Lifts, and Family Values: Masculine Norms in the Best Blue-Collar Jobs

The best jobs available for working-class people are in blue-collar work; the only alternative is a low-paying service work or a pink-collar job. Yet women's presence in traditionally male blue-collar jobs remains minuscule. Forty-five percent of men, but only 10 percent of women, hold blue-collar positions. This figure underestimates the extent of sex segregation, for most blue-collar women work as operatives, not skilled tradespeople, in factories that employ only or predominantly women. Even where men and women work in the same job category, women tend to end up in lower-paying, lower-status jobs: as in-store bakers, for example, rather than as commercial bakers. The best blue-collar jobs, in precision, production, and craft occupations, have the largest concentration of white males of any job category. White females hold only 2.1 percent of such jobs. Black women hold about 2.2 percent.[41]

As noted above, the mechanisms of exclusion from blue-collar jobs differ from those in white-collar work. Whereas women typically have little trouble stepping onto the job ladders for managerial and professional positions, typically they are excluded up front from blue-collar positions by three types of masculine norms: equipment and industrial processes designed around men's bodies, schedules designed around men's access to a flow of family work from women, and eligibility for the jobs defined in terms of masculine gender performance.

Cockpits and Lifts: Designing Blue-Collar Work Around Men's Bodies

Equipment used in traditionally male jobs typically is designed to specifications that make it fit most men but a much lower proportion of women. Said Beth Szillagyi, a sheet metal worker,

There was a slight problem with the safety belt, as they are all made to fit men. On the tightest adjustment it was still rather roomy, but Larry tugged on it hard to make sure it wouldn't go over my hips. "It's hard to find shoes, too," I said, grinning.[42]

The most famous example is the "cockpit case," in which a court found that airplane cockpits fit 25.8 percent of men but excluded 93 percent of women. The cabs of trucks often present similar problems. In addition, when companies brag that their factory equipment is designed ergonomically, women may well have difficulty using it because the specifications assumed a male operator. Equipment may also be designed in ways that make it inconvenient for women, as when women miners find they have to disrobe almost completely to go to the bathroom because coal miners' overalls are designed on the assumption that all miners will be male. Finally, job ladders in traditionally male blue-collar jobs often require workers to start out in positions that require heavy physical work, say lifting loads of 125 pounds, thereby excluding women from promotion to jobs most women could handle without difficulty.[43]

While equipment design is easy to visualize, probably more important sociologically is the design of industrial processes around men's bodies. As a practical matter, an employer will provide lifting equipment when loads become too heavy to lift; the question is where that point occurs. Up to now, that point has often been set based on the assumption that the worker is a European-American man. (Note that this disadvantages not only women but also Asian- and Latino-Americans to the extent that they are, on average, smaller than European-Americans.) Even in workplaces where certain jobs will continue to require more strength than most women can muster, the question is whether inability to perform those particular jobs will exclude women from every job in that workplace. Tasks in factory work are often bundled so that each worker on the factory floor must be able to lift a certain weight, say 125 pounds, even if the job in question requires such lifting only once or twice a day. The result is that no women can work either on the factory floor or in the management positions with job ladders that start on the factory floor. In many situations, the necessary lifting could be delegated to a few workers working with assistive equipment. This rebundling would avoid situations where virtually all women (and smaller men) are excluded from not only most entry-level jobs but all higher-level jobs as well.[44]

Policing Masculinity at Work
While the gendering of white-collar jobs is often subtle, traditionally male blue-collar jobs typically wear their masculinity on their sleeve. Intensely gendered job descriptions send messages that women are inherently unsuited for these positions, which are described as "heavy" and "dirty," in contrast with women's jobs, characterized as "light" and "clean." Women's jobs are thought of as clean and light even when they are not; one court accepted a rule barring women from a number of jobs in a meatpacking plant on the grounds they were too physically demanding, ignor-

ing the fact that the company hired women for lower-paying jobs in the meatpacking departments where they regularly had to carry boxes of meat weighing eighty to ninety pounds. Blue-collar males also sometimes masculinize their jobs through the use of foul language and pornography.[45]

The insistent quality of the masculinized image and culture of blue-collar jobs relates to the hidden injuries of class. In a society where masculinity is often measured by the size of a paycheck, white-collar men define the norm. "With their masculine identity and self-esteem undermined by their subordinate order-taking position in relation to higher-status males . . . men on the shop floor reconstruct their position as embodying true masculinity. They use the physical endurance and tolerance of discomfort required of their manual labor as signifying true masculinity."[46]

This is why women in traditionally male jobs regularly report men's egos are threatened when women do the job men have defined as proof they are "real men." A subway conductor reports, "[W]e were a threat . . . to their self-image. They saw themselves as doing a man's job. They had a big stake in believing that they were doing a job only the superior sex could handle emotionally as well as physically."[47]

Women who don't get the message often are subjected to severe sexual harassment designed to drive women out. Some of it is explicitly sexual, as when a co-worker twice exposed his genitals to one tradeswoman; another relieved himself against the women's changing-room wall; others "constantly" dropped their pants in front of a female electrician; a builder's foreman put his hand farther and farther into her underwear as he held her belt to steady her as she worked on window trim; a subway conductor was propositioned so insistently that she joked about giving a civil service exam, complete with filing fee and a physical to identify the most qualified candidate.[48]

But though much of the harassment was sexual, much was not. Much of it is simply dangerous, as when a police officer's partner aimed his gun at her to "see how fast women can run"; or " when you are calling in for help and someone cuts you off . . . or they don't show up when you call for help"; when a female ironworker was forced to use single-handedly a sixty-pound piece of equipment (a "hell dog") that usually required operation by two people; or when tradeswomen's work partners intentionally drop heavy equipment in attempts to injure them. To quote a woman welder:

> It's a form of harassment every time I pick up a sledgehammer and that prick laughs at me, you know. It's a form of harassment when the journeyman is supposed to be training me and it's real clear that he does not want to give me any information whatsoever. . . . It's a form of harassment when the working foreman puts me in a dangerous situation and tells me to do something in an improper way.

Molly Martin, an electrician and founder of Tradeswomen, Inc., explained the two distinct kinds of harassment as follows:

> Whenever tradeswomen gather together. . . , one topic of conversation is certain to be sexual harassment: the unwelcome touching and requests for sexual favors that almost all of us have experienced sometime during our careers. But we also face another pervasive and sinister kind of harassment . . . aimed at us because we are women in a "man's job," and its function is to discourage us from staying in our trades.

The combination of various kinds of harassment produces "alarmingly high" rates of turnover of women in nontraditional blue-collar work. "No doubt about it," concludes a stationary engineer, "the work is a breeze, any woman who wanted to could do it, but the male environment adds a lot of stress to the job." A sprinkler fitter notes that some women left her apprenticeship program because they didn't like the work, "[b]ut for many I am sure the main reason is the men." Almost as many women leave nontraditional work as enter it; high turnover is the reason sex segregation in these jobs has declined only slightly.[49]

Another key issue is that the bulk of training in traditionally male blue-collar jobs is acquired informally on the job. "Thus, a woman's ability to succeed depends on the willingness of her supervisors and co-workers to teach her the relevant skills." Often they don't. An operating engineer reported, "In my entire year with that company my journeyman refused to answer my questions or do anything for me, except make my job harder." A sprinkler fitter recalled a time when she was assigned to do gofer work for two male apprentices junior to her. When she protested after a couple of days, she ended up with a bad character report and "serious bad vibes from most of the guys on the job." In another case, a worker was demoted to her previous job because she was unable to adequately perform the required tasks. Instead of helping this employee learn how to perform her new production job, her co-workers had locked her in a closet.[50]

Family Values: Designing Blue-Collar Jobs Around Men's Access to Family Work
As we have seen, masculine norms can be social as well as physical. To the extent blue-collar job ladders require uninterrupted market work and penalize workers for interruptions, working-class women who take time off for child rearing are barred from stepping onto them. This has a particularly strong impact because seniority often plays a crucial role in blue-collar work—in deciding who is eligible for what job, and in deciding who will be laid off or "bumped" from their current job to a less desirable one in the event of layoffs. Current seniority policies, under which many women lose their seniority forever if they interrupt their workforce participation, tend to keep mothers in low-status positions, where they are vulnerable to layoffs. Working-class women are particularly vulnerable because they generally have less education, and women with less education are more likely to take time off from market work (presumably because their wages are so low that they are left with little take-home pay after paying for infant care).[51]

Promotion tracks also tend to require a flow of family work mothers generally lack. Promotion in skilled and semiskilled blue-collar jobs typically depends not on outside schooling but on on-the-job training. Skilled workers such as electricians and plumbers are trained through apprenticeships, many of which require nighttime classes for several years. This may contribute to the fact that women were only 7 percent of registered apprentices in 1991. Semiskilled workers learn their jobs often in training programs that take place in overtime. This means that women are excluded from such training because they are less likely to have a family member available to care for their children.[52]

Overtime also increasingly excludes women from many of the best factory jobs. The Bureau of Labor Statistics reported that factory workers in 1994 put in the highest levels of overtime ever registered in the thirty-eight years the agency has tracked it.[53] Overtime has doubled since 1980 in the manufacturing sector overall. In recent years, some factory workers have been required to do so much overtime that even male workers have rebelled, saying that they want more time with their families; the statistics on mothers and overtime suggest that the rebellions did not take place until long after most mothers had quit. Overtime requirements are concentrated in "good" (male) factory jobs because employers aim to increase overtime to spread the load of benefits (which often approaches one-third of labor costs) over the maximum number of hours per employee in order to reduce costs.[54]

Finally, sick leave policies in many traditionally male jobs are designed for adults without primary child-care responsibility. One study in a factory where blue-collar workers earned more than clerical workers found that few women requested transfers to the floor, because those workers were entitled to only two days of sick or personal leave, whereas clerical workers were entitled to twenty.[55]

Requirements for full-time work also push women out of traditionally male jobs in factories and highly paid craft jobs. Only about 6 percent of skilled craft positions are available on part-time schedules. Blue-collar work also presents other scheduling issues that have been studied far less than those in white-collar jobs. A 1995 study found that almost half of low-income parents (compared with one-quarter of working-class and middle-class mothers and one-third of higher-income fathers) work on rotating schedules, which often creates severe difficulties in finding day care. For example, a study by DuPont found that employees in manufacturing jobs had more difficulty balancing their work and family lives than other employees; rotating shifts and emergency care for dependents were cited as major difficulties. A study for the Labor Department found that high-income employees have greater access to flexibility than others, and that nonminorities have greater access than minorities. "For single mothers with small children," said one steelworker, Trudy Pat Farr, "the schedule is pure hell. Some might call it irony; I call it injustice: Single mothers who so desperately need these relatively well-paying jobs have to face impossible conditions. And no exceptions can be made. (Although I've seen a man get a 'special schedule' to accommodate his working wife.)" Farr noted that, when the steel mill where she worked closed down, some women went back to previous jobs "that pay less, but are less dirty, less dangerous, and, most importantly, have a decent work schedule—a schedule more compatible with raising kids.[56]

The irony is that many craft jobs could easily be restructured in ways to make them compatible with the norm of parental care. Here's a woman operating engineer:

> Now . . . , after living through ten years in the trade . . . , I still enjoy both sides of my life. On my winter side (when operating engineers are typically laid off) I'm a laid-back, full-time mom. I cook and bake from scratch, cuddle my kids, and work at training my dogs. On my summer side . . . I'm up and gone long before my husband Curt wakes up. He does all the morning chores on our small farm, gets the kids up and takes them to preschool.

Another woman, a carpenter, notes that one thing she likes about the job is that you can take a long vacation whenever you like with no job consequences. Many skilled craft workers travel from job to job; if you take a break between jobs or for the summer, no one cares.[57]

In conclusion, even if employers were to select employees for "good" blue-collar jobs with no intentional discrimination whatsoever, and even if women in nontraditional jobs were not subjected to severe sexual harassment, a disproportionate number of women still would be excluded from those positions because they are designed around men's physique and men's ability to maintain an unbroken full-time or overtime schedule while their wives (or ex-wives) care for their children. Although the mechanisms of exclusion are different in blue- and white-collar work, in each context the required schedule operates to exclude large numbers of women.

"WOMEN'S WORK" OFFERS A REFUGE FROM MASCULINE NORMS

> Most women still work in jobs that are located near residential areas; are open to part-time workers; are easy to start, drop, and start again; and don't require skills that get stale with time.[58]

A majority of working women in the United States hold low-paid, traditionally female jobs. In 1993, women were 99 percent of dental hygienists; 98 percent of secretaries, typists, and kindergarten teachers; and 98 percent of registered nurses, speech therapists, and billing clerks. Men were still 99 percent of auto mechanics; 97 percent of firefighters and airplane pilots; and over 90 percent of precision metal workers, surveying technicians, and sewage plant operators. Nearly 60 percent of women hold jobs in traditional women's work such as clerical, sales, and service occupations, which typically pay half to two-thirds of the wages in blue-collar craft work.[59]

Classic studies of sex segregation by job category far underestimate the rate at which women work with other women in jobs that pay less than similar jobs staffed by men. Two national studies covering the years 1959 to 1983 found that 90 to 93 percent of women would have to change jobs to have the same job titles as men. A more recent study found that in North Carolina that number was 77 percent.[60]

Studies often focus on the supposed psychological match between women and the jobs traditionally held by them. In fact, masculine norms play an important role in keeping women in women's work. Women who stay where they "belong" avoid the virulent harassment experienced by women in nontraditional work. They do not have to deal with social patterns framed around sports, hunting, or other forms of masculine gender performance. They do not risk injury or discomfort from equipment designed around the bodies of men. They do not require women to have the flow of family work or the ability to move their families, privileges generally available to few mothers.[61]

Scheduling is one important factor keeping women in traditional women's work, which tends to have regular hours with little mandated overtime. Lawyers work lots of overtime; librarians do not. Autoworkers work lots of overtime, whereas waitresses do not. A British study noted that employers build gender into the way they structure hours: in male jobs, they achieve flexibility through overtime; in female ones, they do so through part-time work.[62]

Traditionally female work is also more likely to offer established part-time tracks. The jobs with readily available part-time options are traditional women's work: clerical, administrative, or retail nonprofessional work, or work in professions with a long history of female segregation, such as nursing and library science. Only 6 percent of workers in railroad, mining, and manufacturing are voluntary part-timers; 25 percent of those in the retail and wholesale trade are. Evidence also suggests that subsequent earnings are unaffected by part-time work in these traditional female fields, in sharp contrast to the situation in traditionally male fields.[63]

The third pattern is that in jobs traditionally held by women, taking time off work for childbearing or child rearing does not knock a worker off a career path leading to a much better job. Nurses, librarians, retail sales workers, waitresses, and other women in traditional women's jobs typically can leave and reenter with few long-term consequences. The reason is that these are dead-end jobs with no career trajectory: "Extensive research demonstrates lack of advancement opportunity in all types of female-dominated low-paying jobs." Jobs with more opportunities for promotion are more likely to be filled with males. The best men's jobs—both blue- and white-collar—have career paths that often penalize career breaks and place the key years for career advancement at precisely the period when most people have young children.[64]

"Choosing" women's work typically allows workers to preserve dependable amounts of time for family life, to be able to leave market work completely without jeopardizing their ability to return, and to follow husbands without loss of investment in human capital. This "choice" also lets women avoid both job situations that require masculine gender performances and those with the virulent sexual harassment frequently seen in blue-collar work.

Not surprisingly, women in traditionally female professions report lower role conflict than do women in male-dominated professions or women in nonprofessional jobs. They were the happiest group surveyed. Note, however, that traditional women's work did not offer more flexibility, autonomy, or unsupervised break time; it was too low-status for that. The gains of women who resolve work/family conflict by taking traditional women's work come at the expense of permanent consignment to low-status, low-wage, dead-end work. Workers in such pink-collar jobs did not report the high satisfaction levels of women in traditionally female professions such as nursing, social work, and library work.[65]

If a significant sector of the economy already accommodates people in women's social position, why not declare victory and go home? The reason is that women pay a steep price for jobs not framed around masculine norms. Schoolteachers and mothers who own small home-based businesses do not run the world. Nearly 60 percent of full-time female employees are paid less than $25,000 a year, and nearly 70 percent of the full-time female labor force is in low-paying occupational categories. Note that if this figure included part-time workers, the percentage of low-paid women would climb even higher. Nor do traditionally female jobs offer much chance of advancement. Women represent 76 percent of the workers in the jobs with the fewest advancement opportunities and only 5 percent of those in the jobs with the most.[66]

A final point is in order about how women avoid masculine norms. A sharply increasing number work in woman-owned businesses. The number of woman-owned businesses surged 43 percent in the five years before 1992, double the rate of growth for all except very large firms in the same period. The rate of growth of woman-owned businesses is four times faster than for businesses owned by males, and exceeds the national average in nearly every region and industry. In 1994 woman-owned businesses employed 35 percent more people than the Fortune 500 companies did worldwide. In 1975 women were about 25 percent of self-employed workers; today they account for about 33 percent. Today women own about one-third of all firms. While the top woman-owned businesses used to be in crafts, day care, and beauty salons, today they have shifted dramatically: Now women who own businesses tend to continue to do the white-collar and service work they did in their old jobs. While not all woman-owned businesses are structured to accommodate women's load of family work, many are. "The main thing is that I'm number one a mom and a wife," said one business owner. Self-employed women are consistently more likely than other workers to be married with spouse present. They are also more likely to work part time. A study by the National Foundation of Women Business Owners found that women entrepreneurs are more likely than their male counterparts to offer flexible work arrangements. "Overall," concluded another study, "the data suggest that self-employed women faced (or at least exercised) more choice in terms of hours worked." The many women who start businesses so that they can do the work they want and have the schedule they need dramatize the pent-up productivity that can emerge if work is restructured to eliminate the traditional ideal-worker norm.[67]

The conclusion is dramatic, and rarely recognized: Most women work in workplaces that do not adhere to key elements of the masculine ideal-worker norm. Note that this is different from the human capital theory argument that women "choose" women's work solely because of their family responsibilities. That literature ignores the type of stereotyping experienced by Ann Hopkins in addition to the well-documented sexual harassment of women in traditionally male blue-collar work (and sometimes in white-collar work as well). It also mixes up causation in a way the analysis of domesticity can remedy. The human capital literature is a classic "choice" argument, which leaves domesticity outside the frame of reference. Once the analysis of domesticity is added back in, we see that women's "choice" takes place in a context that requires of ideal workers the social power available to men, to relocate their families, for example, or to enjoy a flow of family work most fathers but few mothers enjoy. A system that requires workers to command the social power of men in order to get "good" jobs is one that discriminates against women. It does so both in the vernacular sense of being inconsistent with our ideals of gender equality and in the technical sense of having a disparate impact on women that is not justified by business necessity and that may violate federal antidiscrimination law. Before we reach the technical argument, however, let us address an issue that arises both in the policy context and in litigation. It may be well and good to reconceptualize "choice" as discrimination, but isn't it just downright impractical in an era when the United States is part of a competitive global economy? The following section addresses this important issue.

IS IT FEASIBLE TO RESTRUCTURE THE WORKPLACE TO ELIMINATE MASCULINE NORMS?

> When they were working on the Mars probe, they needed people on the job twenty-four hours a day. How do you think they did it? Job sharing. If we can do it on Mars, why not on earth?[68]

Andy Marks is a successful Washington lawyer with an intensive commercial litigation practice. Two part-time lawyers work with him at a senior counsel level on litigation matters. This is remarkable because the nigh-unchallenged common knowledge is that part-time work is impractical in litigation because lawsuits proceed according to court deadlines over which lawyers themselves often have little control.

None of which deterred Marks or his firm. "Both of these extremely talented and experienced attorneys were in the process of leaving their existing firms and were looking for a new firm that would enable them to spend more time at home with their young children than a full-time commitment would permit. We decided that we could and would hire them on a less than full-time basis." In thinking this through, Marks recalled an incident several years earlier.

> We had an outstanding woman associate who had been working with me on a piece of major litigation and who became involved in a second matter that required her to work two days a week outside the office for a different partner. I was faced with the choice of whether to have her continue to work on my case three days a week or to find a different associate who could devote full time to my case. I decided to take three days a week. And

then I realized: Virtually every associate who works with me works on cases for other partners and is therefore a part-time lawyer as far as my cases are concerned.[69]

All lawyers regularly find ways to accommodate the demands of other cases; finding a way to accommodate an attorney's desire to work on less than a full-time basis is not all that different.

The part-time lawyers work for Marks a target number of hours *per year,* which means that they can handle the intense work periods characteristic of litigation. Then, when the crunch is over, they take time off. (Arthur Andersen, the accounting firm, has a slightly different approach, in which workers take half the client load instead of half the hours.) Marks' associates like the arrangement because they get to spend time with their children. He likes it because he gets committed workers who do high-quality work.[70]

This story challenges the notion that it is impossible or too expensive to require employers to "accommodate women's private lives." Note how the old-fashioned formulation loads the issue. What's at issue is not the private frolic of flighty women but the clash of two deeply held social norms: the norm of parental care and the ideal-worker norm.

Can we reconcile these norms?

Over the past twenty years many employers have become convinced that they can, and that businesses have to take steps in that direction in the interests of maximum efficiency. In a highly respected survey, 80 percent of corporations agreed that they could not remain competitive in the 1990s without addressing work/family and diversity issues. A survey of two hundred human resources managers by the Conference Board, a business group, found that two-thirds named family-supportive policies as the single most important factor in attracting and retaining employees.[71] This high level of interest is in response to expected shifts in composition of the work force in the twenty-first century. Because a high percentage of new entrants will be female, employers will have to expand their field of vision to include women and minorities.[72]

These realizations led to the growth of a new type of consultant, one specializing in work/family management, and a new focus on work/family issues in personnel departments. Prominent consultants and nonprofits working in the field include the Families & Work Institute, in New York; New Ways to Work, in San Francisco; Felice Schwartz, of Catalyst (whose proposal triggered the "mommy track" debate), in Boston; Fran Rodgers, of Work/Family Directions, in Boston; Susan Seitel, of Work & Family Connections, Inc., in Minneapolis; Dana Friedman, of Bright Horizons Family Solutions; and the group that includes Lotte Bailyn and others at the Sloan School at MIT and the Radcliffe Institute on Public Policy.

"Family-friendly" policies include some well-known benefits such as childbirth leave and part-time work. Newer options include telecommuting, where the employee works from home part or all of the time, and job sharing, where two people become jointly responsible for performing one job, and split the hours between them. A variety of scheduling options has also arisen, the most popular of which are flextime, where workers need to work during a core of hours, say 10 A.M. to 2 P.M., but can choose when to begin and end work, and compressed workweeks, typically composed of four ten-hour days. Employer support for childcare and elder care ranges from referrals to providers (widespread), to subsidies (rarer) or on-site child care centers (rarest). The National Study of the Changing Workforce found in 1993 that 88 percent of all workers have access to some childbirth or parenting leave, 57 percent have access to part-time work, and 29 percent have access to flextime. A 1993 Catalyst study of 1,006 employers, each with more than a thousand employees, found that 53 percent offered flexible schedules. A recent study by the William M. Mercer management consulting firm in New York found in a survey of eight hundred companies that employ a thousand or more workers that 34 percent of the companies used compressed workweeks for some of their workforce and 14 percent were considering them.[73]

One strong message of the existing work/family literature is that no single solution works best in all workplaces. Oshkosh B'Gosh, with plants in rural Tennessee and Kentucky, went at workers' request to nine-hour shifts and four-and-a-half-day workweeks in order to leave workers large chunks of time to work on family farms. The Engelhard Corporation addressed the 150 percent rate of turnover, high absenteeism, high accident rates, and large amount of product waste in its Huntsville, Alabama, chemical plant by allowing workers to vote on a flexible schedule. They chose a four-day workweek with work beginning at 5 A.M and ending at 3 P.M. When the schedule was implemented, absenteeism dropped from an average of twenty to three days a year and both turnover and product waste decreased to less than 1 percent.[74]

What schedules work best vary greatly from workplace to workplace. In the accounts processing department of First Tennessee Bank, employees work longer shifts at the start of the month, when work is heaviest; each takes a day off later in the month. A number of companies and government offices have instituted "dawn patrols," employees who avoid traffic and child-care problems with shifts that start at 6:30 or 7:00 A.M. This schedule is particularly useful to employers in the West who do a lot of business in the East, since when businesses open in New York, it's only 6:00 in California.[75]

For other businesses, flexible hours are less important than on-site child care. Marquette Electronics president Michael Cudahy called the company's on-site child-care center "the best business decision [he] ever made in business." One of the nation's largest design and construction firms, BE & K Engineering and Construction Company, provides a mobile child care center that follows workers from one construction site to the next.[76]

False Truisms

A common assumption is that flexibility does not work in high-level professional jobs. Many employers have found otherwise. Andy Marks' comments suggest this is untrue, as does the analysis of the Big Six accounting firm Deloitte & Touche discussed below. A study by a Chicago-based management consultant, Myerson Smagley, who studied ten large companies headquartered in Chicago, found that nine of the ten had professionals in sharing arrangements, and all were successful. Half of those arrangements involved individuals with significant amounts of travel, client contact, and supervisory authority. According to the Bureau of Labor Statistics, 3.5 million managers and professionals worked part time in 1992.[77]

Another common assumption is that flexible scheduling is not possible for manufacturing workers. Again, many companies are challenging this view. Nearly all automobile tire companies and most big semiconductor companies have now shifted to new schedules, often in order to keep plants running nonstop. While some of these schedules severely disrupt workers' lives, others can offer more family time than traditional schedules. For example, one AT&T factory that produces silicon chips went to a schedule in which employees work three consecutive days one week and then four days the next. One key is stability: The DuPont study found that rotating shifts, as when a worker works nights one week and days the next, can cause high levels of stress in two-job families. Even schedules that have men complaining about lost weekends are welcome to some women. For Tonya Bowden, a single mother of two, the four-day, ten-hour-a-day workweek at GM's Saturn plant was a welcome switch from the prior schedule, which allowed her to see her son just half an hour a day.[78]

A third assumption is that family-friendly policies do not work for clerical staff. At the Minneapolis law firm of Maslon, Edelman, Borman, and Brand, 15 percent of the clerical staff work part time, a system that often offers better coverage than conventional scheduling. "Job sharing means someone is always here. It's transparent. If one is sick or takes vacation they work it out and the other shows up." Some employers have found that job sharing and flexible hours allow them to stay open longer hours at little or no extra cost.[79]

A fourth assumption is that flexibility can work only if it is limited to a few employees. A number of companies have shown this is not true. At Xerox, everyone is allowed flexible schedules; employees publish monthly calendars showing how they'll back each other up to cover absences. At Bank of America, roughly 2,000 of its 96,500 employees job share. Twenty percent of DuPont's more than 100,000 employees use its LifeWorks family resource program, which has flexible scheduling as one of its components.[80]

A final truism is that only large corporations can afford flexibility. Once when I was on a radio talk show, I received a call from the owner of a shoe store. "You know, Joan," he said, "I don't see how what you are saying is anything more than good management and common sense. If I have an employee with a sick child and I don't let her go home, I'm not going to keep her long. If you want to retain good workers, you've got to be flexible." Small businesses do not like turnover, and one consultant advised, "Flexible policies are one way to get people to stay." While large corporations are more likely to have official policies, smaller companies are more likely to react on an individual basis.[81]

The work/family literature reports successes not only in large corporations but in smaller ones. Kern Dermatology, with twenty-two employees, instituted flexible work schedules, parent education classes, and a 20 percent discount at the family care center next door. The company has had a zero turnover rate in the past seven years, and estimates it has saved $27,000 in retraining costs. Mervyn's Department Store's one hundred employees can participate in flexible schedules and job sharing (including trading child care to each other); a discount child care program is also available. The company cut its turnover in half, from 33 to 16 percent, and saved an estimated $48,000 in turnover costs and $61,000 due to the efficiency of flexible scheduling.[82]

Employers who dismiss scheduling flexibility as inefficient typically do not take into account how inflexibility costs them money. Surveys indicate that inflexible policies generate costs due to impaired job performance, absenteeism, and turnover, and that the costs of implementing a work/family program may be less than the costs of not having one. A report on elder care to the Metropolitan Life Insurance Company enumerates the costs associated with current policies. These included replacement costs for caregivers who quit due to job inflexibility and costs both to the employer and to other employees of workday interruptions and absenteeism. Other studies have shown that flexibility also often increases worker productivity and the ability to recruit high-quality workers.[83]

Retention and Recruitment

> The firm invests millions of dollars recruiting and training these talented people, and if they leave prematurely we have, in effect, squandered our investment. Not only that, but clients aren't served as well if you pick your partners out of only half the people hired. You want all the best people to stay with you, men and women.[84]

At Amerco, the company studied by Arlie Hochschild, it cost $40,000 to replace each skilled employee who quit. Other figures suggest that the costs of replacing a skilled worker are typically .75 to 1.5 times the worker's annual salary. These costs quickly add up in workplaces that hire large proportions of women who leave after the birth of children because they have professional husbands and cannot justify raising children when both parents are gone ten hours or more each day. (Recall the attorney cited above who rarely saw her children awake.)[85]

Evaluations of individual companies' family-friendly policies typically find that their most consistent benefit is the ability to retain valued employees. In a recent survey of two hundred human resource managers, two-thirds named family-supportive benefits and flexible hours as the two most important tools for retaining and recruiting workers in the future. A report by the Conference Board, a business group, found that family-supportive benefits were an employer's most important recruiting tool.[86]

The Big Six accounting firm of Deloitte & Touche provides a dramatic example of a company committed to improving retention. Key players at Deloitte became concerned because of the high attrition of women, who comprised 36 percent of its workforce but only 5 percent of its 1,400 partners. Although a 95 percent male partnership rate is about average for the industry, chairman and CEO Michael Cook felt Deloitte's low retention of women was bad business. Low levels of retention persisted even after it instituted a first generation of mommy-track policies, which allowed part-time work for associates, not partners or managers.

Deloitte's data showed that at the entry level, men and women left the firm at about equal rates, but that women left at a faster rate than men after that, at the three-, six-, and nine-year junctures when they could expect to be promoted. And the women who left had often shown real professional promise. This pattern is reminiscent of the pattern we saw in the best, traditionally male blue-collar jobs. In both contexts, a major reason why the percentage of women has not grown appreciably is that the turnover among women reaches extraordinarily high levels.

In 1991 Deloitte hired Catalyst, a nonprofit research firm that advises corporations on how to retain and promote women. Catalyst found that women were leaving because of a combination of the glass ceiling and the maternal wall. Some male managers confided that they hesitated before putting a woman on a high-profile assignment because they were worried the woman might quit and leave the client in the lurch. They assumed that the women who had already quit were home raising families, and that the woman in question would follow suit.

Women in focus groups reported a lack of mentors, and cited being passed over for plum assignments, frozen out of informal social networks, and left out of social events with clients. One reported having to enter through the back door of a men-only private club to attend a company lunch. Interviews with forty promising women who had left showed that over 70 percent were working full time; only 10 percent were home full time. These women cited not only long hours but also glass-ceiling frustrations. One reported frustration at her inability to work with foreign companies. When she asked her boss to allow her to move into areas typically handled by men, he discouraged her: "But you're so good at what you do." Finally, one of the members of Deloitte's Task Force on the Retention and Advancement of Women shocked the other task force members by announcing she was leaving the firm. She had given up partnership status and taken a pay cut to work a part-time schedule but ran into resentment from mostly male co-workers. "The attitude was, 'If *you're* working part-time, *I* have to work harder,'" said a Deloitte human resources director. Despite the support of her superiors, she found the situation unworkable.

By 1995 Deloitte not only had instituted rigorous measures to control glass-ceiling effects but also had changed its policies on flexible work. Too, it put in place a new generation of family-friendly policies that did not penalize those who took them. Under the new policies, reduced hours, telecommuting, and other flexible arrangements became widely available to men and women at all levels, including to managers and partners, so that flexibility was no longer linked with being barred from interesting work and promotion. The prior generation of policies, which sent the message that those who worked flexible schedules were not ideal workers eligible for plum assignments and promotion, had failed to stem women's exodus from the firm. Yet under policies that restructured work, the turnover rates for senior women managers dropped from 26 to 15 percent in three years.

This experience was confirmed at DuPont. When DuPont became concerned that it was losing valuable people because of lack of flexibility, it first offered part-time work at the same rate of pay but without benefits, merit increases, or opportunities for promotion. This approach failed; DuPont has now replaced it with an approach that treats part-timers identically to full-timers with respect to not only salary but also vacation pay, holidays, merit increases, and promotion, with prorating of benefits being phased in gradually.[87]

A Conference Board report noted that 51 percent of companies instituting flexible work plans listed preventing unwanted turnover as one of their reasons for doing so. Another study found that mothers working for bosses who offer flexibility are seven times less likely to quit. A study out of Notre Dame found that new mothers are more likely to return to their old jobs when employers offer flexibility. A 1992 survey of IBM employees found flexibility and work support were the second most important factor given by high-performing employees for remaining with the company. One Tennessee bank estimated that they would otherwise have lost 85 percent of those employees who switched to a new program designed to reduce working hours.[88]

A number of companies have also documented the savings gained from better employee retention and recruiting. After Aetna Life & Casualty introduced a number of flexible work options to improve employee retention, it reported cutting postmaternity attrition rates from 24 to 12 percent, and savings of more than $2 million a year due to decreases in employee turnover. Helene Curtis' flextime program increased the return rate of new mothers from 69 to 93 percent in just three years, resulting in savings (in 1992) of $360,000. Nations Bank's work/family program resulted in a drop in turnover from 30 to 18 percent. Steelcase, Inc., credits their program with reducing turnover from 12 to 3 percent. A widely reported survey by the National Council of Jewish Women for the Department of Labor found that women who were allowed flexible hours worked longer into their pregnancies, returned to work earlier, and were more likely not to leave their jobs after the birth of the baby. Flexibility holds advantages not only in retaining workers but in recruiting them. The Minneapolis law firm mentioned above advertised a job share in a human resources support position, and got a "deluge" of applicants. "We had a hot ticket!" said the human resources director. They had no trouble filling the position. Automatic Data Processing found that flexibility gave them a competitive edge in attracting as well as keeping skilled workers.[89]

On-site child care has a particularly dramatic effect on employee turnover. Patagonia estimates that it saved $160,000 in 1993 alone in recruitment and retraining costs by offering on-site child care. The SAS Institute, a computer company, kept its turnover at 3 percent, far below the industry average of 20 percent. Virginia Mason Medical Center, in Seattle, found zero turnover among employees using on-site day care, compared with 23 percent among other workers. Research also indicates that the turnover rate for on-site child-care center users at 53 percent of the companies studied was zero.[90]

Decreasing turnover appears even more important because of the strong link between retaining employees and retaining clients. When Deloitte instituted its second-generation work/family program, it gave clients the option of switching to a new person when an accountant reduced work hours. They found that virtually all of them choose not to start with a new person.[91]

The Deloitte case dramatizes that women's exodus from high-status jobs is not only because of scheduling concerns but because they see the writing on the wall in jobs where advancement is still linked with masculine gender performance.

Absenteeism

Family-friendly policies also sharply reduce levels of absenteeism. One national survey found that absenteeism and tardiness are dramatically reduced by flextime. A survey by the American Management Association found that allowing workers flexibility not only cuts absenteeism by as much as 50 percent but also improves work quality and morale. The 50 percent figure was confirmed by Chemical Bank, which built an on-site child-care center after surveys found that 52 percent of absences were caused by family-related issues; the on-site child-care center constructed by Intermedics, Inc., resulted in a 60 percent reduction in absenteeism and savings of $2 million.[92]

A government department and a wide variety of kinds of companies, from manufacturing to banking to department stores, all report dramatic improvements in retention under flexible policies. Pella Corporation, which produces windows, found that job sharing not only decreased absenteeism by 81 percent, but also increased performance reviews, which generally went up from "satisfactory" to "high professional." Steelcase, Inc., found that scheduling flexibility reduced turnover, decreased absenteeism and tardy arrivals, increased productivity, and improved customer service and employee morale. In Union County, New Jersey, scheduling flexibility cut absenteeism "dramatically" while increasing the quality of customer service in the Division of Employment and Training.[93]

Upon reflection, none of this is surprising. People need to go to the doctor, the dentist, the school play. If no other method is available, they will simply call in sick or disappear discreetly in the middle of the day. What employers find is that if workers are allowed to schedule in that time, many will do those errands on personal rather than company time. This is noted as an advantage of the flextime program instituted in Union County, New Jersey, where human services director Frank Guzzo reported that employees seemed to be scheduling appointments on their days off.[94]

Productivity

I need 15 percent core workers who work regular hours or longer. If benefits for part-timers were pro-rated, there would be no cost—in money or efficiency—to splitting one job into two, or two jobs into three, or instituting flextime. It would probably increase the plant's efficiency.[95]

A standard argument is that while flexibility would be nice, we cannot afford it in this increasingly competitive global market. In fact, we cannot afford to do without it; increasing productivity is a major reason companies institute flexible work plans. "[W]hen someone cuts back from one hundred to seventy-five percent they become a lot smarter about the way they work, so they're more productive instead of less," said one employer. In summarizing ten studies of managers' experiences, Simcha Ronen found that most supervisors feel their part-time workers are more productive, less likely to quit, and less likely to miss work than full-time workers.[96]

Experience bears this out. A bank with an active second-generation work/family program more than doubled its loan volume with no increase in staffing or major systems improvements and a decrease in overtime pay from $36,000 in 1993 to $6,000 three years later; the accounts processing department also cut the time required to process customer accounts from ten days to four. A Ford Foundation study of Xerox found that one unit of seventeen engineers ended up working very long hours because more than half their time was eaten up with interruptions and impromptu meetings. Once they instituted "quiet times" during the day, hours fell and they had the first on-time product launch in their history. Indeed, some companies have cut hours without cutting pay, financing the cut through increased productivity. At Metro Plastics, in Indiana, employees shifted to two six-hour shifts but continued to be paid for eight hours. "If you count the time it would take to go to lunch, eat, and settle down to work again," said an executive, "they're probably not putting in that much less time, but it feels like a lot less to them; they sure love going home at noon."[97]

Flexible policies can improve productivity in four basic ways: by allowing employers to stay open longer hours with the same number of employees; by improving staffing during vacations or illness; by increasing worker loyalty and job commitment; and, in the case of part-time schedules, by providing a fresh worker at just the point when full-time workers are slowing down.

The first way flexible policies increase productivity is by lengthening the hours that customers are served or machinery is used, often without need for extra staff or overtime. Canadian autoworkers and Chrysler Canada replaced mandatory overtime with a third shift, allowing the plant to stay open around the clock. The full-time schedule was reduced from eight to seven and a half hours (with no reduction in pay), and eight hundred new jobs were added. The company put unutilized capacity to productive use, and avoided the need for an expensive new plant. The Pella window company found that its flexible policies saved money by eliminating the need to overstaff in order to compensate for absent workers. StrideRite found it could add thirty hours onto the workweek at a cost of only 3 percent more when it put one of its customer service units on flexible scheduling. Bank of America found that its regular part-time employees had greater output than either their hourly or full-time counterparts; New York State found that its four thousand job sharers get more done than their colleagues.[98]

The second way flexible policies increase productivity is by improving staffing during employee vacations and illness. When the City of Phoenix began an innovative program of child care for sick children, it saved the city $11,000 in sick leave in just six months. One Aetna manager said he would like a whole department of job sharers, because "when one is sick or on vacation, the other one is always there." At the Minneapolis law firm with 15 percent of its clerical staff on flexible schedules, they have never had to hire a temp. At Marquette Electronics, where work teams can stagger the work to allow a member to come in late or to accommodate a family emergency, employees who miss work can make up the time during another shift. The firm's philosophy is that "[e]veryone has bad days and days when they give 120%." The human resources director at Maslon, Edelman, Barman and Brand notes that a key advantage of flexibility plans is that finding replacements becomes the responsibility of the job-sharing employee rather than the supervisor; this format can be used in manufacturing as well as other types of jobs.[99]

The third way flexible policies increase productivity is by avoiding the "TGIF syndrome." Organizations from state governments to manufacturers to banking and insurance companies have found job sharers and part-time workers are more productive because they start fresh when other workers are flagging. New York State, which allows all of its 200,000 employees flexibility, has found that two people produce more than one in the same job because of the fatigue factor. A vice president at Schreiber Foods found that when an executive assistant job was split between two people, she got a fresh person at midweek, just when others in the office were starting to tire or reacting to job stresses. The Northwestern Life Insurance Company found that flexible scheduling reduced employees reporting burnout from thirty-nine to twenty-eight percent. The Royal Bank of Canada found that workers with flexible schedules "ha[ve] more energy and a more positive attitude, were absent less often, less stressed and better able to balance work and personal obligations."[100]

A fourth way flexible policies increase productivity is by increasing work loyalty. "How could I not be grateful to a company that granted me this, that helped my son incredibly?" asked one Bell South worker who took six months off to care for a sick child. Numerous studies have found that employees offered flexibility are more likely to "go the extra mile," to "go out of their way to make the job work," to be "more loyal." Increases in loyalty can translate into direct increases in productivity: At Fel-Pro, a manufacturer of auto parts in Skokie, Illinois, workers who used family benefits submitted twice as many quality-improvement suggestions as those who didn't.[101]

A final way flexible policies increase efficiency is by increasing the pool of competent workers. Employers currently are losing 50 to 90 percent or more of the qualified employee pool because many mothers refuse to work full time or overtime. Recall the Amerco manager's statement that the people who currently rise to the top are not necessarily the most competent: they are that small minority of people ready, willing, and able to work eighty hours a week.

A recent study by three economists provides an important perspective on why employers continue to demand long hours despite the costs that accompany such a practice. In a study of law firms, they find that it is very difficult for a single firm unilaterally to decrease its hours of work. "Things will be different, however, under a law compelling *all* firms to simultaneously abandon" the current equilibrium of everyone requiring long hours. "A maximum hours law would, in this situation, make current partners better off without making any of the associates worse off." If employees begin to win scheduling suits, described below, the effect would be similar. In other words, the current long hours of work reflect not efficiency but what economists call the prisoner's dilemma: No one actor, acting alone, can change a system that disadvantages everyone.[102]

In summary, the current system forces many men to work long hours, way past their peak efficiency, and wastes many women's productivity, to the extent that one-fourth of mothers of childbearing age are out of the labor force altogether. A system that produces overwork for men and underemployment for women is not efficient. Allowing workers greater flexibility would enhance productivity.[103]

From the Mommy Track to Restructured Work

One point that emerges strongly from the work/family literature is the ineffectiveness of first-generation mommy track policies that link flexibility with marginalization. *Newsweek* observed that "a company may pay lip service to offering alternatives for working mothers, but asking for them can be the kiss of death." According to a report written for the Glass Ceiling Commission, "Many employees and employers view the use of family-friendly policies and the desire for career advancement as mutually exclusive choices." For this reason, actual usage of these policies "is so small, it's shocking." A 1990 study of 188 Fortune 500 manufacturing firms found that while 88 percent offered part-time work (either informally or as part of a formal program), only 3 to 5 percent of their employees took advantage of it. Another survey showed that less than 3 percent of lawyers took advantage of part-time policies despite the fact that 90 percent of the firms surveyed offered it.[104]

Simply adding a marginalized mommy track does not work. Levels of retention will rise only after employers redefine the ideal worker. "Rather than appending 'family-friendly' policies to a traditional conception of office life, [second-generation policies] . . . are redefining the nature of work itself." Such policies will not be effective if they are "grafts upon an unchanging core."[105]

Four elements seem vital to the success of second-generation work/family policies designed to restructure work rather than simply to introduce a mommy track. The first is a shift away from the head-count system of measuring productivity. Managers are discouraged from allowing part-time work in companies that use the common practice of measuring productivity by counting "heads." Under this system, a manager's productivity is assessed based on how much he produces per person employed, without taking into account whether the employees are full- or part-time. Under this system, a manager with two part-time workers is counted as having two "heads," which makes it appear he is not using workers efficiently. Some companies are starting to replace the old head-counting system with a system of counting personnel in terms of "full-time equivalents" (FTEs), a shift in practice that decreases managers' resistance to flexible policies. For example, when Aetna Life & Casualty examined how to generate stronger corporate support for work/family policies, supervisors overwhelmingly said, "Change head count. If I'm encouraged to allow flexible work options, then I shouldn't have to explain why I have 'more heads' at the end of every quarter." The Department of Labor confirmed this finding in a recent study, as have other experts.[106]

Another factor often mentioned in the literature is that top management should communicate support for family-friendly policies; in fact, employees are more likely to use flexible policies when managers use them themselves. A work/family program should be introduced by the CEO of the company, with strong signals of support.[107]

But the literature often fails to highlight what is no doubt the most important single factor in ensuring the success of a family-friendly program. If an employer is serious about restructuring work, *managers' success in implementing flexibility should be a significant factor in their annual review.* It only makes sense that if an employer does not include its managers' success in implementing family-friendly policies as part of its periodic review process, the implementation of such policies will be stalled as managers respond to other priorities.[108]

Another important factor is education. Workshops need to train both employees and managers. Though managers' resistance sometimes stems from the way they have run their own lives, it also sometimes stems from a literal inability to imagine a new way of doing things. In one company with a demonstrated commitment to work/family issues, managers played a board game in which they were given a set period of time to solve an employee's work/family dilemma.[109]

DuPont, a leader in the field, has found that it takes time to shift company culture. Lotte Bailyn, now head of the Sloan School of Management at MIT, has written extensively on the need to shift to a new style of management that focuses on results, not "face time." Bailyn argues that supervisors who have always depended on face time need to shift their attention to output. They need to be less concerned with *how* things get done and more with *whether* they get done. In response to managers' question "How do I know he's working if I don't see him," Bailyn asks, "How do you know he's working when you *do* see him?" The work of Bailyn and others has proven widely influential.[110]

The traditional way to coordinate schedules is to require everyone to be at the office at the same time. An alternative is to require employees to coordinate their schedules on their own. At Hewlett-Packard, nearly everyone uses flextime; workers design their own schedules. One unit found that a compressed workweek increased productivity because the time-consuming process of setting up equipment took place four days a week instead of five. When one Hewlett-Packard facility went into twenty-four-hour operation, some chose twelve-hour shifts and an eight-hour stint every other Thursday. Perhaps not coincidentally, the company's earnings recently rose 41 percent.[111]

New forms of supervision are becoming more common because of the shift to contingent work, which includes part-time employees, temporary workers, day laborers, and independent contractors. Estimates are that from 20 to 30 percent of the economy already has been restructured as "contingent" work. During the United Parcel Service (UPS) strike in 1997, a major issue was that 57 percent of the company's employees were part-time workers. There appears to be general agreement that the growth of contingent workers indicates "structural change, rather than merely a cyclical phenomenon." Although employers often complain it is impossible to supervise restructured work, this structural change shows that many employers already are. The growth of contingent work has given employers experience in new methods of supervision, both of part-time workers and of workers such as independent contractors, whose productivity must be measured directly rather than in terms of face time.[112]

Restructuring work is not impossible. In fact, the process is already well under way. The huge economic shift to contingent work shows that supervisors can maintain quality control without relying on face time. Several decades of experience with family-friendly policies has shown that flexibility is often *more* efficient than traditional practices. But experience also shows that mommy-track policies that link flexibility with marginalization will be used by very few workers. What is needed are not "grafts on an unchanging core," but a redefinition of what it means to be an ideal worker. In place of the rigid, gendered definition of an ideal worker without significant caregiving responsibilities, workplaces need to be structured so that women can perform as ideal workers even if they do not have immunity from family work.[113]

Punish People Who Work Hard? What Kind of a Proposal Is That?

Some feminists have argued that people should be barred from working more than a certain number of hours each day. My approach is different. I do not propose to forbid overtime or to argue that people who work part-time or other flexible schedules should progress *at the same rate* as those who work long hours; I suggest only that they should be paid and promoted *in proportion to the amount they work.*

Nationwide data also suggest that employers typically exact a price for part-time work in terms of pay, benefits, and promotion. Wages of part-time workers are much lower than those of full-time workers. Fully one-fourth of all part-time workers earn the minimum wage (one-twentieth of full-time workers do). As has been noted, the average part-time worker gets paid 60 percent of the average wage rate of a full-time worker. In part this is because part-time jobs tend to be clustered in traditionally women's work where even full-time workers are poorly paid. However, according to one study, only about half of the differential between the pay rates of full-time and part-time employees can be explained by "objective" factors such as sex, race, age, etc.[114]

Someone who works half-time should be paid at the same rate as full-time workers are. This is not a novel proposal. The International Labor Organization has proposed a convention that would end discrimination against part-time work. The operative language requires that "part-time workers [shall] receive the same protection as that accorded to comparable full-time workers." This includes proportional benefits as well as wages. The AFL-CIO Executive Council has recently endorsed the principle of equal pay rates for part-time work.[115]

The Argument That People Work Because They Need the Money and "Flexibility" Is for the Privileged

> When my daughter was born, my boss agreed to let me work part time. But then I found that I was getting all the scut work and none of the design work I was doing before. Also, it gradually became clear that the only responsible way to work part time was, in his view, to work full time. I ended up working close to forty hours a week and being paid for twenty-five. I'm not going to do scut work at slave wages. I quit.[116]

Another common response to proposals for restructuring is that they are unrealistic because American families need the money. This is a legitimate criticism that requires a response.

The most important point is that less affluent families would benefit tremendously if the principle were established that wage rates had to be identical in full- and part-time work, except where significant differences in productivity exist. While today both parents work full time in about half of working families, this may well be because many families cannot afford the severe wage penalty currently involved in part-time work. Assuming, as suggested in the quote above, that many women quit work entirely rather than work part-time because of the poor conditions that are common in part-time work, significant numbers of working-class people have a stake in flexible policies that would allow them to work less than full time without getting paid 60 percent of the full-time wage rate for doing so. This is particularly true of the many working-class couples who split shifts. The stress level might well fall considerably in such families if each parent worked for thirty hours a week at a full-time wage rate.[117]

In addition, flexible policies do not involve only part-time work. In working-class families where both parents have to work full time, other forms of flexibility may be even more important. Chief among these is the ability to take time off work to care for sick children, to be at the school play, to attend a teacher's conference, or to take children to the doctor or dentist. Working-class families, as well as more affluent ones, stand to benefit substantially from more workplace flexibility.

A society where flexibility was built into the economy would be far less unfair to working-class and poor workers than the current situation, where high-status workers are far more likely to be offered flexible policies than lower-status ones. According to one report, such policies typically are enjoyed today primarily by a few workers: highly placed college-educated professionals with annual incomes over $35,000. The rank-and-file worker rarely has access to policies offering work-place flexibility.[118]

Many families might well not lose much income in a restructured system. Today husbands on average earn 70 percent of the family income. In a system where thir-ty-hour-a-week jobs are available at full-time wage rates, the end result might often be that each parent would work three-quarters time and earn closer to 50 percent of the income, rather than having fathers work overtime and mothers part time in "women's work" or on the mommy track.

Wouldn't This Proposal Pit Workers Against Each Other and Reinforce the Association of Women with Caregiving?

Recall the Deloitte partner who quit in part because of resentment by co-workers who felt her part-time schedule meant they would have to work harder. Managers today often feel caught: "If I let one leave early to take her daughter to ballet class, then the others are angry because they feel they should be able to leave early, too." Single and childless people complain that they are left to take up the slack for workers who have families.[119]

This raises issues both for management and for unions. From a union stand-point, will the proposal to restructure work impede unions' ability to organize workers, by pitting women with caregiving responsibilities against people with-out them? From a management standpoint, won't managers be trapped between the threat of discrimination litigation if they don't allow for flexibility and worker resentment if they do?

Starting first from the management side, the threat of litigation could actually help employers handle work/family conflict by ameliorating the rancor that some-times accompanies grants of flexibility today. Managers would be placed in a less awkward position if they were subject to a legal requirement to accommodate care-giving. Moreover, if workplaces were restructured, employers would be less likely to arrange for flexibility in ways that create resentment by placing sudden, uncompen-sated burdens on the remaining employees. Employers instead would build into their work arrangements permanent ways to structure work that provides flexibility and meets their business needs, yet does not overburden the remaining employees.

Moreover, existing incentives would encourage employers to draft flexible poli-cies to apply to all workers. Obviously, employers could not offer flexibility only for women; that would be discrimination based on sex. While no legal difficulty exists with policies that allow flexibility only for caregiving, from a management view-point it makes sense to draft a policy that avoids getting into judgments about why someone needs flexibility, in favor of an exclusive focus on whether a given proposal for flexibility will work. Recall the panel of experts who recently recommended policies in which supervisors ask not "why do you need it?" but "will it work?" The existing pressures in favor of these kinds of policies will help ensure that the union fears that flexible policies will pit workers against each other will not materialize.[120]

Another fear is that requiring employers to restructure will reinforce the association of women and caregiving, because women will request flexibility whereas men
will not. This fear may prove unfounded. The sociological evidence in chapter 1 suggests that the major reason caregiving has continued its association with women is
that men have felt they cannot increase their level of family work so long as doing so
leads to marginalization at work. But if the traditional linkage of family work and
marginalization is ended, many more men could be expected to participate more
equally in family work. Recall that more than half of men surveyed by Robert Half
International said they were willing to have their salaries reduced by twenty-five
percent to have more personal and family time. Thus, allowing flexibility could be
expected to decrease the association of women with caregiving rather than increasing it. If that trend gathered steam, ultimately those alleging discrimination (the
plaintiffs) could no longer prove a disparate impact on women. That would simply
mean that the problem of women's marginalization had been solved.[121]

Working Out the Details

The principle for restructuring work should be that part-time workers should receive proportional rates of pay, benefits, and advancement. If a lawyer would make
partner in seven years of full-time work, she should be able to make partner in
fourteen years of half-time work. This raises the question of how to handle manda-
tory-overtime environments. How should pay, benefits, and advancement be handled in workplaces where full-time means fifty to seventy hours a week?

In those contexts, the number of hours the part-time employee actually works
should be compared to the number of hours worked by the relevant group of full-
time employees. For example, if a lawyer worked twenty-five hours a week in a
firm where full-time attorneys worked fifty hours a week, she should be entitled to
one-half the salary, benefits, and rate of advancement.

Calculating one-half of salary is easy. Benefits and advancement deserve more
discussion. Some companies offer full benefits to part-time workers, presumably
on the grounds that even if you are working part-time, your whole body still gets
sick. An alternative approach is to offer a benefits package worth half as much.
Some employers, notably Starbucks, currently offer prorated benefits to employees
who work at least twenty hours a week.[122]

With respect to advancement, the principle is that part-time employees should
be required to put in the same amount of time before becoming eligible for promotion—but no more. If the full-time track requires seven years before partnership,
someone working half-time should become eligible for promotion, at the latest, in
fourteen years. Of course, most people will not be working part time for the entire
relevant period. If someone worked full time for five years and then part time after
the birth of children, her partnership track would be extended from seven years to
nine years.

Note that in a system of restructured work employers might well feel *less* pressure to accommodate nonstandard schedules than they do today. Given the wage

penalty currently associated with part-time work, only one parent can work part time. Particularly since part-time work for one parent often entails a more intensive work commitment for the other, this means that employers of part-time workers find themselves faced with demands for, say, a three-day week or a twenty-hour-per-week schedule. In a situation where restructured work did not involve penalties in terms of pay and advancement, parents would be much more likely to split the difference so that the employer of each would face requests for thirty-hour rather than twenty-hour weeks. This differential may seem minimal, but sometimes it is not. Recall the manager quoted in chapter 2 who could have accommodated an employee with a thirty-hour-per-week schedule but not with a twenty-hour week.

Would the employee in question have been more flexible if she could have gone to her husband and said, "I can keep my job if I can work four days a week instead of three; why don't you also work four days a week"? Given the level of anger that exists in many American households over the issue of family work, the desire of many fathers to spend more time with their children, and a social context where the father would not suffer catastrophic career consequences for his part-time commitment, many fathers might just agree.

In fact, men who already have significant caregiving responsibilities would benefit from restructuring even more than women, because today they suffer the worst penalties for failing to perform as ideal workers. "Many employers, including many who have progressive policies accommodating family responsibilities of working mothers, believe that working fathers should leave all family responsibilities to their wives." Human resources managers interviewed for the same study said their companies would take a very negative view of fathers who took parental leave. One study found that 63 percent of large employers considered it unreasonable for a man to take any parental leave, and another 17 percent considered parental leave reasonable for a man only if it was limited to two weeks or less. In other words, roughly 80 percent of the employers surveyed opposed even the minimum. And this does not consider the more significant issue that a short period of parental leave after the birth or adoption of a baby does not begin to cover the time required to raise a child.[123]

Restructuring would help integrate more men into family life. Recent studies in Sweden show that men's relative absence from the home perpetuates the view, within the household and outside of it, that mothers are more competent with children. This in turn decreases fathers' involvement and leads to the situation where children turn to mothers, not fathers, when the chips are down.[124]

In summary, a system of restructured work would yield children raised by two parents, rather than by an overburdened and absent father and a marginalized and economically vulnerable mother. A system that provided care for children without marginalizing their caregivers would increase women's power within the family, make women and children less vulnerable to impoverishment upon divorce, and enable fathers to decrease work time and increase family time. It is both feasible and desirable to restructure market work.

LEGAL REMEDIES TO ELIMINATE
MASCULINE NORMS IN MARKET WORK

The early proponents of a Title VII remedy for sexual harassment were . . . told that the practice was so pervasive and of such long standing, the difficulty of drawing a line between the permissible and the impermissible . . . was so insurmountable, the problems of proof so complex, the issue so far from the core prohibitions of Title VII, that nothing could or should be done by the courts.[125]

Suing your employer is not the ideal mechanism of social change. Lawsuits are costly in many ways. The most obvious is that they cost a lot of money. In addition, suing your employer can be emotionally draining in the short run and can hurt your career in the long run; who wants to hire a "troublemaker"?[126]

Nonetheless, legal liability has a remarkable ability to focus the mind. Sexual harassment has been around a long time; employers got serious about it only once they faced legal liability. The threat of legal liability, rather than the damages awarded in individual lawsuits, is what leads to social change.

Employers violate antidiscrimination laws when they apply existing rules differently to women and to men. In the Ann Hopkins case, for example, the Supreme Court found that Price Waterhouse required both men and women to be aggressive go-getters—but then penalized women for acting in the ways that qualified them for partnership on the grounds that they were not sufficiently feminine. This is known as disparate treatment, and it is relevant whenever an employer treats female ideal workers differently from male ideal workers. Glass-ceiling practices that give women less access than men to mentoring and promotions can be challenged as disparate treatment under Title VII of the Civil Rights Act of 1964, the basic statute forbidding discrimination in employment. So can persistent patterns of excluding women from social networks where business gets done, through such practices as scheduling firm functions at all-male clubs. Sexual harassment also violates Title VII.[127]

In other words, current interpretations of Title VII law reach many of the practices that keep women out of the best blue- and white-collar jobs. But mothers have never had a cause of action under federal antidiscrimination law to challenge workplaces designed around men's social power, and only in very rare cases have women challenged male physical norms. Once the design of work around masculine norms is reconceptualized as discrimination, the question becomes whether it is discrimination that is actionable under existing law. I will argue that it is.

SUITS UNDER THE EQUAL PAY ACT

Disparate Treatment Suits to Challenge Discrimination Against Mothers

In December of 1998, a federal district court held that Joann Trezza had started a sex discrimination claim when she was passed over for a promotion, despite the fact that the person who received the promotion was a woman. Trezza, a lawyer in the legal department of The Hartford Inc. and the mother of two young children, was passed over in late 1991 or early 1992 in favor of a woman lawyer without children. When Trezza asked why, she was told that the reason she had not been considered for the job was that, since she was a mother, management assumed she would not be interested.[128]

In 1993 she was up for promotion again. Once again she was passed over in favor of two other employees, one an unmarried woman and the other a father. She contacted a senior vice president and told him she believed that the failure to promote her reflected sex discrimination. Two months later she received a promotion.

Finally, in 1997, she was not considered for the position of senior managing attorney despite the fact that she asked to be considered and had consistently received excellent job evaluations. Instead the company considered two men with children, and then offered the job to a nonmother with less experience than Trezza.

Trezza sued, alleging sex discrimination under a so-called "sex plus" disparate treatment theory. This theory, first articulated in 1971 in *Phillips v. Martin Marietta*, forbids discrimination against mothers even if equal opportunity is offered to non-mothers. In *Phillips*, the employer refused to allow the mothers of school-age children to apply for jobs that were open to the fathers of school-age children. The court in *Martin Marietta*, like the court in *Trezza*, held that the fact that men and women without children were treated the same did not excuse discrimination against mothers; the *Trezza* court explicitly rejected Hartford's contention that no sex discrimination existed because the job in question had been awarded to a woman. Trezza pointed out that only seven of the forty-six managing attorneys at Hartford were women and none were mothers with school-age children. In contrast, many of the male managing attorneys were fathers.[129]

These new "I had a baby, not a lobotomy" suits have tremendous potential, for discrimination against mothers remains very open today, precisely because it is not now conceptualized as discrimination. *Trezza* and similar suits may have begun to change that, in contrast to prior cases in which plaintiffs often lost.[130]

Suits Under the Equal Pay Act

In some law firms, attorneys who switch from full- to part-time work receive contracts providing that they will be paid 60 percent of a full-time salary to work 80 percent of the hours worked by a full-time attorney. This may be a violation of the Equal Pay Act (EPA), which requires that men and women in the same establishment must be paid equally if they are doing substantially equal work.

A key challenge in EPA suits will be to prove that part-time workers are doing "substantially equal" work. This requirement means that plaintiffs could not win EPA suits in situations where their part-time status was used as a reason not to offer them plum assignments, or where they otherwise were not doing work substantially equal to that of full-timers. But a suitable test case might involve, for example, a law firm where a woman is in a highly specialized, technical field that does not ordinarily require travel, say a Washington lawyer involved in agency litigation, trusts and estates, or a specialized tax practice. A promising plaintiff would be an employee with excellent evaluations who had worked full time for a significant period, then switched to part-time work, where she continued to get excellent evaluations but found herself making less per hour than full-time attorneys doing similar work.

One key issue will be whether a plaintiff can dislodge judges' sense that only people who meet the masculine ideal-worker norm are really "serious" and "committed": This is precisely the kind of unconscious discriminatory norm that equality theory should begin to target. Another is whether the plaintiff's work requires the same level of effort. The challenge for plaintiffs will be to convince the courts to define effort as *effort per hour,* based on the management literature stressing the need to redefine productivity in terms of output rather than in terms of face time. Surely the notion that employers should be required to measure productivity in terms of output cannot be seen as a radical claim.[131]

In some cases, a track record may exist that will be helpful in proving that the full- and part-time jobs actually are substantially similar. For example, at a large bank in California, permanent bank tellers were laid off and then rehired as part-time workers. During the UPS strike in 1997, employees made a number of statements to the effect that part- and full-time workers did the same work. This kind of data would be useful in meeting the standard that requires male and female workers to be doing jobs that require equal "skill, effort, and responsibility."[132]

An important issue is whether this type of case can be distinguished from comparable-worth cases, in which plaintiffs argued that employers are required by antidiscrimination law to pay workers in predominantly female jobs the same wage as in predominantly male jobs that are rated as requiring equal levels of skill, effort, risk, responsibility, and so on, according to job evaluation systems generated by employers themselves. Comparable-worth cases arguably made courts nervous because they involved courts in comparing two groups of plaintiffs, say a dental assistant and an electrician. Although the logic of comparable-worth cases is clear—presumably an employer would not give equal rankings to jobs that were not equal—many courts felt that such cases were asking them to dictate wages instead of allowing the market to do so. What EPA masculine-norm cases ask is far less ambitious. Instead of requiring courts to mandate equal pay for a laundry worker and a laborer, they would only require courts to mandate equal pay for, say, two trust and estates lawyers in the same firm doing the same highly specialized work, or two UPS workers in a context where the company itself has said that no difference exists between part- and full-time workers doing the same job. This prospect may prove less unsettling.[133]

The second step in an EPA lawsuit, if the plaintiff can successfully prove that the full- and part-time jobs are substantially similar, is that the burden shifts to the employer. Because the EPA prohibits only pay differentials based on sex discrimination, the employer can defend by proving that the wage differential is due to a "factor other than sex." Is a part-time schedule a factor other than sex?

Although case law exists in both directions, it should be clear that the EPA is broader than the situation where an employer has lower-paying jobs explicitly set aside for women and higher-paying jobs explicitly set aside for men. No employer in the United States today would openly discriminate in this way; in fact, as will be argued in greater detail in chapter 8, much discrimination today is based on a gendered sense of who is a "good candidate" in contexts where employers themselves are not aware that their notion of who is "good" reflects masculine norms. In this social context, if the EPA does not apply whenever employers clothe a discriminatory job description in a gender-neutral veneer, then employers can easily evade the EPA by differentiating jobs on the basis of a factor that correlates highly with sex but does not refer to body shape. It makes no sense to assume that Congress intended to make the EPA so easy to evade.

In *Corning Glass Works v. Brennan*, the Supreme Court held that employers could not pay a wage differential for night-shift work because the different schedule was not a "factor other than sex." Because the schedule difference between night-shift work and day work seems more significant than the schedule difference between a part-time and a full-time worker, *Corning Glass* provides support for the view that part-time work is not a "factor other than sex." This interpretation is reinforced by the *Corning Glass* court's narrow limitation of the factor-other-than-sex language to working conditions—such as toxic chemicals and/or other, more conventional "work hazards." In addition, an old bulletin issued by the agency in charge of implementing the EPA defined part-time work as a factor other than sex; when that bulletin was superseded after an important law review in which Martha Chamallas analyzed discrimination against part-time workers as gender discrimination, the new rules were silent on whether part-time work was a "factor other than sex."[134]

In summary, the EPA provides significant opportunities to challenge the practice of paying women in part-time jobs less than full-time workers who do substantially equal work. Masculine-norm EPA suits should be of particular interest to unions, for they provide a potent tool against the practice of cutting wage costs through a shift to contingent work. (Note, though, that these suits would work only in contexts where the part-time track consists disproportionately of women). But the EPA has several signal limitations. First, as noted above, in many situations employers consign part-time workers to the more routine, less desirable work. Although this practice is part of the problem, employers can defend against an EPA suit if they can prove that full- and part-time workers do not have equal responsibility. Second, the EPA covers only wages, so it does not offer a way of challenging the common practice of penalizing part-time workers in terms of benefits. Neither does the EPA require the employer to change promotion practices that currently marginalize many part-time workers, as when part-time lawyers are taken off the promotion track. To address these issues requires a suit under Title VII.[135]

Disparate-Impact Suits to Challenge Masculine Social Norms

Two different types of lawsuits could challenge masculine social norms under Title VII. One focuses on the design of the promotion track in blue- or white-collar jobs. Another contests an employer's decision not to allow part-time work.

Disparate-impact suits involving nonfinancial issues entail three steps. First, the person complaining of discrimination (the plaintiff) carries the burden (called her prima facie case) of proving that a facially neutral policy has a disparate impact on women. This might involve a comparison between the sex composition of the workforce in entry-level positions with that in high-level positions. If the plaintiff carries her burden of proving disparate impact, the burden shifts to the defendant (the employer) to prove that the employment practice being challenged, despite its disparate impact, is required by business necessity. If the employer prevails by proving business necessity, then the plaintiff can still win the case by proving the existence of a less discriminatory alternative (LDA): an employment practice that will serve the employer's business goals but create less of a disparate impact than the current practice (or practices) being challenged.[136]

In masculine-norm scheduling suits, the key challenge is to present, early and often, a vivid picture of how *this particular workplace* can be restructured in ways that meet the employer's legitimate business needs. Probably the ideal is to have a study by a work/family consultant that shows how to restructure the particular workplace at issue: After all, reimagined workplaces are their business. The most important role of this report is to help offset, early on, the heavy (if unofficial) burden of the "But that's impossible!" reaction.

The picture of the reimagined workplace is also relevant to several legal inquiries. The first concerns an ambiguous provision of Title VII that may (or may not) require the plaintiff to present, at an early stage of the lawsuit, a viable proposal that the employer subsequently refuses to adopt. The provision states that disparate impact is established if the plaintiff proves that there is an alternative employment practice "and the respondent refuses to adopt" it.[137] The consultant's report can also help rebut the employer's claim that business necessity requires no change to current practices, as well as helping to establish the existence of less discriminatory alternatives. In some cases, the relevant data for restructuring will be available from first-generation mommy-track work/family policies, which often are implemented as the result of a consultant's report on what policies are practical and desirable from a business standpoint.

Challenging the Design of the Promotion Track

Consider a large corporation that hires roughly equal proportions of men and women at the entry level but has a promotion track that yields disproportionate numbers of men in top-level positions. Given that roughly 95 percent of upper-level management positions are staffed by white males, this must be a very common situation. We have examined above the relevant policies that contribute to this situation: perhaps the promotion track requires the executive schedule; perhaps it requires relocation; other factors may play a role as well. In the blue-collar context, male physical norms may play a role, as well as norms designed around men's access to a flow of family work from women: large amounts of mandatory overtime, training programs that occur in overtime, stringent sick leave policies that exclude people with primary responsibility for children, job ladders that severely penalize work interruptions.

Let us first consider a white-collar promotion suit. After generating a picture of a restructured workplace, the plaintiff could file a disparate-impact suit alleging that the design of the promotion track has a disparate impact on women. She would first be required to establish that, say, 50 percent of entry-level positions but only 20 percent of jobs in the top four corporate levels and a mere 5 percent of top management positions are held by women.

The second issue is whether the relative paucity of women in higher-level jobs is caused by the actions of the employer or by women's choice to quit. Employers will argue that whatever the documented disparities between men and women, they are caused not by the employers' discrimination but by women's lack of interest in the jobs in question. The causation requirement in disparate-impact suits was codified in the Civil Rights Act of 1991, which requires plaintiffs to establish that the challenged policies caused the impact documented. The argument over causation takes us back to the analysis of choice in chapter 1. When women use choice rhetoric, they speak as people struggling with the constraints handed to them by a world they did not invent. Courts considering Title VII claims are in a different position: Their mandate is to consider whether the constraints women face constitute discrimination. If they do, the fact that many women may have internalized those constraints does not provide employers with an excuse for continuing the discrimination.[138]

The third legal requirement is that the plaintiff must articulate the specific policies that produce the discrimination alleged. An example of a specific policy is the common law-firm policy that takes part-time workers off the partnership track. If the impact in question is produced by an integrated set of policies that cannot be separated, then the plaintiff may be able to challenge the entire integrated set by showing that the "bottom-line" results are discriminatory.[139]

Once an employee has (1) proven the statistics showing disparate impact, (2) refuted the employer's argument that women's predicament is not caused by the policy but reflects only women's own choice, and (3) delineated the policy or policies at issue, she has proven her prima facie case. The burden of proof then shifts to the employer, who is given the opportunity to show that the policy that produces the disparate impact is a business necessity.

The law on business necessity is complex. In 1971 the United States Supreme Court held that an employer had the burden of proving that the challenged policy was "job related" and had "a manifest relationship to the employment in question." Whereas this decision originally placed a heavy burden on the employer, eighteen years later the Supreme Court greatly strengthened the employer's hand. In *Ward's Cove Packing Co., Inc. v. Atonio*, the Court required only that the employer be able to articulate a reasonable "justification for his use of the challenged practice," and stated "there is no requirement that the challenged practice be 'essential' or 'indispensable' to the employer's business for it to pass muster."[140]

Congress overturned *Ward's Cove* in 1991. Unfortunately, it did so in language that was so ambiguous that it remains unclear what precisely is the current test for business necessity. However, it appears that the current test is closer to the old requirement that a discriminatory practice be essential to the business, rather than simply capable of some conceivable business justification. Assuming that is true, it would seem that many current practices could not be justified by business necessity. The description of masculine norms in high-level white-collar work strongly suggests that, at best, the executive schedule and other practices "are not actually job related but merely 'corporate convenient.'" Indeed, the challenged policies may not even be "corporate convenient," for flexible policies properly implemented would improve productivity and lower the costs of absenteeism, turnover, and recruitment in many contexts.[141]

A crucial issue concerns the role of costs in establishing business necessity, for employers will argue that promoting only people who work long hours ensures maximum profits. Employers are, of course, entitled to engage in cost containment; that is a crucial part of management's job. The issue is whether they are entitled to structure cost-containment measures in ways that systematically disadvantage women. The alternative is to contain costs in ways that do not perpetuate practices that produce "built-in headwinds" for anyone without the social resources typically available to men (although not all men). If plaintiffs follow the proposal presented here, the fact that they request only *proportionate* pay, benefits, and advancement for part-time work will mean that the per hour costs of full- and part-time employees should be similar. As a legal matter, federal courts have not treated consistently the issue of whether or not costs are relevant in determinations of business necessity.[142]

If an employer is successful in proving business necessity, the plaintiff still can win if she can prove the existence of a less discriminatory alternative, an alternative way of structuring the promotion track that has a less harsh effect on women. This is where the plaintiff's vividly reimagined workplace is most directly relevant from the viewpoint of legal doctrine. Even at this final stage, the employee may be able to prevail if she can show specific changes that are feasible and less discriminatory.

Individual Redesign Suits

Another type of lawsuit would involve an individual woman who, after working for a number of years in her job, is denied a request to have her schedule changed to part-time. This is a common situation in federal government offices in Washington, D.C., as I know from talking with individual women. No doubt it exists elsewhere as well.

The ideal plaintiff is someone who has been working for the employer for many years and has received consistently excellent work evaluations. She needs to present a plan that is clearly workable and meets the employer's needs. (Again, a work/family consultant may be helpful in framing her proposed plan.)

Proof of disparate impact would require her to show that a large number of employees (disproportionately women) have requested to have their hours cut, that they left when their requests were turned down, and that a disproportionately low number of women now hold the jobs at issue. This actual workplace data, which provides evidence of disparate impact, will sometimes be hard to come by. In my experience, however, certain key women have served as mentors for women seeking part-time work in specific agencies of the federal government, and serve as a kind of institutional memory of requests denied. Similar situations may well exist elsewhere. The issues of business necessity and less discriminatory alternatives will be much the same as in promotion suits.

The challenges involved in litigating work/family conflict would be lessened if a proposed amendment to the Equal Pay Act is adopted. In 1994 the Contingent Workforce Equity Act (CWEA) proposed to amend the Equal Pay Act to prohibit employers from paying part-time employees at a rate different from that paid to "full-time employees in such establishments for equal work on jobs the performance of which requires equal skills, effort, and responsibility, and which are performed under similar working conditions." Now that unions have begun to take an interest in the issue of equal pay rates for part-time work, the time may be ripe to resurrect this proposed statute. The International Labor Organization's proposed convention on part-time work, mentioned above, has many of the same provisions as CWEA, notably its guarantees that part- and full-time workers will receive equal wage rates.[143]

Disparate-Impact Suits to Challenge Physical Masculine Norms

Title VII can be used to challenge not only norms framed around men's life patterns but norms framed around men's bodies. In the leading case, *Boyd v. Ozark Air Lines*, an airline employed only men as pilots. After antidiscrimination laws were enacted, fifteen women applied and were denied employment. The company maintained a rule that all pilots be five feet, seven inches tall, a requirement that excluded 93 percent of women but only 25.8 percent of men. The trial court held that this rule had a disparate impact on women.[144]

Then the airline claimed business necessity, on the grounds that pilots had to be a certain height to fly its planes. The courts accepted this argument. The Eighth Circuit stated that "an individual's ability to operate all the instruments in the cockpit and reach the design eye reference point is dependent upon an individual's height and is essential to the safe and efficient operation of a plane." However, the trial court found that the design of the airplanes required pilots to be only 5´5´´, not 5´7´´, as the company rules stated. It held that this was a less discriminatory alternative, and required the airline to adopt it as the new rule.[145]

As in many of the situations involving norms framed around men's bodies, employers instituted the height requirement only after antidiscrimination laws no longer allowed the outright exclusion of all women. Many police and fire departments throughout the country formulated height, weight, and strength requirements as a way of excluding women once they could no longer be openly excluded on the grounds that these were "men's jobs." In some contexts, one could prove that the employer's intent was to discriminate against women and that the height, weight, or other rules are mere pretexts where the real goal was to eliminate female candidates. For example, in *Boyd*, why did the airline require pilots to be 5´7˝ if the equipment in question required only 5´5˝? Was this evidence that its articulated concern over safety was a mere pretext, and that its real goal was to exclude women?[146]

If this can be established, the employee may have a disparate-treatment claim; the other possibility is to claim disparate impact, as did Mary Roth Boyd. Disparate-impact suits need not come out as Boyd's did. Courts should recognize that designing equipment or industrial processes around male bodies operates to exclude women from the best blue-collar jobs today. The ability to function in an environment designed around men's bodies is not a legitimate job qualification. The purchase of new equipment, modification of existing equipment, redesign of industrial processes, or creation of job descriptions designed around male bodies are employment practices that violate Title VII.

Clearly employers cannot be expected to scrap all their airplanes or redesign all their factories tomorrow. But they do not need to. In many situations where women are excluded by workplaces designed around men, adjustments short of a total redesign will solve the problem, as where factories install platforms for workers too short to reach equipment without them. In other workplaces, as noted above, job redesign can limit the number of jobs on a factory floor that require heavy lifting: instead of requiring every worker to lift 125 pounds once a day, job tasks can be rebundled so that heavy lifting is required of only a few people.[147]

Both jobs and equipment are redesigned from time to time as a matter of course. Airplanes wear out; airlines buy new ones. Suppliers come out with new models, often at the insistence of their customers. Employers often play an active role in establishing specifications for equipment and industrial processes. No doubt many design changes have occurred since Mary Roth Boyd lost her suit in 1977, yet only 4 *percent* of airline pilots are women even today. The sole issue is whether the exclusion of women (and smaller men) will be built into the design specifications for generation after generation.[148]

In workplaces where women are excluded by requirements that they lift heavy loads, mechanical lifts will often be available, or will be more likely to become available in the future, due to the Americans with Disabilities Act (ADA). In factories that require lifting of heavy loads, back injuries are common. The ADA often will require that employers install mechanical lifts to help disabled workers do their jobs. Thus, in many workplaces, the only issue will be whether existing lifts, which will become more and more common as more post-ADA back injuries occur, are used only by the disabled worker or by women and other workers as well.[149]

In summary, in many workplaces, male physical norms can be eliminated by minor modifications of existing equipment, rebundling of tasks, or increased use of existing equipment. In a disparate-impact suit, all of these, and more, can be proposed as less discriminatory alternatives even where immediate redesign is not feasible.

Moreover, where expensive equipment must be replaced, this does not mean it has to be replaced tomorrow. In contexts where immediate modifications are not feasible, companies may have a legitimate business necessity to hire mostly men today, while antidiscrimination principles require them not to perpetuate this system into the indefinite future. The key point is that courts should take the long view. Instead of assuming that the only two alternatives are an immediate replacement of all equipment versus perpetuating into the indefinite future a system that excludes women, courts and plaintiffs should explore the many intermediate solutions. The guiding principle is to proceed in a measured and orderly fashion toward a society where workplaces are designed around the body of the average person, not the average man.

In disparate-impact cases, the legal issue is whether an employer has a business necessity to continue, decade after decade, to provide jobs designed around men's bodies. Where redesign of costly equipment is the only practical remedy, plaintiffs should ask for delayed relief. This is commonplace in cases involving the Occupational Health and Safety Administration (OSHA). In OSHA cases where an employer has to make costly or substantial changes, plaintiffs often agree that the changes should be stretched out over a significant time period. The length of the period involved depends on the equipment. If the problem is that the employer provides safety shoes only in men's sizes, then the replacement period may well be short. If the problem lies with truck cabs or plane cockpits, then the period required will be longer.[150]

ELIMINATING MASCULINE NORMS IN BENEFITS AND OTHER GOVERNMENT PROGRAMS

The ideal-worker norm is embedded not only in workplaces but in government benefits, which often were designed in an era when it was assumed that women were at home (or, as in the case of Social Security, was designed with the express intention of discouraging wives from working). In addition to Social Security, these include unemployment insurance, pension benefits, labor laws, the plant closing act, and (ironically) the Family and Medical Leave Act. Policy makers need to redesign these social programs, which currently provide a safety net for working men but not for many working women.

Many of the necessary changes have already been proposed. The CWEA, mentioned above, proposed to give collective bargaining rights to part-time and other contingent workers, and to include them under occupational health and safety laws and the federal plant closing act (which requires employers to notify employees of plant closings), the Family and Medical Leave Act, ERISA (the federal act regulating pensions), antidiscrimination laws, and unemployment laws. In addition to government benefits, the ideal-worker norm is built into the tax system, a complex topic that will not be discussed here, but which is the subject of a growing literature.[151]

Fair Labor Standards Act

The Fair Labor Standards Act (FLSA) fuels the current ideal-worker/marginalized-caregiver pattern in important ways. Passed in 1938, it was part of the labor unions' long effort to establish an eight-hour day and a five-day week. Originally its requirement that employers pay time and a half for overtime work encouraged employers to limit hours to forty a week. However, as the cost of benefits increased, employers gradually found it more lucrative to require large amounts of mandatory overtime from their existing workforce, rather than to hire more workers. This allows them to amortize their existing benefit load over a large number of hours worked by a smaller number of workers.[152]

The result is that the FSLA has become a key element in the current pattern of overwork by men, which in turns feeds the pattern where mothers cut back their workforce participation because fathers are virtually never available to share the burden of family work. Consequently, amending the FSLA is a matter of pressing concern. It could be amended in several ways to discourage long hours and end the marginalization of part-time work. Common proposals include lowering the hours standard from 40 to 37.5 or 35 hours a week, increasing the premium paid to overtime workers from time and a half to double time, redefining the administrative, professional, and other exemptions so that fewer people are excluded from the overtime requirements, or banning mandatory overtime (employers would have to use voluntary overtime systems instead).

Unemployment Insurance

Eligibility for unemployment insurance is set at the state level. Common requirements reflect the ideal-worker norm in several ways. Many states impose monetary requirements that are difficult for part-time workers to meet, for two reasons. First, earnings during the base period must exceed a minimum level that is higher than what many part-time workers make. Second, most states also have a "high-quarter" requirement, which specifies the minimum an individual must earn within at least one calendar quarter in the base period. Some workers whose overall earnings meet the base period requirement cannot collect unemployment insurance because they did not earn enough in a single quarter to meet the high-quarter requirement.

In addition, in order to qualify for unemployment insurance, a worker must be "able and available" for work. Twenty-five states require a worker to be available for full-time work; five states have conflicting statutes or regulations. Of the nine states that do allow part-timers to collect unemployment, five require a history of part-time work, so that a worker fired because he or she was no longer able to work full time due to family responsibilities would be denied compensation.

In states that do cover part-time workers, the issue arises as to what is "good cause" to limit a worker's search to part-time work. The National Employment Law Project, after a fifty-state review, recommended California's definition of good cause, which offers access to part-time workers in return for reasonable evidence of the conditions requiring part-time work. Finally, when an employee has been discharged due to failure to show up because of difficulties in obtaining child care, the question arises whether their failure to appear is judged to be misconduct (in which case the employee is not entitled to unemployment). CWEA proposed changes that would require unemployment laws to provide unemployment compensation to people available for part-time but not full-time work.[153]

Family and Medical Leave Act

It is ironic that the Family and Medical Leave Act (FMLA), passed in response to parents' need for flexibility, does not cover workers who work less than twenty-five hours a week. CWEA proposed to include part-time workers in the FMLA. Some states (Connecticut, New Jersey, and North Dakota) allow medical leave for workers who work at least twenty hours a week. Others (Maine, Oklahoma, and West Virginia) require only three to twelve months of continuous service, without requirements for a minimum number of hours a week. CWEA proposed changing the FMLA to cover part-time employees by decreasing the coverage threshold from 1,250 hours to 500 hours per year (about ten hours per week).[154]

Pensions

The Employee Retirement Income Security Act of 1974 (ERISA) governs private sector employee benefits, notably pension plans, voluntarily established by employers. Several ERISA requirements preclude part-time workers from participating in pension plans. First, ERISA disregards any year in which a worker accrues less than 1,000 service hours, so an employee working less than twenty hours a week may never become eligible to participate in her employer's pension plan, no matter how many years she has worked. Even if a part-time worker meets the threshold requirements, ERISA allows his benefits to be forfeited unless he becomes vested under circumstances that may well affect part-time workers. As of April 1993, only 15 percent of part-time workers had pensions, as opposed to 56 percent of full-time workers. CWEA proposed to lower the ERISA threshold from 1,000 to 500 hours per year (about ten hours/week).[155]

Social Security

Under the current system, the amounts dual-earner families pay into Social Security subsidize the benefits of ideal-worker/marginalized-caregiver families. This occurs because the current system offers women a choice: claim Social Security based on their own earnings, or claim 50 percent of their husband's benefit. Because men generally earn more than women, it is more advantageous for most women to claim 50 percent of their husband's benefit, which means that working wives typically receive no return whatsoever on all the years they have worked and have paid into the Social Security system. Indeed, the system was consciously designed to discourage working wives and to subsidize homemakers, which it does to this day. As usual, the resulting impoverishment of working women emerges in clear profile only when divorce causes them to cease to be linked with an ideal-worker man.[156]

The current system severely penalizes divorced women because the system's design reflects the husband-owns rules described in chapter 4. Indeed, a divorced wife is not entitled to any Social Security benefits derived through her husband unless the marriage lasted for at least ten years. Mary Becker has pointed out that a divorced man gets twice the Social Security benefits his ex-wife gets, no matter how long the marriage; if he remarries, he and his new wife get three times what his ex-wife gets. Although the retired worker's remarriage can only increase his draw, the divorced wife's remarriage—before or after her ex-husband's death—may terminate her claim.[57]

Labor and Antidiscrimination Laws

Nearly half of all working women are denied labor representation because of their status in the workforce. The National Labor Relations Act needs to be amended to cover part-time and other contingent workers. In addition, antidiscrimination laws often cover only establishments with a specified number of employees working a specified number of weeks, thereby barring antidiscrimination claims by part-timers and other contingent employees.[58]

CONCLUSION

This chapter argues that most American women remain economically marginalized because the best blue- and white-collar jobs integrate masculine norms, notably the ideal-worker schedule, equipment designed around men's bodies, and social norms based on masculine gender performance.

Designing work to require the ideal worker to command a flow of family work and other privileges most men enjoy, but most women do not, discriminates against women. Many individual workplaces designed around masculine norms exclude a disproportionate number of women in violation of Title VII. In some situations employers may well be violating the Equal Pay Act as well.

Although some employers will argue that current practices are required by business necessity, many already have realized that flexibility creates workplaces that are often more, rather than less, efficient. This accounts for the spread of family-friendly policies as employers seek to cut down on absenteeism, to increase productivity, and avoid the huge replacement costs that result from high rates of turnover.

The results thus far are disappointing. Few employees use family-friendly policies because flexibility continues to be linked, in first-generation mommy-track policies, with marginalization. Moreover, asking managers to implement these policies has proved difficult: Supervisors who still live in the patterns established by domesticity are often reluctant to dismantle a system that has framed their logic all of their lives.

Until now, flexible policies have been discussed largely within the frame of management consulting, which emphasizes the bottom-line benefits of flexibility. It has now become apparent that effecting changes this deep requires a cause of action to focus attention on how the current design of work discriminates against women. After over a decade, work/family consultants have articulated a new vision of restructured work. But they have never had a cause of action. Courts should give them one.

CHAPTER FOUR

•

*Deconstructing the Ideal-Worker Norm
in Family Entitlements*

"*Some people say you can't put a price on a wife's twenty-seven
years of loyalty and devotion. They're wrong.*"

But do not women *now* work right earnestly? Do not ... our market women labor right earnestly? Do not the wives of our farmers and mechanics toil? Is not the work of *mothers* in our land as important as the work of the father? "Labor is the foundation of wealth." The reason that our women are "paupers," is not that they do not labor "right earnestly," but that the law gives their earnings into the hands of manhood.

—LETTER FROM FRANCES GAGE TO GERRIT SMITH,
DECEMBER 24, 1855

Leo Cullum © 1993 from the New Yorker Collection. All Rights Reserved.

I've never met a mother who doesn't work. Women who do only family work labor roughly the same number of hours as men; women who do market work as well work much longer.[1] Yet American women and children constitute nearly 80 percent of those in poverty: as noted in chapter 2, the United States is a rich nation whose poor are predominantly mothers and children.[2]

The problem is that women's work does not get translated into entitlements because the law delivers their earnings "into the hands of manhood."[3] Under the common law that delivery was formal and explicit: The doctrine of coverture defined family property as belonging to the husband. Today the relevant law is in the divorce courts, where mothers are impoverished by a double application of the ideal-worker norm. First mothers marginalize to enable fathers to perform as ideal workers while the children are raised according to the norm of parental care. This pattern means that the wages of most mothers are much lower than their husbands': men typically earn 70 percent of family income. Then, upon divorce, courts generally treat the ideal-worker's wage as his sole personal property. The wage is seen as "his," while his family's claims are relegated to the discretionary realm of family law. In other words, the chief asset of most marriages—the ideal-worker's wage—continues to be treated as the property of the husband. In this context it is hardly surprising, as noted in the introduction, that nearly 40 percent of divorced mothers end up in poverty.[4]

The impoverishment of women upon divorce is an impoverishment of custodial mothers, who almost always suffer a considerable decline in economic well-being upon divorce. Commentators agree that men's standard of living increases while women's and children's declines sharply upon divorce. Poverty in families headed by divorced women not only is more common than poverty in two-parent households but it is also more likely to be chronic. Even where mother-headed families' incomes do not fall below the poverty line, typically they decline sharply. Middle-class wives often do not have the resources to maintain a middle-class lifestyle because their own earning power is at a low working-class level. Wives of affluent men suffer the sharpest declines in standard of living.[5]

A growing movement proposes to remedy postdivorce impoverishment by limiting access to divorce. Some twenty-two states have considered reforms limiting people's ability to divorce. Most proposals require mutual consent or proof of fault, eliminate no-fault divorce when minor children are involved, or impose waiting periods or predivorce counseling.[6]

The no-fault divorce debate has produced much heat but little light. As other commentators have noted, divorced women's impoverishment stems not from the shift to no-fault divorce but from the way economic entitlements have been defined under both the fault and no-fault regimes. Under both, a major problem faced by divorced women "is not the lack of a male presence, but a lack of a male income."[7]

This chapter proposes to solve the problem of postdivorce impoverishment not by limiting access to divorce but by questioning who owns the "male" income. It will argue that when divorce courts treat the ideal worker's wage as the sole personal property of the husband, they ignore the fact that the husband can perform

as an ideal worker only because he is supported—after divorce as well as before—
by a flow of family work from his wife. An asset produced by two adults should
not be unilaterally awarded to only one of them. This chapter proposes to treat the
ideal worker's wage as joint property: to stop delivering women's earnings into the
hands of manhood.

IS COVERTURE DEAD?

"Suppose your wife had done nothing, as would have been the case if you
had supported her, could you, out of your fifteen dollars a week, have kept
your family? If you had paid for the cooking, baking, washing, ironing,
sweeping, dusting, making and mending of clothes, would your wages
have kept you, your wife, and five children as comfortably as you have
lived, and enabled you to lay by a little each year?"

"Certainly not, certainly not; thirty dollars a week would not have
done it."

"Then your wife made the extra fifteen dollars by her hard work and
economy. She came almost as near supporting you as you did supporting
her, did she not?"[8]

The story begins with coverture, the common-law system that defined the family
property as belonging to the husband. Coverture began as an integral part of patriarchy, the starkly hierarchical gender ideology that preceded domesticity. Under patriarchy, as noted in chapter 1, women were viewed as the "weaker vessel," in need of
men's control and guidance. In a society that considered women inferior, it was natural to vest ownership in husbands, who were seen as having the wisdom to manage
the family's economic life. Thus, under coverture a husband owned his wife's personal property as well as his own. He also had full rights to manage his wife's real estate,
including ownership of all rents and profits. Finally, he owned the wife's labor, both
the wages from her market work and the right to her services within the household.[9]

Although coverture began under patriarchy, important elements of coverture
persisted under domesticity. Reva Siegel's extensive historical analysis shows that
the passage of the MWPA (Married Women's Property Acts) did not eliminate the
economic disenfranchisement of married women. Rather than abolishing coverture, the MWPAs just gave it a new form.[10]

Siegel uncovers a vivid debate concerning whether the MWPAs would emancipate only a wife's right to the wages generated by her market work or whether they
would emancipate her family work as well. Nineteenth-century "joint-property"
advocates argued they should emancipate both. They complained that the "wife
owes service and labor to her husband as much and as absolutely as the slave does
to his master," and argued that women's family work should give rise to joint ownership of family assets: "[I]n a true marriage, the husband and the wife earn for the
family, and . . . the property is the family's—[it] belongs jointly to the husband and
the wife." The joint-property advocates challenged the traditional notion that

wives were supported by their husbands: "Do not the majority of women in every town support themselves, and very many of their husbands, too?" asked Elizabeth Cady Stanton. Said the resolution of a women's rights convention in 1851:

> [S]ince the economy of the household is generally as much the source of family wealth as the labor and enterprise of the man, therefore the wife should, during life, have the same control over the joint earnings as her husband, and the right to dispose at her death of the same proportion of it as he.[11]

MWPAs ultimately emancipated only wives' labor in the market. Some statutes explicitly excluded wives' family work from coverage; in other states, the exclusion was accomplished through the courts. Though husbands' ownership of wives' family work continued, its rationale shifted. Gradually its defenders abandoned the original openly hierarchical justification and turned instead to rationales drawn from domesticity. Home was where a man

> *seeks a refuge from the vexations and embarrassments of business, an enchanting repose from exertion, a relaxation from care by the interchange of affection:* where some of his finest sympathies, tastes, and moral and religious feelings are formed and nourished;—where is the treasury of pure disinterested love, such as is seldom found in the busy walks of a selfish and calculating world.

Domestic ideology turned labor into love. "Ironically," observed Reva Siegel, "the moral elevation of the home was accompanied by the economic devaluation of the work performed there." The "pastoralization of housework," discussed in chapter 1, reinforced the social right of husbands' claim to women's labor. Turning labor into love preserved men's traditional access to women's work by arguing that any attempt to link such work with entitlements would sully the home sweet home with the market values of a "selfish and calculating world."[12]

This argument lives on in two types of contemporary cases where wives seek to turn their family work into entitlements. The most important is the "degree cases," where the wife finances her husband's degree only to have him file for divorce shortly after he has begun earning his professional salary. Courts often respond with outrage at the suggestion that the wife's work should result in entitlements upon divorce. For example, a 1980 Wisconsin court asserted that awarding entitlements to the wife "treats the parties as though they were strictly business partners, one of whom has made a calculated investment in the commodity of the other's professional training, expecting a dollar for dollar return. We do not think that most marital planning is so coldly undertaken." A 1988 West Virginia court protested that "[m]arriage is not a business arrangement, and this Court would be loath to promote any more tallying of respective debits and credits than already occurs in the average household. . . . Characterizing spousal contributions as an investment in each other as human assets," it continued, "demeans the concept of marriage." Courts' anxiety about commodification is echoed by the criticism of commentators. "Divorce," scolded one, "does not represent a commercial investment loss." She continued: "[A]nalogizing marital educational financing to invest-ing in a commercial enterprise ignores the personal basis behind the institution of marriage by reducing the marital relationship to an arm's length commercial trans-action." Language like this shows the anxiety triggered by the prospect of com-modifying women's work in the sense of having it give rise to entitlements.[13]

Commodification anxiety serves to police traditional gender boundaries, as when the fear of a world sullied by commodification of intimate relationships feeds opposition to granting wives' entitlements based on household work. This is part of a larger pattern. For example, in chapter 1 we saw how anxiety over dele-gating child care to the market persuaded women to stay at home rather than to give over child care to "strangers," another example of commodification anxiety policing domesticity's gender roles. Commodification anxiety serves several differ-ent purposes and does not always signal the policing of gender boundaries. But it often does, in ways that have rarely been recognized.

This analysis represents an important shift in the analysis of commodification by legal scholars. The legal literature on commodification stems in significant part from the work of Margaret Jane Radin, whose work focuses on the potential for commodification to sully human relationships. "[M]any kinds of particulars—one's politics, work, religion, family, love, sexuality, friendships, altruism, experi-ences, wisdom, moral commitments, character, and personal attributes [are] . . . integral to the self. To understand any of those as monetizable . . . is to do violence to our deepest understanding of what it is to be human." In response to a literature in law and economics that seeks to extend the reach of the market, for example by instituting a market for adoptable babies, Radin has argued against such proposals by trying to articulate what it is about them that makes most people regard the selling of babies and similar proposals with dismay.[14]

Radin is right that excessive commodification can threaten human flourishing. Yet the legal literature on commodification rarely notes that women's key problem has been too little commodification, not too much. While too much commodifica-tion has the potential for harm, so does too little: women's historic poverty stems in significant part from the way successive legal regimes have turned their labor into love, leaving property the province of men.[15]

Commodification anxiety provides the current rationale for the he-who-earns-it-owns-it rules that originally were justified on patriarchal grounds. The specter of family life corroded by strategic behavior is powerful rhetoric for policing male privilege in an egalitarian age. Yet commodification anxiety glosses over an impor-tant point: The issue is not *whether the family wage will be owned* but *who will own it*. Note the unstated assumption that having wives' work give rise to entitlements will import strategic behavior into the family sphere, while having husbands' work give rise to entitlements raises no such problem. Husbands' work takes place in the market, so it "naturally" is commodified.

This logic veils an important step. Entitlements within the family have never followed automatically from entitlements within the market. Under coverture, the fact that a wife earned a wage did not make it hers, nor did courts worry that giving her husband a legal entitlement to it sullied the marital relation with strategic behavior. Only when wives began to point out that a husband's ownership of his wage with respect to his *employer* did not necessarily mean he owned it with respect to his *wife* do courts become concerned that having family relations give rise to property rights would sully the marital sphere. This worry arises only when family-based entitlements redistribute husbands' wealth to wives. A wife's claim that family work should give rise to entitlements is ridiculed as the claim that "twenty-seven years of loyalty and devotion" have a price. Note the exclusive reference to loyalty and devotion. No mention is made of the laundry.

Coverture has been updated; it is not dead. The most direct continuation, documented by Reva Siegal, is the doctrine of marital service. After the MWPAs abolished coverture's prohibition on contracting by married women, cases arose in which wives sued to recover on contracts with boarders or others for household work, and on contracts with husbands for work on the family business. Courts refused to allow the wives to recover on the grounds that a wife still owed to her husband the duty to perform household work. Said an 1897 court:

> A man cannot be entitled to the services of his wife for nothing, by virtue of a universal and unchangeable marriage contract, and at the same time be under an obligation to pay for those services, by virtue of a contract made before marriage.

Courts therefore prohibited wives from recovering for contracts involving household work.[16]

This doctrine survives today. A striking example is the 1993 California case of *Borelli v. Brusseau*, mentioned in chapter 1. *Borelli* involved a May-December marriage in which the elderly husband wrote a will that left the bulk of his estate to his daughter from a prior marriage. After he was severely disabled by a stroke, his doctors advised a nursing home, as he needed twenty-four-hour-a-day care. He persuaded his wife to provide the care herself, promising he would leave her considerably more of his estate than he originally had planned. "She kept her promise but he did not keep his," to quote the majority opinion. The wife discovered, upon the death of her husband, that he had never changed his will as promised. She sued, alleging breach of an oral contract.[17]

The court ruled against her, citing marital service cases holding that because husbands already owned their wives' family work, promises based on that work were unenforceable for lack of consideration. (The consideration doctrine forbids the enforcing of contracts where one side receives no benefit because it has given no "consideration.") The majority's rationale relied heavily on commodification anxiety. "[E]ven if few things are left that cannot command a price," proclaimed the majority, "marital support remains one of them." The majority insisted that Mrs. Borelli's full-time nursing fell within a gender-neutral requirement that spouses owed each other a duty of support. The dissent pointed out the absurdity of this argument. "Appar ently, in the majority's view [Mrs. Borelli] had a preexisting . . . nondelegable duty to clean the bedpans herself. . . . To [so] contend in 1993 . . . means that if Mrs. Clinton becomes ill, President Clinton must drop everything and personally care for her."

Though the doctrine of marital service is the most direct way that coverture has been updated, it is not the most important. Divorce law is dominated by covert and largely unconscious assumptions, drawn from coverture, that husbands' work gives rise to entitlements but that wives' work does not.

THE IDEAL WORKER IN THE DIVORCE COURTS

It's no accomplishment to have or raise kids. . . . Any fool can do it.[18]

The most important continuation of coverture in the divorce courts is rarely recognized: the he-who-earns-it-owns-it rule that men own their wages with respect to their wives as well as their employers. No rationale typically is offered for this heroic leap, which reflects assumptions drawn from coverture that are inconsistent with current commitments to gender equality. The result is a system that places men's claims in the nondiscretionary realm of property, while it relegates women's and children's claims to the discretionary realm of family law. This means that women's and children's claims are dependent on courts' willingness to redistribute a man's property. Given Americans' reluctance to redistribute wealth, this gendered allocation places women and children at a severe disadvantage.

The common understanding is that family work is an expression of love. Love it may be, but it's labor as well. Credible estimates place the value of unpaid family work at between 20 and 60 percent of gross domestic product. The only reason why love's labor's lost is that courts refuse to recognize it.[19]

The he-who-earns-it-owns-it rule shapes not only the allocation of men's claims to property law while wives' claims are relegated to family law, but also shapes the assumptions that inform the way divorce courts handle property division, child support, and alimony.

Property Division

The amount of money she'd end up with irrespective is more than enough for anything she would ever want to do. I have a lot of other goals and aspirations and if I were picking places to charitably expend my money, this would not be the first.[20]

This quote, from the husband in the largest divorce case ever filed in the state of Washington, accurately reflects the continuing sense of husbands and many divorce courts that husbands own the assets of a family and that any claims forwarded by wives are claims for charity. In the context of property division, the irony is that wives are often awarded "equal" shares when the estate is small, but are much less likely to get half when the estate is a substantial one. Note that in the typical case, where a divorcing family has few assets, "equal" shares often means that the wife receives an equal share of a nominal amount, or else receives an equal share of the family's mortgage debt. In sharp contrast, studies both in the United States and in Australia have found that wives do not typically receive an equal share in families with significant assets.[21]

This pattern disadvantages both affluent wives and less affluent ones. Less affluent wives often find that "equal division" means they have to sell the family home so that the husband can get his equity out of it, while his children and their mother move to an apartment or smaller home in a cheaper neighborhood. One study found that two-thirds of the children of divorce move to less affluent surroundings within three to five years after divorce.[22] Thus "equality" is imposed in contexts where that gives wives less than they would have gotten under the old dependence-based fault system in which custodial mothers typically were given the family home.

Where the estate is a substantial one, equality goes out the window. One study found that three-fourths of wives in families where the husband owned a business or professional license received less than half of the family assets. The North Dakota Gender Bias Report found that whereas 80 percent of judges and nearly half of male attorneys felt that judges always or often consider a homemaker's contribution when dividing a privately owned business, only about one-fifth of women attorneys agreed.[23]

What explains these patterns? It seems that divorce courts are informed by the same assumption that underlies the "charity" quote with which this section began: Husbands own, wives need. Wives are entitled only to an amount necessary to meet their reasonable needs, while no limit is placed on husbands' entitlements because they are conceptualized as owners. Thus a wife is entitled to half of an estate if that is necessary to meet her reasonable needs. But she is not entitled to half if her needs can be met with less.

The he-who-earns-it-owns-it assumption is so strong that it is not overcome even by explicit statutory language directing courts to give wives entitlements that reflect their domestic contributions. The original version of the Uniform Marriage and Divorce Act (UMDA) provides that courts, in dividing marital property, should consider the contributions of each spouse. Contributions as a homemaker are named as one factor to be considered, but no weights or presumptions are provided to direct courts how to balance the many factors enumerated. In this context, most courts have given little weight to family work, or have ignored it completely. More recent versions of the UMDA added many more factors for a court to consider, making it even more unlikely that courts will give substantial weight to family work. Studies have found that what influences courts are monetary contributions, not domestic contributions or even need. Consequently husbands are awarded the bulk of property.[24]

Alimony

If judges use their discretion to perpetuate coverture's husband-owns assumption in the context of property division, this assumption literally is written into state statutes on alimony, and it is incorporated into standards for child support in more subtle ways.

Alimony statutes typically refer to need explicitly. Wives' lack of entitlement is dramatized by the low incidence, and the low amounts, of alimony awards. Although one study found that 80 percent of women assume they will be able to get alimony if they need it, in fact few women are awarded alimony today (about 8 percent), or have ever been. In addition, the amount of alimony typically awarded is low. In addition, today two-thirds of alimony awards are temporary. Alimony as an institution eloquently expresses the view that the wife has no entitlement if she is not her former husband's favorite "charity."[25]

This impression is reinforced by the fact that courts generally do not require husbands to pay alimony in amounts that would diminish the husband's lifestyle. One study noted "a judicial reluctance to require a financially independent spouse to reduce his or her lifestyle to support a financially dependent spouse." Most respondents to a questionnaire agreed that "a wife's alimony is based on how much the husband can give without diminishing his current lifestyle." Courts' theory seems to be that a property owner cannot be expected to put a crimp in his own style to give to the poor.[26]

The he-who-earns-it-owns-it rule also explains why it is so hard to get an alimony order modified when the father's income rises. The stringent rules that often allow a modification only if the circumstances of the parties have changed so much that the order has become unconscionable once again reflect unspoken assumptions about entitlement and need, as do certain procedural rules. The theory seems to be that just because the father has become wealthier, this doesn't mean his children or their caregiver are entitled to share in that wealth. They may not be his favorite charity at the moment.[27]

Child Support

The award of the ideal worker's wage unilaterally to the husband affects not only his former wife but his children as well, given that mothers remain the primary caregivers in roughly 90 percent of divorces. Levels of child support have risen over the past decade, in response to the child-support guidelines put in place by states in response to a 1984 federal law. In theory, these guidelines have moved away from need as the basis for calculating child support. In practice, child-support standards continue to reflect the underlying assumption of husbands' ownership in a number of ways. Most states' child-support guidelines rely on studies that include only day-to-day expenses associated with child rearing. While the studies typically provide for child-support levels linked with the overall income of the parents, they exclude from consideration the ways children in intact families benefit from parental savings, investments, and other forms of wealth accumulation. Moreover, only three states use the Melson formula, which produces a greater degree of income equalization than either of the two approaches used in most states. Another proposal by Judith Cassetty, which suggests equalizing not incomes but standards of living of the two postdivorce households (to account for the fact that the household of the custodial mother typically has two or three people while the household of the father typically has only one), has not been adopted in any jurisdiction. Thus although the two chief templates for child-support guidelines (the income-shares method and the percentage-of-income method) provide for some sharing, many state guidelines still reflect the assumption that the ideal worker's wage "really" belongs to him. As a result, a 1992 California study of conditions after the implementation of the guidelines reported that household income of employed custodial mothers was roughly two-thirds that of fathers, though mothers' households typically were two or more times larger.[28]

Another very explicit signal that children's entitlements are limited to their needs is the use of an income cap when the father's income is high. Such caps are commonplace. One example is Minnesota, which caps the income considered in determining child support at $60,000 per year. Ohio guidelines cap awards at 10 percent of the father's income if he earns over $100,000. Caps in Ohio and other jurisdictions clearly send the message that an affluent father is expected to share his wealth with his own children only if he is still married to their mother.[29]

The impact of rules excluding a man's family from sharing in his wealth emerges clearly when one considers what middle-class families use wealth for: housing and college education. A family's housing is intimately tied to its creation of an environment suitable for raising children. In the classic scenario, divorce means that children move to less expensive housing in a cheaper neighborhood. This relocation takes the children away from their friends and their support network during a time of acute stress. Moreover, since quality of schools is often tied to the price of housing, cutting the children off from their father's wealth may affect their long-term future.[30]

Child-support standards also jeopardize some children's chances for college, which has severe consequences, given the correlation between a college education and future earnings. This occurs in two ways. First, to the extent that child support does not provide for the sharing of family wealth, this may well make it difficult to finance college tuition. Second, many courts refuse to award child support to children over the age of eighteen (and in eleven states, courts are precluded from doing so). Although no large-scale study is available, a study of forty-nine families in California found that many middle-class fathers gave little or no financial support to their children after high school, or attached burdensome strings to it. These difficulties may account for the studies documenting that the "fear of falling" out of the middle class often becomes a reality for the children of divorced families. Children of divorced parents "are less likely to equal or surpass their parents' social and economic status." In these and other ways, the divorce courts are a key engine for our society's massive disinvestment in children.[31]

In summary, the he-who-earns-it-owns-it rule updates coverture in a very concrete sense. At common law, when a typical family's chief asset was land, the law awarded *to husbands* the control of land and the rents and profits that issued from it; in today's cash-flow society, where a typical family's chief asset is the ideal worker's wage, once again the law defines that as the property of the husband.[32]

THE JOINT-PROPERTY PROPOSAL

The impoverishment of children and their caregivers is as much a product of law today as it was under coverture. Because that impoverishment stems from the way entitlements are allocated, an effective solution will require those entitlements to be redesigned. American courts have always felt free to update the common law to suit current conditions. In assessing how to change the rules upon divorce, we must begin with an understanding of modern marriage.

The Dominant Domestic Ecology

Prior chapters have contested the accepted wisdom that it used to be "a man's world" but that "men and women are equal now." A more accurate description is that our system has shifted from one where (middle-class) men were breadwinners and (middle-class) women were housewives to one where men are ideal workers and their wives (or ex-wives) are workers marginalized by caregiving. Chapter 1 showed that the contemporary version is a domestic ecology that consists of three elements: the gendered structure of market work, a gendered sense of how much child care can be delegated, and gender pressures on men to structure their identities around work.

The gendered structure of market work is the crucible in which the dominant family economy is forged. Under the current definition, the ideal worker is away from home nine to twelve hours a day, so that an ideal-worker parent with preschool children typically sees them awake for only an hour or two a day. When children reach school age, the issues shift: who will pick them up from school, help with homework, and take time off for medical appointments, illnesses, or the school play? An ideal worker needs to delegate all, or virtually all, of this care in the manner of the typical father. Typically he delegates to the child's mother, who either drops out of the workforce to provide this flow of household services (in the pattern of traditional domesticity, c. 1780–1970) or remains a market participant but is marginalized by her inability to perform as an ideal worker (the predominant pattern today). This gendering of market work is the first important element of the dominant family ecology.[33]

The second is the gendered sense of how much child care can be delegated. The norm of parental care discussed in chapter 2 is covertly gendered. Because fathers delegated virtually all of child care under traditional domesticity, many fathers retain a sense that virtually all child care is delegable. Most mothers do not. These gender traditions form the background of powerful cultural expectations that frame the attitudes of the current generation, aptly captured in the Doonesbury cartoon printed on the next page.

One study found that the typical U.S. father spent an average of only twelve minutes a day in solo child care; another estimated twelve to twenty-four minutes. A third reported that mothers spend about three times as much time as fathers in face-to-face interaction with children. Mothers are far more reluctant than most fathers to delegate child care past a certain point: I have called this the domestic nondelegation doctrine.[34]

The structure of market work and the domestic nondelegation doctrine combine with a third element of the current family ecology: gender pressures on men. As discussed in chapter 1, conventional genderings tie men's sense of themselves to their success in market work. These gender pressures leave the typical man with little emotional alternative but to perform as an ideal worker to the extent his personality, class, and race enable him to do so.

The result is a dominant domestic ecology that enhances men's market potential while eroding women's. Fathers earn 10 to 15 percent *more* than men without children, while mothers earn 10 to 15 percent *less* than women without them. This wage differential represents the value of family work performed by mothers. As a result, most wives earn far less than their husbands. Among married white couples between the ages of twenty-five and sixty-four, three out of four husbands earn more than their wives. When both spouses are the same age and have the same education, the odds against a wife's earnings equaling her husband's are three to one.[35]

The family work of a full- or part-time homemaker allows her husband to concentrate his efforts on market work, as courts and commentators have acknowledged. Thus studies show that men with wives at home earn more and get higher raises than similarly educated men whose wives do no market work. Single fathers, who lack the flow of domestic services that typically supports married fathers, often find they have to cut back on work commitments because of their caretaking roles. A 1983 survey found that nearly a third of the single fathers polled had to reduce their work-related travel, a third had to arrive late or leave early, and roughly 10 percent had quit or been fired because of work/family conflicts. These data show that in the typical marriage where most family work devolves upon the wife, "she [comes] almost as near supporting [him] as [he does to] supporting her."[36]

Absent Coverture, An Asset Produced by Two People Should Be Jointly Owned by Them

Once family work is acknowledged as *work*, a new rationale emerges for income sharing after divorce: An asset produced by two people should be jointly owned by them. The only reason to award the fruits of the dominant domestic ecology one-sidedly to the husband is an unacknowledged continuation of coverture. The alternative is joint ownership.[37]

This approach to income sharing differs markedly from those of other commentators whose goal is to present a new theory of alimony. They typically rely on strained analogies to commercial partnership law that trigger commodification anxiety. The theorists of alimony also overlook that the he-who-earns-it-owns-it rule operates not only in the context of alimony but also in property division and child support and, at a more fundamental level, in the initial decision to allocate husbands' rights to property law while consigning women's and children's rights to the discretionary realm of family law.[38]

The joint property proposal provides an answer to an important question: "[T]he marriage has not continued; why, then, should [the wife] continue to share in her former husband's income?" A Georgia family court judge expressed this sentiment less delicately: "I don't know my feelings about child support, but alimony is like feeding hay to a dead horse."[39]

The description of the dominant domestic ecology provides a simple answer. A divorced husband may not have to share his income if no children were born of the marriage. But once they are, typically the children's mother will do the child rearing and other family work that allows her husband *both* to perform as an ideal worker *and* to have his children raised according to the norm of parental care *after divorce as well as before.*

The important point is that most divorcing fathers retain the primary benefit of the domestic ecology even after the marriage has ended. In the nearly 90 percent of divorces in which mothers are awarded custody—even in states such as California where joint custody is favored—mothers typically remain the children's primary caregiver. In this context, noncustodial fathers continue to be supported by a flow of domestic services from their ex-wives. If they were not, they too would have to "choose" a job that allowed them to stay home with the baby, to pick children up from school, to take time off when children are sick, or otherwise to provide care (or partially delegate it, at considerable expense) as their ex-wives now do.[40]

Husbands' continuing financial obligations reflect the continuing dependence of their children and the continuing caretaking obligations of their ex-wives. The typical husband and father is benefiting from the dominant family ecology long after the marriage has ended. The relevant comparison is not to the husband's situation *if he had never had children*, but to his situation *if he had to raise his children without a wife who serves as primary caregiver.*

The current reluctance to make a father continue to support his children and their caregiver reflects the sense that divorced men are entitled to a "clean break." A central thrust of the no-fault revolution was to introduce the view that divorce was simply the unfortunate breakdown of a love relationship; once the marriage was dead, both parties should be free to make a "clean break" and a "fresh start."

The problem with the "clean break" theory is that a mother who has previously marginalized cannot subsequently simply "move on." If she still has children at home, she still has to raise them. Even if she doesn't, she is stuck with the long-term impacts of her eroded career potential; one study found that women lose 1.5 percent of earning capacity for each year out of the labor force.[41]

In fact, the father in a family organized around the dominant family ecology does not want a "clean break" either. What he wants (and generally gets) is the ability to take with him the career benefits he received as a result of the division of labor within the marriage. The "clean break" imagery is nothing more than a way to characterize rules that allow the husband to walk away with this income transfer from his former wife as the optimum in freedom for both parties.

This is not to minimize the extent to which the "clean break" feels like an apt description to the husband. Keep in mind the close association of maleness with "success." A man who is deprived of the benefits of "his" success because of his commitments to a prior family would not have the freedom men now enjoy to seek emotional and sexual fulfillment on the secondary marriage market. This freedom is alluring; taking it away no doubt feels like a threat. The predominant self-understanding is: "She hurt me; I hurt her. Now we both need to put it behind us and move on."[42]

With the initial characterization I do not take issue: Most divorces hurt both parties. Nor do I contest the need to move on. The issue is who will move on with what. Today a man can overinvest in his career secure in the knowledge that if his marriage fails, he can walk with his wallet and enter another marriage with his financial assets substantially intact. He can put his prior marriage behind him in a way his marginalized wife and children cannot. This is the freedom I am proposing to constrict, in the interest both of treating both spouses fairly and of encouraging investment in existing marriages and existing children. To quote one California court, "As to deterring remarriage, we can only say that to the extent that the rule makes people realize that they may not pursue their own pleasures in utter disregard of an earlier marriage of twenty-two years that has produced four children and a dependent spouse, it is to be commended rather than faulted."[43]

Courts' decisions to preserve fathers' freedom to seek future emotional and sexual fulfillment at the expense of their existing children are indefensible. They can be dispensed with in a sentence: Mothers always have understood that having children decreases future freedom. Fathers need to learn the same lesson. Mothers never have had the option of disinvesting in existing children in favor of having new ones. Offering this option to fathers seems equally bizarre.[44]

The underlying message of the joint-property proposal is that once a wife has marginalized for the sake of her husband and/or their children, the mutual interdependence within the family unit is a long-term arrangement whether the parents stay married or not. This message fits well with new thinking that sees divorce less as a complete rupture than as a rearrangement of family relationships. Having children limits future freedom. Mothers have always known this, and fathers need to learn it too.[45]

How the Current System Destabilizes
the Marriages of Very Successful Men

A recent spate of well-publicized divorces of very successful men suggests a rarely recognized dynamic: Courts' continuation of husband-owns rules works in conjunction with the other social forces to destabilize the marriages of the rich.

The first step in this dynamic is that such men tend to become very detached from family life. Sociologists have found that the more successful the husband, the less likely he is to share household work. Recall the absentee affluent fathers discussed in chapter 1 whose wives "don't bother [them] with petty domestic details." Their lack of involvement in family life is the first social force destabilizing the marriages of such men.[46]

The second destabilizing force is that, as noted in the introduction, sociologists have long recognized that husbands' market power typically gets translated into power within the family realm. Thus a husband worth a billion dollars can expect a lower level of family work and a higher level of deference than an ordinary Joe. Yet men who have become very affluent during long-term marriages probably do not have the same level of authority in a long-established marriage with a woman their own age, contracted when both were young and relatively equal in terms of wealth, as they would have in a new marriage with a younger woman, contracted when the wealth disparity between the partners was very great. Thus, in the most famous of the "executive divorce" cases, involving Gary Wendt of General Electric, the wife felt that her husband became dissatisfied when she developed interests of her own; his alternative was to marry a new wife whose life would revolve around him to a degree that better suited his tastes.[47]

The third destabilizing force is the so-called marriage market. As Lloyd Cohen puts it, "[W]omen in general are of relatively higher value as wives at younger ages and depreciate much more rapidly than do men," in large part because "physical beauty and sexual attractiveness of women, while subjective in nature, is a sharply inverse function of age." Feminists would agree, although they attribute this phenomenon to the fact that different things are eroticized in men and women: youth and looks are eroticized in women, while success is eroticized in men. This practice increases the desirability of successful older men while decreasing the desirability of their wives. Statistics show that men in general find it easier to remarry than do women; successful men probably enjoy even greater comparative advantages.[48]

Courts cannot end these social forces destabilizing existing marriages. But they can stop adding to them. The he-who-earns-it-owns-it rule works in conjunction with these forces by making it virtually costless for men to walk away from long-term marriages in order to negotiate a new May-December marriage in which they enter from a much stronger bargaining position. Thus we see the commonplace occurrence of highly successful men "turning their wives in for a newer model." One suspects that this habit of highly successful people would change if they had to leave half their wealth behind them.

The Specifics of the Joint-Property Proposal

The joint-property proposal contains two separate elements. The first is that property should be divided equally in cases where substantial assets are at stake as well as in cases where they are not. Courts should stop asking what wives of wealthy men "need." In our society we generally do not ask whether owners "need" what they own. I will raise no objection to asking it of wives only when we begin to ask this of property owners in general.[49]

In most families, ownership of accumulated property is not the most important issue. We live in a cash-flow society where most people's primary asset is their human capital, their ability to earn a wage. Very few divorcing families have substantial property because most have invested instead in the ideal-worker's wage. One study found that the average family had only $3,400 in savings upon divorce. This is why income sharing is the key to ending the postdivorce impoverishment of women and children.[50]

In designing an equitable system of income sharing, the crucial question is how to split the income between one household where the adult is the primary caretaker of the family's children and another household where the adult is not. Splitting the postdivorce income equally between the households fails to consider both the direct costs of supporting the children and the indirect costs associated with caregiving in a society that marginalizes caregivers. Simply dividing the total combined incomes of the adults by the number of people in the family presents a different problem: It ignores the differences between children and adults. The better alternative is to equalize the standards of living of the two postdivorce households.[51]

The next issue is how long income should be equalized. The widespread, but incorrect, assumption is that incomes must be shared forever if a property law rubric is adopted. This assumption flows from the model of the fee simple in land. But, of course, even some "classical" interests (such as tenancies, life estates, and conditional estates) do not entail eternal ownership. Moreover, the "disintegration" of property shows that property entails a bundle of rights defining legally recognized interests with respect to some valuable asset. This definition may, but need not, entail permanent rights.[52]

If the concept of property does not require granting a permanent interest, how long should income equalization last? The first step in defining the desirable period relates to children's dependence. Because the dominant family ecology typically continues for the period of the children's dependence, so should income equalization.[53] The second (and harder) step is to account for the impact of caregiving on the income potential of the wife once the children have ceased to be dependent.

My proposal is to adopt a guideline that does not attempt to calculate the actual period required for the wife to regain her income-earning potential, but focuses instead on generating equitable solutions in two situations. The first is where a long-married homemaker is divorced after the children are grown. The second is where a caregiver is divorced when the children are still young.[54]

Any proposal that limits income equalization to the period of the children's dependence yields unacceptable results for long-married homemakers. Take a homemaker married at twenty-four whose thirty-year marriage ends the year she turns fifty-four and her last child leaves home. A proposal mandating income equalization only for the period of the children's dependence would deliver her onto the job market at age fifty-four with thirty-year-old job skills. In this situation, her husband has enjoyed the full benefits of the dominant family ecology and should share in its impact on the homemaker's income potential. Moreover, the wife has relied for thirty years on the expectations of mutual dependence built into the dominant family ecology. To reflect both facts, I propose adding a second period onto the period of the children's dependence, equal to one year of income equalization for every two years of marriage, to begin at the date of divorce. This calculation would mean that the longtime homemaker described above would be entitled to income equalization for fifteen years after the date of divorce, until she was sixty-nine years old. This approach would eliminate the situation where a long-married wife suddenly is thrown onto the labor market without adequate time to plan her future. She would be free to use the money available from income equalization either to retrain (if she is able) or to save (if she is not). The ex-wife would not by any means be guaranteed her former standard of living, but her position would be a great improvement over the current situation, in which long-married homemakers are abruptly reduced to poverty.[55]

In the prototypical divorce the marriage breaks down after four years and the birth of two children. In this situation, income equalization under the proposed formula would persist for two years after the youngest child ceased to be dependent. A wife married at twenty-four and divorced at twenty-eight when her youngest child was a year old would be entitled to income equalization for the period of the children's dependence plus two additional years. Although a two-year period clearly is not enough to remedy the erosion of her earning potential, this short period reflects that she relied only for a short period on the expectation that the dominant family ecology would provide her with long-term support.[56]

The incentives built into this proposal are different from those implicit in the traditional scheme of lifelong alimony. Income equalization for the young mother would end in her forties. This provides a significant incentive for both parents to do market work. Former wives' incentive is that, in the paradigm case, income sharing will end a short time after the children's dependence ends, leaving the woman to support herself on her own. Former husbands also have an incentive to support their ex-wives' ability to work, because the more she earns, the less the ex-husband will owe to achieve income equalization.[57] In this context, one would expect that divorced mothers typically would build up their work experience for much of the period of the children's dependence, and would have an additional period after children's dependence ends when they could perform as ideal workers before income equalization ends.[58]

Joint-property proposals could be implemented by statute or case law. Passing new statutes would have two signal advantages. First, it would allow states to eliminate language in alimony and child support laws that define women's and children's entitlements in terms of need, leaving property ownership as the province of men. To the significant extent that current child-support guidelines sharply limit the amount of child support, these also need to be changed; a new statute would provide a good opportunity.

A new statute would also allow states to formulate an approach to postdivorce entitlements that does not artificially separate the entitlements of children and their caregiver. Separating the entitlements of women and children makes no sense in a society premised on the norm of parental care. Implementing the joint-property proposal by statute also would allow states to incorporate a "self-support set-aside," that is, a certain minimum amount of money required for the father's self-support, in cases where income sharing would bring the father's income down below what he needs to survive. This is particularly important in the context of Aid to Families with Dependent Children (welfare), where the funds paid by the father will go not to his children but to the government, which is assigned the right to child-support payments as partial reimbursement for AFDC paid to his children. A support system without a set-aside will serve only to land even more low-income (and disproportionately minority) men in jail in a social context where the solution to family poverty lies not in redistribution between equally poor husbands and wives but in a more general redistributive program.[59]

Income equalization could also be implemented immediately by the courts in one of two ways. First, courts could introduce a new category into family law. One lower court took a step in this direction by recognizing a homemaker's claims to "equitable restitution."[60] Alternatively, courts could implement income equalization through awards of child support and alimony. A court could calculate the award necessary to equalize the standards of living of the two postdivorce households, and then, as a second step, allocate it between alimony and child support. Courts have ample discretion, which they are now using to award ownership to men, to award alimony for only short periods, or to award low levels of child support. (To the extent that courts' discretion is limited by the child-support guidelines, courts will be forced to characterize their awards as alimony or equitable restitution.)

In conclusion, the only thing blocking the joint-property proposal is a decision by courts and legislatures to continue patterns inherited from coverture, in which men's claims give rise to entitlements while women's claims are treated as charity. To the extent that this decision is conscious, it is rationalized into three objections.

OBJECTION 1: WOMEN'S WORK DOES NOT FIT THE DEFINITION OF PROPERTY (DEGREE CASES)

I will tell you what the value of a law school education is. It is zero.[61]

Despite some early support for using the language of property to address the issue of postdivorce impoverishment, it is an article of faith among many family law courts and scholars today that property language is out of place in this context.[62]

This dismissal is ironic because conclusions about ownership are inevitable in this context: The issue is not over whether the family wage will be owned, but over who shall own it. The typical case in which courts have considered these issues involves a wife who supported her husband through professional school and claims "property in his degree" when he divorces her shortly after finishing training. Courts, with few exceptions, have rejected wives' claims that the degrees are marital property, often using broad language to the effect that human capital does not have the attributes traditionally associated with property. To justify this rejection, courts rely on Blackstonian image of property rights as the absolute dominion of people over things. This imagery, however, was never an accurate description of property law and was formally abandoned in the First Restatement of Property in 1936. The 1936 restatement adopted instead Wesley Hohfeld's view that property rights defined the relationships among people in a context where courts attach the name "property" as a signal they have accepted someone's claim. From a Hohfeldian perspective, the joint-property proposal emerges as a redefinition of family relationships, away from coverture's hierarchical allocation of ownership exclusively to the husband, to reflect the more egalitarian expectations of the modern era.[63]

The degree cases project a very different image of property rights. The most famous statement is from a Colorado case, *Graham v. Graham*:

> An educational degree, such as an M.B.A., is simply not encompassed even by the broad views of the concept of "property." It does not have an exchange value or any objective value on an open market. It is personal to the holder. It terminates on death of the holder and is not inheritable. It cannot be assigned, sold, transferred, conveyed or pledged. An advanced degree is a cumulative product of many years of previous education, combined with diligence and hard work. It may not be acquired by the mere expenditure of money. It is simply an intellectual achievement that may potentially assist in the future acquisition of property. In our view, it has none of the attributes of property in the usual sense of that term.[64]

Other courts have used similar reasoning: "Since a professional license does not have the attributes of property, it cannot be deemed 'property' in the classical sense," said one court after quoting the passage from *Graham*. "[A]n advanced degree," it concluded, "such as a medical license, is not 'property' under our Divorce Code."[65]

Note the form of the argument. The court starts out with a set notion of what "property" entails. It then inquires whether a degree fits that image. Upon deciding that it does not, it concludes that no property right exists. In sharp contrast to the Hohfeldian view that property reflects evolving relationships among people, this old-fashioned formalistic style of legal thought carries the message that judges' conclusions about property flow nigh automatically from the category "property."[66] In contrast to the Hohfeldian view's message that property is a word courts use to signal their legal conclusion that someone has an entitlement, the *Graham* court's language sends the message that judges play no active role in determining entitlements. But they do. Conclusions about property are legal conclusions, made in a context where the court has to allocate the asset to someone.

Courts' eagerness to disguise their role in allocating entitlements has led to the metaphysical style legal realists decried as "transcendental nonsense." In 1980 a Wisconsin court concluded that if a wife were to win in a degree case, she "will have been awarded a share of something which never existed in any real sense." What never existed? Conclusions about property rights are legal conclusions, not observations of some preexisting reality. Another court asserted: "The medical license may be used and enjoyed by the licensee as a means of earning a livelihood, but it is not ownership." Degrees are not property because they cannot be the subject of ownership? The courts' circular statements blur their role in allocating entitlements between husband and wife.[67]

In addition to circular and metaphysical arguments, courts also argue that degrees are not property because they cannot be sold or inherited. Yet many property rights cannot be sold or inherited. Life estates cannot be inherited, nor can other common law estates such as the fee tail. Property interests that cannot be sold include the interest of a life tenant with an inalienable life estate and that of a beneficiary of certain types of trusts (notably the "spendthrift trust"). These examples illustrate that even some "classical" estates do not fit the court's absolutist model.[68]

Many modern property rights also clash with the court's absolutist imagery. Examples are pensions and goodwill, which are widely recognized as property despite their lack of heritability. Inalienable property rights also include stock in closely held corporations, partnership interests, rights in cooperatives, and pension rights. Moreover, in some contexts courts recognize property rights in jobs, which again are not inheritable. The question is why they refuse to do so in the context of postdivorce entitlements. Courts' refusal to recognize "new property" rights in the family context stems not from the logic of property but from unstated assumptions about who is entitled to what.[69]

Courts also commonly point to the "intangibility" of the proposed interest as a reason why professional degrees are not property. In the words of one such court, degree cases involve "an intangible property right, the value of which, because of its character, cannot have a monetary value placed upon it for division between spouses." Yet property rights often involve intangible assets; indeed, the "dephysicalization" of property rights is a widely noted modern trend. Today many valuable, intangible interests are considered property, including pensions, goodwill, trademarks, and trade secrets.[70]

If courts' projected image of property rights is so inaccurate and their property theory half a century out of date, why have the degree cases proved so convincing? I have argued that contemporary property law combines absolutist rhetoric with an actual practice of property law that reflects a more Hohfeldian view. In cases where courts refuse to redistribute the bundle of sticks between a landowner and the public or another landowner, they often mobilize the mythology of property as a justification. In sharp contrast, if courts decide to grant such a request, they ignore the mythology of property altogether and offer substantive reasons for their reallocation of entitlements. Similarly, in degree cases, courts use the mythology of property to insist that they could never disturb coverture's allocation of owner- ship to the husband. If they were committed to reallocating the marital bundle of sticks, the mythology of property would recede into the background.[71]

In short, courts' use of the mythology of property in degree cases tells us less about their authority to reallocate the bundle of sticks than it does about their de- sire to do so. We must therefore examine why courts are so reluctant to accept wives' claims of entitlement. As the economists tell us, the first place to look in discerning human motivation is self-interest. In the degree cases there is plenty at work. For the judges that hear them, they often strike close to home.

Family court judges, almost by definition, are successful lawyers. Most are men who have conformed to an ideal-worker pattern in a profession notorious for long hours. This workaholic culture tends to marginalize the ideal workers' wives even as they assume more and more family responsibilities to allow for their husbands' "success." It is also the (upper-middle-) class context in which the ideology of gen- der equality is strongest. In short, the judges in degree cases are heavily invested in the polite fiction that the husband's career success and the wife's marginalization both result not from a system that privileges men because they can command a flow of domestic services from women, but from the idiosyncrasies of two individ- uals residing in the republic of choice.[72]

The degree cases also reflect judges' sense that they worked long and hard for their degrees. Their reaction is colored by their struggles in law school and their sense that they have earned everything they have achieved through their own hard work. That degree holders worked long and hard is not the issue. So did their wives, both in the home and (often) at boring, dead-end jobs, passing up opportu- nities for better positions. The issue is not who worked hard, but whose hard work gives rise to entitlements. If courts hold that only men's hard work gives rise to en- titlements, they need to give reasons for continuing the allocation that stems from coverture.[73]

In summary, the degree cases are loaded against women because they strike so close to entitlements enjoyed by the judges in charge of deciding the cases. In addi- tion, the cases are unrepresentative, since only about 12 percent of the U.S. popula- tion has a professional degree. Thus it is unfortunate that the issue of allocating income upon divorce has been addressed almost exclusively in the context of de- gree cases. Judges should reassess the issue of who owns what after divorce, in- stead of treating that issue as having been decided by the degree cases.[74]

OBJECTION 2: PRECEDENT FORBIDS JUDGES FROM ADOPTING THE JOINT-PROPERTY PROPOSAL

Almost universally (the exception is New York State), U.S. courts have refused to treat degrees as property. Since this is the only context where courts have considered whether wives have access to husbands' human capital, we must examine whether wives' lack of success in these cases precludes courts from implementing the joint-property proposal. If we examine the reasons courts have given for their decisions, we find that the degree cases do not preclude them from implementing the joint-property proposal, since the rejection of wives' claims in the degree cases has been closely tied to the rationale and the design of the proposed entitlement in those cases, which are different from the rationale and design of the entitlement delineated in the joint-property proposal.

In the degree cases, wives' lawyers, relying on human capital theory, defined an entitlement equal to the present value of the difference between what the husband would have earned without the degree and his projected earnings with the degree. This proposed entitlement had two basic drawbacks. First, it was framed in the language of investment, which made the entitlement appear to involve unhealthy commodification of intimate relations. Second, the proposed entitlement was defined in a way that courts found overly burdensome on the husband. Third, the proposed entitlement required complex calculations that necessitate expensive expert testimony that many wives cannot afford. I will discuss each in turn.[75]

The proponents of human capital theory rely on commercial analogies that seem jarring and out of place when applied to family relations. Joan Krauskopf, in an early application of the human capital theory to postdivorce entitlements, characterized the family as "a firm seeking to maximize its total welfare" and the wife as someone seeking "a fair return on her investment." Ira Ellman pursues a long analogy of the wife to a company that supplies specialized parts to IBM and argues that both the wife and the parts supplier make "investments a self-interested bargainer would make only in return for a long-term commitment." Ellman explains in another context that if the wife "invests in herself and does poorly, she has no one else to cover her loss. There is no reason why someone else should cover it if she invests in her husband instead and he does poorly" any more than if she had invested in the wrong building. In one of the most recent expositions of human capital theory, Cynthia Starnes speaks of the "income-generating marital enterprise" in which "a dissociated spouse should receive a buyout of her investment."[76]

Human capital theorists' highly commercialized language weakens wives' claims in two ways. First, this language reinforces the sense that such theorists are flailing around for inherently unconvincing rationales. Second, it sends the message that granting wives an entitlement threatens intimate relations with undesirable commodification. Human capital theory triggers fears of a world in which all human relations assume a market model of commercialized self-seeking. Its commercial analogies and its focus on wives' "return on investment" imply that the only alternative to a one-sided allocation of the ownership of the family wage to the husband is the specter of a family life corroded by strategic behavior.[77]

Courts' negative response to human capital theory reflects not only commodification anxiety but also their rejection of the relief wives typically demand in degree cases: a percentage of the amount by which a degree enhanced the earning power of the husband. Even though courts perform the same computation in wrongful-death and other tort cases, degree-case courts commonly reject this calculation, which requires a projection of the husband's earning power, as "too speculative" and as "a gamut of calculations that reduces to little more than guesswork." The question is why courts are willing to engage in such calculations in wrongful-death cases and other contexts but are reluctant to do so when a wife is claiming an interest in her former husband's degree.[78]

One rationale courts commonly give is that awarding the proposed entitlement impinges unduly on husbands' freedom. The most vivid protest is from a court that argued that an award to the wife "would transmute the bonds of marriage into the bonds of involuntary servitude contrary to Amendment XIII of the United States Constitution." Another court referred to the potential to subject the husband to "a life of professional servitude." The same court continued: "In reality, however, after a divorce a person may choose not to practice his or her chosen profession, may later change to a less lucrative specialty, or may fail in the chosen profession. Such developments cannot be anticipated at the time of divorce."[79]

This language requires some unpacking. The underlying point made by these courts is that, given the widespread rule forbidding modifications of marital property divisions, a holding that a degree is marital property would forbid courts from making any adjustment if a husband did not in fact earn the income a court projected he would earn. The expressed fear is that a husband's job choice would be limited by his need to earn the income a court projected for him. Underlying this expressed fear, I suspect, is a reaction against making the husband a lifetime provider, even though a marriage is over.[80]

The joint-property proposal very explicitly does not make the husband a lifetime provider; the entitlement it envisions ends once the effects of the dominant family ecology have ended. It builds in incentives for wives to return to work because the proposed entitlements end once the children are grown and the wife has recovered (to some extent) from the impact of the dominant domestic ecology on her employment prospects. Nor does it give wives a permanent "ownership interest" that limits husbands' future freedom. If a husband takes a lower-paying job, the total amount of income to be equalized will fall automatically.[81]

In conclusion, courts' rejection of wives' claims in the degree cases is in response to the rhetoric used and the specific entitlement demanded. The joint-property proposal avoids both language that signals an unhealthy commodification of family life and the demand for a permanent entitlement for ex-wives in the earnings of their former husbands. Therefore the degree cases do not bind future courts considering the joint-property proposal, which offers a time-limited entitlement framed around widespread notions of marital sharing within the context of the dominant family ecology, rather than in off-putting language that seems to commodify intimate relations.

OBJECTION 3: THE JOINT-PROPERTY PROPOSAL
IS UNFAIR TO MEN

Stephen Sugarman has raised a number of objections from a male perspective. In degree cases, he argues, the wife conferred no real benefit on the husband because "he would often have gone to medical school anyway" and financed his purchase through a loan from his bank instead of his wife. In the case of the mother at home, he argues, she sacrificed for her children, "but that is different from saying that her sacrifice was the cause of his career development."

The degree-case argument needs little comment. Suffice it to say that if the medical student received a loan from the bank, he would be expected to pay it back, with interest that often adds up to a total repayment roughly three times the size of the original loan. Instead, he received a loan from the wife, who expected to be repaid by accessing human capital through her man rather than her job, or by being supported at a later point while she built up her own human capital. Even if her expectations of a permanent claim on her husband's income cannot be realized, she should be repaid by sharing her husband's professional income for the same period for which she shared hers with him.[82]

Sugarman's hypothetical mother-at-home reflects the dominant formulation in the society at large: that mothers stay home for the benefit of the children. Chapter 1 shows that an integral part of mothers' decision to stay home is the father's assumption that he is entitled to perform as an ideal worker, regardless of the burdens that imposes upon his wife or ex-wife. Again, the mother stayed home so the children would receive the societally accepted level of care *while the husband's ability to perform as an ideal worker remained unimpaired.*

A third objection made by Sugarman is that ex-husbands should be held accountable only for the disadvantages the wife suffered from her marriage, not for the disadvantages she suffers because of general societal discrimination. This argument often focuses on the hypothetical case where the wife earns a low salary doing "women's work" (say $20,000 as a librarian) and a husband earns a much higher salary doing traditionally male work (say $80,000 as a businessman). If the husband were forced to share his income, the argument goes, he would be recompensing the wife for the general societal discrimination against women workers, which should be borne by society as a whole rather than by him alone. "Even though men as a class have partly caused women's condition in the job market, I do not see why the particular man, who now happens to be a former husband, should be responsible for redressing this much larger societal problem."[83]

This argument is based on the premise that individual husbands do not benefit from the current organization of market and family work. Chapter 1 shows they do. Most men benefit from the construction of market work around the ideal-worker norm, combined with their entitlement within the family to perform as ideal workers while their wives accept marginalization to the extent "necessary" to enable the family to meet the norm of parental care. To the extent that traditional "women's jobs" are underpaid because of the devaluation associated with women and women's work, even men who do not themselves discriminate enjoy privileges that stem from societal discrimination against women.

Another possible objection from a male point of view is that income equalization would penalize the husband in a situation where he wants to continue the marriage but his wife is determined to leave because she has fallen in love with someone else. Why should a man in this situation share his income with his ex-wife? He need not unless children were born of the marriage. In a society that chooses to deliver care by marginalizing the caregivers, fathers need to share their income not only with their children but also with their children's caregiver; otherwise the children will suffer. Note that in the hypothetical case, the caregiver mother still is delivering to the father the flow of services that allows him to perform as an ideal worker while having his children under parental care. The jilted father should not be legally enabled to take out his fury at his former wife by depriving his children of needed resources. This is not to minimize the outrage of the ex-husband. The source of this fury, however, is a society that tips the balance in favor of the freedom of self-expression rather than in favor of preserving existing marriages. We may, as a society, want to rethink this balance by making divorce more difficult where one party wants to divorce and the other doesn't. This is a complex topic that cannot be fully developed here. For now, the important point is that the children of a marriage should not have to suffer financially in order to protect their father from the sometimes infuriating consequences of a society that values amatory freedom so much more than marital stability.

CONCLUSION

A prominent legal scholar once reassured me that most divorced women don't stay poor because, "they pull themselves out of poverty if they remarry." But surely the solution to female impoverishment is not to require that women, to escape the consequences of coverture, "cover" themselves with another man. The time has come to bury coverture by ending the various husband-owns rules at work in family law, rules that keep alimony and child support awards low and give women equal shares of property in small estates but not in large ones.

The unfair allocation of entitlements upon divorce holds tremendous potential as an organizing tool. "Divorce creates a rupture, leading to a raised consciousness about marriage." An abiding problem for feminists, dramatized in chapter 1, is that many women are so deeply enmeshed in domesticity that a critique is as likely to alienate them as to enlist them. A crucial issue is how to frame critiques of our gender arrangements in ways such women can hear. At the present, divorced women are a key audience for critiques of domesticity, for women are much more likely to launch a gender critique after divorce than within marriage. Notes one study, "[I]t was separated or divorced women *with* children who were most likely to challenge the dominant culture's views of gender roles." Since Lenore Weitzman's brilliant study in 1985, feminists have recognized the power of the "divorce revolution" as an organizing tool. Most of this fervor has gone into lobbying for increased child support and (even more important) improved enforcement of existing child-support obligations.[84]

Both are important issues. But this chapter suggests that the real cause of women's impoverishment upon divorce is not the level of child-support payments, but a double application of the ideal-worker norm: women first are marginalized at work because of their inability to perform as ideal workers, and then upon divorce are cut off from the ideal-worker wage they helped create. Feminists need to channel divorced women's anger, and their clarity of vision, into potent forces for eliminating the ideal-worker norm in market work and family entitlements.

One crucial step is to link the way the ideal-worker norm impoverishes women marginalized by caregiving with the way it deprives ideal-worker women of custody. For if women who marginalize expose themselves to poverty upon divorce, women who don't risk losing custody of their children. The best-known recent case is that of Marcia Clark, the prosecutor in the O. J. Simpson case, whose husband sued for custody of their two children after the trial on the grounds that she spent all her time at work. "Like all moms, Marcia Clark can't have it all," concluded an article in the *Detroit News*, glossing over the fact that fathers have always had both jobs and children. (Clark ultimately retained custody.)

In another well-known case, Sharon Prost, a mother who was chief counsel for the Republicans on the Senate Judiciary Committee, lost custody of her two children to her husband despite her testimony that she got up at five-thirty A.M. to spend time with her children, spent more hours with them than her husband did, and routinely picked up the children from day care by six. Nor did the judge mention the testimony by one of the children's teachers that she saw the mother almost every day and relied on her as a "surrogate room mom," focusing instead on the two or three times a semester the children's father participated in school activities. The judge faulted Prost for failing to make the children her first priority: "[H]er devotion to her job and/or her personal pursuits often takes precedence over her family." She was awarded only six days of visitation a month and ordered to pay $23,000 a year in child support, although by arrangement with her ex-husband, she got the boys overnight twelve to fourteen days a month and continued to drive them to school, stayed home with them when they were ill, did their laundry, attended soccer practices, and chaperoned school field trips. (One year after the appeals court awarded custody to her former husband, Prost was awarded half-time custody when she took a job that allowed her to leave work by 3:00 P.M.)[85]

In a third case, a college student nearly lost custody of her three-year-old daughter when she placed her child in day care in order to attend classes at the University of Michigan. The trial judge held that custody should go to the father, whose mother had agreed to care for her granddaughter at home. This decision ultimately was reversed. In another South Carolina case, Ruth Parris lost custody of her son when a judge held she was "not particularly family-oriented" because of her "aggressive, competitive" career as a real estate agent. The judge ignored the fact that she had taken a year off work after her son's birth and was closely involved in his daily care. The court instead was impressed by the father's commitment to parenting, as evidenced by his cooking on weekends, attending his son's swim meets, and taking his son for doctor's visits. In a New York case, a mother lost custody of her eight-year-old to her unemployed ex-husband, on the grounds that he was better able to care for the child since he was home while the mother worked full time. Numerous other similar cases have been documented.[86]

In a fourth highly publicized case, a mother (Alice Hector) who was a partner at a major Miami law firm lost custody of her children to her former husband, an unemployed architect. Despite the fact that the case has been described in the press as the award of custody to an at-home father, the facts differ substantially from the classic case involving a mother at home. The most notable is that the mother had spent a year and a half as, in effect, a single parent while the father lived apart from the family, hunting treasure in New Mexico. Moreover, unlike most cases where the homemaker is a mother, the court noted that this family always had either a live-in nanny, a housekeeper, or an au pair to help care for the children; no inquiry was made into how much care the father actually did. From the testimony cited in the court opinion, it appears that in this family, as in most families where the mother does not do virtually everything, a complex allocation arises in which the mother continues to do many caregiving tasks that the ideal-worker father does not usually do. The most obvious is that the mother took responsibility for providing the children with continuity of care. There are other examples as well. Though the father made weekday play dates, the mother did the sleepovers; though the father picked up the kids from school, the mother took over on weekends. The court seemed much impressed by the father's volunteer work at the children's school, which started, according to the mother, only after he had an affair, she filed for a divorce, and he started to worry about losing custody.[87]

In *Burchard v. Garay*, a lower court in California awarded custody to a father who had denied paternity and never lived with the child in question, on the grounds that he had greater job stability, owned his own home, and was "better equipped economically . . . to give constant care to the minor child and cope with his continuing needs." The appellate court reversed, noting in a concurring opinion that "[t]o force women into the marketplace and then to penalize them for working would be cruel. It is time this outmoded practice was banished from our jurisprudence."[88]

It ought to be, but it is not. The lawyer for Hector noted, "Every moment that you're not with your kids is a moment that can be used against you. . . . This means that if you work, there is a danger that you could lose your kids." When these custody cases are juxtaposed with the massive documentation of the ways courts impoverish women upon divorce, it becomes clear that married women are being placed in exactly the kind of catch-22 the Supreme Court decried in *Price, Waterhouse v. Hopkins*.[89] If they perform as ideal workers, they risk losing their children upon divorce (even, it appears, if they have performed as primary caregivers as well). If they do not perform as ideal workers, then divorce will impoverish both them and their children. To say this is a nondiscriminatory system is indeed a stretch.[90]

From Sameness and Difference to Reconstructive Feminism

According to the conventional categories of feminist jurisprudence, chapter 3's market-side proposal recalls sameness feminism in its desire to create a world where men and women play similar roles with respect to market and family work. In sharp contrast, this chapter's family-side proposal would be seen as championing difference by advocating increased rights for caregivers. This accounts for the fact that I have been labeled a cultural feminist as well as a radical feminist and a proponent of sameness. In fact, my proposals reflect a new paradigm that combines elements of sameness and of difference. From sameness feminism it draws its vision of equal parenting; from difference feminism it draws its respect for family work.[91]

The goal of reconstructive feminism is to deinstitutionalize domesticity by deconstructing the ideal-worker norm. Taken together, the two major proposals presented in part I will do so. The market-side proposal in chapter 3 reflects the premise that men will never pay the price women now pay for their commitment to the norm of parental care: marginalization. Because men cannot afford to be marginalized, they will perform as ideal workers and will refuse to share equally in family work so long as doing so precludes ideal-worker status. The insight that men will never share family work if it continues to be linked with marginalization gives rise to the proposal to restructure market work so that parents can live up to the norm of parental care without experiencing marginalization.

This eliminates the stick that keeps men in the ideal-worker role. The family-side proposal eliminates a crucial carrot: ownership of the family wage. Men today know they can overinvest in work and create a family premised on their absence from daily life, secure in the knowledge that if at any point they want to reverse their priorities, they can walk with their wallets, get a younger wife, and reinvest in a new and improved family, taking with them the asset that embeds not only their market work but their ex-wife's family work as well.

The strategies presented in chapters 3 and 4 rest on the assumption that in a world where family work as well as market work gives rise to entitlements, and where workers are not gratuitously penalized for living up to the norm of parental care, more adults—men as well as women—would lead lives that balance their work and family ambitions.

This concludes part I, which has focused on an analysis of why gender has proved so unbending in social life. The shifts in market work and family entitlements explored in part I will remain elusive unless we can build coalitions for gender change. Part II examines how we need to change the ways feminists and others talk about gender, which currently pit women against each other and against men.

PART II

•

Unbending Gender Talk (Including Feminism)

> If I cannot get further, this is because I have banged my head against the wall of language. Then, with my head bleeding, I withdraw. And want to go on.[1]

Because the ways we talk about gender remain imprisoned within models framed by domesticity, they give rise to fights among women in everyday life ("mommy wars") as well as to fights within feminism. These fights often have an impacted, interminable quality. An example is the debate over whether men and women are the same or different. Very brief reflection tells us they are both; which is relevant depends on the question being asked. Yet despite the fact that U.S. feminists announced an end to the sameness/difference debate nearly a decade ago, in many discussions much still seems to turn on whether men and women are the same or different.

The subject of maternity leaves came up in a conversation with a Ukrainian feminist. "We are not going to try to deny the differences between men and women," she said firmly. "We need to fight to preserve maternity leaves." As I learned more, it emerged that (like most women from East-Central Europe) she had no hope that women in her country would be able to count on men for any significant contribution to family work. Men did not do "women's work" and she thought they never would. The government, in sharp contrast, had helped women in significant ways. Many of the formerly Communist countries had extensive systems of socialized support for child care, including not only maternity leaves, but also state-run day care centers, child-rearing leaves of up to three years, even (in Germany) a paid day off each month for housework.[2]

The Ukrainian's assessment was that her best hope was to protect socialized benefits rather than (as have U.S. feminists) to focus on getting men to do more family work. This strategic judgment had little to do with whether men and women are "really" different. Although she expressed her conclusion in terms of difference, in fact it reflected a sophisticated political assessment of the optimal gender strategies in her own political culture.

One goal of part II is to show feminists how to translate this kind of political assessment out of the language of sameness and difference, which turns out to be a confusing and divisive way to talk. This project is important because as feminist movements grow in Latin America, East-Central Europe, and other areas, the same stale debates are being re-created in new arenas. For example, key documents of the Inter-American system require equal treatment in general but allow special protection for children and women during pregnancy and nursing;[3] Latin American feminists already have begun to split over Carol Gilligan's description of women.[4]

These debates are being exported to other countries because we have never resolved them ourselves. Once we place domesticity at the center of feminist analysis, we can begin to recognize and defuse the ways our gender talk pits us against each other. In the four chapters that follow, the analysis of domesticity will lead to new ways of talking about gender across class and race divides (chapter 5), of talking about what men and women are really like (chapter 6), of assessing what policies are feasible and desirable for changing the practice of domesticity, notably the way it structures market work and family entitlements (chapter 7), and of talking about the relationships of gender, power, and truth (chapter 8). Chapters 5 and 6 are designed for a general audience; chapters 7 and 8 are addressed to policy makers and theorists, respectively.

Problems created by the deep patterning of our language "are solved ... by looking into the workings of our language, and that in such a way as to make us recognize those workings; *in spite of* an urge to misunderstand them. The problems are solved, not by new information, but by [re]arranging what we have always known. Philosophy is a battle against the bewitchment of our intelligence by means of language."[5] The goal of part II is to break the bewitchment that keeps us talking, thinking, and doing gender in ways that place the project of reconstruction beyond our reach.

CHAPTER FIVE

•

How Domesticity's Gender Wars
Take on Elements of Class and Race Conflict

Dear Ann Landers:

This is in response to "A.C.T. in Houston," the stay-at-home mom who complained because her husband wanted her to get an outside job. My question for her is this: Who does she think does the cooking, tutoring, sewing, laundry and housekeeping in a home where both parents work? Does she think the Keebler elves come in and cook meals, wash clothes and help with homework?

No matter how many hours a day a woman works outside the home, all these chores still need to be done. For working women, they are done late at night, early in the morning or on a lunch hour.

Stay-at-home moms have it easy. Next time "A.C.T." wants to complain about how hard her job is, she should think about how hard it would be to squeeze it all in after 5 P.M.

—Alabama

Dear Al:

You spoke for a great many women today, but instead of arguing among yourselves, why don't you lean on the men to do more?[1]

The traditional feminist assumption is that gender binds women together. In fact, gender divides them. Domesticity's organization of market work and family work pits ideal-worker women against women who have made a conscious, often painful, decision to reject the ideal-worker role in favor of a life defined by caregiving.[2]

The resulting gender wars threaten feminist coalitions. This chapter will show how the full-commodification model exacerbates these conflicts, enshrining ideal-worker women as the ideal and thereby alienating women whose lives are framed around caregiving. The gender wars that result often take on elements of racial and class conflict because of the distinctive relationships of the working class and people of color to the ideals and social practice of domesticity.

A key message of antiessentialism is that gender is different as lived and imagined by different social groups. The full-commodification model translates those differences into gender, race, and class conflict that erodes the potential for effective alliances. This chapter explores strategies designed to transform these differences into resources for gender change.

But first an important proviso. In the past decade feminists have often pondered how to provide a description of women that avoids essentialism. This question involves a category mistake. What follows is a description not of individual women but of gender traditions. My goal is to describe the fields of social power that affect women of color and working-class women. This clarifies why I can offer a unified description: I am describing only the dominant strains, not the full complexity of all counterhegemonic trends. This also explains why my description does not fully capture the complexity of the experience of any individual woman. No woman is only a woman; individuals are much more complex than the social forces within which they negotiate everyday life.

HOW DOMESTICITY CREATES GENDER WARS AMONG WOMEN, AND HOW THE FULL-COMMODIFICATION MODEL EXACERBATES THEM

"How *nice* that you can walk little Bobby to school every morning," gushes a stay-at-home mother to a harried working mom as she arrives at her son's school. "Otherwise, you'd never *see* him." (Opening salvo.)

"Listen, Sophie *really needs* some fake fur for her princess costume," wheedles a working mom talking to her next-door neighbor. "Since you're home with *so much time*, would you mind picking up some at the store for me?" (Direct hit.)

"Oh, you're a lawyer. How *exciting*. It must be *so much fun* to get dressed up and go to an office all day. And I'm sure that Joey does *just fine* at the day-care center." (Heavy artillery.)[3]

The war of "mommy versus mommy" came to national attention when Hillary Clinton defended her career, saying, "I suppose I could have stayed home, baked cookies and had teas, but what I decided was to fulfill my profession." This comment outraged many homemakers. Note the dynamic. Hillary Clinton felt embattled: One of the country's top hundred lawyers, she found herself having to defend her career in a context where a man would be required only to avoid too obvious a strut. When she defended herself, she made a comment that seemed to endorse society's devaluation of caregiving. The result was that homemakers focused their anger on Hillary rather than on the system that punishes both her for performing as an ideal worker and them by devaluing important family work.[4]

Domesticity divides women against themselves. Until feminists acknowledge this dynamic and defuse it, alliances among women will remain fragile and difficult. Gender wars are not limited to conflicts between employed women and homemakers, for American women are not divided into two dichotomous groups. Instead, they are on a continuum. Some are as devoted to success at work as the most "high-powered" men; others do no market work. But most American women lie somewhere in the middle, or shift between various points on the continuum at different stages of their lives. These infinite gradations are divisive, as each woman judges women more work-centered than herself as insensitive to her children's needs, and those less work-centered as having "dropped out" or "given up."

Any mother with a full-time career fights gender wars every day. Recall the conversation I had with my daughter's nursery school principal, who announced, "It's not so easy, is it, to combine being a mother with a full-time career?" (chapter 2). The principal felt she was standing up for traditional feminine roles and values against a woman captured by masculine norms. Mothers at home, and their defenders, have a substantial investment in the notion that "working mothers" take on an impossible task, and ultimately fail to meet their children's needs. The small cadre of feminist reporters provides examples. A Minneapolis video producer reported that a disapproving at-home mother counted up the number of times the producer went to her son's soccer practice and "made sure she let me know she couldn't *imagine* not being there when her child came home from school." Another working mother told of her son's kindergarten teacher who would send home last-minute notes saying the child needed a mango or wooden craft sticks by the next morning, apparently assuming that she was at home when her child returned from school. "I told her we needed more notice, but she didn't stop. She thought, you're home, or you should be, and you just do it. She's a stay-at-home mother now." Another gender war pits mothers against women without children. An editor with an important job in Washington, D.C., met a co-worker as the editor was leaving work one day at 5:30. "Oh," quipped the co-worker, "working half a day today?" The editor was going home to her children. The co-worker was single and childfree.[5]

Mommy wars extend beyond everyday sniping. Two studies of the failure to ratify the ERA both identify a gender war between homemakers and career women. Jane Mansbridge argues that two perceptions fed homemakers' receptivity to what ERA supporters considered "Phyllis Schlafly's lies." The first was that the ERA would have eliminated some protections homemakers traditionally enjoyed, notably the "tender years" presumption that custody of young children belonged with their mothers. The second was that homemakers felt that feminism had contributed to their loss of status.* "Many people who followed the struggle over the ERA believed—rightly in my view—that the Amendment would have been ratified by 1975 or 1976 had it not been for Phyllis Schlafly's early and effective effort to organize potential opponents." In other words, the ERA was defeated when Schlafly turned it into a war among women over gender roles. The full-commodification model, with its belittlement of homemaking, contributed to this defeat.[6]

A second study of the defeat of the ERA in North Carolina reached similar con-

---

*Although Mansbridge argues that feminism probably did contribute to homemakers' loss of status, the historical analysis presented in chapter 2 suggests that feminism was itself a reaction to the fact that by the 1960s homemaking had already lost the status "moral mothers" had enjoyed in an earlier period.

clusions. Donald Mathews and Jane DeHart, in a nuanced and subtle study, found that the ERA was defeated in North Carolina by "family-oriented women" who felt deeply threatened by a vision of equality that seemed to belittle the gendered roles that had structured their lives. The full complexity of their analysis cannot be captured here, but the gender war aspect of the North Carolina ERA fight emerges clearly. As one anti-ERA activist explained to students in a junior high school, "libbers" had launched a "total assault on the role of American wife and mother." As DeHart and Mathews are careful to note, millions of housewives and mothers supported the ERA—in fact, housewives were no less likely to support it than employed women. But ERA opponents typically saw the ERA as an assault on the domestic arrangements that provided the basic framework for their lives:

> He works for me, takes care of me and our three children, doesn't make me do things that are hard for me (drive in town), loves me and doesn't smoke, drink, gamble, run around or do anything that would upset me. I do what he tells me to do. I like this arrangement; it's the only way I know how to live.

Such women feared that feminist notions of fluid roles threatened to "subvert behavior that expressed for some people the very sources of their personality." They also felt that feminists' "equality" threatened their support and Social Security as housewives. DeHart and Mathews argue that these women understood very well their dependency and vulnerability, and felt that ratificationists were threatening female solidarity. "'You Olympic swimmers,' nonfeminists seemed to be saying, 'should not rock the boat for the rest of us who cannot swim—especially after you have stolen our life jackets.'"[7]

Rebecca Klatch's study of antifeminist women (many of them anti-ERA activists) similarly found that "[t]he conflict between feminists and homemakers is a tug-of-war between two lifestyles." She found that most antifeminist women were white, middle-aged housewives, religious (typically Protestant fundamentalist or Catholic), married or widowed, new to politics, and oriented toward single issues. Feminists, she found, tended to be younger, more career-oriented, and often divorced or unmarried. Said one anti-ERA activist, "The women's liberation movement really resents homemakers. . . . They caused resentment to grow between homemakers and working women. . . . The women who used to say 'I'm a homemaker' with pride now say 'I'm just a housewife.' That's a terrible change in attitude." Feminists feel these accusations are unfair. Fair or not, the important question is how to avoid having gender wars of this type mobilize opposition to equality for women.[8]

A similar dynamic is at work in the abortion debate. The usual feminist analysis—that antiabortion activism represents men's attempt to control women—aptly captures important elements of the debate. But it misses others, for it fails to take account of the fact that the majority of activists on *both sides* of the debate are women. Studies of the abortion debate suggest that, in significant part, it is a gender war between ideal-worker women and women whose lives are framed by caregiving.[9]

In Faye Ginsburg's study of abortion activists in North Dakota, she once again found career women pitted against homemakers. It comes as no surprise that the career women were pro-choice while the homemakers were pro-life. What is surprising is that the pro-life homemakers were substantially younger than the pro-choice feminists. The pro-choice activists typically were women with a substantial career commitment who had been deeply influenced by feminism in the late 1960s and early 1970s. The pro-life activists tended to be younger women who came of age in the 1970s and whose major life-defining step was to drop out of the workforce to have children.

Pro-life advocates embraced the notion that family life is meant to provide a haven from the heartless world of the material values. Said one:

> I think we've accepted abortion because we're a very materialistic society and there is less time for caring. To me it's all related. Housewives don't mean much because we do the caring and the mothering kinds of things which are not as important as a nice house or a new car.[10]

Ginsburg argues that these pro-life advocates are modern-day "moral mothers," embracing the language of domesticity to critique the premise that society is better off if adults pursue their own self-interest. The women she interviewed saw their pro-life stance as part of a system of values that chooses nurturance over material success. They belittled the "man's world" of self-interest as selfish and materialistic, in contrast to the maternal world of "unconditional nurturance." Linda Gordon aptly captures their commodification anxiety, their fear that allowing market values into family concerns will be destructive to the family and to society at large. Abortion opponents, she says,

> fear a completely individualized society with all services on cash nexus relationships, without the influence of nurturing women counteracting the completely egoistic principles of the economy, and without any forms in which children can learn about lasting human commitments to other people.[11]

Another study of abortion activists again found commodification anxiety policing traditional gender roles:

> I think women's lib is on the wrong track. I think they've got every [possible] gripe and they've always been that way. The women have been the superior people. They're more civilized, they're more unselfish by nature, but now they want to compete with men at being selfish. And so there's nobody to give an example, and what happens is that men become *more* selfish. See, the women used to be an example and they had to take it on the chin for that . . . but they also benefitted from it because we don't want to go back to the cavemen, where you drag the woman around and treat her like nothing.[12]

Again, we see themes from domesticity: men are selfish, women are selfless, women are more moral than men. These themes are linked with the sense that if women begin to act like men, they will lose their moral hold over men in a world where they are vulnerable to male power.

Ginsberg's findings suggest that gender wars are not something time automatically will cure. Instead, they are re-created in every generation of women, including our own. If gender wars have led to the defeat of the ERA and to significant losses in the abortion context, feminists sorely need to better understand this dynamic.

Ginsberg's study is important because she highlights that the wars between ideal-worker women and women who have framed their lives around caregiving often involve women who are similar along other dimensions: Like Deborah Fallows, they may have been educated as ideal-worker women and started out on similar careers. But no one, including Ginsberg, makes another important point: Women whose lives are framed by family rather than market work may be as feminist as ideal-worker women. After all, if one strong theme in feminism has been to hold up ideal workers as the ideal, a second is to stress the importance of undervalued family work. This is the point put forth strongly by feminists who framed their lives around caregiving. They share the feminist goal of empowering women; they just think that should occur within the sphere of life domesticity assigns to women, rather in the sphere domesticity assigns to men.

Feminism's full-commodification model feeds gender wars in several ways. Its long-standing association with the devaluation of homemaking triggers a conflict between ideal-worker women and women who have framed their lives around caregiving. Its focus on market child care triggers commodification anxiety over the intrusion of the market into family life. Its insistence that women should enter into employment on the terms traditionally available to men feeds the sense that feminists are male-identified women out of touch with the values associated with traditional femininity. Its failure to address the small matter of who will take care of the children when women work feeds the sense that children's welfare is dependent on the continued marginalization of their caregivers.

The full-commodification model also reflects the social location of privileged white "essential" women in important ways. As a result, gender wars often turn into class and race conflicts in ways detailed in the remainder of this chapter.

WHY GENDER WARS TAKE ON DIMENSIONS OF CLASS CONFLICT, AND HOW TO AVOID IT

> Perhaps we need to rethink what we mean by feminism, recognizing how much our image of what it means to be "liberated" is based on access to opportunities which are only available to middle-class women.[13]

Does the full-commodification model embed class privilege? Upon reflection, it does. Its imagery of market work as liberating and of domesticity as drudgery are framed around the kinds of jobs available to women from the professional middle class. Its vision of the market as a benign force that can enhance family life is one most often held by women with enough wealth to gain access to rewarding work and quality child care. Its image of men as oppressors reflects a view held by the partners of privileged men; less privileged women are more likely to see their men as vulnerable and in need of solidarity. Feminists need to think through the different meanings of gender for different social groups when they formulate their rhetoric and their goals.

This section examines the relationship of working-class women to the key gender axes of domesticity; the following section examines crucial issues related to women of color. Obviously these are overlapping categories. For now, the important point is to recognize them as two distinct social force fields that need to be taken into account in building coalitions for gender change.[14]

The potential for class conflict over gender issues emerges clearly in Kristin Luker's study of abortion activists in California. Luker found that pro-life activists tend to come from the working class, whereas pro-choice women tend to come from the middle class. "Almost without exception pro-choice women work in the paid labor force, they earn good salaries when they work, and if they are married, they are likely to be married to men who also have good incomes." Nearly all worked (94 percent), and over half had incomes in the top 10 percent of all working women in the country. Very few pro-life married women worked. "Thus pro-life women are less likely to work in the first place, they earn less money when they do work, and they are more likely to be married to a skilled worker or small businessman who earns only a moderate income." Pro-choice women tended to be college graduates; pro-life women tended to have graduated only from high school. Education is a standard proxy for class in the United States.[15]

Luker does not fully analyze the implications of her finding that the gender war over abortion has elements of class conflict. Linda Blum does, in a thoughtful discussion in which she argues that "much of the difference in worldview that leads women to embrace or reject feminist reforms stems from class differences." Why should gender wars have dimensions of class conflict? The reason, explored below, is that working-class people have different gender traditions that stem from their different relationships with the key gender axes of market work, market child care, and family work.[16]

Market Work

> I may be subordinate here, but I express myself fully at home. For factory hands, and especially for the women among them, family photos sometimes meant: I may not be the boss here, but I have another life where I am.[17]

For Betty Friedan or Luker's California pro-choice advocates, market work offered substantial salaries and a respected social role in a professional or managerial position. Working-class people often have more mixed feelings about market work. "Take this job and shove it" is a theme common to their descriptions of work life. Working-class kids complaining about their jobs are told, "Of course you don't like it, that's why they pay you." Studs Terkel's 1972 classic *Working* contains ample evidence of the alienation felt by workers whose jobs offer little autonomy or opportunity for advancement. Lillian Rubin, in her 1976 classic *Worlds of Pain*, quotes a twenty-nine-year-old warehouseman:

> A lot of times, I hate to go down there. I'm cooped up and hemmed in.... It seems like all there is to life is to go down there and work, collect your pay check, your bills, and get further in debt. It doesn't seem like the cycle ever ends. Every day it's the same thing; every week it's the same thing; every month it's the same thing.

Some of the men Rubin interviewed reacted with resignation ("I guess you can't complain. You have to work to make a living, so what's the use"—a twenty-six-year-old garageman); some with boredom ("I've been in this business thirteen years and it bores me. It's enough"—a thirty-five-year-old machine operator); and some with alienation ("The one thing I like is the hours. I work from seven to three-thirty in the afternoon so I get off early enough to have a lot of the day left"). These images contrast sharply with Friedan's image of market work as the key to personal fulfillment.[18]

That labor is alienating comes as no surprise. Marx placed workingmen's alienation at the center of his analysis in the latter half of the nineteenth century, and Rubin confirmed his analysis more than a century later. For men in working-class jobs, she reported,

> bitterness, alienation, resignation, and boredom are the defining characteristics of the work experience. "What's there to talk about?"—not really a question but an oft-repeated statement that says work is a requirement of life, hours to be gotten through until you can go home.

The middle-class custom of asking a new acquaintance "What do you do?" is met with confusion and discomfort in working-class settings. As a black working-class informant told John Gwaltney:

> One very important difference between white people and black people is that white people think that you *are* your work.... Now, a black person has more sense than that because he knows that what I am doing doesn't have anything to do with what I want to do or what I do when I am doing for myself. Now, black people think that my work is just what I have to do to get what I want.

Studies of the white working class confirm that "achievement in a specialized vocation is not the measure of a person's worth, not even for a [working-class] man," and certainly not for a woman. Working-class women's identity is "multifaceted," framed not only around work but around family and other roles as well. This is true in part because some three-fourths of working-class women hold low-status, low-paying, traditionally female jobs.[19]

Friedan's unconscious assertion of privilege in her imagery of market work sheds light on the oft-repeated assertion that the women's movement is "a bunch of middle-class women who don't have anything else to do, going to meetings and rallies and stuff. It hasn't done anything for us at the bottom of the social and labor scale." Friedan's dream is of a professional job; her anger is that of a woman whose gender has blocked her from claiming the job that otherwise would be hers by virtue of her race and class. Gender has always seemed the most important axis of social power for privileged white women because it is the only one that blocks their way. This is not to say that the injustice meted out to them is not injustice. It is. But if privileged women want others to join their struggles, they must reimagine themselves in ways that take into account the perspectives of their proposed allies.[20]

The potential for cross-class coalitions is greater today than thirty years ago because of the dislocations wrought by the postindustrial economy. Feminists' focus on market work seemed alien to many working-class women twenty years ago because they did not see themselves as permanent committed workers (despite the fact that a majority of them were in the labor force). In sharp contrast, the demise of the family wage means that today's working-class women know they probably will continue in the workforce even after they have children. Rubin notes in her 1994 *Families on the Fault Line,* "Although the women I interviewed for this book are the class and status counterparts of those I spoke with twenty years ago, they no longer think that women's issues don't have much to do with them. Quite the opposite!"[21]

Feminists, too, have changed in ways that enhance the potential for cross-class coalitions. They have changed Friedan's argument that women *want* to work to achieve self-development into an argument that women *need* to work to help support their families. This is a good start, but it does not go far enough. Feminists need to rethink their inheritance from the viewpoint of working-class women to assess how to appeal to women whose relationships with the key gender axes are different than their own. This includes not only market work, but also family work and market child care.

Market Child Care and Family Work

> Among many poorer Americans, liberation means the freedom of a mother finally to quit her job—to live the life of a capitalist stay-at-home mother as it were. Of course work for her has meant scrubbing floors or scouring toilets or sewing endless buttons on discount smocks.[22]

For a short period after World War II, working-class men in good blue-collar jobs could deliver the "good life"—the house, the car, the washing machine—on their salaries alone, or with only intermittent, part-time work from their wives. Those days are gone. The family wage today is what it was originally: a prerogative of the middle class. "I know she doesn't mind working, but it shouldn't have to be that way," said Doug, the white thirty-year-old forklift operator quoted in the preface. "A guy should be able to support his wife and kids. But that's not the way it is these days, is it? Well, I guess those rich guys can, but not some ordinary Joe like me." Our generation has seen the demise of the family wage working-class men fought so hard to achieve.[23]

Feminist commentators often assume that this means working-class women are ready to embrace the full-commodification model. Rubin quotes thirty-four-year-old Victoria Segunda, the assistant manager of a children's clothing store and mother of three: "I started out as a part-time salesperson and now I'm assistant manager.

One day I'll be manager. Sometimes I'm amazed at what I've accomplished; I had no idea I could do all this, be responsible for a whole business like that. My husband, he keeps looking forward to when all the bills are paid and I can stay home again. But I don't ever want to stop working. Why would I?" Rubin's informants sometimes sound like middle-class women in the 1970s. "I couldn't believe what a difference it made when I went to work," said Joy Siri, a thirty-nine-year-old white woman married eighteen years with three teenage children. "I felt like I've got my own life. I never felt like I really ruled my life before. You know, I went from my parents' house to my husband's. He's a good man, but he's bossy. Now I'm working just like him, so he can't just boss me around so much anymore. I mean, he still tries, but I don't have to let him." Phyllis Kilson, the mother of four grown children who is quoted above, also notes that her husband always made all the big decisions: "I never felt like I had a right to my say. I mean, I tried sometimes, but if he said no, I figured I didn't have a right to contradict him. Now I make money, too, so it's different."[24]

These women's children are grown; they lived for years in single-earner households where the husband's word was law: No doubt they find the sudden shift in the power dynamics exhilarating when they go to work. But to working-class women with younger children, domesticity may still look like an attractive alternative.

When working-class wives join the workforce, their families face all the pressures faced by middle-class families, but with fewer of the resources to ease the way. Lillian Rubin found that "[f]or most working-class families, child care often is patched together in ways that leave parents anxious and children in jeopardy." In one illustrative family, the nine-year-old was a latchkey child, alone at home after school. The babies, under three years old, went to the wife's mother two days a week. "But she works the rest of the time, so the other days we take them to this woman's house. It's the best we can afford, but it's not great because she keeps too many kids, and I know they don't get good attention. Especially the little one. . . . She's so clingy when I bring her home; she can't let go of me, like nobody's paid her any mind all day." This kind of painful reality no doubt feeds the nostalgia for the days when working-class women could stay home; many of the quotes describing the norm of parental care in chapter 2 are from working-class mothers. In general, child care used by middle-class parents emphasizes child development and learning opportunities, while working-class parents often can afford only the most basic services from unlicensed providers.[25]

Not only are working-class families forced to make sharp trade-offs in choosing child care, but they cannot so readily turn to market solutions to help with housework. Because they cannot hire outside cleaners, working-class women spend weekends scrubbing floors and toilets. Because they cannot send out laundry and dry cleaning, they find themselves washing and folding clothes late at night. Because they can't afford take-out, they find themselves pressured to prepare dinner just when babies are needy and older children need help with homework. The time famine that has received so much publicity in middle-class life is much worse for working-class families.

"Leisure," snorts Peter Pittman, a 28-year-old African-American father of two, married six years. "With both of us working like we do, there's no time for anything. We got two little kids; I commute better than an hour each way to my job. Then we live here for half rent because I take care of the place for the landlord. So if somebody's got a complaint, I've got to take care of it, you know, fix it myself or get the landlord to get somebody out to do it if I can't. Most things I can do myself, but it takes time. I sometimes wonder what this life's all about, because this sure ain't what I call living. We don't go anyplace; we don't do anything; Christ, we hardly have time to go to the toilet. There's always some damn thing that's waiting that you've got to do."

Even sex "becomes a problem that needs attention" in this "whirling dervish" world.[26]

Lack of time for family life is even more of a problem for the large number of working-class families who fulfill the norm of parental care by having the parents split shifts, with one parent caring for the children while the other is at work. One-fifth of the families Rubin interviewed did this, although this number tends to fall as the economy improves. The impact of the split-shift solution on family life is harsh. When Rubin asked one split-shift couple when they had time to talk, she got a look of annoyance at a question that seemed stupid. "Talk? How can we talk when we hardly see each other?" "Talk? What's that?" "Talk? Ha, that's a joke." Tina Mulvaney, a thirty-five-year-old white mother of two teenagers, gave a fuller description:

> Mike drives a cab and I work in a hospital, so we figured one of us could transfer to nights. We talked it over and decided it would be best if I was here during the day and he was here at night. He controls the kids, especially my son, better than I do. . . . So now Mike works days and I work graveyard. I hate it, but it's the only answer; at least this way somebody's here all the time. I get home at 8:30 in the morning. The kids and Mike are gone. It's the best time of the day because it's the only time I have a little quiet here. I clean up the house a little, do the shopping and the laundry and whatever, then I go to sleep for a couple of hours until the kids come home from school.
>
> Mike gets home at five; we eat; then he takes over for the night, and I go back to sleep for another couple of hours. I try to get up by 9 so we can have a little time together, but I'm so tired that I don't make it a lot of times. And by 10, he's sleeping because he has to be up by 6 in the morning. So if I don't get up, we hardly see each other at all. . . . It's hard, very hard; there's no time to live or anything.

Rubin notes she seems listless.[27]

Though the split-shift solution creates many difficulties, it is more likely to lead to a more equitable distribution of family work. Rubin found family work split roughly equally in only about 16 percent of her sample, most often because parents worked split shifts. In many of the families Rubin talked with in the nineties, the allocation of household work was a source of conflict. Working-class women's willingness to engage in struggle around the division of family work is one of the most striking changes Rubin noted when she compared the situation today with that twenty years ago. The women who once felt indebted to a husband who "helped out" now demand more equal sharing of family work.

> "It's not fair," said a white 36-year-old manicurist, married 17 years. "Why should he get to read the paper or watch TV while I run around picking up the kids' toys and stuff, cooking supper, cleaning up afterward, and trying to give the kids some quality time? It would be different if I didn't work; then I wouldn't look for him to do any housework. But I put in my eight hours every day just like him, so I think he should do his share.[28]

Feminists hear this as evidence that working-class women are finally ready to join the sisterhood.[29] Though the potential is there, the opportunity could be squandered by a mistake in tone. The classic contemporary text on work/family conflict, Arlie Hochschild's *The Second Shift*, threatens to make this mistake. As discussed in chapter 2, she makes several moves characteristic of the full-commodification tradition that have proved off-putting to many working-class women, notably her focus on privileged women's access to professional careers.

Hochschild's text sends two other messages that could easily undercut the potential for cross-class coalitions. The first is her hostility toward domesticity. The best place to begin understanding the sharp class difference in the meanings of domesticity for middle- and working-class homemakers is with a 1972 interview by Studs Terkel of a working-class housewife named Therese Carter. Housework may have looked like drudgery to Betty Friedan, but it looked attractive to Carter when she compared it to the jobs she was familiar with as the wife of the foreman in an auto body repair shop:

> I don't look at housework as drudgery. People will complain: "Why do I have to scrub floors?" To me, that isn't the same thing as a man standing there— it's his livelihood—putting two screws together day after day. It would drive anybody nuts. That poor man doesn't even get to see the finished product. I'll sit here and I'll cook a pie and I'll get to see everybody eat it. This is my offering. I think it's the greatest satisfaction in the world to know you've pleased somebody. Everybody has to feel needed. I know I'm needed.

Family work holds a different aura in working-class contexts. Notes Ellen Israel Rosen, "While domestic work is burdensome it also is seen as providing rewards in terms of intimacy, pride and autonomy, things not available in the commodity-oriented, exploitative marketplace."

Commentators often note that family work is seen as important political work by African-Americans, because it helps sustain a family life that is seen as protection against racism in the outside world. A similar dynamic is at work in white working-class households. Despite the fact that the family places women in a position of subordination, it also "is almost the only institution in capitalist society that bears both an ideology and a reality of love, of sharing, and of generosity." Feminists' imagery of the family as the locus of subordination seems most convincing to women otherwise privileged by class and race; to working-class women, it may seem instead (or as well) a haven against the injuries of class.[30]

Domesticity holds other attractions in the working-class context. As noted in chapter 1, domesticity was invented as a strategy to differentiate the middle class from the working class. For well over two centuries, having a wife at home has signaled middle-class status. This may carry little weight with women who feel themselves solidly middle-class and want to pursue careers, but for many working-class families, having a mother at home seems a desirable way of "giving the kids a good start in life," or, less subtly, signaling that the family has achieved a certain level of gentility.[31]

Domesticity is linked with middle-class aspirations for another, very practical reason. As discussed in chapter 1, having a wife at home is the only way to deliver to working-class children the same kind of care received by middle-class children. The hidden assumption behind the proposal to delegate child care to the market is a family income high enough to buy quality care; implicit is an image of the market as the benign deliverer of quality goods. This image holds true only for the affluent. Working-class children can be protected from their parents' disadvantaged market position only if child care is handled outside of the market. Many working-class families feel they can access high-quality care only by relying on grandmothers or other relatives. This is why care by family members is so much more common in the working class than among the more privileged: One study of DuPont workers found that 40 percent of women in manufacturing used relatives for child care as opposed to only 8 percent of professional women.[32]

As discussed in chapter 1, strong forces propel American families toward domesticity in a society without publicly supported child care. Thus even when working-class women praise market work, they may not share the hostility to domesticity common in the dominant strain of feminism. "What happens when your kid gets sick?" asked Faye Ensey, a twenty-eight-year-old office worker. "Or when your babysitter's kids get sick? I lost two jobs in a row because my kids kept getting sick and I couldn't go to work. Or else I couldn't take my little one to the babysitter because her kids were sick. They finally fired me for absenteeism. I really don't blame them, but it felt terrible anyway. It's such a hassle, I sometimes think I'd be glad to just stay home."[33]

Twenty years ago, white working-class women typically praised domesticity and held typical working-class attitudes toward market work. Today the situation is more complex. Yet feminists need to remember that, if they had a choice, many working-class women would prefer that their men earned higher wages so that they could care for children in the manner of a middle-class family.[34] To avoid class as well as gender wars, feminist proposals need to maintain a tone of respect for domesticity.

Feminism Versus Traditionalism in the Working Class

The common stereotype that working-class men do less family work than middle-class ones appears to be untrue; one study found that "[c]lass location is simply not a powerful determinant of the amount of housework husbands perform." This section concerns not the walk but the talk: whether or not working-class men espouse traditionalist attitudes rather than whether they carry them out. Research suggests that men with lower incomes are more likely than men with higher ones to disapprove of married women earning money.[35] Ellen Rosen's 1987 study of women in blue-collar work in a New England mill town found that her subjects supported the notion of separate spheres and did "not seek an egalitarian division of labor within the family." Male authority, she reports, "is still an integral part of most working-class relationships." Thirty percent of Rosen's informants told the interviewer in an open-ended question that their husbands were not happy about them working; an additional 34 percent said things like, "He doesn't really mind." Rosen's evidence suggests working-class husbands' objections to working wives relate to their desire to feel like the family breadwinner. "He wants her to stop working, while she, because she is earning well, may not want to. . . . A man's ability to provide is, after all, a source of self-esteem."[36]

As has been noted, working-class men today often need considerable reassurance in their status as breadwinners. The narrowing of the wage gap represents, in significant part, the recent "skidding" of the incomes of high-school-educated men. In a society where manhood is linked with breadwinning, high levels of gender traditionalism are predictable under these conditions, especially the sense that "the women should be women, and let us be the men." A 1983 study found high levels of traditionalism in working-class males of all races.[37]

Rosen found considerable traditionalism among the women as well. The women Rosen studied, who had blue-collar jobs and so earned considerably more than most working-class women, nonetheless were acutely conscious of the fact that "every woman is only a husband away from welfare." Their commitment to separate spheres "is a way of reinforcing a husband's obligation and willingness to provide continuing support for his wife and children." The wage-earning "help" they offer to husbands is intended to engender an obligation for "reciprocity." "Fairness requires that if she helps him, he should also help her." Feminist demands for equality may well seem threatening because an insistence on equality seems tantamount to "forfeiting the right to be taken care of in a work world which offers them few opportunities to take care of themselves." The parallels with ERA opponents are striking. Rosen found many working-class women who opposed women taking traditionally male jobs on the grounds that such women deprive another wife of her rightful due. Said one, "When I see the women go and drive the bus or deliver the mail, when there are so many young men who need jobs, I think men should have these jobs, not women. I think women hurt themselves by being equal to men." Ironically, working-class women's disadvantaged position in the job market thus serves to reinforce their endorsement of men's privileged access to "good jobs."[38]

Rosen's data were from older couples, since older women predominated in the blue-collar work she studied. Two recent studies by Roberta Sigel and Lillian Rubin argue that an important generational shift has taken place, with working-class men under forty considerably less conservative than older ones. Yet a close reading of Sigel's study suggests that she may have exaggerated the shift. She reports that "[v]irtually no one, not even among the older women, had any desire for a return to traditional sex-role definitions," but she also notes that in telephone interviews nearly 5 percent of the women identified themselves as "strongly traditional" while 22 percent "professed harboring varying degrees of traditionalism." A finding that over one-fourth of women hold some traditional views seems to contradict her earlier statement.[39]

Sigel also found persistent traditionalism in men—although this often came out only in her blue-collar focus groups, from men who expressed less traditional gender views in telephone interviews. Said Tony, an electrical worker in his mid-forties whose wife had recently entered the workforce:

> I wouldn't let my wife work. I told her; I said, "Look, you got the kids, you stay home. When the kids go to school all day, then you work." That's fine, up to a point. I tried to do it on my own. Working 20 hours a day to make everything go. She said, "Hey look I gotta go to work." Well, I was against it, but it had to be done. As far as I was brought up, Pop did the work; Mom stayed home with the kids. Alright? I was raised that way, and that's the way I saw it.

"That is also pretty much the way other middle-aged and older blue-collar men saw the situation. The husband as the breadwinner and the wife as the homemaker describes their image of the normal and good life." Sigel found that men over forty are close enough to the era of the family wage to be replaying the patterns documented by Ellen Rosen.[40]

The question is how much younger men differ. Sigel asserts that "the younger men [in the blue-collar focus group] did not subscribe so much to the traditional script." They assumed their wives would have to work and were more willing to acknowledge that their wives might have needs for self-fulfillment outside the home. Many also conceded they should do more family work. Indeed, the younger working-class men seemed more like middle-class men, with their formal embrace of gender equality accompanied by their refusal to share equally in family work. Like middle-class men both twenty years ago and today, many working-class men under forty talk the talk but do not walk the walk.[41]

Yet both Rubin and Sigel include a number of examples of younger working-class men espousing very traditional views. Rubin quotes Gary Braunswig, a twenty-nine-year-old white drill press operator:

> "I know my wife works all day, just like I do, but it's not the same. She doesn't *have* to do it. I mean, she *has* to because we need the money, but it's different." He stops, irritated with himself because he can't find exactly the words he wants, and asks, "Know what I mean? I'm not saying it right; I mean, it's the man who's supposed to support his family, so I've got to be responsible for that, not her. And that makes one damn big difference.
> "I mean, women complain all the time about how hard they work with

the house and the kids and all. I'm not saying it's not hard, but that's her responsibility, just like the finances are mine."

"But she's now sharing that burden with you, isn't she?" [asked Rubin.]

"Yeah, and I do my share around the house, only she doesn't see it that way. Maybe if you add it all up, I don't do as much as she does, but then she doesn't bring in as much money as I do. And she doesn't have to be looking for overtime to make an extra buck. I got no complaints about that, so how come she's always complaining about me? I mean, she helps me out financially, and I help her out with the kids and stuff. What's wrong with that? It seems pretty equal to me."[42]

This is not a striking example of a revolution in gender consciousness. Rather, it sounds like separate spheres updated rather than abandoned. Younger working-class men may now talk the language of equality to strangers on the telephone, but many of them sound pretty traditional to me.

Integrating Class and Gender Analysis

In her influential *Brave New Families*, Judith Stacey bids "[f]arewell to Archie Bunker." "If this ethnography serves no other purpose," she writes, "I hope it will shatter the image of the white working class as the last repository of old-fashioned . . . American family life."[43]

A key strength of Stacey's book is the sensitive way she captures the complexity of her subjects' negotiations with gender. Yet her insistence that her subjects are feminists, not traditionalists, sometimes oversimplifies these negotiations, particularly in view of her acknowledgment that young working-class women often vehemently reject a feminist identity. Stacey calls one of her subjects a feminist because she had ended her husband's domestic abuse and gained a more equitable division of household work. However, this occurred only after the wife had left him and had returned "to him (and his pension)" after he was disabled by a severe heart attack. Surely this proves no more than that Archie Bunker disabled does not exercise the same family power as he did as a breadwinner in good health. Stacey's other case study describes Pamela Gama, a middle-class woman who temporarily fell out of the middle class when she divorced her engineer husband. She ultimately made it back into the middle class as the administrator of a social service agency, and married a working-class man. In labeling her feminist, Stacey glosses over the price Gama paid for the concessions she gained in her second marriage: a formal acknowledgment, as a born-again Christian, that her husband was ordained by God as the head of the family. Is this situation better described as feminism, or as a complex deal in which Gama gained practical benefits in return for formal deference?[44]

Stacey's book is best read as a reminder that working-class women have good reasons for what they do, and that (like all women) they negotiate complex and shifting relationships both with traditional gender ideals and with feminism. To the (significant) extent that Archie Bunker was a caricature designed to make working-class people look silly, the stereotype deserves to die. But feminists should not overlook the fact that working-class women have some very good reasons to feel the continued allure of domesticity.

Traditionalism among working-class men is equally persistent, for reasons that are astutely explored by Karen Pyke in her analysis of "class-based masculinities." Pyke points out that the dominant masculinity of white, heterosexual, middle- or upper-class men who make good salaries and occupy "order-giving positions" differentiates them not only from women but from lower-status men whose "masculinity and self-esteem [are] undermined by their subordinate order-taking position in relation to the higher-status males." Whereas the careers and good salaries of high-status males typically are sufficient to establish their authority at home, lower-status men "must either concede power to wives or maintain dominance by some other means." Pyke argues that the traditionalism of lower-status men reflects the fact that, lacking "career success," they must establish their authority through less subtle means. She documents both higher levels of domestic violence in the marriages of lower-status men and more direct and explicit demands for submissiveness and/or rigid gendered divisions of labor. "In the absence of legitimated hierarchical advantages, lower-class husbands are more likely to produce hypermasculinity by relying on blatant, brutal, and relentless power strategies in their marriages, including spousal abuse. In doing so, they compensate for their demeaned status, pump up their sense of self-worth and control, and simulate the uncontested privileges of higher-class men."[45]

The studies by Rubin, Rosen, Sigel, and Pyke suggest an important conclusion: *Domesticity is a system that ties gender performance inextricably to class status.* Because working-class people have a particular relationship to gender ideals, and because gender ideals serve in significant part to differentiate among classes, analyzing gender without simultaneously considering class makes no sense. Despite this, many feminists rarely speak of the linkage of gender and class. Law students in my feminist jurisprudence class have told me that after four years of majoring in women's studies, the first mention they ever heard of working-class women was in my classroom.

HOW THE FULL-COMMODIFICATION MODEL TURNED A GENDER PROBLEM INTO A RACE PROBLEM

> There are so many roots to the tree of anger
> that sometimes the branches shatter
> before they bear.
>
> Sitting in Nedicks
> the women rally before they march
> discussing the problematic girls
> they hire to make them free.[46]

In sharp contrast to the dearth of feminist analysis of the ways gender is experienced differently by people of different classes, a deep and rich literature exists on gender and race. It documents how racial hierarchy affects the ways women of color experience gender. Some of these differences stem from the fact that a higher proportion of people of color are poor or working-class; those differences are reflected in the prior discussion of class. This section focuses on differences attributable to race and ethnicity. The primary focus is on African-Americans because that literature is so richly developed; some of its analysis applies to other communities of color as well. The literatures on Latinas and Asian-Americans are developing so rapidly that we will soon be in a position to examine in detail the similarities and differences among communities of color.

A delicate situation exists whenever a white woman describes the experience of traditionally subordinated groups. One response is "No—absolutely not—white women should not write about black women or any other group of non-white women."[47] While the risks are great, the project of constructing coalitions for gender change requires a working description of the traditions of people of color. The following is offered in that spirit.

A Heritage of Anger Against White Privilege: Women of Color and Market Child Care

> [E]very time the housewife or working woman buys freedom for herself with a domestic, that very same freedom is denied to the domestic, for the maid must go home and do her own housework.[48]

Feminists of color have criticized Friedan and others for their emphasis "on the professional careers of those women who are already economically privileged and college educated." A highly developed body of work explores the way the full-commodification strategy alleviates white women's gender disenfranchisement by using their privileged class and race position.

> [D]omestic labor may be subordinating to [white middle-class women] as women, but if they hire others to do it (mostly Black, Latina, or Asian women), domestic labor becomes (low) paid work—thus gender subordination becomes gender, class, and race subordination.[49]

Reproductive labor divides along racial as well as gender lines. During the great period of immigration in the nineteenth century, large numbers of foreign women worked as domestic servants, many of them Irish at a time when Irish were not considered white. For a long period after slavery, domestic work was one of the few jobs open to black women. In the South, black women were coerced into performing domestic work when they resisted it. Even as late as 1940, 60 percent of all African-American women workers were domestic servants (and many more were laundresses). The percentage fell to about 25 percent in 1967, and 8 percent in 1980.[50]

Many black women escaped domestic work as soon as alternative jobs opened up to them. Said the owner of one domestic service agency, "I never get any American black women. I once asked a friend of mine who's black and she said that her mother did that already. American black people have been slaves and domestics for years. And after they scrub somebody's floor, they get up saying, 'My child will never do this.'" "I worked hard to serve God and to see that my three girls didn't have to serve nobody else like I did except God," said a former domestic worker. "My girl's in an office, and the baby—my son—over twenty years in the Army. I get full thinking about it. I had it bad, but look at them." Despite the steady flow of African-American women out of domestic work, they are still more likely to work in domestic service than are women of any other group.[51]

Latinas are also heavily represented in household work. A 1995 study found that more than three-fourths of the domestic workers in Los Angeles, and half of those in New York, were not U.S. citizens. "[I]n other words," says Mary Romero, "hire a woman of color and pay her as little as possible to fulfill your housework duties and responsibilities. . . . [M]iddle-class American women aim to 'liberate' themselves by exploiting women of color—particularly immigrants—in the underground economy, for long hours at relatively low wages, with no benefits."[52]

No doubt exists that domestic workers often are paid low salaries for long hours. "Maids" in the nineteenth and early twentieth centuries were expected to work six and a half days a week for twelve or fourteen hours a day; even today, a sixty-hour week is common for live-in nannies. Live-in workers in particular find their employers' families a "greedy institution"; historian Elizabeth Clark-Lewis documents the struggle of black domestics in Washington, D.C., to shift from live-in to day work in order to gain autonomy, control over their hours of work, and the ability to care for their own families. Contemporary commentators note the irony: Live-in domestics have to leave their own children, often in less-than-ideal conditions, to care for the families of their employers. This pattern is particularly common among immigrant women.[53]

Domestic workers not only work long hours; most receive low wages as well. When my mother paid $40 a week in the 1950s, another neighborhood lady got into her car one day at carpool time and told her that "she was spoiling it for everyone else." The pattern of low wages continues to the present day; the low wages paid to child-care workers were discussed in chapter 2.[54]

In short, the full-commodification model has often meant that white women hire women of color to do their domestic work in exploitative employment relationships.[55] Evelyn Nakano Glenn concludes, "Domestic service has played a critical role in the distinct oppression of women of color. White middle-class women benefitted from the exploitation of women of color." In this cultural context, a shift away from the full-commodification model to a model whose aim is to give all workers time for family work takes one step toward defusing the racial anger that surrounds domestic work.

Exclusion from Domesticity as an Expression of Racial Hierarchy:
The Distinct Meanings of Family, Work, and Domesticity Among People of Color

> I presume there are no class of people in the United States who so highly
> appreciate the legality of marriage as those persons who have been held
> and treated as property.[56]

A second step toward defusing the racial anger surrounding the full-commodification model is to recognize that marriage and domesticity have different meanings in different communities. One way of expressing racial hierarchy in the
United States has been to cut people of color off both from marriage and from domesticity's gender ideals. Under slavery, black men were acutely aware that they
were deprived of the basic perquisites of conventional masculinity, including the
right to protect and provide for their families. The ideals of southern womanhood
also excluded black women. Whites saw those ideals as applicable only to whites;
black women were seen not as "ladies" but as mammies and jezebels. In addition,
"[t]he primary role of the slave mother, if compared with the 'mainstream' American gender convention, also was deeply compromised, for she was never able to
give the needs of her husbands and children greatest priority. Even though most
slave children were part of matrifocal families, the slave woman's most important
daily activities encompassed the labor that she performed for her owner, not for
her family."[57]

Disrespect for slaves' family ties played an important role in humiliating and de-
moralizing them, as Peggy Davis has documented with force and eloquence. Slave
marriages had no legal status, leaving owners free to sell their slaves in disregard of
kinship bonds. The best evidence available suggests that "about one in six (or
seven) slave marriages ended by force or sale." Slavemasters did not respect
parental bonds either. Sale of slave children away from their families was common.
Davis quotes one observer who "recalled children who instinctively clung to their
mother's neck at any sign of unusual activity" for fear of being sold. According to
Davis, "[M]arriage—together with desertion of the plantation system and armed
struggle against Confederate slaveholders—was the most dramatic and powerful
means by which former slaves laid claim to citizenship." "When the institution of
slavery began to crumble, former slaves seized the right to marry enthusiastically
not only for its private but also for its social meaning."[58]

Slaves also laid claims to domesticity's sex roles, which were considered integral to civilized living. Male slaves regarded many domestic tasks as unsuitable or
degrading. Those living "abroad" (on plantations other than the ones where their
wives lived) brought their laundry home: "Saturday night, the roads were . . . filled
with men on their way to the 'wife house,' each pedestrian or horseman bearing his
bag of soiled clothes." When masters required male slaves to do laundry or other
domestic tasks, it was to punish or humiliate them.[59]

Blacks' exclusion from gender ideals was compounded by the practical costs of
wives' inability to work for their own families. Note that the work slave women

did for their own families was the only work not expropriated by their masters. In this context, family work took on a special meaning: "They did it because they wanted to. They were working for themselves then," said one slave. They were also working for their families in a context where masters appropriated so much of slaves' time that children suffered.

> On many plantations women did not have enough time to prepare break-
> fast in the morning and were generally too tired to make much of a meal or
> to give much attention to their children after a long day's labor. . . . Fed ir-
> regularly or improperly, young black children suffered from a variety of ills.

A contemporary observer reported that the number of children was low on the plantations he was familiar with because "[t]he mothers had no time to take care of them—and they . . . [were] often found dead in the field and in the quarter for want of care of their mothers."[60]

Because one of the key expressions of white supremacy, from slavery until today, is the assault on the black family, African-Americans have often seen the preservation of family life as a deeply important political goal. Peggy Davis, relying heavily on the stories from slavery, has argued recently that preservation of family life is so important that it deserves constitutional status.[61]

In view of the symbolic and material dimensions of slaves' exclusion from domesticity and stable family life, it is hardly surprising that once slavery was abolished, freedmen not only married but also placed a high priority on withdrawing wives from field work. "Where the Negro works for wages, he tries to keep his wife at home," noted a contemporary observer. Said another, "Until colored men attain to a position above permitting their mothers, sisters, wives, and daughters to do the drudgery of . . . other men's wives and daughters, it is useless, it is non-sense . . . to talk about equality and elevation in society." Former masters belittled freedmen's attempts to claim for black women a "true womanhood," which whites saw as appropriate only for white women; in other words, gender remained a battleground in the struggle over whether blacks were full people. One of the reasons planters tolerated sharecropping was that it was the only way they could tap the labor of free women and children. Said a sharecropper named Ned Cobb: "I was a poor colored man but I didn't want my wife in the field like a dog."[62]

Although black women worked outside the home in much higher proportions than did white women until very recently, "the majority of wage-earning women, especially mothers and wives, usually did not believe that their presence or their position in the labor force was an accurate reflection of who they were or of how they should be viewed by members of the black community." In her study of blacks in Washington, D.C., Sharon Harley found that "[f]or a group of people one generation out of slavery, gender-defined work and domestic responsibilities were symbolic of their new status." "The race needs wives who stay at home, being supported by their husbands, and then they can spend time in the training of their children." While most black mothers were in the labor force, "this did not preclude members of the black community from articulating what they believed was the ideal role for black married women." "Black women wanted to withdraw from the labor force," concluded Patricia Hill Collins, "not to duplicate middle-class white women's cult of domesticity but, rather, to strengthen the political and economic position of their families." In sharp contrast to white feminist imagery of the family as the "gender factory" that represents a key source of women's disempowerment, the family is often seen by blacks as well as by working-class whites as a haven in a harsh and unyielding world: "[B]lack women see their unpaid domestic work more as a form of resistance to oppression than as a form of exploitation by men." In this context, the work of mothering can take on a marked political dimension, simultaneously protecting children from the racism they might otherwise meet in market child care, and offering mothers the opportunity to train their children to deal with racism. This sense persists up into the present. In Elsa Barkley Brown's memoir she remembers her college-educated mother's decision to stay home with her children as "an act of resistance."[63]

In part this reflects black homemakers' tradition of working for "the betterment of the race." As did white women during the nineteenth century, black women often turned their domestic roles into social activism. "All during my college course I had dreamed of the day when I could promote the welfare of my race," said Mary Church Terrell in 1940; she taught school and worked for the District of Columbia's school system beginning in 1887. Said one contemporary commentator, "Community workers got involved 'through my kids.' It is in their roles as the principal caretakers of children that racial-ethnic women pose the largest threat to the dominant society." This pattern persisted into the 1970s, when Lois Davis, "at home" with two children ages one and four, helped lead the effort to desegregate the Montgomery County, Maryland, public schools. "Her racial vision of domesticity as political space entailed a shift from the work of earlier club women in two ways. First, she was united with white women, while the earlier club women worked in all-black groups. Women of her generation also had a feminist consciousness that earlier generations lacked: many of them worked with the La Leche League as well," notes her daughter Adrienne Davis, now a law professor.[64]

The different meanings of marriage and family work persist in a social context in which marriage remains much more accessible to whites than blacks. Fewer than 75 percent of black women can expect to marry sometime in their lives, compared to 90 percent of white women. The black divorce rate has soared as well. Both factors no doubt feed the sense that marriage and family need to be nurtured, not attacked. In addition, contemporary sociological data suggest that middle-class and working-class black women have significantly more "traditional" outlooks than do same-class whites. "African-Americans believe very strongly that it is still the man's responsibility to provide, far more so than white men or women."[65]

White women's failure to understand the distinct meanings of domesticity and family work in different racial contexts has created conflicts since the beginning of the second wave of feminism in the late 1960s. Rayna Rapp's description of a typical feminist meeting in that period captures the pattern of conflict:

Many of us have been at an archetypical meeting in which someone stands up and asserts that the nuclear family ought to be abolished because it is degrading and constraining to women. Usually, someone else (often representing a third world position) follows on her heels, pointing out that the attack on the family represents a white middle-class position and that other women need their families for support and survival.

Many African-American women do not share white feminists' assumptions either about the oppressiveness of the family or about the homemaker role. bell hooks writes:

Contemporary feminist analyses of family often implied that a successful feminist movement would either begin with or lead to the abolition of family. This suggestion was terribly threatening to many women, especially non-white women. While there are white women activists who may experience family primarily as an oppressive institution (it may be the social structure wherein they have experienced grave abuse and exploitation), many black women find the family the least oppressive institution. . . . We wish to affirm the primacy of family life because we know that family ties are the only sustained support system for exploited and oppressed peoples.

Deborah King agrees: "Many of the conditions that middle-class, white feminists have found oppressive are perceived as privileges by black women, especially those with low incomes. For instance, the option not to work outside of the home is a luxury that historically has been denied to black women. The desire to struggle for this option can, in such a context, represent a feminist position, precisely because it constitutes an instance of greater liberty for certain women." The "attributes of the white women's status currently criticized by many feminists as examples of sexism," adds Elizabeth Clark-Smith, "were seen (and are still seen) by many black women as representative of the unique privileges of women of the dominant group."[66]

While other people of color have not been as rigorously excluded from gender ideals as blacks, their sense of the importance of family nonetheless reflects attitudes more similar to blacks' than to whites'. For Latino/as, "the family is by far the single most important unit in life. . . . It is the basic source of emotional gratification and support."[67] The reluctance of Latinas to delegate child care outside the family (except to fictive-kin *comadres*) stems from the traditional Latin focus on family life as well as strong traditions that "cast employment as oppositional to mothering. The reluctance to use market care may reflect the high cost of market care for big families, since some groups of Latino/as have higher-than-average birth rates. One study of Chicana families found that over 70 percent used relatives to care for children while mothers worked. In addition, more Latinos than other men express disapproval of married women earning money, even after age, education, income, and marital status are taken into account. One study of Chicano/as found strong support for domestic mothers and provider fathers. Perhaps as a consequence, fewer Latina mothers are in the labor force than are either black or white mothers, although labor force participation differs among different groups of Latinas. Differences among Asian-Americans exist as well, although as a group they tend to have fairly high rates of labor force participation.[68]

In both Latina and Asian cultures, male dominance is tied to custom and religion rather than to the provider role. "Within Asian communities, the Asian family (especially the immigrant one) is characterized by a hierarchy of authority based on sex, age, and generation, with young women at the lowest level, subordinate to father-husband-brother-son." Rubin found that Asian and Latino men "generally participate least in the work of the household and are the least likely to believe they have much responsibility beyond bringing home a paycheck." Men who live in ethnic neighborhoods, Rubin notes, "find strong support for clinging to the old ways." Families who assimilate into the larger society are more like other Americans of the same social class. Recent data suggest that men in Latina families, like other American men, are under pressure to increase their level of contribution to family work, as are men in Korean immigrant families. Research among Korean immigrants suggests that the view that wives are responsible for family work persists long after the belief that men lose face if they do "women's work" has been discarded. In an era when half of all Asian-Americans are foreign-born, the old ways retain considerable influence.[69]

Racial Anger as a Fact of Feminist Coalition Building

Gender in communities of color is different from gender as lived and imagined among whites. The full-commodification model ignores this in ways that trigger racial divides. First, the strategy of having women perform as ideal workers while child care is delegated to the market in effect has meant delegating devalued and underpaid work to women of color. Second, because of the distinct significance of domesticity and family work in the black community, the full-commodification model's devaluation of domesticity and family work often does not resonate among African-Americans. This is also true among Latina/os and perhaps many Asian-Americans as well.

White feminists need to be attuned to the ways that assumptions that embed class and race privilege can alienate potential allies. A tone of respect for family and for domesticity are important in a social context where gender ideals and the denial of family life have been key elements of a system of class and race oppression.

A shift to new feminist strategies will not completely defuse tensions that stem from racial privilege. Such tensions emerge both in the literature on domestic workers and in the literature on feminism. White feminists intent on building interracial coalitions need to be capable of dealing with the racial anger that often emerges in such coalitions. In a country where "[w]hite women did less demanding work at home and secured better jobs in the labor market," such anger is a fact of life in feminist coalition building.[70] The conclusion to this chapter suggests some ways to transform anger against racial hierarchy into a force *for* gender change rather than a force that undercuts it.

THEMES OF EQUALITY AND ANGER AGAINST MEN

> We identify the agents of our oppression as men. Male supremacy is the oldest, most basic form of domination. All other forms of exploitation and oppression (racism, capitalism, imperialism, etc.) are extensions of male supremacy.[71]

> Anti-male sentiments alienated many poor and working-class women, particularly non-white women, from the feminist movement. Their life experiences had shown them that they have more in common with men of their race and/or class group than bourgeois white women.[72]

The distinct social location of nonprivileged women not only creates different relationships with domesticity but also creates different relationships with feminism. The literatures on class and race rarely meet, but when they are read together some parallel points emerge about both groups' relationships to feminism. I will first discuss the class literature and then the literature on race.

Every recent study has noted the complexity of working-class women's relationship with feminism; what they *say* about feminism, notes Lillian Rubin, is different from what they *do* about it. General agreement exists that most working-class women are reluctant to identify themselves as feminists. One study found that 73 percent of working-class women did not embrace feminism. A 1998 survey found that "education more than anything else determines whether a woman defines herself as a feminist"; again, education tracks class position. The same survey found that 53 percent of college-educated white women living in cities self-identify as feminists in a country where only about 28 percent of all women do.[73]

The temptation is to dismiss this, given that most women support many of feminism's traditional proposals. It would be a mistake to do so. Lillian Rubin astutely explains the complexity of working-class women's relationships with feminism. She quotes Maria Acosta, a white twenty-eight-year-old secretary: "I'm a firm believer in making your man feel like a king." Yet Acosta rejected the example of her mother, who "waits on my father all the time," and claims an entitlement to reciprocal "care" from her husband. Yet Acosta notes as well the very practical limitations imposed on women who deal with men: "The problem is that men need to feel important, so if you want to live with them. . . ."[74] Rubin notes Acosta's pain at acknowledging "the distance between what her life is and what she'd like it to be." Roberta Sigel concludes that working-class women mute their demands for equality because "they feel they have too much invested in [the survival of their marriages] to insist on the genuine equality to which they feel entitled." Rosen agrees, arguing that working-class women fear that demands for equality may threaten family stability in a context where divorce can lead to grinding poverty.[75]

Rubin sees working-class women's distancing themselves from feminism as

> their way of making a public statement that they're "real" women—soft, nurturing, caring; their way of trying to reassure themselves about their

femininity, about their capacity to be good wives and mothers; and their attempt to appease the hostility of their husbands. And this, too, is their gift to their husbands—a gift to compensate for the men's pain, for the knowledge both husbands and wives carry inside about the fragility of their lives and their families; a gift that seeks to ease the men's anxiety about their manhood by allowing them to believe they retain the power to define what a woman ought to be.

The men sigh with relief. "These goddamn feminists and their crazy ideas, they're making women nuts today," says Acosta's husband, Joe. "Don't get me wrong, Maria's not one of them, no way. She knows who wears the pants, not like those, excuse me, ball-busting feminists." Rubin heard similar sentiments from three-quarters of the working-class husbands she met. Perhaps the most dramatic instance of women embracing patriarchal language as a gift to their husbands is Judith Stacey's description of Pamela Gama, discussed above, who became a born-again Christian and embraced the traditional notion that the husband is the head of the household even as she used Christian language to gain concessions from her husband. Evidently she felt she could gain more in terms of the concrete conditions of her everyday life by giving her husband (at least outwardly) the deference his father's generation had enjoyed.[76]

Middle-class feminists need to recognize that one of the reasons they feel so free to attack "their" men is that the men hold such a powerful social position. To women whose men are walking wounded, open rifts may appear disloyal and unseemly. "Many blue-collar wives recognize that their husbands' sense of manhood is contingent on their shared belief they are supporting their families." With the demise of the family wage, working-class women often eschew (open) feminism in favor of "gifts" to assuage egos bruised by the injuries of class. In this context, feminism's traditional language of anger toward men can trigger a circle-the-wagons response by working-class women of all hues.[77]

The relationship women of color have with feminism is further complicated by the use of gender ideals as instruments of racial oppression. "[T]he call to be 'treated like a man' is based on extending to men of color the full 'rights' of manhood in the United States." From this perspective, the full-commodification model is seen as the decision by privileged white women to remedy their own relative deprivation in relation to privileged white men by taking advantage of white women's position in the racial hierarchy. As a result, many blacks see feminism as a fight between white men and white women that ultimately leaves them out. This is not to discount the rich tradition of African-American feminism, from Angela Davis to bell hooks to Alice Walker to Audre Lorde; black women's relationships to gender and to feminism are complex. But anyone seeking to build a broad feminist coalition needs to be aware of the dominant strains in the black community.[78]

White women need to remember that black women often relate to them not so much as women but as whites: "To a black woman the issue is not whether white women are more or less racist than white men, but that they are racist." Moreover, when men of color are stripped of the privileges of masculinity, "women of color are caught between the need to assert their equality and the desire to restore the prerogatives of masculinity to their men." Notes bell hooks:

> Currently, they know that many males in their social groups are exploited and oppressed. . . . While they are aware that sexism enables men in their respective groups to have privileges denied them, they are more likely to see exaggerated expressions of male chauvinism among their peers as stemming from the male's sense of himself as powerless and ineffectual in relation to ruling male groups, rather than an expression of an overall priv-ileged social status.

A poor or working-class man, particularly one of color, is "constantly concerned about the contradiction between the notion of masculinity he was taught and his inability to live up to that notion. He is usually 'hurt,' emotionally scarred because he does not have the privilege or power society has taught him 'real men' should possess." Such men, hooks continues, "know the sufferings and hardships women face in their communities: they also know the sufferings and hardships men face and they have compassion for them. They have the experience of struggling with them for a better life." Black women in particular are well aware that black men have often been cut off from steady work and that black men's labor market posi-tion has sharply deteriorated since 1970, more so than that of white men. Hispanic and Asian-American men also have experienced a long tradition of workplace dis-crimination. In this cultural context, a call by white women to challenge "men's" access to market work may be read as envy and anger on the part of one privileged group, white women, against an even more privileged group, white men, for deny-ing them an equal share in class and race privilege."[79]

"As long as racism limits opportunities for black men, black women will contin-ue to express some ambivalence about competing with black men inside the black community and will also strive to avoid direct confrontation and overt conflict." It should not be overlooked that a strong and articulate movement of African-Ameri-can feminists now challenges a tradition where demands for civil rights are often translated into calls for civil rights of black men. But when feminists of color de-mand equality, they often articulate those demands somewhat differently than do white feminists, avoiding the language of anger against men. As bell hooks astutely points out, feminist goals can be pursued in terms that bring men into alliance with women: "Men *do* oppress women. People *are* hurt by rigid sex role patterns. These two realities co-exist." hooks proposes new feminist strategies designed to keep both in focus. They would teach men not "to equate violent abuse of women with privilege" at the same time that they show men the potential benefits of being re-leased from the oppressive aspects of the male role, notably the cultural mandate to be the provider, which today is inaccessible to poor and working-class men.[80]

This analysis holds the promise of a challenge to traditional male privileges with-out triggering charges of sowing discord within the black community. White women have often failed to recognize that a coalition based on gender requires delicate interracial negotiations in which minority women may well be wary of publicly criticizing in interracial contexts actions they would not hesitate to challenge in private. This hesitance in part reflects healthy racial solidarity: "Racial solidarity has been a fundamental element of black women's resistance to domination." In part, however, it reflects pressures from within the black community to identify what is good for "the race" in terms of what is good for black men. Asked a recent newspaper article, "Cannot black women remain seriously concerned about the brutal effect of racist domination on black men and also denounce black male sexism?" Black feminists are increasingly arguing that "[b]lack liberation struggles must be re-visioned so that they are no longer equated with maleness." Other feminists of color agree, from Michelle Wallace, Toni Morrison, and Alice Walker to Kimberlé Crenshaw and bell hooks.[81]

Not only African-American but also Latina and Asian-American feminists regularly get "criticized for weakening male ego and group solidarity." Notes one commentator, "[F]or Chicanas to challenge Chicano male privilege renders them susceptible to the charge that they are acting 'like white women'—an act of betrayal to *la cultura*." Chicana feminists have been attacked for developing a "divisive ideology." Asian-American women have had similar experiences.

> Asian-American women are criticized for the possible consequences of their protests: weakening the male ego, dilution of effort and resources in Asian-American communities, destruction of working relationships between Asian men and women, setbacks for the Asian-American cause, co-optation into the larger society, and eventual loss of ethnic identity for Asian-Americans as a whole. In short, affiliation with the feminist movement is perceived as a threat to solidarity within their own community.[82]

In summary, not only do women of color have different relationships with the key gender axes of domesticity; they also have different relationships with feminism. As will be further discussed in chapter 8, reconstructive feminism avoids the language of anger against men in contexts where such language will interfere with the process of building coalitions for gender change.

CONCLUSION: IMPLEMENTING ANTIESSENTIALISM

> Black women's conceptions of womanhood emphasize self-reliance, strength, resourcefulness, autonomy, and the responsibility of providing for the material as well as emotional needs of family members. Black women do not see participation in the labor force and being a wife and mother as mutually exclusive; rather, within Black culture, employment is an integral, normative, and traditional component of the roles of wife and mother.[83]

For the last decade or more, feminists have been faced with protests that their agenda is shaped around the worldview of privileged white women. This tradition of protest against an agenda shaped by "essential" women is called antiessentialism. Catharine

MacKinnon and others have protested that antiessentialism has hurt feminism. Other prominent feminists, notably Martha Fineman, Christine Littleton, and Robin West, have protested that women *are*, in fact, bound together by their gendered experiences despite race, class, and other differences. Fineman asserts that women have "a common gendered-life reference point that unites them in interest and urgency around certain shared cultural and social experiences." "Therefore, if women collectively have different actual and potential experiences from men, they are likely to have different perspectives—and different sets of values, beliefs, and concerns as a group."[84]

Most women do have different experiences than most men, but this does not mean that women are bound together by gender. In fact, as this chapter has stressed, women's experience of gender divides them as much as it unites them. They are divided as individuals by the different deals they strike with the gender pressures upon them. Thus, a focus on "women collectively" leaves out women who construct gender identities that run counter to the traditions of femininity: women who perform as ideal workers and have little interest or sympathy with the plight of women marginalized by motherhood. The intense gender pressures on women to embrace motherhood as traditionally defined often cause women who resist to condemn the traditional feminine life pattern with more fervor than do men. An example is when women professionals without children condemn their colleagues who fail to return to work after childbirth on the grounds that they are "hurting everyone" by reinforcing traditionalist stereotypes.

Women are divided not only by the different life paths they choose; even women who share classically female experiences interpret those experiences very differently. As Angela Harris pointed out long ago, different groups of women may react differently even to quintessentially female experiences such as being raped.[85] This chapter makes a similar point. Even women united by the *experience* of family formation and motherhood may *interpret* that experience differently, in ways that have important implications for coalition building. The descriptions presented above, while no doubt imperfect, are meant to specify how gender is lived and imagined differently in different communities.

New language proves useful to capture this important axiom. If one imagines gender as a force field pulling men and women back into domesticity's "traditional" roles, the force field differs depending on one's placement in other fields of social power. To privileged white women, as noted above, gender often seems the only force pulling them down, jeopardizing their access to power and privilege. Among less privileged people, as discussed above, women may experience the housewife role not as dragging women away from their goals in life but as offering a refuge from the bad jobs and poor-quality child care that would otherwise be their fate due to their class and race position. The housewife role is experienced differently because of the intersecting force fields of race and class. If gender is a force field, the configuration of the force depends on the interactions between gender and other fields of social power.[86]

When white feminists (typically behind closed doors) protest that antiessentialism has undercut feminism, they miss a central point. The problem is not that antiessentialism eroded coalitions that *used to exist*, but that certain coalitions that white feminists *thought* existed never did. Both working-class women and women of color have had many hesitations about joining up. If feminists want to build broad gender coalitions, they need to change their strategies to take account of complex interrelationships of gender, race, and class.

A shift away from the full-commodification model to a strategy of reconstruct- ing the relationship of market work and family work can help defuse gender, class, and race conflicts in a number of ways. Most important is that, instead of focusing on gaining access for women to the kind of meaningful work generally available only to the privileged, the proposals in part I aim to *democratize access to domesticity*. A restructuring of market work will give to working-class women and women of color greater access to the parental care that remains a widespread social ideal.

Feminists need not to decry domesticity but to use it as a weapon, to argue that if we truly value caregiving, we should restructure market work to end the mar- ginalization of caregivers. This strategy should appeal equally to ideal-worker women who feel they need more time for family life or other goals, and to margin- alized caregivers who feel their family work is undervalued. It should also appeal to working-class women. While the full-commodification strategy reflected priv- ileged women's attitudes toward market work, domesticity, market child care, and family work, reconstructive feminism maintains a tone of respect for family and for domesticity, and holds the promise of allowing nonprivileged people as well as privileged ones more flexibility to care for their own children without jeopardiz- ing their position at work. (This is not to say that parents don't still need high- quality, low-cost child care for the time they are at work.)

A shift away from the full-commodification model also may help defuse the her- itage of racial anger surrounding work and family issues in the black community. Helpful in this context are its avoidance of the language of anger against men, its tone of respect for family life and for domesticity, and its proposal to democratize domesticity.

Yet it is unrealistic to expect this heritage of anger to disappear. One means of avoiding it is for feminists to turn to communities of color for alternative models of masculinity, femininity, and family life. The black community in particular provides rich lodes of tradition that offer important cultural resources. One is its imagery of motherhood. A strong tradition in the black community sees market work as an in- tegral part of motherhood rather than as inconsistent with it. This tradition is not uncontested; as discussed above, domesticity's imagery of mothers at home also holds considerable sway. But black mothers often have had to operate in less-than- perfect conditions that generated ideals of community responsibility for child rear- ing: "African-American mothers can draw upon an Afrocentric tradition where motherhood of varying types, whether bloodmother, othermother, or community othermother, can be invoked as symbols of power." Notions of "kin-scription" and other forms of community responsibility for children contrasts with the peculiarly Euro-American insistence that child rearing is a private matter that does not involve community support. The sense that "it takes a community to raise a child" is in sharp contrast to the dominant white tradition in the United States, which takes a more privatized view of child rearing than do most other communities in the world. (As discussed in chapter 6, this peculiarly American viewpoint is not shared by most Europeans.) Recent books by Marion Wright Edelman and Cornel West (co-authored with a European) show that many of the most important voices calling for more community support for child rearing are African-American.[87]

Another resource from the black tradition is the sense that family work is important political work. This stands in sharp contrast with the dominant white tradition, which tends to belittle family work as part of the just-a-housewife syndrome. Related to this is the usage that distinguishes between someone's biological father and his "daddy." Being someone's daddy means that a man has played the social role of male child rearer, a tradition that stresses that biological ties do not exhaust men's role in child rearing. In addition, imagery of mothers as strong and capable women ("My mother was much of a woman") contrasts with the dominant imagery of mothers as selfless and self-effacing ("My mother was a saint"). Moreover, African-American traditions contain precious imagery of "independent, self-reliant, strong, and autonomous" women who are not so much feminine as womanly. This imagery provides important resources for reconstructing not only motherhood but womanhood more generally: "[a] new definition of femininity for *all* American women."[88]

The black community also offers resources for reimagining the middle-class family. Because of the difficulty black men have experienced in getting jobs, a much smaller disparity exists between the wages of men and women in black families than in white ones. Whereas in white middle-class families the husband typically earns about 70 percent of the family income while the wife earns only about thirty percent, in black middle-class families the contributions are considerably more equal: the husband earns roughly 60 percent while the wife earns roughly 40 percent. Another, related pattern is that black married fathers contribute more to family work than do white married fathers. In short, despite domesticity's hold, the black community offers counterhegemonic gender imagery that provides important cultural resources.[89]

This focus on the cultural resources of the black community reflects the strategy of using new gendered ideals to displace old ones. This strategy holds far more promise for achieving gender flux than the traditional white feminist antidote to the disempowerment associated with femininity: androgyny. The classic statement is Carolyn Heilbrun's, originally published in 1974.

> The ideal toward which I believe we should move is best described by the term "androgyny." This ancient Greek word—from *andro* (male) and *gyn* (female)—defines a condition under which the characteristics of the sexes, and the human impulses expressed by men and women, are not rigidly assigned. Androgyny seeks to liberate the individual from the confines of the appropriate.

Heilbrun, in a way common at that period, cites as evidence of the desirability of androgyny that creative men score high on scales of femininity, and that in a graph showing the frequency distribution of athletic ability, a wide intermediate range will include both boys and girls despite the fact that the top of the distribution will be all-male.[90]

One way to react to these studies is to seek a world (to quote a famous article by Richard Wasserstrom) in which sex is as unimportant as eye color. But the project of unloading meaning from sex seems unrealistic, for two reasons. The first is that sex is an insistent social marker: We live in a world where most people feel awkward if they don't know whether you are a he or a she. A world where sex was as unimportant as eye color, many people feel, would leave them literally speechless. (The alternative of inventing a new language, which holds considerable appeal for intellectuals, probably holds little appeal for most others.)[91]

Not only would a genderless world leave people speechless in the literal sense, it would leave them bereft in other ways as well. As will be discussed in more detail in chapter 6, most people rely on gender performances to structure feelings they experience as pressing concerns; the role of gender performance in sexual arousal is the most obvious. The reliance on gender to structure emotion, arousal, and speech means that linking liberation to the project of downloading meanings of sex makes gender flux seem simultaneously alarming and implausible. An alternative is to seek not androgyny but a widening of the accepted range of masculinities and femininities. In this context, an appreciation of the different ways gender is lived and experienced in different communities becomes an important resource for enriching our imaginations for the future.

Once feminists reframe their language and their strategies to avoid the kind of gender, race, and class wars sketched in this chapter, they can begin to sustain a focus on deconstructing the masculine norms that all feminists oppose. But first feminists need to change the ways they talk about femininity. This is the subject of chapter 6.

•

CHAPTER SIX

Do Women Share an Ethic of Care?: Domesticity's Descriptions of Men and Women

"Despite my best efforts, you're still the man and I'm still the woman."

One day a little boy went to school wearing pink barrettes. The other boys confronted him. "You're a girl," they said, "you have pink barrettes." He protested he was a boy, to no avail. Finally he pulled down his pants and showed them his penis. They were unimpressed. "Everybody has one of those," they said. "You're still a girl. Only girls wear pink barrettes."

This chapter and the next analyze a series of patterned conflicts within feminism called the sameness/difference debate. The way to defuse those conflicts, I argue, is to recognize them as disagreements over women's relationship to domesticity: as conflicts not about penises but about pink barrettes. The first step is to recognize that the sameness/difference debate is in fact two distinct debates: one about the *ideology* of domesticity, the other about its *practice*. This chapter first distinguishes these two debates. It then focuses on the debate over the ideology of domesticity and the claim that women have a different voice, or culture.

Everyday conversation echoes the issues discussed in this chapter. "You give a boy a Barbie, he just uses it for a gun." "I used to think boys and girls were the same, but now I know better." "I never would have believed it, but boys and girls really are different. Boys just naturally gravitate toward trucks." A Y-linked truck gene? People never quite get this far in a vernacular discourse in which people commonly fail to distinguish between biology and domesticity's norms of gender performance. Thus the cartoon printed on page 177 identifies the ideal-worker/marginalized-caregiver dyad as the biological fate of men and women. Is it biology that makes this woman responsible for all the housework and child care while the man leisurely reads a newspaper?

The goal of this chapter is to change both vernacular and professional gender talk by charting a new relationship to the ideology of domesticity. I examine the striking parallels between the descriptions of women by cultural feminists and those in vernacular texts such as John Gray's *Men Are from Mars, Women Are from Venus*. Both track domesticity's description of men focused on achievement and autonomy and women focused on an ethic of care. The key problem with this form of gender talk is that it embraces domesticity's description and calls it the voice of women. This creates conflict among women based on their relationship to conventional femininity, between *femmes*, attracted to feminism by its promise to revalue the traits and roles domesticity associates with femininity, and *tomboys*, attracted by feminism's promise to deliver them from domesticity's prescriptions. The chapter explores how to neutralize these conflicts, outlining new strategies and patterns of gender talk that hold the promise of avoiding gender wars and refocusing both femmes and tomboys on the masculine norms all feminists oppose.

DISTINGUISHING THE TWO BRANCHES OF
THE SAMENESS/DIFFERENCE DEBATE

> Carol Gilligan's delineation of women's moral reasoning in *In a Different Voice* resonates strongly with the intuitions of vast numbers of people.[1]

The standard description of the sameness/difference debate conflates two distinct issues: whether men and women are "really" the same or different (the different-voice debate) and whether men and women should be treated the same or different in the policy arena (the special-treatment debate).* The different-voice debate involves not practices but ideology: domesticity's "system of perception and appreciation of practices," notably its linkage of women with an ethic of care. The

---

*I use the term "special treatment" only as a historical artifact. As the discussion in the text makes clear, both sides of this debate were demanding (different visions of) equality. In chapter 7, I propose replacing the terms "equal treatment" and "special treatment" with the terms "maternalists" and "equal-parenting advocates."

special-treatment debate involves proposals to redesign our practices by redesigning our institutions.[2]

The debate over Carol Gilligan's "different voice" was the most important manifestation in feminist jurisprudence of the debate over "cultural feminism," the view that men and women belong to different cultures. Gilligan's *In a Different Voice* was published in 1982; the famous *Buffalo Law Review* "Conversation," deeply influenced by Gilligan, came out three years later. When I submitted my article "Deconstructing Gender" in 1988, an editor of a major feminist law journal told me she had never before seen an article criticizing Gilligan.[3]

The special-treatment debate peaked at roughly the same period. The initial round revolved around a California maternal-disability statute challenged in *California Federal Savings & Loan Association v. Guerra*. The special-treatment group supported the statute, which gave mothers up to four months of unpaid leave for disabilities related to birth and pregnancy. The equal-treatment group opposed it on the grounds that it did not treat men and women equally. The controversy began with a 1983 article by Linda J. Krieger and Patricia N. Cooney advocating special treatment. Wendy Williams' response came out about a year later. Martha Fineman published her first article criticizing equality in family law in 1983; her analysis was extended by Mary Becker. Lucinda Finley's 1986 "Transcending Equality Theory" and Christine Littleton's 1987 "Reconstructing Sexual Equality" are commonly considered the theoretical resolutions of the debate.[4]

The special-treatment and different-voice debates were, and still often are, lumped together. This captures the fact that many proponents of special treatment also embraced Gilligan's description of women. Ann Scales argued for both Gilligan and special treatment in her influential *Yale Law Journal* article of 1986. Lucinda Finley used the keywords of cultural feminism ("values of interconnectedness and care") in her *Columbia Law Review* article published in the same year. Though Littleton was rigorous in her avoidance of cultural feminist language when her goal was to build a coalition during the *CalFed* controversy, she embraced Gilligan's description of women once the demands of coalition building had ended.[5]

The two debates, though, are logically independent. Although many special-treatment feminists believe that women really are different, others do not. Two prominent examples are Herma Hill Kay and Sylvia Law, who argued that legislatures should be able to treat women differently from men only so long as those interventions are strictly limited to biological differences. (Note how this proposed resolution again defines the issue as one of biology.) The logical independence of these debates means that one can imagine someone who does not believe that women share an ethic of care but who does support a statute designed to give mothers pregnancy disability leave. (Indeed, I am such a person.)[6]

If the special-treatment and different-voice debates are logically independent, what links them? Both concern feminists' relationships with domesticity. As Catharine MacKinnon pointed out long ago, sameness/difference formulations represent only one way of framing the issues they address. This chapter's goal is to articulate an alternative formulation that does not simply change the subject, as did MacKinnon when she shifted the focus from work and family issues to the eroticizing of dominance.[7]

THE DIFFERENT-CULTURES HYPOTHESIS AS
AN EXPRESSION OF THE IDEOLOGY OF DOMESTICITY

Having geared themselves up to obtain the [jobs] which once were men's only, [women] discover within themselves a different scale of values.[8]

Unlike many baby boomers, driven to prove that they could juggle a full-time career and motherhood, [Cheryl] Jones, 37, made relationships her priority.[9]

The parallels between vernacular gender talk and cultural feminism are rarely noted. This section first explores those parallels and then shows how both forms of gender talk are tied to the ideology of domesticity.

When Gilligan set out to record the self-descriptions of mostly privileged women in the 1970s, what she found was domesticity alive and well in Boston. As noted in chapter 1, domesticity gendered personality to justify its role allocations; women belonged at home because of their natural focus on "gentleness, sensitivity, expressivism, altruism, empathy, personalism, and tenderness," while men belonged in the public realms of the market and politics because they are naturally competitive and instrumental. Gilligan expressed this gendering of personality in the metaphor of voice, replacing the prior metaphor that men and women have different cultures.[10]

Gilligan's informants provided self-descriptions that rely heavily on themes from domesticity. The selflessness of the "moral mother" was a central theme in the different voice Gilligan celebrated. One informant described the "moral person [as] one who helps others; goodness is service, meeting one's obligations and responsibilities to others, if possible without sacrificing oneself." Gilligan quoted subjects who referred to the influence of their mothers: "endlessly giving," "selfless," "her mother's example of hard work, patience, and self-sacrifice." Other interviews reflected the moral mother's traditional responsibility for emotion work. Gilligan reported that "interpersonal, empathetic, fellow-feeling concerns . . . have long been the center of women's moral concern." She emphasized her informants' stress on empathy and compassion, a theme she transmuted into a focus on relationships and an "ethic of care." Gilligan describes Claire, whose "ideal of care is thus an activity of relationship, of seeing and responding to need, taking care of the world by sustaining the web of connection so that no one is left alone." Eleven-year-old Amy sees Gilligan's famous Heinz dilemma as "not a math problem with humans but a narrative of relationships that extends over time." Gilligan quotes and endorses Jean Baker Miller's description that "women's sense of self becomes very much organized around being able to make, and then to maintain, affiliations and relationships."[11]

Gilligan's description clicked with many women. "I felt she was describing me," one student told me after reading Gilligan, echoing many others. Robin West claimed that every woman she knows has recognized herself in Gilligan's descriptions. While this proves that Gilligan described something that resonates within our culture, it does not prove she was describing differences in the way men and women actually behave. In seeking to reinterpret clichés and stereotypes, what Gilligan had found was women's voice in a much more literal sense.[12]

Much of what Gilligan and her followers cite as evidence of an ethic of care I see as evidence that women justify their decisions by reference to different social norms than those applicable to men. Consider the case of Denise, a Gilligan interviewee who decided to have an abortion. She felt guilty and conflicted; when she finally decided to go ahead with the abortion, she described her decision as self-sacrifice.[13]

This seems an odd choice of words. I can think of many good reasons for having an abortion, but *self-sacrifice* is not a word I would choose. For Denise, it came to mind because she lives in a culture that requires women to become mothers and requires mothers to be selfless. Domesticity intimates that women who act for themselves rather than for others are selfish, as in "selfish career woman." Women seeking abortions know some would consider their decision to abort a selfish one; they counter by arguing that their decision is more selfless than motherhood would have been. This proves less that women act pursuant to a consistent ethic of care than that conventionally gendered women are under social pressure to describe whatever they do as selfless and caring. It proves the continuing influence of the ideology of domesticity on the self-descriptions of ordinary women. The "moral equation of goodness with self-sacrifice," as Gilligan herself recognizes, is one of the conventions of femininity.[14]

What Gilligan described, as she herself acknowledged, was the "conventional feminine voice." What her study showed is that conventional femininity continues to be structured by domesticity. Gilligan herself tried to chart a more complex relationship with domesticity than many of her followers did. Whereas commentators advocated redesign of a wide variety of basic social institutions to reflect the "different voice" (and Gilligan herself sometimes seemed to make this argument as well), Gilligan's main thrust was to critique both the mainstream voice and the different one, arguing that each needs to learn from the other. She articulated her ideal as a "dialectical mixture" of the different and mainstream voices.[15]

Though *In a Different Voice* can be read as a celebration of domesticity, it also contains a critique of it. In the media coverage and among Gilligan's followers, the celebration quickly swamped the critique. The book's tremendous popularity, and its staying power despite powerful methodological critiques, reflects the fact that it feels true to many women. This is hardly surprising, given that Gilligan was describing conventional femininity. Meanwhile, her theme that conventional femininity has limitations was largely lost.

Vernacular descriptions of men and women typically parallel Gilligan's in many ways, for they too describe women through the lens of domesticity. The quote from *Newsweek* about Cheryl Jones, cited above, shows how domesticity's formulation that women are focused on relationships is still used, as it originally was, to justify domesticity's split of men in the market and women at home. Critiques of working mothers typically follow the framework set by domesticity. Psychology professor Faye Crosby summarized this pattern astutely:

> Men are still seen as providers, working to support their families, an un-selfish act. Women, on the other hand, are seen as selfish because they are stepping out of their social role. They are not seen as providers, so working is seen as something they do only for themselves. Working becomes a self-ish act.

Women who stay home are selfless because, as caregivers, they suffer the marginal-ization demanded of caregivers under domesticity's organization of market and family work. Keep in mind that women need to be selfless only because they live in a system that marginalizes caregivers. But because they do, going to work becomes evidence of selfishness and unwomanliness.[16]

Domesticity's descriptions of men and women also serve other purposes. A recent example is the bestseller, John Gray's *Men Are from Mars, Women Are from Venus* (1992). Like Gilligan, Gray describes women as focused on relationships. Virtually his first bit of advice is that "[a] woman's sense of self is defined through her feel-ings and the quality of her relationships." "Instead of being goal oriented, women are relationship oriented; they are more concerned with expressing their goodness, love, and caring." Note Gray's linkage with relationship and care; he refers not to the hierarchical relationships of the Great Chain but to the emotion work allocat-ed to women by domesticity. Gray and Gilligan both contrast women with men's focus on achievement, autonomy, and getting things done; in other words, with the instrumental focus of breadwinners under domesticity.[17]

Gray's book covers the same ground as Deborah Tannen's earlier bestseller, *You Just Don't Understand*, which has the subtlety Gray lacks. Tannen's elegantly detailed de-scriptions stress that her goal is to explore not the true voice of womanhood, but gender differences in men's and women's conversational rituals. Tannen reports that the goal of women's talk is typically to establish connection and rapport, whereas the goal of men's talk typically is to negotiate status. Her descriptions of conventional gender perfor-mances, particularly conventional masculinity, are startlingly precise. While Gilligan described men as the freestanding actors of liberal theory, focused on rights, Tannen de-picts them as anxious people engaged in constant negotiations over status. She ties their focus on problem-solving and their reluctance to talk about emotions to this quest for status. Thus women reporting their troubles, who often want no more than a sympa-thetic ear, are often answered by men who assume that they are being asked to provide solutions. Men tend to turn requests for emotion work into requests for instrumental action to reaffirm their sense of themselves as competent and manly males.[18]

Tannen's description of U.S. men, like Gilligan's description of women, had an eerie resonance for many women. "It's as if she knew my boyfriend," said another student of mine, "I guess all men are like that." Tannen, like Gilligan, distances herself from the claim that she is describing the way men and women "really" are. A distinguished linguist with a long career of studying class and ethnicity, Tannen included careful disclaimers noting that not all women are alike, and that influences other than gender affect people's behavior. These were all but ignored in the press; her description, like Gilligan's, was used to confirm "commonsense" descriptions derived from domesticity.[19]

Also ignored was Tannen's message, stressed more in her academic texts than in her popular ones, that her analysis of men and women as belonging to different cultures was not an alternative to the analysis of gender and power but an elaboration of it. "That men dominate women as a class, and that individual men often dominate individual women in interaction, are not in question: what I am problematizing is the source and workings of domination and the intentions and effects." Tannen asserts that "societally determined power differences are an element of cultural difference theory and research."[20]

What Tannen terms the "unfortunate dichotomy" between the cultural-difference and dominance theories disappears if we view difference feminists as describing not the voice of women but the conventions of femininity. In that context, difference feminism becomes a careful tracking of how the default modes of conventional behavior systemically advantage men. Thus, in the hands of deft cultural feminists such as Robin West and Leslie Bender, cultural feminism becomes a way to critique the systematic power differentials and distortions of values that result from conventional notions of masculinity and femininity.

Vernacular gender talk often tracks the patterns of cultural feminism, as when soccer moms savage their current or former husbands for their dissociation from the emotion work of family life, calling them "men from Mars." While the striking parallels between feminist texts and popular ones are rarely noted, upon reflection it is not surprising that when feminists talk about gender they often follow the patterns of vernacular gender talk. Feminism, after all, is gender talk. This makes it all the more pressing for feminists to invent new ways of talking so that descriptions of men and women do not trigger gender wars among women with different relationships to domesticity. The remainder of this chapter begins that process of invention.

THE "DIFFERENT VOICE" DEBATE AS A GENDER WAR
BETWEEN THE FEMMES AND THE TOMBOYS

[Robin] West has stated that every woman she knows has recognized herself in *In a Different Voice*. I *literally* recognized myself in the book and not in the way that West suggests. When I was a college student I participated in one of the psychological surveys discussed in the book. . . . I was one of the women who gave the "archetypical" masculine response. . . . My "different voice" and the voices of the other women in the study who gave similar unladylike responses (and the male subjects who gave "sissy" answers), even if we were in the minority, apparently were not worthy of discussion because we did not fit her story.[21]

Feminists from Betty Friedan to Ruth Bader Ginsburg rejected domesticity's linkage of women with an ethic of care as part of their vehement rejection of domesticity. Their goal was to rid women of the ideology as well as the practice of domesticity. The rise of Carol Gilligan in the 1980s represented a return to the earlier strategy of embracing domesticity as a tool for women's empowerment. Gilligan's *In a Different Voice* embraced domesticity's descriptions of women to argue that commonly accepted theories of moral development had been framed around masculine norms. The burden of Gilligan's argument, which sameness feminists often forget, was that values and behavior traditionally associated with women should be respected on a par with the values and behaviors traditionally associated with men.[22]

Nonetheless, Gilligan's methods for critiquing masculine norms set off a gender war that dominated feminist jurisprudence for a decade. Suddenly, in the 1980s, the assumption was that if you were a feminist, you accepted Gilligan's description of women. Women who did not were often called "male-identified." The Gilligan debate quickly deteriorated into an intense conflict within both women's history and feminist jurisprudence.

In women's history, animosities reached a fever pitch when historians of women testified on both sides of the *Sears* case, discussed in chapter 1. Sears attorneys called Rosalind Rosenberg in support of their position that women lacked interest in commission sales positions because they disliked the highly competitive atmosphere in commission sales as well as the requirement for night work and travel to customers' homes. Rosenberg cited Gilligan and historians' documentation of a distinct women's culture in the nineteenth century in support of Sears lawyers' contention that women dislike competition, and that their focus on relationships at home and at work made the noncommission work more attractive to them. Rosenberg linked her willingness to testify with her belief that women need maternity leave and other maternalist policies to enable them to compete successfully in the labor market.[23]

The furor over *Sears* tore apart both women's history and feminist jurisprudence. For years law reviews were full of articles in favor of Gilligan and articles against her. The focus of feminism shifted away from the masculine norms all opposed, centering instead on recriminations over the accuracy of Gilligan's description of women's voice.

A key goal of reconstructive feminism is to focus sustained attention on deconstructing the masculine norms embedded in domesticity; the ideal-worker norm is the most obvious example. To accomplish this requires ending the eternal skirmishing between different-voice feminists and their opponents. Until now, the only way to avoid this gender war has been for different-voice feminists to qualify their statements with the assertion that they are describing "most women" rather than "women." They aptly point out that they should be able to make statements about women that do not accurately describe every single woman, so long as those statements say something valuable about women as a group. The question is how to enable feminists (and women in general) to talk about the pressures of conventional femininity without triggering gender wars about what is "the" voice of women.

If we start from Gilligan's assertion that what she describes is conventional femininity, the next step is to recognize that many women have a conflictual relationship with femininity's conventions. After all, though many women read Gilligan's description of Amy and Jake and announced they were Amy, many others read it and announced they were Jake. If the Amys are femmes who accept domesticity's description of women, the Jakes are tomboys who do not. They are Jo (note the male name) rather than Beth in *Little Women;* Laura rather than Mary in the Little House on the Prairie books; George (again a male name) rather than Nancy in the Nancy Drew series. Tomboys disdain the tools of femininity and may have an affinity for boy culture as well—for toads, burps, and baseball diamonds.[24]

Of course, this simplifies women's often complex relationships with the conventions of femininity, as will be discussed further in chapter 8. I propose to simplify these negotiations for the moment, and to use *femme* and *tomboy* to signal women's relationships to one specific aspect of femininity: domesticity's descriptions of men and women. Let me also say clearly that in referring to women as femmes I do not assume that is a bad thing to be. I do not accept the cultural devaluation of femininity. I am involved in both caregiving and feminine gender display on a daily basis. I believe that traditional femininity is a valuable tradition.

My central message is that *both* femmes *and* tomboys offer important insights into what it means to be a woman. Both offer important resources with which to end the traditional linkage of femininity to disempowerment. If some femmes do not approach femininity as a critical tool with which to revalue the tasks and values traditionally associated with women, others do. If some tomboys merely echo society's devaluation of women, others don't.[25]

Women with sharply different attitudes toward conventional femininity can be feminists. That said, the point that anti-Gilligan feminists are the tomboys to Gilligan's femmes offers some insight into the fury each group expends upon the other. For the tomboys, women's empowerment means escaping domesticity: playing Dracula instead of dolls. For this reason, tomboys hear Gilligan's description as legitimating the same old, oppressive stereotypes that conflate women and conventional femininity—and calling it feminism. This infuriates them.

Femmes see the source of women's woes very differently. Their dissatisfaction lies not in the gender performance required of women but in the devaluation associated with it. Femmes, therefore, see tomboys as having lined up with the strong social forces that belittle the traditions they are trying to defend.

In short, the different-voice debate is a war among women over gender. Gender wars not only pit ideal-worker women against women marginalized by caregiving (as discussed in chapter 5) but also pit women who embrace domesticity's description of women against those who feel violated by it. To avoid these gender wars, both femmes and tomboys need to change the way they talk. I first discuss the situation from the tomboys' point of view. Then I will discuss it from the viewpoint of the femmes.

TOMBOYS

Sex, Sameness, and Eye Color

The traditional strategy of sameness feminists, introduced in chapter 5, was to escape domesticity by making sex differences less freighted with social meaning. The classic exposition is Richard Wasserstrom's 1977 article arguing that, in the ideal world, sex would be no more important than eye color: "A nonracist society would be one in which the race of an individual would be the functional equivalent of the eye color of individuals in our society today." Wasserstrom notes that this ideal is harder to imagine in the context of sex. "On the attitudinal and conceptual level, the assimilationist ideal would require the eradication of all sex-role differentiation. . . . Just as the normal, typical adult world is virtually oblivious to the eye color of other persons for all major interpersonal relationships, so the normal, typical adult in this nonsexist society would be indifferent to the sexual, physiological differences of other persons for all interpersonal relationships." Wasserstrom notes that bisexuality would be the norm in such a society. He concludes that there "seem[s] to me a strong presumptive case for something very close to [this] ideal." The classic expression of the Wasserstrom approach is the refrain of sameness feminists that the differences among women are greater than the differences between men and women. Often mathematical curves were used to make the notion that one day sex would be unimportant seem plausible.[26]

It did not seem plausible for long, or to many people. It soon came to be seen as unappealing even to leading feminists such as Lucinda Finley.

> Many men and women of a wide variety of political outlooks wish not to dispute pregnancy's uniqueness, but to celebrate it. For example, when I contemplate Richard Wasserstrom's [proposal for] an ideal world where a person's sex will make about as much difference as eye color, my reaction is disquiet and sadness. I sense that we will have lost something very fundamentally human in such a world of no "real" differences. My sense of loss stems from a feeling that I as a woman want to be able to revel in the joy and virtually mystical specialness of having a baby. What I do not want is to be punished for this wonderful gift at the same time. My feeling that something will be missing in this ideal androgynous world also comes from a fear that it rests on a vision of equality that says we can all be equal if we just strip away our differences. Life in such a world would be boring, impoverished, and unenriching.[27]

Note the instinctive sense that a proposal to make sex differences less freighted with social meaning would lead to a literal loss of sexual functioning. Surely women still could have babies in a world where Toys R Us did not offer black bikes for boys and pink for girls. An unloading of the metaphorical meanings we attach to sex would not result in the end of sexual functioning.

Yet Finley's main point is that off-loading meanings from sex sounds unappealing. Why? Finley, like most of the rest of us, is constituted in part by domesticity. Like most women, her identity is tied up with domesticity's celebration of motherhood. The project of making sex as unimportant as eye color failed in significant part because sex is so loaded a metaphor that it shapes the way we define our dreams.

A case in point is what Erving Goffman calls gender display: dressing and acting in feminine ways. Radical feminists of the early second wave often attacked the accouterments of femininity on the grounds that they made women into sex objects and used women's sexuality to sell products.[28]

They do. Yet most younger feminists have rejected this attack, and in my experience, even older feminists who once associated femininity with exploitation now dress and act far more femme than they ever imagined they would. I certainly do. This is another instance of the axiom that gender is too central a metaphor to simply abandon. It frames not only the way we dress but the structure of the erotic, our daydreams for ourselves and our children, and much more. For these reasons, most people literally cannot imagine a world where sex is no more important than eye color. Feminists should not allow their agenda to hinge on people's ability to do so.

Domesticity as a Powerful Interpretive System

The goal of making sex as unimportant as eye color is impractical for a second, related, reason. Domesticity—like Christianity, psychoanalysis, and other powerful interpretive systems—has sophisticated mechanisms to neutralize counterevidence and reinforce its own canonical interpretations. Thus the psychoanalyst insists that when a patient resists an interpretation, in fact that just proves its validity: The analysis cuts so close to home, it has produced resistance. Similarly, the unbeliever's protest that wine cannot turn into Christ's blood is met with the assertion that one's ability to make that leap of faith is the true test of a Christian.

Domesticity bewitches in similar ways. People who see men and women as fundamentally different have that interpretation constantly reinforced through a variety of false feedback loops that make it difficult for people to break out of domesticity as an interpretive system.

Biological Differences as Proof of Domesticity

Once I was on a panel with Linda Chavez, and she started out by saying that feminists want to deny the fact they are women; then she went on to make an argument that rested in part on women's "unique role as childbearers." When my turn came to speak, I began: "I have gone through nineteen months of pregnancy and thirty-one hours of labor, and I never forget that I am a woman. That's not the sort of thing you forget."

What was going on? Chavez was trying to use the biological fact that women can bear children and men can't to support a whole series of assertions about women's ideal social role that have nothing to do with biology. I embraced her observations about biology but contested her interpretation of those biological differences.[29]

The first false feedback loop is this: The existence of biological differences is cited as support for domesticity's description of women as naturally focused on an ethic of care. It isn't. The fact that women do the birthing does not mean that the allocation of child rearing to women is inevitable, or that child rearing inevitably is linked with marginalization.

A note of explanation is in order. Some feminists today have become dissatisfied with the distinction between sex and gender. It is true that sex, like gender, is a social construct. People born with both male and female organs typically are operated on within days of their birth to make their bodies fit our metaphor of male and female as opposite and mutually exclusive. Sex and gender also are intertwined in the sense that gender performance is eroticized. The mutually constitutive nature of sex and gender sometimes plays an important role in work/family issues where they overlap with the eroticizing of dominance. An example is the custom of women marrying men who are older, taller, and richer—a pattern that often makes it "logical" for the woman, less advanced in her career, to move to follow her partner, to cut back on work, or to quit. However, while the intertwining nature of sex and gender is important in the overlap between work/family issues and the eroticizing of dominance, the traditional feminist differentiation between sex and gender remains indispensable for focusing attention on the differences between body shape and the social allocation of market and family work.[30]

Differences in Social Role as Proof that Men and Women Have Different Cultures

The second false feedback loop is more subtle: Any attempt to deny domesticity's description of women is taken as a nonsensical attempt to deny the existence not of biology but of gender roles. How can you deny that women are focused on an ethic of care, goes the argument, when women do the overwhelming proportion of the caregiving?

The fact that women comprise virtually all of the marginalized caregivers does not prove they share an ethic of care. Women may end up as marginalized caregivers for quite different reasons than that they share a uniform psychology focused on a web of relationships. Chapter 1 began by showing the social forces that get encoded as women's choice to devote themselves to caregiving rather than to market work. These included objective factors such as the lack of affordable, high-quality child care, employers' entitlement to marginalize anyone who does not live up to the ideal-worker norm, and fathers' felt entitlement to perform as ideal workers. These objective factors create strong force fields pulling mothers toward marginalization. Recall the *Doonesbury* cartoon (reprinted on page 125) that pointed out that women can feel guilty even when they are doing a lot more family work than men, because men compare themselves to their fathers (who did very little) whereas women compare themselves to their mothers (who did virtually everything). This cartoon aptly pinpoints that men and women live in different force fields, and so experience very different social cues. As a result, most well-adjusted people become gendered. Consequently, women develop various skills and traits required for the modern caregiving role, such as the ability to do six things at once, family executive skills (from locating suitable resources to coordinating schedules), and the ability to sustain the complex social relationships associated with childhood (with friends, parents, teachers, and so on). Are these skills evidence of women's ethic of care, or are they evidence that most rise to the occasion once they are assigned the role of primary caregiver? If the latter, it makes no sense to cite these skills as reasons for continuing women's exclusive responsibility for caregiving, since any competent adult assigned to caregiving would develop them.

A concrete example of how the social pressures on men and women can produce gendered behavior is the case of two managers given an assignment by a superior who has traditional attitudes toward gender. The male manager may well conclude that he is being judged on how commandingly he takes charge of the situation and motivates people to act on his analysis. In other words, he is assessed on his ability to present the classic management style, traditionally associated with males. The female manager, on the other hand, may conclude that she is being judged on how well she gets people together to talk through the issues; if she orders people around, she may be told she "needs to go to charm school," just as the man may well be judged as ineffective if he uses a consultative style rather than a commanding one. The result in each case would be gender-appropriate behavior, produced not by the man's and woman's different voices, but by their (accurate) individual assessments that it was wiser to act in ways traditionally associated with men and women respectively.[31]

Citing the differences in men's and women's psychology as the reason for their different social roles is the most sophisticated version of the habit of citing differences in social roles as support for domesticity's descriptions of men and women. People do not develop in a vacuum; most of us adjust to the social realities we encounter and attempt to make the best of them. This strain of the different-voice argument holds up a mirror to the world and labels the reflection the voice of women. Many women end up as they do not because they, from the beginning, shared an ethic of care. Maybe they were just making the best of a bad deal.

The Role of Gendered Words in Policing Domesticity

Words are often gendered in covert ways. The clearest example of this is the word *nurture.* The fact that women, but not men, nurture stems in part from the hidden gendering of the word *nurture.* Although its broadest definition is "the act of promoting development and growth," the word derives from nursing a baby and still has overtones of something only a mother can do. Men are involved in all kinds of relationships in which they promote another's development in a caring way: as fathers, as mentors, as camp counselors, as Scout leaders. But we tend not to describe these relationships as nurturing. Instead, women nurture; men mentor.[32]

Language polices gender in a different, related way. Feminists have long noted the use of different words to describe the same behavior in men and in women. Men are assertive; women are strident. Or, as in *Hopkins*, women aggressive enough to make partner at a major accounting firm "need to go to charm school": What would be praised as appropriate behavior for men is, in women, viewed as a personality defect—and not, therefore, as counterevidence to domesticity's descriptions of men and women.

Related to this is an intriguing trope on the theme of emotional expressiveness. While emotional expressiveness in women is often cited as the reason why they do family work, emotional expressiveness in a man often gets channeled into his career. If a woman is insightful about people, she ends up as a mother; if a man is, he ends up a psychiatrist. "The kids really prefer their father, he really seems to understand their needs," said one at-home mother. But they rarely saw him. He worked long hours building up his psychiatric practice. Four years later the mother was deeply hurt when, after she had spent many hours volunteering at her children's nursery school, her husband was offered a position on its board of directors. After all, she was "only a housewife." He was a child psychiatrist.

The Use of Counterevidence to Confirm Domesticity's Descriptions

Perhaps the most astonishing false feedback loop is the use of counterevidence to confirm domesticity's metaphor. "Mr. Mom" deflects attention from the fact that men nurture, by coding any man who nurtures as a woman. Even feminists talk about "men who mother."[33] Well, if men do it, I guess it isn't something only a person with a vagina can do.

But note how the gender boundaries are policed by language that confuses penises with pink barrettes, by classifying people who play a certain social role as women regardless of the shape of their genitals. Back in the height of the Gilligan days, women who did not accept Gilligan's description of women were often called "male-identified": the evidence that Gilligan had not provided an accurate description of women was discredited on the grounds that the women who rejected Gilligan's description were, ipso facto, men. This form of argument dates back at least to Victorian times, when women who engaged in behavior judged gender-inappropriate were referred to as "unsexed."

The Observer Effect

Another false feedback loop, rarely noted, is aptly described by sociologist Barrie Thorne in her fascinating study of children's play on school playgrounds. Thorne points out that children's playground play is very gendered: most boys play with boys at activities associated with boy culture, while girls play with girls at jump rope, hopscotch, and other games traditionally played by girls. In sharp contrast, Thorne notes, when the same children play in neighborhood groups, they tend to play in mixed-sex groups at games that are not gender-marked. To gain a full understanding of the role of gender in children's play, Thorne points out, one needs to examine not only school playgrounds but also neighborhood groups, and to build into one's analysis an assessment not only of situations where gender comes to the foreground as the key social force but also of situations where gender does not play an important role.[34]

This gender theorists virtually never do. People looking at gender tend to look at situations where behavior is gendered and to come up with totalizing theories that assume gender is important in every arena of social interaction; not that women behave in gendered ways in certain situations, but that they share a gendered "different voice."

Barrie Thorne points out that commentators on gender tend not only to overestimate the pervasiveness of its influence but also to generate descriptions that confirm the conventional descriptions of men and women. When academics focus on gender, their eye is likely to be caught by the people who are most obviously gendered. Thorne cites the "big man bias" in research on masculinity, which leads commentators to focus their attention not on the gentle creatures among the male population, but on the boys who best reflect macho ideals. A study of the macho men and the femme girls has obviously been successful in its thesis that gender is an important social variable.[35]

This tendency holds true not only for scholars but in everyday life as well. People tend to treat situations where behavior is very gendered as relevant to gender, whereas situations where behavior is not gendered are not processed as evidence undermining the importance of gender as a determinant of social behavior. All this serves to associate girls and women more closely with feminine gender performances, and boys and men with masculine ones.

Many studies have documented that people do not see evidence that contradicts their stereotyped assumptions. For example, when people are shown movies of babies they are told are male, they see behavior that is vigorous and assertive; when they are shown the same movies and told the babies are female, they observe behavior that is gentle and cute.[36]

These studies are artificial in their creation of a situation where the observers have no gender cues. But one can see a similar phenomenon when mothers watch their toddlers on a playground. They tend to see their gender stereotypes confirmed because of the way they classify information: gender-appropriate traits are attributed to gender, whereas gender-inappropriate traits are attributed to personality, birth order, or some other explanatory system. That Johnny hits people needs no explanation: after all, he is a boy. The fact that Ben refuses to play with guns doesn't disprove the thesis that boys are aggressive; it just proves he's a gentle soul or a freethinker. The fact that Peter is a fire-eater who bosses everyone around proves how macho he is; the fact that Emma does the same means only that she has a strong personality.

The observer effect starts with an observer. Why are mothers invested in the notion that boys and girls are "really" different? The mother who noted that boys just naturally gravitated toward trucks suggests an answer. She made that comment on the tot lot on a weekday at 3 P.M. I was there because I had an option available to few: As a tenured law professor, I had both a flexible schedule and a nonmarginalized job. She did not. She and most of the other mothers had made sharp trade-offs to be there on the playground. They had given up careers in favor of staying home or the mommy track. The accepted way of describing their situation, as discussed in chapter 1, is to insist that their "choice" to marginalize reflects their own priorities as women; those priorities just turned out to be different from those of their husbands. Thus most mothers at the playground had a personal stake in describing their children in gendered terms, for at risk was their self-description as women enjoying free choice under a system of gender equality.

Pressures Toward a Conventionally Gendered Self-Presentation
A final force contributing to domesticity's description of men and women is that men and women themselves often use stereotypes strategically. Consider an ad run during the 1996 Olympics.

> My name is Jackie Joyner-Kersee. I can throw a shot put 100 yards, and I can run faster than all but 128 men in the world. . . . I have red toenails.
> [Voice-over] Just another Avon lady.

The standard feminist response is outrage that one of the best athletes in the world should need to present herself as just another Avon lady. This is true, but it is only half the story. It also provides an important message about how people accommodate gender flux.

Note that from the time we are very small, "appropriate" gender performance is a key test of basic social competence. "Something is clearly wrong with" the little boy in pink barrettes. This is why young children, whose major job is to establish social competence, are so religious in their policing of gender proprieties—for them, knowing that boys don't wear pink barrettes is analytically indistinguishable from knowing you get run over if you walk in the middle of the street, or that big kids poop in the toilet and not on the street.

The close link between gender performance and social competence presents challenges for women who take on traditionally male roles, be they rainmakers or Jackie Joyner-Kersee. The danger is that they will end up like Ann Hopkins, who adopted male gender performance not only in her go-get-'em attitude as a rainmaker, but also in her use of profane language and other macho mannerisms.

What Hopkins got, it is important to remember, was a lawsuit. This is not the result most women desire. The more risk-averse approach is to counter one's go-getter ethic with exaggerated messages that one is not clueless about femininity, but in fact is completely competent in all elements of feminine gender performance except deference, demureness, and other qualities inconsistent with go-getting. Successful women in male-dominated fields often stress femininity in their day-to-day gender performance. Egyptian women take the veil in order to work in mixed-sex environments where women have not worked in the past. Professors tend to give gendered classroom performances in response to the gendered expectations of students as reflected in student evaluations.[37]

The result is that everyday observation tends to confirm the truism that men and women "really are different." This highlights an important point about gender, rarely noted: its infinite availability as an interpretive system. People regularly turn to gender to explain phenomena they do not understand, or to avoid more painful explanations they would rather not face. One common example is mothers' use of gender to explain the behavior of their children. When parents have a boy who is very aggressive, they will often resign themselves to the "fact that boys will be boys"; it is easier than seeking reasons for antisocial behavior. Similarly, mothers who find themselves at home after a long marital battle will often explain their situation as evidence that women "are just different from men; I didn't used to believe it, but now I do." It is less painful to turn back to domesticity's description of women as sharing an ethic of care than to describe their situations in the language of struggle and defeat.

Gender is too useful an explanation, in too many situations, to make it feasible to simply eliminate the meanings we attach to differences in body shape. This strategy should be abandoned in favor of a strategy of disinvesting in the debate over domesticity's descriptions of men and women.

Disinvesting in the Debate

Nature, Mr. Orner, is what we are put in this world to rise above.[38]

Thirty years of second-wave feminism have seen many accomplishments, but dislodging the ideology of domesticity is not one of them. Most people, feminists or not, believe some version of domesticity's descriptions of men and women.

Domesticity is such a powerful interpretive system that feminism should not hang its success in empowering women on people's ability to see though domesticity's descriptions of men and women. This suggests the need to disinvest in the debate over what men and women are "really" like. The structure of this book suggests one way to do so: Feminists should avoid mixing up discussions of whether men are from Mars and women are from Venus with discussions of how to redesign social roles. A societal consensus exists that men and women should share family work; feminists should avoid being derailed into conversations about whether mothers "naturally" end up as primary caregivers because of their ethic of care. To quote Robin West, "It simply doesn't follow, from the existence of a biological difference between men and women, that a behavior associated with that difference or attribute is impervious to social or legal pressure."[39] Nature is what we are put on earth to rise above.

Shifts in social role are more important than shifts in symbolism. Once we change social roles, the metaphors will take care of themselves, for whatever men do will come to be described as manly. In a family in which the father cooks, he enlists his son as a sous-chef, with messages that cooking is a manly thing to do. In the workplace, jobs performed by men are described in masculine metaphors, but they are abruptly redescribed in feminine terms if the job is reclassified as women's work. Thus when the job of secretary was a man's job in the nineteenth century, it had the aura of a manly apprenticeship in which young men observed, helped, and learned from older men of the same social class, making social contacts through the job that would stand them in good stead in business or professional life. When the job was gendered female in the 1920s, its ruling metaphor changed. The secretary's social status fell; she became an "office wife" who performed wifely services such as buying presents for the boss's family and making coffee. A dramatic example of how (straight, conventional) men will describe whatever they do in masculinist terms is the following description of housework by a househusband:

> A day of cooking, cleaning, child care and household management is not unlike climbing a mountain. Some of it is sweaty, grueling work, but the pleasures, such as sunlight through the mist on Mount Washington, or seeing a toddler learn a new game, are constant enough to make it worth it. . . . Housework may not be Everest, but it is an adventure that awaits any man who wants to forge ahead and meet the challenges of unexplored territory.

Producing shifts in social roles will lead naturally to a new metaphor of manly nurture. Feminists need to focus on changing institutions; our sense of what men and women are "really" like will follow.[40]

In conclusion, tomboys should not allow feminism's future to hinge on people's ability to see through domesticity's descriptions of men and women. Femmes also need to establish a new relationship to domesticity.

FEMMES

The key to attaining a truce between femmes and tomboys is to maintain a rigorous distinction between the conventions of femininity and the voice of women. This section discusses how femme practice needs to change in order to accomplish this.

Gender Talk in the Vernacular

Domesticity reemerges whenever people of good faith hold up a mirror to the world and find domesticity reflected—in women's conversational style, behavior, or self-descriptions—and then describe their findings as insights about "women." Today the accepted corrective is to critique these descriptions as essentialist, pointing out that women are not all alike. As noted above, cultural feminists reply that they should not be forbidden from offering a description of most women even if it does not apply to every single one.

The key point, however, is *not* simply that domesticity's description does not apply to all women. Instead, it is that tomboys feel violated by a description of women that marginalizes their alternative definitions of womanhood. This problem can be remedied by presenting descriptions of the kind offered by Gilligan, Gray, and Tannen as descriptions of *conventional gender performance* rather than of *women*. This leaves popular writers free to bracket the extent to which people's actual behavior conforms to the gender pressures upon them and academic writers free to explore resistant genderings.

Domesticity as Social Critique:
The Philosophy of Femininity

Nancy Cott has shown that domesticity, from its inception, has functioned as an internal critique of capitalism: "In accentuating the split between 'work' and 'home' and proposing the latter as a place of salvation, the canon of domesticity tacitly acknowledged the capacity of modern work to desecrate the human spirit." Cott argued that domesticity forwarded the kind of critique expressed in Marx's analysis of alienated labor. "The canon of domesticity embodied a protest against that advance of exploitation and pecuniary values" that occurred under capitalism. Under domesticity, Cott concluded, "women's self-renunciation was called upon to remedy men's self-alienation." In a political culture with few viable languages of critique, domesticity offers a Marxism you can bring home to mother, one of the few available languages with widespread vernacular resonance available for critiquing the excesses of liberal individualism. This is one reason why modern feminists are attracted to domesticity.[41]

If we look at Robin West's "Jurisprudence and Gender," we can gain a deeper appreciation of how domesticity functions as a language of critique. West begins by showing how mainstream political philosophers, from critical legal studies on the left to Robert Nozick on the right, take as a starting point what West calls the "separation thesis": "the claim that human beings are, definitionally, distinct from one another . . . the claim that we are individuals 'first,' and the claim that what separates us is epistemologically and morally prior to what connects us." These claims, she says, "while 'trivially true' of men, are patently untrue of women. Women are not essentially, necessarily, inevitably, invariably, always, and forever separate from other human beings: women, distinctively, are quite clearly 'connected' to another human life when pregnant." Women are connected, West argues, by other experiences as well, including the experience of "heterosexual penetration, which may lead to pregnancy"; by menstruation, "which represents the potential for pregnancy"; and by breast-feeding. "Indeed, perhaps the central insight of feminist theory of the last decade has been that women are 'essentially connected,' not 'essentially separate.'" West's connection thesis is that "[w]omen are actually or potentially materially connected to other human life. Men aren't. This material fact has existential consequences."[42]

In West's critique of "masculine jurisprudence," she should pay more attention to the word *masculine*, which refers to a social construction rather than a biological fact. She is correct that political theory is tied to masculine gender performance: The enshrinement of freestanding individuals with rights at the core of most modern liberal political theory is intertwined with notions of masculinity.[43]

To understand how this occurred requires some intellectual history. The rise of domesticity was accompanied by a shift in its complement: mainstream liberalism. Historian James Kloppenberg has noted that, as of the eighteenth century, the predominant versions of liberalism were "oriented more toward ideals of virtue rather than toward simple acquisitiveness." Locke's liberalism, he argues, "dissolves if it is removed from the context of divinely established natural law, which encumbers the freedom of individuals at every turn with the powerful commands of duty." Liberalism enshrined self-interest, but only within the bounds prescribed by republicanism, religion, and Scottish moral philosophy. Kloppenberg calls these "the virtues of liberalism."[44]

During the nineteenth century, in precisely the period that saw the rise of domesticity, liberalism began to flatten out into a celebration of the individualistic pursuit of self-interest that was unconstrained by liberalism's ethical dimensions. What was left was the image of men driven by self-interest in pursuit of material gain. This version of liberalism set up a public sphere composed of men pursuing self-interest in the market realm, while virtue was allocated to women at home. This is the sense in which domesticity is the dangerous supplement of liberalism, and liberalism as a political theory is gendered.[45]

West offers her philosophy of femininity as a corrective to this gendered strain of liberalism. The version of liberalism she critiques is masculine in the sense that it is part and parcel of the gender system that made separation integral to masculinity and connection integral to femininity. Note that these associations did not exist under patriarchy, which defined *men as well as women* as connected in bonds of interdependence with social superiors and inferiors in the Great Chain of Being.

West conflates the gendering of liberalism with the physical state of maleness. For this reason, she fails to recognize that her interpretation of what it means to be a woman—framed in terms of motherhood and an ethic of care—does not follow inexorably from biological differences. Instead, it represents only one interpretation of the meaning of sex differences, the interpretation that stems from domesticity.

Why does it matter? After all, West correctly describes the dominant definitions of the culture we live in. It matters because another key value of our postmodern age is the way we "fit loosely into our traditions." One hundred years ago, for middle-class women, the only alternative to being a "lady," whose personality and social role were framed by domesticity, was social death: think of the isolation of George Eliot "living in sin" in the mid-nineteenth century. The same is not true today. We allow today a much broader range of femininities, from the self-parodying femme performance of Madonna to the gender-ambiguous k. d. lang; from Rebecca Lobo to Whoopi Goldberg to Hillary Clinton; from soccer moms to born-again virginity pledgers to bisexual intellectuals rejecting compulsory heterosexuality. Women have always given a wide range of gender performances; the difference today is that a much wider scope of performances has been invited into the mainstream.[46]

In this context, to speak in a way that defines women in terms of pregnancy and the ethic of care may strike many people as gender-policing women back into domesticity's rigid formulas of womanhood. This is bound to create rifts within feminism, between femmes attracted to feminism because of its promise to revalue traits and roles domesticity associates with women, and tomboys attracted to feminism by its promise to deliver them from domesticity.

What's the solution? Political theorist Joan Tronto offers one approach in *Moral Boundaries: A Political Argument for an Ethic of Care*, in which she carefully dissociates the ethic of care from women, linking it instead with thinkers of the Scottish Enlightenment. Tronto identifies an important rhetoric of liberal sympathy with potential to help restore the virtues of liberalism, but when she associates that rhetoric with "care" we begin to notice that the experience of care is heavily gendered. Other than relief work, the caring she describes is mostly done by women: by mothers, by medical personnel (largely female, with the exception of doctors), by cleaning staff, by "the neighbor helping her friend set her hair." When Tronto does use a consciously male-gendered example, the result sounds distinctly forced, as when she associates the ethic of care with piano tuning. When she discusses who staffs the jobs involved in caring work, the sense that most caregivers are female emerges even more strongly. The result is that the reader ends up feeling that it is hard to avoid the association of women and caregiving. The capacious language of liberal sympathy turns out to be somewhat different from the practice of caring in a society structured by domesticity.[47]

In a 1996 review of her book, Carrie Menkel-Meadow asks Tronto: "Can we have a degendered theory of care with a gendered practice of care?" The obvious question is: Do we want one? Robin West argues we do not.

> It is a premise of this book . . . [that] an ethic of care is a vital moral perspective. . . . Given that, it is certainly fair to ask—as Tronto does—why connecting such an ethic with a complicated and controversial claim about gender differences is either necessary or wise. . . . [T]here are two reasons why it might be necessary, whether or not wise. . . . [I]f it is defensible, it is so in part because of the importance and value of the experiences that inform it. And if those experiences are largely the experiences of women, then we need to know that. . . . Second, if an ethic of care has been undervalued, we need to know *why*, if for no other reason than to dispel the presumption that it has been assigned a low value because it is of little value.[48]

If women do most of the caring, it does not make sense to erase the linkage between caring and women. This chapter pinpoints a third path, different from the classic choices of enshrining care as inherent to womanhood or denying the links between gender and care. That alternative is to link the ethic of care not with *biology*—not with body shape—but with *gender*, with the traits and the role allocations domesticity assigns to women. West and other cultural feminists can use important cultural resources from the traditions of femininity without characterizing what they find as "the" voice of women.

If we distinguish between women and gender, we need not disavow the connection between gender and care: Women do indeed do most of the caregiving. But to the extent that care is part of women's gender assignment, it is an assignment not always "carried out according to expectation." All women are under pressure from domesticity; not all women accede. I join West in embracing domesticity in significant ways, even as we both seek to change the subordinated context in which family and caring work occurs.[49]

But some women feel that domesticity has been imposed upon them. They reject it, and feel that feminists should not be in the business of telling them how to be a woman. "The potential for material connection with the other defines women's subjective, phenomenological and existential state." Isn't it more tactful, and truer, to say that this defines the experience of women who carry out their gender role assignment according to expectation and interpret it through the lens of domesticity?[50]

A theory of care should attribute its insights to the *tradition of domesticity*, not to *the voice of women*. This distinction may not feel important to the femmes, but it feels very important indeed to the tomboys, who otherwise are left feeling that feminists, of all people, are aligning with the forces that have told them all their lives to behave more femininely.

RECONSTRUCTIVE FEMINISM

The twin goals of reconstructive feminism are to use domesticity in strategic and self-conscious ways and to destabilize it from within.

Strategic Uses of Domesticity: Domesticity in Drag

Sameness feminists of the early second wave strove to deconstruct gender in the literal sense of divorcing sex differences from the load of social meanings heaped upon them. My goal is to deconstruct gender in the more postmodern sense of trying to manipulate a system of meaning from within. This should, up front, be distinguished from the Derridian use of *deconstruction*, which insists that language is a system in which meanings are always unstable and deferred. While language is often ambiguous, at best ambiguous language is like a stool with three legs: A fourth leg is not needed because the stool works fine with three. Often language's ambiguity does not get in the way of its ability to function as a system of meaning. Indeed, to the extent that language is ambiguous and undecidable, ambiguity is often an integral part of the message being sent. This is true in situations ranging from sexual innuendo to statutory drafting.[51]

Gender is a system of meaning so pervasive and inescapable that it shapes our identity. It cannot simply be tossed aside; it must rather be changed from within, through parody, performance, or a new interpretation that presents the system in a novel light or plays off one element against others. Judith Butler often uses deconstruction in this sense, and she offers important insights into how to destabilize a system that structures our identities and our dreams. While Butler has a different agenda, her bottom line—that the system we inherit structures our sense of the erotic—has implications for deconstructing domesticity. We need to approach domesticity as Butler approaches feminine gender display, not with a peremptory demand for its immediate abandonment, but with the goal of gender bending: of focusing attention on the contingent and stitched-together quality of our performances, thereby opening up ways to bend the elements of domesticity into new configurations. Suppleness and a sense of open-ended play are important weapons if the goal is domesticity in drag.

The strategy of destabilizing domesticity from within appeals to me in part because I have come to agree with the philosophers of femininity that domesticity offers a political language that is too important to abandon. Instead, the goal should be for feminists to use domesticity self-consciously. Four such uses come immediately to mind: to restructure market and family work; to inform progressive strategies on welfare reform and "family values"; to use gender as a language of class entitlement; and to change feminist strategy in the abortion debate.

Using Domesticity to Restructure the Relationship of Market and Family Work

Part I of this book represents an attempt to use domesticity against itself. The strategy is to use one norm from domesticity—the norm of parental care—to challenge a second norm also derived from domesticity—the ideal-worker norm. Note that the norm of parental care is not a simple carryover but a transmutation of domesticity's norm of mothercare into a norm applicable to all parents regardless of the shape of their genitals. This illustrates how one can use the language of domesticity as a weapon for ending the devaluation of tasks and traits associated with femininity by transmuting the heritage of domesticity.

"Welfare Reform" and Family Values

The welfare debate could benefit from an understanding of how domesticity functions as a political rhetoric. A review of census data suggests that access to parental care differs according to class. In 1994 (before welfare reform was implemented) over a third of poor women were full-time homemakers, whereas less than a fourth of working-class women were. Indeed, more poor women were full-time homemakers than in any other income group.[52]

These figures help explain the dynamics of the welfare debate. Conservatives' success in stirring up working-class anger against poor single mothers reflects not only racism but also envy. As noted before, union polling shows that the number one concern of union members is that both parents have to work to support a family. This makes sense for a generation whose fathers could support a wife at home on a working-class salary, who feel they have lost access to domesticity. In view of the paucity of attractive alternatives to mothercare, anger over the loss of working-class access to mothercare is understandable. In this context, a federal welfare program that contributes to a higher rate of domesticity among poor women than among the working class is clearly vulnerable. Note that I do not endorse the process of directing class anger at welfare, or at African-Americans. I only note it to point out that those involved in designing policies to help poor people should take gender politics into account.

An understanding of how domesticity interacts with class provides important insights into how conservatives have been able to forge such an effective alliance with the working class using the rhetoric of "family values." "Family values" generally refers in part to the traditional family enshrined by domesticity. Thus far, progressives have generally ceded family values to the conservatives. Given domesticity's cultural power, this is very unwise. Instead of ceding domesticity to the right, progressives need to articulate their own vision of family values.[53]

I believe in three basic family values. First, as noted in chapter 1, I believe that families are healthier when alternatives exist to family life. So long as people with little predisposition toward family life are policed into it, families will suffer. Alternatives always have existed—for monastics, for bachelors, in Boston marriages. Expanding the category of "others" need not alarm us. There are many ways to lead a productive and ethical life.

I believe, second, that family life is so important that everyone should have access to it. Anyone should be able to make a sincere commitment to start and sustain a family with someone they love, regardless of the shape of their genitals. People should also be able to raise children as single parents. People end up as single parents for all kinds of reasons, and many single-parent families work out just fine.[54]

I also believe in the importance of (a certain amount of) parental care. This does not mean I believe in the mother-as-sole-source model; children and parents alike are better served when both parents are involved with child rearing. Transmuted from the norm of mothercare, the norm of parental care has tremendous potential. It is widely shared: I know radical lesbians who are dead set against the existence of marriage but who embrace as uncontroversial the view that children often need their parents in ways that can interfere with full-time market work.

Feminists need to stop attacking ideals they act upon in their own lives. We need to offer not a fated assault on domesticity but a new interpretation of it, one that "uses the master's tools to dismantle the master's house," identifying the parts of domesticity that must be left behind if we are to move closer to our ever-elusive ideals of equality.[55]

Gender as a Language of Class Entitlement

It would not have occurred to industrial workers in the nineteenth century that they were entitled to a domestic ideal that was, at the time, still explicitly identified with the middle class. But today (at least in theory) domesticity is not class-linked, so it can be used by workers to demand an entitlement to a standard of child rearing once reserved for the privileged.

In a culture with few languages of solidarity, domesticity offers an important resource. The radical potential of the norm of parental care is that although American workers often do not feel entitlements as *workers*, they often do feel entitlements as *parents*. Partly these relate to time. In a society where workers complain they have no time for family life, the sense that children are entitled to the attention of their parents becomes a way of challenging the great American speed-up. Women workers are insistent that their employers should accommodate their "needs as mothers." This can translate into resistance to mandatory overtime or demands for personal time off to care for infants or sick children, take children to doctors' appointments, or attend the school play. It may even translate into demands for health benefits and decent wages, on the grounds that someone who works hard is entitled to a decent standard of living for her children. In addition, women's sense of children's needs—and of their own vulnerability in our system of providing for children's care by marginalizing their caregivers—makes them far more willing to demand a significantly larger role for government in providing social benefits. What political analysts call the "gender gap" contains a profound message: the "fact" that Americans don't like big government is a more accurate description of American men than American women. "Over the past sixteen years men have become much more antigovernment; women have not."[56]

Public opinion surveys also find acute concern over the impact of working conditions on family life. When the respondents to one survey were asked to rate the accuracy of thirteen descriptions of the economy, the most widely endorsed concerned pressures on the family. Nearly three-fourths of all respondents said that "reducing stress on working families with policies like flexible hours and affordable child care" would be a very effective way of improving their economic situation. Concerns over the pressures on families outweighed even people's desire for increased salaries and concerns over layoffs.[57]

Unions have already begun using gender as a language of class, both in organizing and in their efforts to turn out the vote in national political campaigns. Consider the following ad:

SOME POLITICIANS DON'T KNOW MUCH.

They don't know what it's like saving for both an education

AND AN ELECTRIC BILL

They don't know second mortgages, second shifts or second-hand

THEY CERTAINLY DON'T KNOW THE PRICE OF

MACARONI AND CHEESE

OR HOW TOUGH IT IS TO FIND A GOOD JOB.

OR HOW TOUGH IT IS TO LOSE ONE.

At the end of the day, the health care problem isn't crying in their laps.

THE ECONOMY ISN'T ASKING THEM FOR

A NEW PAIR OF SNEAKERS . . .
PLEASE VOTE[58]

Note that two of the three items in big type are explicitly related to children. The ad shrinks traditional political issues and rhetoric (health care, the economy) and pops out the message that voters should vote a redistributive agenda to protect their children. Family values have enormous redistributive potential in a culture with few viable languages of social democracy.

Abortion, Caring, and Motherhood

The classic abortion rights rhetoric is the "pro-choice" argument that women should have the right to control "our bodies our selves." In the early 1990s the National Abortion Rights Action League (NARAL) changed its approach, as epitomized by the slogan "Pro-Children, Pro-Family, Pro-Choice."

The classic abortion rights rhetoric ignores the covert gendering of the liberal language of individual rights. That language excludes mothers from the republic of freestanding individuals making choices in pursuit of their own self-interest. The linkage of domesticity and liberalism, in effect, mandates selflessness for mothers and self-interest for others. When pro-choice forces ignored the gendering of liberal rhetoric, this made it easier for "pro-life" advocates to argue that women seek abortions for petty and selfish reasons, and that allowing women to stray from the path of selfless motherhood will lead to a world in which market values are not balanced by women's traditional caring role. Recall the pro-life women quoted in chapter 5, who linked opposition to abortion with their desire to avoid an excessively individualistic and materialistic society. The key for feminists is to frame their demands for women's liberation in ways that do not trigger these fears.

I have argued, in a proposal that has proved extremely controversial within feminist jurisprudence but parallels the strategies taken by NARAL, that abortion rights should be defended in the name of responsible motherhood. Most women, after all, choose to abort when they feel they cannot live up to their ideals of motherhood. This includes young women who do not feel they can offer a child the kind of economic security and undivided attention that are required to meet their ideals of motherhood. It also includes married women who abort because they feel another child would interfere with the obligations they have to existing children. It even includes women who do not want to become mothers simply because their priorities lie elsewhere than a life dedicated to caregiving—who know that the children of mothers who are not particularly focused on caregiving suffer in ways that children of fathers not particularly focused on caregiving often do not.

As tomboys have long recognized, domesticity as a political rhetoric holds important pitfalls for women. But, as femmes have shown, it also provides important opportunities. My sense is that few feminists would oppose creative uses of domesticity if such uses were divorced from claims about the way women "really" are. Once tomboys no longer feel misdescribed as women, I suspect most would agree that women's gender traditions contain some things worth preserving.

Destabilizing Domesticity from Within

Even if feminists embrace domesticity as a potential tool for social change, they will continue "to make gender trouble, not through strategies that figure a utopian beyond, but through the mobilization, subversive confusion, and proliferation of precisely those constitutive categories that seek to keep gender in its place." Gender flux remains an important goal of reconstructive feminism.[59]

One step in this direction is to focus attention on the deleterious impacts of domesticity. Take its impact on our emotional life. Women were associated with sentiment long before the rise of domesticity, but it was domesticity that institutionalized emotion work as characteristically feminine and "real men" as doers, not feelers. Social psychologist Carol Tavris traces the translation of these truisms into social science terminology in the mid-twentieth century:

> When I was growing up, social scientists maintained that men were "instrumental" and "task-oriented," whereas women were "expressive" and "person-oriented." This was a fancier way of saying that men were best suited for the world of work and women were best suited for motherhood.[60]

Latin cultures dramatize the point that male power is not inconsistent with emotional expressiveness. The narrow emotional range associated with masculinity in the United States stems from domesticity's symbolic association of masculinity with the tight self-control deemed necessary to achieve success in the middle-class world of work.

As domesticity split the world into a women's domestic sphere and a male sphere of work, sentiment was associated with the home and perceived as feminine. "To the extent that women are encouraged to talk about their emotions, men are in general expected to remain controlled and silent about theirs." Recall the working-class man who told Lillian Rubin, "Guys talk about things and girls talk about feelings." Note that when we think of emotionally controlled and distant men, we do not think first of the typical gender performance of Italian- or African-American men (although ambitious ones—think of Colonel Delmore in the 1996 film *Lone Star*—may be more likely to conform to stereotype).[61]

My experience of teaching young women about feminism for nearly two decades shows that this pattern produces a lot of pain for women as well as for men. Tapping this pain was key to the success of Deborah Tannen's *You Just Don't Understand*, which showed clearly how masculinity focuses men on a method of "problem solving" that often creates situations where the only real problem is lack of empathy. Once this issue is translated out of the language of "men are like this" and "women are like that" into an analysis of *gender pressures on men and how to change those pressures*, the issue of how to change "the strong silent type" can be moved toward the center of feminists' agendas. This is important not only to improve people's lives but because male withdrawal from emotional life has important implications for family work. Many men who currently rely on their wives to foster and maintain friendships and family networks haven't a clue about what's involved.[62]

If domesticity creates men from Mars, it also takes an important toll on our politics. One obvious example is the way domesticity identifies issues related to caregiving simultaneously as women's issues and as matters that "naturally" belong in the private sphere. In France and many other countries, as has been mentioned, such issues are felt to be of pressing public concern, relating to the future health (indeed, existence) of the community at large. Domesticity, American-style, is an integral part of the mind-set that leaves the United States the only major industrial nation that offers no paid maternity leave as a matter of national policy.[63]

Domesticity impoverishes our politics in subtler ways as well. As Joan Tronto shows so well, domesticity marginalizes not only the care of children but all tasks related to caring and caregiving. At a more sweeping level, the rise of domesticity was an integral part of the process that drove the virtues out of liberalism. To understand this process, it is best to begin with republicanism (lowercase *r*), the amorphous ideology that explained in the early modern world of monarchies how to sustain a republic. The health of a republic, went the theory, depended on having citizens with sufficient property to give them the independence to pursue the common good rather than their own narrow self-interest. Property gave men the virtue necessary to participate in public life. In most versions of republicanism, virtue and selflessness played central roles in public life.

This shows how the domesticity/liberalism dyad served to marginalize both virtue and selflessness by associating them with women. Virtue came to be associated with bourgeois sexual propriety rather than civic life; selflessness came to be associated with motherhood rather than with the citizen's pursuit of the common good.

To reverse this state of affairs, as communitarians have sensed, requires resuscitating nongendered rhetorics of community. But precious few retain any substantial vitality. Many communitarians suggest a return to republicanism, which is deeply flawed in ways an enormous literature has explored in excruciating detail. Much of the literature on republicanism misses the point. The goal is not to excavate a historical republicanism, but to build a new one suited to modern needs. The crucial quandary is how to uphold a vision of a unitary common good in a diverse world full of incommensurable notions of the good.

In addition to or instead of republicanism, religion offers another rhetoric capable of countering the devaluation of virtue and selflessness that accompany domesticity's association of both with women. Religion offers a nongendered language of selflessness and virtue with considerable political bite. Christianity has a nongendered rhetoric of selflessness with wide resonance: "Christ offered himself up as a sacrifice for the whole world." Moreover, the themes of selflessness that turned into Christianity derive from vital currents in Judaism. Hillel, who lived before Jesus, considered the love of man to be the kernel of Jewish teaching: "What is hateful to thee, do not unto thy fellow man: this is the whole Law; the rest is mere commentary." Jesus' commandment to love thy neighbor as thyself stems from that tradition. Both Christianity and Judaism thus offer strong nongendered rhetorics of selflessness that can serve to degender domesticity's allocation of selflessness to women.[64]

When we seek a nongendered language of selflessness and virtue, republicanism and religion both offer nongendered alternatives to domesticity. The ultimate goal of reconstructive feminism is not to embrace domesticity as we know it, but deconstruct its artificial oppositions and to reorganize our institutional and symbolic world. Domesticity needs to be transformed by melding it with other aspirational rhetorics, to make a new language and a new society capable of attaining our humanist ideals.[65]

•

CHAPTER SEVEN

Do Women Need Special Treatment?
Do Feminists Need Equality?

> The working woman shall have the same rights and, for equal work, receive the same remuneration as the working man. Working conditions must allow the fulfillment of her essential family function and assure the mother and child a special protection.
>
> —ITALIAN CONSTITUTION

The second branch of the sameness/difference debate concerns not the ideology of domesticity but its practice, specifically how to change domesticity's organization of (market and family) work. Debates about how to restructure market and family work raise troubling questions about equality. For (to quote Aristotle) while the principle of equality requires treating like things alike, it also requires treating different things differently. Since "common sense" tells us that men and women are different, what does gender equality mean?[1]

This is what Pablo Perez Tremps has called "the great technical problem" in equality theory.[2] It does not remain technical for long. An example that gives many feminists pause is the use of equality rhetoric to undermine women's claims to alimony. Originally alimony was available only to women, as a continuation of the traditional breadwinner/housewife roles. This practice was targeted once feminists began to insist on equality before the law. Alimony then became available to men as well as women, often with highly inequitable results.[3] In a recent U.S. case, a woman divorcing an abusive husband, an artist whom she had supported for a decade, found that the gender-neutral state statute made her potentially liable for alimony, despite the fact that she had earned virtually all the income and done virtually all the housework and child care.

Disillusionment with equality has emerged not only in alimony reforms but in other contexts as well. For example, as of the nineteenth century mothers were presumptively entitled to the custody of children of "tender years," another entitlement that ended with the rise of feminism after 1970. As a result, in divorce negotiations many fathers now act as if they intend to contest custody even when they do not, because husbands' lawyers have found that mothers often will compromise claims for child support and alimony to avoid a custody contest. Citing these and other examples, influential North American feminists such as Martha

Fineman and Mary Becker have argued that equality hurts women, and that feminists should avoid stating their claims in the language of equality.[4]

Yet their proposed alternatives have many limitations. Becker has argued that feminists should advocate rules that give custody back to mothers. Yet such rules would mean that in a situation where a father had maginalized his workforce participation in order to care for his children, he nonetheless would lose custody in a divorce. Thus a return to maternal custody would create yet another institution that polices women back into traditionally feminine roles and men out of them: It would act both as a deterrent to fathers who want to care for their own children and as an argument for fathers to use against wives trying to persuade the men to participate equally in family work.

Martha Fineman has argued that, in the context of allocating family assets upon divorce, feminists should focus not on equality but on what women need.[5] Yet the social mandate is to give women equality, not to meet their needs or those of any other social group. In the United States, the resistance to the language of needs is ideological. "From each according to his abilities, to each according to his needs"— if any principle is anathema in the United States, it is this one.[6] In other areas of the world, resistance to meeting social needs is not ideological but practical. Meeting citizens' needs is off the political agenda in many countries because it seems economically unfeasible.[7]

In sharp contrast, "rights talk" is a key resource for articulating moral claims in legal language. This is not to say that rights talk always works, only that it frames moral claims as legal entitlements in the way they are most easily heard. Thus the claim that women have been deprived of rights through discrimination is one of the most central and least contested elements in human rights law; the economic rights articulated in the Covenant on Cultural and Economic Rights are far more contested. Many national laws and constitutions also promise gender equality. But this does not answer the question of what the principle of gender equality requires.[8]

This chapter reexamines what is commonly called the "special treatment/equal treatment" debate, and will take us beyond the current resolutions.* The first such resolution is that feminists should avoid an emphasis on equality and focus instead on women's needs. The second is that feminists should recognize a small realm of "formal equality" where men and women should be treated the same, along with a much larger realm of "substantive equality" where men and women should be treated differently. To quote Catharine MacKinnon, women should be treated "the same when we are the same, different when we are different . . . [T]hat is the way men have it: equal and different, too."[9]

---

* I use the "special treatment/equal treatment" terminology when describing the debate traditionally called by this name. Yet my goal is to change that terminology, which correctly described neither the "special treatment" nor the "equal treatment" position. Later on in this chapter, I redescribe the relevant split as one between *maternalists* intent on empowering women within their traditional sphere, and *equal parenting advocates* intent on empowering women by moving toward a model of equal parenting.

To say that equality requires that women be treated alike when they are alike, and differently when they are different will often leave women vulnerable. For the traditionalist will respond that it is legitimate to discriminate against married women in the workplace because employers should be entitled to award plum jobs to workers who are not encumbered with family responsibilities that prevent them from devoting their full attention to their work. This is treating women differently because they are different. Is it consonant with the principle of gender equality for women?

Clearly not. What these initial examples show is that treating women the same can leave women vulnerable (as in the case of alimony and custody reform) but treating women differently can leave them vulnerable as well. The language of sameness and difference is not only divisive; it is also confusing and analytically flawed. This chapter translates the "sameness/difference" policy debates into a new language and a new analytical framework. I will argue that treating men and women the same is a strategy that works well where the goal is to eliminate the disabilities traditionally experienced by women, but it can backfire when applied to women's traditional privileges, for treating caregiving women the same as men who do not have caregiving responsibilities only exacerbates such women's gender disadvantage. To correctly apply the principle of treating men and women the same requires that formal equality be combined with an analysis of gender and power.

Once this is accomplished, an analysis of masculine norms takes center stage. Where such norms exist, treating men and women the same will backfire unless they are first dismantled. Otherwise women will be further disadvantaged when they are treated the same as men in the face of norms that favor men because they are designed around men's bodies or life patterns. Sometimes the dismantling of masculine norms can be accomplished simply by changing a single institution, such as the ideal-worker norm. In other situations, neutralizing the effect of masculine norms requires affirmative action, not as reparations for *past* wrongs but as a counterbalance to women's *current* disadvantage.

The result of this analysis is to offer a general theory of gender equality, which requires first the dismantling of masculine norms, and then treating men and women the same in ways sensitive to the linkage of gender and power.

Once this chapter has articulated a general theory of gender equality, it returns to the traditional special-treatment/equal-treatment debate in the United States and examines the ways both sides have mischaracterized their opponents. The first step toward avoiding this in the future is to recognize that these fights are not, in fact, fights over sameness and difference; instead, they are gender wars between femmes and tomboys that reflect differences in personal gender strategy. The fights are between *maternalists*, whose goal is to empower women in their traditional caregiving roles, and *equal-parenting advocates*, whose goal is gender flux.

What is the best way to defuse these battles? The key is to recognize that the divergences in feminists' personal gender strategies are often irrelevant, because in most situations the most desirable policy will be determined by the political culture in which feminists work. That culture will determine which of three potential axes it is most practical to change in a given political culture at a particular moment: the allocation of responsibilities or entitlements between fathers and mothers, the relationship of employers and employees, or the contours of the public and private spheres. Under the approach presented in this chapter, an analysis of which of these three axes to change replaces the traditional fights over sameness and difference.

The goal of this chapter is to take an instance of "language gone on holiday" and to defuse the gender wars that have arisen as a result. These gender wars mean that the two sides in the special-treatment debate have often mischaracterized each other as not "really" feminist. In fact, both groups are "really" feminists in the sense that both are committed to empowering women. They just have different visions of how to do so. Once the two sides stop demonizing each other, they can work together toward a new vision of equality that demands neither equal treatment in the face of masculine norms nor special treatment that leaves such norms intact; instead, it requires the dismantling of such norms. Once masculine norms are eliminated, women do not need special treatment or equality of results. All they need is a level playing field instead of one slanted in ways that currently pull women down.[10]

EQUALITY WITHOUT DISCRIMINATION

What Is Formal Equality and When Do We Need It?

The common understanding is of "liberal feminists" who support treating men and women the same because of their commitment to liberal neutrality. I will contest this view, arguing that formal equality is a position developed in response to a particular feminist agenda: the mandate to eliminate rules that enforce domesticity's allocation of the ideal-worker role to men and the primary-caregiver role to women.

Liberal feminism is associated with a series of cases litigated in the 1970s by Ruth Bader Ginsburg (now a Supreme Court justice and then with the Women's Rights Project of the American Civil Liberties Union), who insisted that men and women receive equal treatment before the law. An early example is *Reed v. Reed*, a 1971 case challenging a Florida state law that provided that were a man and a woman otherwise equally eligible to administer an estate, the man would automatically be preferred over the woman.[11] Florida justified the law by saying that it treated men and women differently because they were not in fact alike: Women's exclusion from public life meant that most women had less expertise in financial affairs than most men.

A closer look at the cases associated with the formal equality position shows that all involve policies that either police men and women into domesticity's gender roles, or punish those who cross gender boundaries. Most of the cases involve penalties imposed on male primary caregivers or female ideal workers. These include *Frontiero v. Richardson*, which involved the rule that servicemen but not servicewomen had the automatic right to claim their spouses as dependents; *Weinberger v. Wiesenfeld*, which challenged the rule that mothers but not fathers could claim Social Security survivors' benefits to care for the decedent's children; *Califano v. Goldfarb*, which contested the rule that automatically awarded survivors' benefits to women but not to men. The two final cases involved traditional disabilities associated with domesticity's allocation of women to the sphere of private life: Both involved challenges to jury systems that required jury service of men but not of women (*Healy v. Edwards, Duren v. Missouri*), overturning a prior case that tied rules excusing women from jury service to their domestic roles.[12]

MacKinnon, among others, has criticized Ginsburg for her choice of male plaintiffs, but this analysis shows why Ginsburg chose them. David Cole has argued that Ginsburg chose male plaintiffs because it was easier for male judges to feel the sting of gender disadvantage when it affected males than when it affected females. But the threshold point is that male plaintiffs served her purpose as well as female ones. Given that her goal was to dismantle domesticity, challenging the role domesticity assigned to men was as effective as challenging the role it assigned to women.[13]

Ginsburg's strategy for dismantling domesticity was to forbid government actors from using categories based on sex. As later articulated by Wendy Williams, this strategy stemmed not from a liberal obsession with neutrality but from an analysis of power, namely from the conviction that if courts and legislatures were allowed to use sex as a category of analysis, they would often use it to police men and women back into traditional roles. Thus Ginsburg's insistence on forbidding the use of sex-based categorizations was not so much a *theory* of equality as a *strategy* to constrain actors who could not be counted on not to discriminate if they were allowed to treat women differently from men.[14]

Formal equality is a strategy of limited usefulness in the United States today, because our manner of discriminating has changed (partly in response to Ginsburg's lawsuits). Domesticity's gender roles are no longer a formal part of our law and personnel policies. Women's traditional disabilities have been abolished, as have rules and policies penalizing ideal-worker women and primary-caregiver men. Yet in other countries women's traditional disabilities remain. A well-known example is the Guatemalan law that still requires women to obtain their husbands' permission before they work outside the home.[15]

Recent events in Peru show that the task of achieving formal equality is not finished once men and women are treated the same before the law. In Peru, the traditional provision that women need their husbands' permission to work outside the home was changed not by eliminating women's traditional disability altogether but by purporting to extend it to men. To quote the statute at issue:

> Each spouse can practice any job or profession that is allowed under the law, and can work outside the home, with the tacit or express consent of the other spouse.[16]

To capture why this remedy is inadequate requires us to introduce an analysis of gender and power, which begins from the fact that men traditionally are considered breadwinners, while women traditionally are not.[17] Though the allocation of caregiving to women has been challenged by feminism, *men's* duty and entitlement to market work has never been seriously questioned. Men have tacit permission to work outside the home, both because of the breadwinner role that is culturally linked with masculinity, and because the gendered structure of market work and the habit of older men marrying younger women means that most men are paid more than their wives.[18]

Given these social conditions, not only do men have tacit approval for working outside the home; few women will have a realistic opportunity to forbid their husbands from doing so. As the Latin American feminist Alda Facio has pointed out, the law must be analyzed not only at the level of formal rules but also at the level of social practice: Giving women a formal right that will never be exercised in practice is not a remedy that offers true equality. The formal grant of veto power to women is in fact a cynical fiction.[19]

The same is not true of men's veto over women's right to work outside the home. At the level of social custom, no tacit approval grants women the right to engage in market work. Not only are women unlikely to be able to show tacit approval for their work outside the home; they are also less likely to obtain formal approval from their husbands. Many husbands will feel free to forbid their wives from working, both because market work is not tied to femininity in the same way it is tied to manhood and because most men earn more than their wives. In this social context, the grant to men of veto power over their wives' labor force participation is not fictional. On the contrary, it is very real.

The Peruvian example shows that the principle that men and women should be treated the same does not answer the question of whether women's traditional disabilities should be extended to men, or whether they should be eliminated for everyone. An analysis of gender and power shows that such disabilities need to be abolished entirely, for purporting to extend them to men will merely perpetuate discrimination against women.

Thus the principle of formal equality is very important in cases involving women's traditional disabilities, where the solution is to treat women the same as men by eliminating those disabilities for everyone. But a different analysis proves necessary when we move from women's traditional disabilities to their traditional privileges.

Extending Privileges Traditionally Granted to Women

Very early in the feminist revolution of the 1970s, the movement to eliminate women's traditional disabilities led to a movement to eliminate women's traditional privileges as well. Early challenges were to women's traditional entitlement to alimony and to the maternal presumption, which gave mothers presumptive custody of children of "tender years."[20] Alimony statutes were changed by allowing men as well as women to qualify for alimony if they could show need.[21] Custody was changed as well, in one of three ways. In most states it was changed to award custody based on the best interest of the child. Other states moved toward joint custody, with the father and the mother sharing either physical custody of the child, or legal rights to make decisions concerning him or her, or both. Finally, a few states moved toward a standard that awarded presumptive custody to the child's primary caregiver.[22]

Many feminists have argued that these shifts have hurt women. While few men are awarded alimony, some of the situations in which men do receive alimony seem unfair to their wives, as in the case of the artist husband mentioned in the introduction to this chapter. Moreover, alimony awards dropped in value, in part because of the new presumption that they would be temporary rather than permanent.[23] As discussed above, the abandonment of maternal custody may have hurt women as well: Widespread reports exist of women giving in on alimony and other economic claims in the face of husbands' new demands for custody of the children (whether they actually want it or not).[24]

This evidence is often cited as proof of the bankruptcy of the formal equality principle of treating men and women the same, or as proof that feminists should avoid grand theory and focus on getting what will help women without worrying about the theoretical justifications involved.[25] This antitheoretical approach holds significant risks, for it sends the message that feminists are giving up their moral claim to equality and are just on the floor scrambling with other political actors for whatever they can get. I will argue that the alimony and custody debates reaffirm the importance of treating men and women the same, but show that avoiding discrimination in this context requires treating them the same by extending the benefits traditionally based on *sex* and linking them instead to *gender*, making alimony and custody available to men as well as women who play the primary-caregiver role.

Alimony. Traditional alimony represented a continuation of husbands' duty to support their wives in a social context where women were granted divorces only if they could prove marital fault.[26] Although need was the traditional test for alimony, that requirement was imposed to limit eligibility to needy wives in a social context in which virtually all wives were economically dependent upon their husbands.[27] Thus, the purpose of the need standard was to limit alimony to a subset of dependent wives: those without the job skills or independent income to support themselves without the help of their ex-husbands.

Reframing this goal in a sex-neutral fashion would provide alimony for anyone, regardless of body shape, who has played the marginalized-caregiver role traditionally played by the wife, so long as need can be demonstrated. Thus, in the case of the artist whose wife had performed both all of the market work and the large bulk of the family work for the duration of the marriage, alimony would not be available. For in that case, the economic dependence of the husband differed from that of the traditional wife. Although the artist husband could prove need, he could not meet the threshold requirement: He did not play the marginalized-caregiver role that provides the basic rationale for alimony.

Custody. Once women's traditional privileges are delinked from body shape and relinked to social role, some of the chief evidence against treating men and women the same before the law disappears. In addition to the alimony example, another example is the experience with the elimination of maternal custody. In that con-

212 • *Unbending Gender Talk (Including Feminism)*

text, the predominant trend in the United States has been toward joint custody. This result may seem necessary in the face of human rights treaties that mandate that fathers and mothers both retain parental rights after divorce.[28]

Joint custody works well in the minority of situations where it is freely selected by parents who are both equally committed to providing half of the child's everyday care: Indeed, in the absence of violence or some other acute problem in family dynamics, this probably is the ideal custody solution. The problem with joint custody, American style, is that when it becomes the presumption in cases where daily caregiving is not equally shared, it in effect gives the father the same rights to control the life and labor of the mother as existed during marriage. In roughly 90 percent of families with joint custody, the child still lives with the mother, yet because legally custody is joint, the father gains important rights. It effectively preserves for fathers the right they currently have in intact marriages: to provide only a small percentage of the day-to-day work of raising a child while retaining equal rights to make important child-rearing decisions. Preserving fathers' right to command how mothers shall perform the caregiving work required to raise a child is a far cry from equality for women. Second, in cases where the parents have joint legal custody courts have been less willing to allow the mother to move in order to take a good job elsewhere or to be near her family or other support networks. This is particularly important because, in intact families, the family most often lives in a location chosen to accommodate the father's job or other preferences. Forbidding the mother from moving after divorce in effect requires the mother to continue to live in a location chosen for her former husband's convenience even after the marriage has ended. In a society where wives are expected to follow their husbands, forbidding a custodial mother to move also means that a mother often will have to choose between her children or a new husband who wants or "needs" to move in order to follow good job opportunities.[29]

Clearly joint-custody provisions cut against women in many ways. So, too, does the predominant approach, which is to open an inquiry into what is in the best interests of the child.[30] This involves an assessment of who is the better parent, and such assessments are made in a social context where judges often will assume that a father doing 20 percent of the family work is more admirable than a mother doing 80 percent, since as things currently stand, many mothers do 100 percent and many fathers do virtually none. The unspoken and very sexist assumption that fathers are entitled to the caregiving work of mothers often distorts the inquiry mandated by the best-interests-of-the-child test.

An alternative is to follow the principle of changing privileges that are traditionally linked with body shape into privileges linked with gender roles. This would mean a presumption of custody to anyone who has marginalized his or her participation in market work in order to provide caregiving. The best proposal is that of Karen Czapanskiy (building on a prior proposal by Elizabeth Scott), which begins from the notion that—in a society that provides for children's care by marginalizing their caregivers—children need to be able to rely not only upon continued care by the adult they have come to depend on, but also on their other parent to support the primary caregiver. Czapanskiy therefore proposes that, after divorce, custody be awarded to reflect the division of child care while the marriage was intact *and* that the adult with primary custody is entitled to the support of his or her former partner. "Support" entails not only financial support; under this model, visitation by the noncustodial parent is part of the support owed to the caregiver. This model provides important sanctions in a society where fathers often show up for visitation only when they feel like it, and leave a disappointed child when they don't.[31]

When Equality Requires Deconstructing Masculine Norms

At this point we encounter the limits of formal equality, for the goal of reconstructive feminism is not simply to allow a minority of women who do not conform to stereotype to enter into traditionally male roles, or to protect women who remain in traditionally feminine roles. The ultimate goal is to deconstruct domesticity, and reconstruct market work and family entitlements.

This requires us to look again at the function of the principle that played such a central role in formal equality cases: that men and women should be treated the same. In *Reed v. Reed*, that rule functioned to strike down an open and explicit masculine norm, namely that males were more suitable to be estate administrators. Today in the United States most of the explicit masculine norms have been eliminated. What have not been eliminated are implicit masculine norms such as the ideal worker norm. As this book has shown, treating women the same as men in the face of norms designed around men's bodies and male social power merely perpetuates discrimination against women. In the context of such masculine norms, the first step in achieving gender equality is to dismantle such norms. This analysis places masculine norms at the center of any assessment of equality between men and women.

The idea that much of the world is designed around masculine norms has long been a staple of feminist analysis. The best single brief statement in North American feminism is from Catharine MacKinnon:

> Men's physiology defines most sports, their needs define auto and health insurance coverage, their socially designed biographies define workplace expectations and successful career patterns, their perspectives and concerns define quality in scholarship, their experiences and obsessions define merit, their objectification of life defines art, their military service defines citizenship, their presence defines family, their inability to get along with each other—their wars and rulerships—defines history, their image defines god, and their genitals define sex. For each of their differences from women, what amounts to an affirmative action plan is in effect, otherwise known as the structure and values of American society.[32]

The ideal-worker schedule is another example of a male norm. This book has argued that, particularly in contexts where ideal workers put in substantial amounts of overtime, performing as an ideal worker is inconsistent with common notions of how much parental care children need. Leaving this system intact means that most married mothers will "choose" not to perform as ideal workers because for them that choice means something different than it does for men. Men know that if they do not provide care for children, women will, whereas women know that if they do not do the caregiving themselves, the only alternative is to delegate it to a domestic worker. Thus ideal-worker mothers typically come face-to-face with the norm of parental care in ways most ideal-worker fathers do not. In this context, leaving intact the ideal-worker norm does not offer equality for women. It bars equal opportunity except for women ideal workers, who, in the United States, earn 90 percent of the average wage of men.[33] Yet mothers, who comprise nearly 90 percent of women, do not earn anywhere near what men do. True economic equality for women requires deconstructing the ideal-worker norm and reconstructing market work.[34]

A substantial literature exists documenting other sorts of masculine norms. An outstanding example is Elizabeth Schneider's early and elegant analysis of the way that judges apply the self-defense doctrine in criminal law. In the United States, the paradigm case for self-defense is a barroom brawl. In that context, appropriately, judges require that the threat to self must be "imminent" in order to justify the use of self-defense.[35]

Schneider points out that this standard for self-defense leaves many women vulnerable in domestic violence cases. The classic example is where a woman's husband has beaten her severely for many years. Then something happens such that his beatings intensify in strength or frequency, often with threats that he will kill her. Say she has tried repeatedly to leave, or has not tried because she believes his statements that he will kill her if she does try. In the United States she is entitled to a protective order ordering him to keep away from her, but obviously the police cannot protect her twenty-four hours a day. Perhaps she has tried to go to the police before, and they have refused to help her, and instead have asked what she did to provoke her husband, and recommended that she try to figure that out and avoid provoking him in the future. Consequently she (justifiably) believes that she cannot count on protection from the police, and that if she tries to leave, he will kill her. She refuses simply to disappear, because that would require her to cut herself off from her children, grandchildren, and other family and go to a strange city where she has no job and no ties. So she waits until, in a pattern that has often been repeated, he gets drunk, beats her, and falls into a stupor on his bed. Then she kills him.

Self-defense? No: no immediate threat. To understand why her behavior *was* legitimate self-defense requires us to recall her gendered characteristics as a typically feminine women. The fact that she has been beaten repeatedly and has not beaten back is the kind of behavior one often sees among women but rarely among men. The fact of domestic violence itself, of course, is a gendered phenomenon, stemming as it does from some men's sense that, in order to have the manly dignity they feel they deserve, they must exercise power over "their" woman. It also often has sexual elements as well: Many batterers find the exercise of brutal power over their lovers erotic. Gendered, too, is the fact that many victims of battering cannot leave the situation, either because they are economically dependent on the batterer, because they are responsible for the care of children, or both. The fact that this victim of violence did not find much help from the police also was gendered: What victim of a violent robbery would find himself interrogated as to what he did to provoke the robbery? Finally, the fact that the perpetrator waited until her batter- er was asleep is gendered: She did so because she did not feel competent to take her batterer on when he was awake, either because he is stronger than she is or be- cause he has been trained to fight in a way that she (as a woman) was not.

In order to understand why a woman in this kind of acute and chronic battering situation would kill her batterer, and why she would wait until he was asleep to do so, one must understand her gendered experience as a woman and a mother. This does not mean that we need one standard for self-defense for women and another for men. Indeed, if a man found himself in the same situation as our hypothetical woman—brutalized for years by someone who was stronger and better trained in fighting, unable to escape from the situation, where the authorities have shown themselves unwilling to offer to her the kind of protection they offer to other similar- ly blameless citizens—he too should be granted use of the doctrine of self-defense. The point is not that women should be treated differently than men, but that anyone in the situation women typically find themselves in should be held to have acted in self-defense in this kind of situation. Offering the self-defense doctrine only to peo- ple who strike back in a barroom brawl—or to someone protecting "his" house from an intruder—constitutes discrimination against women, because it offers the de- fense in the paradigm situations in which men need it while refusing to offer the defense in the paradigm situation in which women need it. Judges who apply the doctrine of self-defense in this way are violating the principle of gender equality.

A similar analysis could be made of rape law. Obviously judges need to differen- tiate between consensual sex and rape. Typically the law does so by means of a re- quirement that the rape victim "resist" her attacker. A more appropriate standard may well be that the victim signal her lack of consent, *taking into account* that rape situations are fraught with violent potential, so that the ways in which victims re- sist will reflect their perception that they may be killed or severely injured; indeed, studies indicate that rape victims are so much more likely to be killed or seriously injured if they resist that many rape counseling materials advise women not to resist. Surely it is not a great burden to insist that men avoid demands for sex in situations so fraught with violence or the threat of it that the object of their atten- tions fears for her life or safety if she says no.[36]

Thus the resistance requirement itself indicates that the law is more concerned with protecting men from false rape allegations than it is with protecting women from rape. Here is the first male norm at work in the law of rape. This norm is exac- erbated when judges apply the resistance requirement in ways that, in effect, require the rape victim either to struggle to the death or to be held to have consented to sex in rape situations. Interpreting the resistance requirement in this way, again, is to adopt the viewpoint of men (naturally concerned with false rape allegations) rather than women (naturally concerned with avoiding the humiliation of forced sex).[37]

Latin American laws holding that an entire gang of rapists is exonerated if one of the rapists marries the victim also reflect masculine norms in two senses.[38] The first is that this law defines rape as a crime against the traditional male entitlement to protect the honor of the family—which traditionally has meant the property interest of the father in controlling the sexuality of "his" women. Women, of course, never have had a property right in the sexuality of their men. The second is that rape law, thus constructed, is primarily concerned with protecting men's sexual prowess and with men's entitlement to "defiled" women; this explains the logic (otherwise obscure) of eliminating the rape charge where one man agrees to "waive" men's traditional right to virgins. Defining rape law to protect two traditional male entitlements—to control the sexuality of the women in his family, and to protect men's prowess—is a failure to give equal protection to men and to women. Legal doctrines designed to protect men's entitlements rather than women's human rights (in this case to sexual autonomy) fail to deliver equality to women.

These examples show that masculine norms structure the three levels of law set out by Alda Facio: formal rules (such as the law of rape), the way rules are applied (such as the way courts define what constitutes resistance in the context of rape), and social custom (such as the way employers structure market work). Equality requires changing each type of norm: not only changing the formal rules, but also changing the way judges apply the rules, and changing social customs (such as the ideal-worker norm) that are embedded in informal rules and unspoken expectations.

Often these types of masculine norms can be changed by changing a single rule (such as the code provisions concerning rape) or the way judges apply a rule (such as the way judges apply the resistance requirement). In other contexts, however, women are disadvantaged not merely by a single rule or interpretation, but by processes involving many different actors motivated by a variety of stereotypes of which they are barely conscious, or blissfully unconscious.

Take the example of women candidates for political office. They are disadvantaged, first, by reporters who cover male candidates with questions on their political positions, but cover female candidates with questions that focus more on the shape of their legs than the quality of their ideas. Or they are disadvantaged when they face questions about whether their children will suffer if they are elected, or whether their spouses object to their candidacy. These questions would never be asked of men, and send subtle messages that women's true role is to serve her husband and children; conduct that would be interpreted as public spirited in a man is subtly transformed into selfish and irresponsible in a woman. Women candidates also are disadvantaged when candidates are selected through the old-boy network, because they are less likely to be included in the male bonding that often provides the accepted idiom and the key activities, be they sports or hunting or extramarital sex. Together these forces and others form a powerful force field that pushes women out of traditionally masculine roles and into traditionally feminine ones. This force field is not insurmountable, which is why some women—particularly those with male biographies—can surmount it. But it drags women down and out of political roles of power and responsibility.

Where women's disadvantage stems not from a single male norm kept in place by a single institution or actor, but rather from many people (women as well as men) acting in a decentralized way who are driven by (often unconscious) stereotypes, then no effective method exists to eliminate the masculine norms at their source. The problem becomes complex indeed, because the only effective way to, for example, change people's stereotypes about women candidates is to have more women candidates, as The White House Project has pointed out.[39] But the force field dragging women down currently is so strong that few women candidates survive it—not because they are less able than men, but because they face challenges their male counterparts do not face.

In this kind of context, the only way to give equal opportunity to women is by affirmative action. Note that affirmative action is necessary not to remedy women's *past* disadvantage; it is necessary to remedy the way stereotypes and other types of masculine norms create *contemporary* disadvantage for women. The force fields that pull women down operate not only in politics but also in the workplace, where they drag women out of high-status positions in management and the professions. This topic will be further discussed in chapter 8.

In conclusion, gender equality requires that men and women be treated the same, but treating men and women the same requires not only equal treatment but changing existing institutions. When those institutions are designed around men's bodies or life patterns, the first step in achieving gender equality is to dismantle masculine norms.

CRITIQUE OF THE TRADITIONAL SPECIAL-TREATMENT/ EQUAL-TREATMENT DEBATE

This section addresses in more detail the so-called special treatment/equal-treatment debate in the United States. It makes two original contributions to this well-plowed field. First, it provides an integrated analysis of two sets of controversies whose relationship has never been adequately explored: the debate in the early 1980s over the design of workplace-leave policies, and the debates in family law over the design of child custody and economic entitlements upon divorce.

Both situations, upon reflection, concern the practice of domesticity, specifically the design of caregivers' entitlements. The work-side debates examine how to design entitlements on the job so that child rearing does not marginalize caregivers. The family-side debates examine how to design entitlements for caregivers upon divorce. Both debates concern the design of policies to redesign the relationship of market work and family work to replace the ideal-worker/marginalized-caregiver dyad inherited from domesticity.

My second contribution is a close analysis of the ways both sides in the special-treatment debate have mischaracterized their opponents. Difference feminists charge that sameness feminists deny difference and require women to adhere to masculine life patterns. They also charge that sameness feminists overlook the interests of marginalized-caregiver women. Sameness feminists charge that difference feminists perpetuate old roles and stereotypes of women. None of these charges is entirely justified. This section reexamines these charges, and then suggests that what really divides "special treatment" from "equal treatment" feminists is a gender war between *maternalists* whose goal is to empower women within their traditional caregiving roles and *equal parenting advocates*, whose goal is to move toward an ideal of equal parenting by men and women. In debates over how to design policies to restructure the relationship of market work and family work, feminists should abandon confusing and divisive language of sameness and difference (or special treatment and equal treatment) and instead use language that acknowledges the divergence in goals between maternalists and equal parenting advocates.

Do "Sameness Feminists" Deny Difference and Embrace Masculine Norms?

[I]n a recent California case *[CalFed]*, feminists actually lined up against a woman who lost her job when she took a disability leave for childbirth.[40]

The accepted description by difference feminists first contrasts their willingness to acknowledge the existence of differences between men and women with sameness feminists who minimize "or den[y] the existence of significant differences between men and women." While difference feminists insist on equality of results, the accepted description continues, sameness feminists are content with formal equality. Martha Fineman paints a picture of sameness feminists in the thrall of the "illusion of equality" and intent on ignoring evidence that equal treatment would hurt women upon divorce. Both Fineman and Mary Becker charge that formal equality helps professional women at the expense of women whose lives are framed by caregiving. Sylvia Ann Hewlett attributes similar traits to all of American feminism: "American feminists have generally stressed the ways in which men and women should be equal and have therefore tried to put aside differences."[41]

This description is repeated over and over again, in textbooks, monographs, and the popular press. Yet on its face it seems wrong. Why would any feminist deny that differences exist between men and women? Isn't the whole point of feminism that significant power differentials exist between men and women? This section will reexamine the texts associated with sameness feminists to reassess the accuracy of the accepted description.

In an early influential article, Linda J. Krieger and Patricia N. Cooney state that liberal feminism reflects two basic assumptions. The first is that no "real" differences exist between the sexes and that differentiation instead reflects illusory sex-based stereotypes. The second is that once all vestiges of discrimination are removed, women will achieve equality through "individual freedom of choice and equal competition in the social and economic marketplace." "Perhaps the most serious flaw in the liberal approach," the authors continue, "is that by virtue of its second assumption, it accepts maleness as the norm and permits a denial of equality ... to women who are either unwilling or unable to assimilate to that norm."[42]

A central theme is that liberal or sameness feminists' goal is to allow women to assimilate into institutions designed around masculine norms, which Christine Littleton labels "assimilationism." MacKinnon criticizes feminists who aim only to help women who can follow the life patterns traditional to men ("social males," Littleton calls them). Fineman decries "liberal feminists" whose "goal is equal participation in existing political, economic, and social institutions" and implores feminists "to do more than merely open the doors to institutions designed with men in mind." "Equal treatment," she notes, has contributed to the oppression of women, "particularly poor, nonprofessional women." Lucinda Finley articulates this as the "ideal of homogenous assimilation" into the masculine norm. Mary Becker, in "Prince Charming: Abstract Equality," argues against "a single general standard of equality" on the grounds that it "is unlikely to effect much real change without seriously risking worsening the situation of many women, especially ordinary wives and mothers."[43]

A review of the work of Wendy Williams and Ruth Bader Ginsburg, both often classified as liberal or equality feminists, shows that neither aspires merely to assimilate women into institutions designed around men. In fact, both are committed to deconstructing masculine norms. Wendy Williams makes it very clear that her goal is to "reduce structural barriers to full workforce participation": "Today the workplace remains unacceptably tailored to the old sex-based allocation of childrearing duties." A fact often overlooked is that *both* Williams *and* her opponents in *CalFed* advocated workplace restructuring. Special-treatment advocates supported restructuring through the California maternal disability statute, which redefined the ideal-worker norm in a way that included workers who bear children; equal treatment advocates supported restructuring by requiring all California employers to offer temporary disability policies that would include pregnancy. Either strategy would have eliminated the masculine norm that assumes that ideal workers take no time off for childbearing.[44]

Ruth Bader Ginsburg's early work says loud and clear that true equality requires "affirmative action" to "eliminat[e] institutional practices that limit or discourage female participation." "In some contexts," said Ginsburg in 1975, "redressing gender discrimination can be accomplished effectively simply by altering recruitment patterns and eliminating institutional practices which limit or discourage female participation." In others, Ginsburg notes, more would be required. "Extended study programs might be provided for students unable to undertake full-time study because of special family obligations that cannot be met by customary financial aid (notably, care of preschool children)." Clearly Ginsburg did not assume that women would assimilate into workplaces designed around masculine norms. Her proposals, while tentative, assumed that true equality for women would require restructuring so that "child rearing burdens are distributed more evenly among parents, their employers and the tax-paying public."[45]

Martha Fineman cites the Wisconsin reformers who worked in favor of an equal-division rule for dividing marital property upon divorce. She argues that marginalized-caregiver custodial mothers may well need more. Chapter 4 shows that I agree; for now, the important point is whether the Wisconsin reformers argued for 50 percent because they were gripped by an equality illusion. Fineman's own data suggest otherwise. She notes that the reformers argued for 50 percent simply because they faced a situation where women typically were being awarded one-third of the marital property, in an unacknowledged continuation of dower. In that context, using equality rhetoric to argue for 50 percent may well not indicate anything more than that reformers asked for what they thought they could get, and that 50 percent represented a substantial improvement supported by a persuasive rationale.[46]

The final and most important question is whether demands for equality have hurt women in traditional roles. To quote Mary Becker, "Formal equality has actually hurt many women. . . . [W]omen have lost many of the traditional sex-based rules which gave them some measure of financial security and protection." She notes the loss of maternal preference in child custody disputes as well as calculations of child or spousal support in which courts assume that the father and mother have had equal access to the breadwinner role. A second common allegation is that "equal-treatment" feminists sometimes have sought to eliminate entitlements for caregivers. Often this is framed as a defense of working-class women. Krieger and Cooney conclude, "The PDA's equal treatment approach simply does not meet the real needs of a vast proportion of this country's women workers," particularly working-class and single mothers. Mary Becker also argues that formal equality tends to harm ordinary wives and mothers, noting that perhaps its proponents view harm to those women as "a justifiable cost of effecting social change." She contends, "The elite who lead the feminist movement should be reluctant to press for change they consider desirable by imposing costs on other women."[47]

These are serious charges. The next task is to assess whether "sameness feminists" have sought to eliminate entitlements for caregivers.

Are Sameness Feminists Insensitive to the Needs of Caregivers?

Ruth Bader Ginsburg is one prominent feminist who has been accused of advocating the elimination of entitlements for caregivers. The only case in which she did so was *Kahn v. Shevin*, a challenge to a Florida law that gave a small property-tax break for widows but not widowers. *Kahn v. Shevin* should be viewed in the context of the series of early formal-equality cases discussed above. An important point is that while the cases involving women's access to traditionally male jobs and job benefits were handpicked by Ruth Bader Ginsburg and litigated by the ACLU Women's Rights Project under her direction, *Kahn v. Shevin* was not. In fact, she believed the case never should have gone to the Supreme Court. The case originally was brought by an ACLU affiliate without coordinating with the Women's Rights Project; Ginsburg got involved only once the case was headed for the Supreme Court, presumably to control the potential damage an adverse decision in *Kahn* would present for the line of precedent she was building on the issue of whether statutes expressing and enforcing domesticity's gender roles were constitutional. Presumably her assessment was that the potential damage of *Kahn* as a precedent outweighed the relatively small benefit it offered to widows (a $500 break on property taxes).[48]

The common assumption is that sameness feminists such as Ginsburg opposed all entitlements to caregiving women. As noted above, though she proposed subjecting all categories based on sex to strict scrutiny, she proposed not to prohibit entitlements for caregivers but to frame them in terms of "functional categories." In other words, a program designed to help women marginalized by gender would have to be drafted as a program to help caregivers, not as a program to help women. Thus a law designed to establish a presumption that mothers who are primary caretakers get custody upon divorce would have to be drafted as a presumption in favor of primary caretakers, not (as in the old days) as a maternal presumption. What Ginsburg opposed was the use of "sex as a proxy." The following, written as part of the debate over the Equal Rights Amendment, illustrates this.

> [The ERA] does not mean that disadvantageous treatment would be shift-
> ed to women whose occupational circumstances permit no alternative.
> But it would require substituting precise functional categories for gross
> gender classification. Functional description should preserve, and indeed
> might enlarge, rights and benefits accorded to women who work full-time
> within and for the family unit.[49]

All Ginsburg is saying is that laws designed to protect caregivers should be drafted to give rights to *caregivers* regardless of sex, not to *women*. She is right. A law that uses sex as a proxy—say, a maternal presumption—otherwise becomes another yet social sanction to police women back into the caregiver role and men out of it, for males who have performed the role of marginalized caregiver would not be awarded custody for the simple reason that they have penises. Surely no feminist wants to add to the social forces that penalize people for nontraditional gender performances.

If Ginsburg stated so often and so clearly that her vision of equality did not preclude remedial programs based on "functional" gender categories, why does the conventional wisdom hold that "sameness feminists" propose to deliver traditional women to the dogs? Part of the confusion stems from Ginsburg's unconventional use of the words *sex* and *gender*. Among feminists generally, *sex* is used to refer to biology, and *gender* to refer to the gender roles and other performances traditionally associated with sex. Ginsburg, in sharp contrast, used *gender* to refer to biology. Her reasons are unclear. Some attribute the decision to personal prudishness. Ginsburg herself seems to have felt that using the word *gender* rather than *sex* would help protect her from the jokes and innuendoes she would otherwise encounter if her opposing counsel and hostile judges could accuse her of talking about nothing but sex in front of all-male courtrooms in the 1970s.[50]

Whatever Ginsburg's reasons for her use of the terms, when she and others opposed the use of categories based on *sex* and articulated their taboo as one on categories based on *gender*, no wonder people became confused. Moreover, some feminists were not as careful as Ginsburg to avoid policies with the potential to penalize women in traditional roles. Some feminists went beyond Ginsburg's injunction against policies designed by reference to sex and opposed as well policies designed by reference to gender.[51]

One example, discussed above, is Herma Hill Kay's brief advocacy of the elimination of alimony for younger women.

> I do not believe that we should encourage future couples entering marriage to make choices that will be economically disabling for women, thereby perpetuating their traditional financial dependence upon men.[52]

Four years later Kay had backed away from this position, under fire from other feminists.

> I do not believe that we have yet come to the historical moment when I would conclude that there is no need to . . . [award alimony in some circumstances]. Before that moment arrives, I believe we as a society must have firmly in place a much more elaborate institutional structure of available child care and health care services, as well as adequate social and economic support systems to enable parents to nurture and rear their children. Moreover, we must have greater confidence than now seems possible that the existing job discrimination against women workers, particularly those with children, can be ended.[53]

Despite many accusations that sameness feminists oppose economic entitlements for women upon divorce, Kay is the only feminist I have found who opposed such entitlements. Most feminists have concentrated their efforts on searching for a new rationale for alimony, not on eliminating it. Among the fifteen-odd leading scholars writing about the impoverishment of women upon divorce, not one opposes alimony.[54]

This makes sense. While work-side commentators can dream of restructuring market work to eliminate traditional gender roles, commentators on the family side pick up the pieces after traditional gender roles have impoverished divorced women. Small surprise that family-side commentators do not question the need for entitlements based on caregiving, even if most assume that feminist strategies should seek to undermine traditional gender roles, not perpetuate them.

Another major example of "sameness" feminists opposing entitlements for caregivers is an article on child-custody standards written by two influential feminists, one a lawyer (Katharine Bartlett) and the other an anthropologist (Carol Stack).[55] Bartlett and Stack argue against a standard that awards custody to the child's primary caregiver, in favor of a presumption of joint custody except in cases of actual or threatened abuse. This is a controversial proposal because a substantial majority of women today are awarded sole physical and legal custody. Bartlett and Stack's proposal would reverse this, and would give fathers significantly more control than most noncustodial fathers have today.[56]

Bartlett and Stack defend their proposal by reference to law's expressive function—its ability to express and change social expectations and norms: "[A]n end to the law's complicity in inegalitarian norms may be a precondition of reform and even a catalyst for it." Bartlett and Stack argue that the joint custody rule "stakes out ground for an alternative norm of parenting" that involves fathers as much as mothers. Instead of saying that fathers will be able to be involved in the lives of their children only if they were involved before divorce (as does the primary-caretaker presumption), it says that "[y]ou, father, have a role to play in your children's lives which is to participate in their upbringing and assume day-to-day responsibility for them jointly with their mother, and you will do so after marriage even if you do not do so during marriage."[57]

Bartlett and Stack clearly identify their goal as having the father and the mother do equal parenting. When the proposal is to abandon the rule most likely to protect women in favor of a strategy that trades off concrete legal protection in the hopes of destabilizing domesticity, however, the question is not whether men and women are the same or different but whether law's expressive function should trump its role in offering concrete protections for caregiving women.

Surely no one answer exists to this question. In significant part it depends on how many women stand to lose from decreased legal protection, how deeply hurt they will be, and whether the proposed change will serve only to express our ideals or also to help us attain them. Each of these is a factual issue, yet the debates on using law's expressive function have been very short on facts. Bartlett and Stack do not present any data to back up their assumption that a joint-custody standard will change the behavior of fathers, leaving open the question of whether courts have the resources necessary to make fathers into active parents. Yet these data seem vital. Surely it makes no sense to adopt joint custody if courts *will not* enforce obligations on fathers but *will* give them significant rights to command how mothers shall do virtually all the family work. Then the symbolic message is worse than ever: that fathers are entitled to substantial control over their children even when they do virtually none of the day-to-day work of raising them. As suggested above, adopting joint custody under these circumstances in effect preserves the father's right to direct and control how the mother performs the caregiving work.

Perhaps for these reasons, Bartlett has backed away from her support of joint custody and now supports a standard very close to that proposed by Czapanskiy. Thus two of the leading proponents of strategies designed to eliminate entitlements for caregivers advocated those policies only briefly, only to reconsider later.[58]

The experiences of Kay and Bartlett confirm that special-treatment feminists are right that eliminating entitlements for caregivers is not a desirable feminist strategy. An analysis of gender and power shows that such a strategy is unlikely to work. Part I shows the powerful force fields that lead many mothers to "choose" marginalization. These include the ideal-worker norms in market work, men's sense of entitlement to family work and other social privileges such as the ability to move their families to follow an attractive job offer, and women's sense of what they owe to husbands and children. Feminists need to ask whether any proposed policy will be sufficient to counter these powerful forces, which influence women day by day. Typically they will not be. For example, Kay's proposal to eliminate alimony for younger women assumes that women will not accept marginalization if they face poverty upon divorce. Women *already* face poverty upon divorce—even with alimony—and they accept marginalization nonetheless. They do so because (like most Americans) they are convinced *their* marriage will survive, or because they see no other way to provide quality care for their children despite fears of divorce. Because women's "choices" are not influenced by the existing threat of impoverishment, there is no reason to think that threatening them with slightly more impoverishment will make the crucial difference.[59]

Feminists need to choose our battles and to attack the gender system where it is weak—not to trade off protections for marginalized caregivers in fruitless assaults where the system is strong. This brings us back to *CalFed*, another case involving entitlements for caregivers, this time the work-side entitlement of parental leave. Does this again involve sameness feminists proposing to trade off to eliminate caregivers' entitlements? Not on the surface: Though discussions of *CalFed* often overlook it, neither group of *CalFed* feminists opposed the leaves proposed by the California statute. The split was over *how to design the leave program*, not *whether to have one*.

Which side was right? An answer requires us to separate two questions that are rarely distinguished. The first concerns the optimal litigation strategy in *CalFed*; the second is whether a *CalFed*-type statute is the optimal way to draft a workplace-leave law. Commentators rarely distinguish between these issues, yet it is vital to do so, for while defending the California statute as written may well have been the right litigation strategy in *CalFed*, this does not prove that the California statute represents the best way to draft a leave law.

On the issue of litigation strategy, this depends on one's assessment of whether there was a realistic possibility that the U.S. Supreme Court would require California employers (as the equal-treatment feminists argued they should) to offer temporary disability insurance for all employees as relief for an antidiscrimination suit. Precedent exists that would have allowed the Supreme Court to do so; clearly the Court *could* have ordered such relief if it had had the will to do so. The question is whether it was reasonable to expect that a Supreme Court consisting of Justices Scalia, Rehnquist, White, Powell, Marshall, Brennan, Blackmun, Stevens, and O'Connor would yield a majority in support of the equal-treatment position.[60]

The key person is Justice O'Connor. In a five-to-four situation, she is what lawyers call the swing vote, the person whose vote will determine who wins the case. The first woman appointed to the Supreme Court, O'Connor has often sided with women in sex-discrimination cases, but she is also a Reagan appointee who often sides with business interests. The question, then, is whether O'Connor, given the choice between a feminist position that did not impose upon business the costs of funding disability insurance for all workers (by merely upholding the *CalFed* statute) and a feminist position that did (the equal-treatment position), could have been persuaded to support the solution that imposed greater costs on business.[61]

Probably not. Given O'Connor's well-documented receptivity to an unfettered market and business concerns, it is highly unlikely that she would have supported the equal-treatment position when the much cheaper alternative of simply upholding the California statute was staring her in the face. The chances of a majority in favor of the equal-treatment strategy were slim; the realistic choice was to strike down the California statute or to uphold it. This again raises the question of whether feminists committed to destabilizing traditional gender norms should effect their goals by opposing entitlements for caregivers. They should not.[62]

But the fact that CREW had the winning strategy in *CalFed* does not prove that the *CalFed* statute represents the best way to design leave statutes. Virtually all commentators have assumed that if CREW was right, this proves that leave laws can legitimately link benefits to sex because they concern pregnancy, a sex difference between men and women. Prominent feminists such as Sylvia Law and Herma Hill Kay adopted this argument; after all, even the staunchest of sameness feminists had argued that the Equal Rights Amendment did not forbid statutes linking benefits to sex in the context of true sex differences.[63]

Did the *CalFed* leave law cover only true sex differences? I would argue not. The answer lies in a judgment about how physicians determine the periods of maternal disability they will certify—typically six weeks for a vaginal birth and eight weeks for a cesarean. Don't these periods reflect the sociological fact that mothers recovering from childbirth typically are expected to do virtually all of the baby care, so that they are sleep-deprived during the recovery period? To answer that a nursing mother must necessarily do all the care herself is unconvincing to someone (me) who spent one pregnancy leave with no daytime help and sitting up for a half hour every two hours for nighttime nursings, and a second, far healthier, recovery period in which I had much more help and became far less run down.

Given existing practice, physicians obviously do the right thing in certifying disability periods long enough to allow mothers to recover under existing social conditions where they have little or no help. Moreover, there are obvious strategic benefits to coding as "physical" the needs created by the current combination of physical recovery plus baby care. But this strategy imposes costs as well, as has been noted by critics who argue that linking postbirth leave to disability ensures that in the important early weeks, when family patterns change to adjust to the new baby, the baby's demands will be tied to the mother alone rather than to the father as well. The FMLA's provision of leave periods for adoptive parents suggests that childbirth leave is linked to the norm of parental care, not solely with the medical needs associated with childbirth.[64]

Thus the ultimate messages of the *CalFed* controversy are more complex than is commonly recognized. Though CREW had the winning litigation strategy, the California statute does not represent the ideal approach to designing workplace-leave policies. The best design for such policies would offer, from the beginning of a child's life, leaves both for recovery from childbirth (available to postpartum women) and for caregiving (available to all parents), with the provision that such leaves could be taken either simultaneously or sequentially.

In conclusion, when we go searching for "liberal" feminists who embrace mere assimilation into a world framed around masculine norms, we find that the major figures to whom this position is attributed do not actually hold it. I suspect that assimilationism exists less in feminist theory than in everyday life. Take the example of the law professor who recently announced that she did not intend to take the semester's leave granted by a parental-leave policy that had been fought for and won by her predecessors, because she did not want "special treatment"; instead she took off two weeks and then returned to full-time work. This is assimilationist feminism: a woman trading off hard-won gains for caregivers in an attempt to conform to the male norms that define being a responsible worker as one who acts like a traditional father. While it is easy to condemn this new mother, more to the point is that feminists need to develop and publicize an effective resolution to the special-treatment/equal-treatment debate in order to clarify the thinking of ordinary women in making their everyday decisions.

That said, another striking conclusion of the analysis thus far is that feminists involved in the special-treatment debate often have inaccurately characterized their feminist opponents. One common description (of feminists committed to assimilation) describes virtually no one. A second (of sameness feminists opposed to entitlements for caregivers) describes very few. These two common misdescriptions of equality feminists are matched by a common misdescription of special-treatment advocates: that their proposed policies simply re-create and reinforce existing gender roles. In fact, as the following section will show, both groups seek to empower women; they just have different visions of how to do so, based on whether they seek to empower women in their caregiving roles or whether to bring about a more equal sharing of family work between men and women.

Maternalists Versus Equal-Parenting Advocates

For without public support policies, few women can cope with motherhood without hopelessly compromising their career goals.[65]

[Justice Ginsburg's] "grand ideal" is to have men and women work together to share equally life's responsibilities and rewards.[66]

A close reading of the "special treatment/equal treatment" debate reveals that the split is not between those who believe that men and women are the same and those who believe they are different, but between two groups I will call *maternalists* and *equal-parenting advocates*. Though both are committed to gender equality, they have very different visions of how to achieve it. Neither is satisfied with formal equality; both insist on eliminating the privileging of men's bodies and biographies through masculine norms. But masculine norms can be eliminated either by empowering women within the role domesticity assigns to them or by deconstructing domesticity's gender roles and replacing them with a new organization of market and family. The first strategy leads to maternalist policies that leave intact the gendered allocation of child rearing to mothers. The second leads to policies designed to encourage equal parenting. The persistent fights between maternalists and equal-parenting advocates can be seen as an integral part of a larger series of fights between femmes (who embrace femininity and seek to empower women within it) and tomboys (alienated from existing gender roles and desirous of changing them). In this context the femme/tomboy split describes not (as in chapter 6) feminists' relationship to the ideology of domesticity; instead, it describes their relationship to domesticity's structuring of market work and family work.[67]

The most influential credo of maternalism is Christine Littleton's "Reconstructing Sexual Equality." Littleton differentiates between "symmetrical" models of equality, which insist on identical treatment of men and women, and "asymmetrical" models, which do not. She advocates a model of "equal acceptance." "Acceptance does not view sex differences as problematic per se, but rather focuses on the ways differences are permitted to justify inequality. It asserts that eliminating the unequal consequences of sex differences is more important than debating whether such differences are 'real,' or even trying to eliminate them altogether." Earlier on, Littleton had explicitly included social as well as biological differences. In other words, her argument embraced the dyad of male ideal worker and female caregiver and sought to empower women within their traditional caregiver role.[68]

Littleton is a classic maternalist; Ruth Bader Ginsburg and Wendy Williams are classic equal-parenting advocates. Williams states clearly that her goal is to destabilize domesticity's allocation of family work to women and market work to men:

> Today's feminists from the outset rejected the separate spheres ideology which assigned men to the workplace and women to the home. The crucial functions of the traditional family arrangement—financial support, housework and childrearing—should not, they asserted, be assigned by sex. To the extent that laws and rules force the traditional preassignment and inhibit choice, they should be replaced by laws and rules that make no assumptions about the sex of the family childrearer or wage earner, but simply address those functions directly. Moreover, the workplace should be restructured to respond to the reality that all adult members of a household in which there are children are frequently in the workforce.[69]

In sharp contrast to Littleton's strategy of empowering women within traditional roles, Williams is committed to *gender flux*, that is, to destabilizing domesticity's gender roles. This central split informed the other disagreements at work in *CalFed*. For example, Williams placed a high priority on avoiding any use of the law that would reinforce the symbolic hold of domesticity's ideology of sacred motherhood; Littleton did not. This highlights that Littleton's aim was not to deconstruct domesticity but to empower women in the domestic role.

Maternalists often charge that feminists who oppose maternalism are blind to women's needs, or hold up as the ideal European programs that provide supports for motherhood. "Instead of applying the antidiscrimination model, which predominates in American jurisprudence, European law affirmatively encourages and even mandates direct accommodation of the special pregnancy-based needs of working women," write Samuel Issachroff and Elyse Rosenblum. Discussions of maternalism often blur the desirability of reconfiguring the public sphere with the question of whether the programs that do so will be designed in ways that reinforce domesticity's allocation of family work to women.[70]

Martha Fineman's work fits the pattern. Fineman begins with the common description of feminists committed to gender neutrality and argues (correctly) that feminism makes no sense without close attentiveness to gender. The "concept of a gendered life is my attempt to create a way to argue that a consideration of differences is necessary to remedy socially and culturally imposed harms to women." The subtext is that some feminists deny difference and that such denial means they deny the importance of gender. As noted above, resistance to policies that link benefits to sex does not necessarily entail opposition to benefits based on gender. The reigning confusion over *sex* and *gender* causes Fineman to blur the distinction between equal-parenting feminists, who reject the traditional linkage of caregiving to sex, and conservative nonfeminists, who declare gender analysis no longer necessary because inequality no longer exists.[71]

As will be discussed further below, Fineman's work has played an extraordinarily important role in insisting that society should "value, and therefore subsidize, caretaking and caretakers." She has been a major influence in shifting the center of gravity within legal feminism to a focus on dignifying family work and insisting that it should give rise to entitlements. But can one take seriously the project of revaluing family work without arguing (as does Fineman) for an embrace of "Mother"? (The capital letter is hers.) Despite her protests that she uses "Mother" as a gender-neutral term of art, Fineman's declaration that the gender-neutral ideal of parenthood is a "tragedy" leaves little doubt that she embraces domesticity's allocation of child rearing to women; in fact, her proposals would eliminate parental status for all fathers except those who somehow qualify as "Mothers."[72]

Christine Littleton's plea for feminists to continue their traditional focus on women crystallizes the split between maternalists and equal-parenting advocates. Her proposed redraft of the FMLA to cover all caregiving performed by women shows how her equal-acceptance theory would reinforce the allocation of child rearing to women. The trouble with sex-linked policies, as noted above, is that they police men out of caregiving roles. The maternalist response is often to charge that equal-parenting advocates obviously care more about protecting a few caregiving men than the large majority of caregiving women. This blurs the basic point: Equal-parenting advocates are concerned about caregiving men not because they devalue women but because their goal is gender flux—a goal that is undercut by linking benefits for caregivers to the shape of their genitals.[73]

Why bother with gender flux if women still do 80 percent of child care? Because though some men do little, large numbers of men do a lot. A few are househusbands. A lot more are primary caretakers part of the time. Nearly 20 percent of men in split-shift families with children under five are primary caretakers while their wives are at work. In many other families, men do substantially more than their fathers did. In my neighborhood alone, I know househusbands who are marginalized caregivers while their wives perform as ideal workers, men who work from 6 A.M. to 2 P.M. in order to pick up the children at school, and men who drop off kids at school so their wives can go to work early. I also know many men with nigh-total immunity to family work and men who literally do not know the names of their children's teachers or the camp their children are attending. One study estimated that one-third of men behave as traditional breadwinners, while another third drop out of family life or avoid it completely; the remaining third have taken on considerable amounts of family work. That study, by Kathleen Gerson, convincingly documents the "demise of a cultural consensus on the meaning of manhood." Sex-linked policies would counteract this trend by policing men out of caregiving roles, reversing the gender flux achieved since 1970.[74]

An additional point is in order. Littleton asserts that her proposed alternative, of paid leave for all caregiving performed by women, would help larger numbers of women than the FMLA. But surely this depends on its ability to be passed by Congress. Such passage seems unlikely. Business took a vigorous interest in the FMLA and for many years blocked its proposal of unpaid leave. In this context, it seems unlikely that a paid leave could carry the day, even if maternalist feminists commanded the support of antipoverty groups and gay activists (as Littleton notes they would). Littleton's proposal probably would not become law, so it seems hard to see how it would help women more than the FMLA, which did. Equal-parenting advocates settled for unpaid leave only because insisting on a paid one would yield no leave at all. Littleton is measuring what equal-parenting advocates had to embrace in the real world against what she would like to embrace in an ideal one.[75]

Littleton's second proposal is to reinstitute the maternal-custody presumption. She discusses an outrageous custody case in which a lower court ordered a mother to move back to the city of her child's father, who had divorced the mother when she refused to abort and played no role in the child's life for several years after his birth. The court ordered the mother to relocate despite the fact that to do so she would have to give up a good job and move to a city where she had no job prospects. (The facts are from Littleton, who helped represent the wife.)

Littleton is right that the lower court's ruling was a scandal; on the other hand, the appellate court found for the wife and reversed the lower court. This does not seem to support Littleton's contention that women need a return to the maternal presumption to protect them, for in this case the best-interests-of-the-child standard (while hardly ideal) seemed to protect the mother just fine.[76]

Yet it would be unwise to stop there. Littleton's underlying point is worth close attention. Don't provisions designed around gender rather than sex present the risk that courts will apply them in ways that reflect and perpetuate the force field of male power over women? This is a vitally important issue.

As Mary Becker has noted, "To some extent, this problem can be avoided by careful drafting and detailed legislative history."[77] A return to the Czspanskiy standard will show how. Many judges bring the kind of gendered expectations to family work expressed in the *Doonesbury* cartoon reprinted in chapter 4. Those judges assess whether or not a father is a "good" father by comparing his contribution to the minimal contribution expected of breadwinners, whereas a mother's contribution is judged by comparing her to a full-time homemaker. This problem of differential baselines makes many judges too easily impressed by fathers and too often critical of mothers, as in the custody cases discussed at the end of chapter 4.

The tendency for judges to be overly impressed by family work done by fathers and underimpressed by that done by mothers shows how women can be made vulnerable by a standard designed around gender rather than around sex. Another example is when divorce courts claim that their commitment to women's equality requires them to treat women the same as men upon divorce—in other words, to calculate postdivorce entitlements on the assumption that marginalized mothers are as able as fathers to support themselves upon divorce. Treating a $100,000-a-year lawyer and a secretary out of the workforce for twenty years as if they were equally able to support themselves is clearly not required by principles of equality. In some contexts, some judges appear to be punishing women in anger over feminism's demands for equality. "Now they think, 'Well, you gals wanted to be in the job market, here is your chance,'" said one prominent family lawyer. Other judges start from unspoken notions of male ownership of the ideal worker's wage, as discussed in chapter 4.

Though situations can be avoided by linking entitlements to sex, the disadvantage of doing so is that sex-linked policies police men and women back into domesticity's gender roles. The alternative is to draft gender-linked policies in ways that make them hard to abuse—and to be ready to litigate if they are abused.[78]

Two basic principles for drafting gender-linked statutes can help avoid abuse. The first is to delineate the factors a nonbiased decision-making process would use. The second is to create a record that makes the decision maker's reasoning process public. For example, in the primary-caretaker example, one needs first to identify the factors a nonbiased decision-making process would consider. In the context of custody decisions, these factors would vary depending on the age of the child but should address the child's normal, everyday activities. For a school-age child, factors would include who takes the child to school, who picks the child up, who maintains steady contact with teachers, who schedules play dates and lessons, who supervises homework, who spots and takes steps to address any academic or social problems that arise, who plans and gives birthday parties, who supervises baths and eating, who buys clothes, who puts the child to bed, and so on. The statute needs to walk the judge through a child's day, so that the judge is forced beyond stereotypes to assess who actually did what. The statute also needs to assess who has given up ideal-worker status in order to accommodate child care, for it is only fair that a parent who has sacrificed social status and economic independence should not lose custody of the child for whom those sacrifices were made.

The second step is to require creation of a public record so that the judge's findings on the issues discussed above will be reviewable by a higher court. This is important because the legal standard for reversal of a trial court's findings is difficult to meet: in the ordinary case, the appeals court must find an abuse of discretion. Creation of a record makes this standard easier to meet. It also serves an independent purpose. In a society with high ideals, publicity is often an effective weapon —judges whose decisions would reflect bias and stereotypes if left unspoken will often be much less willing to make such statements in a formal, written way.

Even with careful drafting, the distortion of gender-linked statutes remains a possibility. The trade-off is this: risk sexist application of a gender-linked statute that will appeal to femmes as well as tomboys, or split the feminist coalition by insisting on sex-linked statutes.

The split between maternalists and equal-parenting advocates is a real one, unlike the prior conflicts within feminism described above. Since women are divided by gender strategy, feminism should give voice to the strongest arguments for each major position (which is what I have tried to do here). On the other hand—precisely because women are and will remain split—feminists seeking to create a wide coalition need to design policies that appeal both to women seeking to empower women within domesticity and those who seek gender flux.

Even in contexts where maternalist policies work best in the short term, they can be drafted as gender- rather than sex-linked policies, so that such policies do not become part of the societal machinery policing men and women back into domesticity's gender roles. Maternalist policies also can be linked with policies designed to destabilize gender roles in the long run. For example, a gender-linked maternalist policy socializing caregiving can be combined with equal-parenting policies that eliminate the carrots and the sticks that keep men in the ideal-worker role. (This describes the strategies set out in chapters 3 and 4.)

Equal-parenting policies should incorporate three elements of maternalism. First and foremost, they should respect family work, and focus as much on entitlements for caregivers as on entitlements for workers. Second, they need to avoid eliminating entitlements for caregivers in the name of equal-parenting goals. Both incorporate the concerns of women whose goal is to empower women in their traditional roles rather than to open up new roles. Finally, equal-parenting policies need to be drafted very carefully, to help ensure they are not interpreted in ways that turn them into weapons against women. When they are used in ways that harm women, they need to be challenged as illegal sex discrimination.

From "Special Treatment v. Equal Treatment" to "Maternalists v. Equal-Parenting Advocates"

The special treatment/equal treatment language carries with it an old gender war in which feminists often mischaracterized each other in ways that have impeded them from designing and advocating effective policies for restructuring the relationship of market work and family work. This section points the way to a new methodology for designing policies to change the practice of domesticity that completely avoids the divisive and misleading language of sameness and difference. Once issues of policy design are divorced from the language of sameness and difference, the following section will show, they can be reformulated in new ways that focus attention on the practical choices policymakers face.

THE THREE AXES

Market and family work can be restructured by changing one or more of three possible axes. First, one can change the allocation of family work within the household or the entitlements that flow from it. I call this *gender redistribution*. Second, one can shift some responsibilities from the *private* to the *public* sphere. Third, one can challenge employers' entitlement to marginalize all employees who have responsibility for family work, thereby *redefining the relationship between employers and employees.*

Policy options lie along one or more of these axes. Note that the resulting discussion does not focus on sameness or difference. Instead, it focuses on which axis or axes to change. Often the particular political realities a feminist faces will prove more important than her own personal gender strategy in determining what is the most desirable policy option in a given situation. The following discussion pays special attention to the relative attractiveness of different options in different cultural contexts.

Gender Redistribution

One way of restructuring the relationship of market work to family work is to redistribute household work and the entitlements that spring from it. On the family side, this involves redefining who owns the wealth generated by the family. On the work side, it involves redistributing responsibilities within the household. This section discusses both types of gender redistribution.

Redistributing Entitlements Stemming from Family Work

Some countries in Latin America do not allow for alimony upon divorce; in others alimony is allowed but typically is awarded in low amounts. Child support, too, typically does not represent a true measure of the actual costs of raising children.

In effect, then, the work of the ideal worker, typically the father, is defined as his sole personal property upon divorce. The only issue is how much of "his" income will be redistributed upon divorce to his ex-wife. If we begin from the principle that the ideal worker's wage reflects the joint work both of the ideal worker *and* of the caregiver(s) whose family work allows him to perform as an ideal worker, then it makes no sense to award ownership of that wage exclusively to the ideal worker: An asset produced by two parties should not be treated as the property of only one of them.

In the Latin American context, as in North America, mothers often are in the labor force. In both cultural contexts, however, they typically continue to be in charge of housekeeping and child-care arrangements even when they are. Thus, even women with jobs either do the family work required to raise children and run a home themselves or supervise those who do. In either case, mothers are providing the flow of family work required to allow fathers to perform as ideal workers, after as well as before divorce, and so should be treated as joint owners not only of the property accumulated during the marriage but also of the wages earned after divorce, for as long as the children are dependent, and for a period of time thereafter to allow the mother to gain the work experience necessary to perform as an ideal worker. True equality requires equalization of the incomes of the ex-husband's and the ex-wife's household upon divorce, to be accomplished by giving each ownership of half the income of the other for the period described above.

Redistributing assets upon divorce is an important strategy to end the impoverishment of divorced women and their children in societies where divorce often means poverty or downward mobility for children. Although redistributing entitlements between ex-husbands and wives is an important feminist project, it is not one that will help all women. In many cases both in the United States and in Latin America, poverty among divorced women often reflects "reshuffled poverty"—in other words, the women were poor even before they divorced. Using gender-based redistribution as the only feminist strategy, therefore, helps richer but not poorer women. It also does not help women in families where poverty results not from an unfair distribution of assets between them and their former husbands but from a lack of assets overall.[79]

Gender-based redistribution strategies must be linked with larger income-redistribution strategies if all women are to be helped out of poverty. (This is why I work on property as well as gender issues.) This does not mean that feminists cannot legitimately focus on helping those women whose poverty is produced by gender, rather than class, disenfranchisement. To require feminists to use strategies that help poor women as much as nonpoor ones in effect requires feminists to stop focusing on gender. This sounds suspiciously like the traditional mandate that women must selflessly focus on others.

Though feminists have the right to focus on gender, they have the responsibility to ensure that the strategies they adopt do not place poor women and their families in a worse position than before feminists intervened. For example, an equalization proposal such as that suggested above must provide that poor fathers be allowed to set aside an amount necessary for their own survival, before income equalization of the two postdivorce households begins; otherwise, income equalization would result in poor men being faced with the choice between making their support payments and paying for their own food and rent.

Whenever feminists use strategies designed to redistribute household income between men and women, they need to think through how to avoid imposing unanticipated and unintended burdens on poor families.

Redistributing Family Work Within the Household

U.S. feminists traditionally have focused on redistributing household work between men and women. Has this strategy worked? The glass is half empty and half full. The empty part is obvious: In the United States women, on average, still do 80 percent of the child care and two-thirds of the housework.[80]

This represents some progress. First, it represents a significant rise (although a small one) in the amount of household work men do as a group . Many men do a lot more work than their fathers did. Men who grew up in households where wives made their husband's coffee now do dishes and change diapers. But although American men as a group no longer expect immunity from family work, few expect to do half of it. A 1988 study of Stanford law students found that the women expected to do from 50 to 90 percent, while the men expected to do 10 to 50 percent. Although some men share equally in household work, such men are only a very small proportion of the population.[81]

Equally important is that significant variation exists in the amount individual men do. Some still do virtually no family work; others do a lot. Indeed, some men today are marginalized caregivers—not many, but feminists committed to dignifying caregiving work need to praise the men who dedicate themselves to caregiving in a culture that requires adults who do so to make themselves economically vulnerable, at odds with domesticity's definitions of manhood.[82]

The most significant change is symbolic. Few Americans now assume that men are immune from obligations for household work. As Arlie Hochschild documents for middle-class women and Lillian Rubin for working-class ones, most men have lost their felt entitlement to a flow of household work from women. The result is that while women still do most family work, anger about men's lack of equal contribution is widespread. At an upper-middle-class party in Cambridge, Massachusetts, in the early 1990s, the wife did everything while the husband didn't lift a finger; the guests were embarrassed. In a more modest home in Connecticut, a cute countrified sign on the dining room wall stated: "Call me Mom, not maid." In a broad range of class contexts, domestic work that used to be considered women's work now is considered family work.[83]

This seems a modest accomplishment until one looks abroad. Commented Colombian television executive Ampara Ortiz, "Men in Colombia don't even know how to break an egg; they couldn't go to the kitchen to begin with." When she came to the United States, she noticed "a lot of sharing responsibilities at home, helping with the kids while the wife went to a meeting, that really shocked me. To see a man cook, that's when I realized that I was in another country with another culture." Old country cultures persist in the United States to the extent that immigrants remain culturally distinct. Rubin quotes Joe Gomez: "Taking care of the house and kids is my wife's job, that's all." And Amy Lee: "A Chinese man mopping a floor? I've never seen it yet." This was true in the United States not so long ago. In a Perry Mason novel of the 1940s, a man pulls the curtains so the neighbors won't "catch him" washing the dishes.[84]

The strategy of redistributing household work between men and women has significant appeal in the United States. Its potential even for very resistant cultures should not be underestimated. Even in Japan, where young husbands still joke they don't know how to use the microwave, attitudes are beginning to shift. A Japanese husband recently lost a court case claiming $38,000 in damages because his wife, who works (as he does) as a full-time public servant, did not fulfill her part of the marriage contract. The husband had demanded that the wife rise early to cook him the traditional breakfast of miso and rice, press his pants, and clean the house. She did not refuse to do "her" duties, but said that in order to fulfill them they had to live close to work; her husband rejected nine suitable homes. The judge found for the wife on the grounds that it was reasonable for her not to continue the marriage under these conditions. Hardly a sex-role revolution, but this case suggests that even in cultures highly resistant to male involvement in "women's work," the strategy of gender redistribution should remain a long-term goal.[85]

Nonetheless, exclusive reliance on the redistribution of family work has proved a failure. Many men still do very little, and men as a group still do far less than half. U.S. feminists need to recognize that many men cannot afford, economically or emotionally, to share equally in family work as long as they have to pay for caregiving in the coin of marginalization. Most families rely on men's wages, so most men cannot afford marginalization at work. Moreover, as I argued in chapter 1, men's identity is typically built around work roles, which makes them psychologically unable to risk marginalization. As long as employers are free to marginalize anyone who does not perform as an ideal worker, and the ideal worker is defined as someone with immunity from family work, most men feel as if they have little choice but to resist demands to share equally in household work.[86]

Few mainstream feminists acknowledge this. For example, Arlie Hochschild's *The Second Shift*, the most influential recent book on work/family conflict, remains firmly focused on redistribution within the household.[87] Early feminists linked their proposals for gender redistribution with proposals for government-funded child care. Contemporary proposals need to recognize that gender redistribution cannot work in isolation. It needs to be paired with a strategy to change the conditions within which families engage in market work.

Reconfiguring the Public and Private Spheres

Another path to gender equality is the reconfiguration of the public and private spheres. This is the path most often taken in Europe. In Sweden, one parent can take parental leave for the first year of their child's life, with nine months fully compensated; parents can work part time until the child is eight years old. In Norway, employees can take one year's parental leave paid at a rate of 80 percent of their earnings for the previous fifty-two weeks. In France, high-quality, government-funded child-care facilities are as common as public schools.[88]

American feminists typically operate within an intensely privatized frame. One reason they have focused so much on gender redistribution is that it can be accom-

plished without challenging the traditional allocation of child rearing to the privatized realm of the family. Some feminists have argued that American feminists need
to shift to a European model and spend a lot more energy working to create public
supports for child rearing. Martha Fineman has proposed that the United States
create a broad-based program, modeled on the Social Security system, that would
provide economic support for mothers and their children.[89]

U.S. feminism has been profoundly affected by the constricted scope of the public sphere. The political debate in the United States tends to focus on the question
of how much to cut existing political programs, rather than on whether to implement sweeping new proposals for parental leave and other family benefits.

In much of the world, the prospect of public financing of maternity leave and
other costs associated with child rearing is not unthinkable in the way such policies are unthinkable in the United States, with its peculiar aversion to the public
sphere. Yet, at least in the short term, the kinds of public financing of social benefits that are common in Europe seem unlikely to appear in Latin America anytime
soon because of practical circumstances: Such programs are very expensive, and
few governments have the resources to finance elaborate child care programs or
paid parental leaves.

To the extent that such programs emerge, however, a key policy issue is whether
they are designed to socialize *mothers'* burdens through programs that do not challenge the allocation of family work to women, or whether their design is aimed at
changing the existing ideal-worker/marginalized-caregiver roles. France is probably a preeminent example of a maternalist strategy: Its extensive system of leaves
and publicly financed child-care facilities reinforces the message that family work
is the province of *mothers*, not *parents*. Sweden is the preeminent example of socialization strategies designed to destabilize the traditional allocation of family work
to women. Sweden has long drafted eligibility for its programs in a sex-neutral
way, and when it found that only women used parental leave despite its gender
neutrality, it set aside a specific period of parental leave that was available only if
leave was taken by the father.[90]

Although public resources for child care outside the home may not be the
whole solution, there is no doubt that an acute need exists for more support for
non-home-based child care. For single parents, and many married ones, child care
remains an important part of the solution even if it is not the magic cure it is sometimes represented to be. As noted before, child care in the United States is under-
funded, with the result that the quality of child care is not what it should be: Child
care workers are paid less than garbage collectors, and turnover is among the highest for any job in the country.[91]

The potential exists for conflicts between feminists committed to ending the
marginalization of mothers by changing the structure of work and those committed to increasing government funding for child care. This conflict need not occur.
Not only is child care an important part of any solution, but ending mothers' marginalization would address a key problem in child care, namely, the low salaries of

child-care workers. Currently, mothers' marginalization depresses the wages of women, and because families typically compare the costs of child care to the salary potential of the mother, it also keeps child-care salaries low.*

To a significant extent I have preserved American feminists' traditional privatized frame—as evidenced by the term "family work." That term is useful because it stresses that the tasks at issue involve *work*, not merely "family *responsibilities*," and because it stresses that the work is the responsibility of the entire *family*, not just the *woman*. Yet it leaves in place the assumption that child rearing will occur primarily within the family realm. That assumption is less normative than an attempt to be realistic, for recent attempts to expand the public sphere in the United States have not been notable for their success. As noted before, Friedan and others expected and lobbied for an extensive system of federally funded child care, yet American feminists' repeated attempts to gain government funding for child care have met with little success. For a long time the United States was the only Western industrialized country with no parental leave; after twelve years of lobbying, the result was the Family and Medical Leave Act (FMLA). While the FMLA is a significant and important accomplishment, it is also a drop in the bucket: It covers only a small percentage of those employed in the United States, and offers only an unpaid leave that many women cannot afford to take. The long struggle to achieve even this minimal level of coverage dramatizes the difficulties American feminists have faced when they try to shift tasks or funding into the public sphere.[92]

Our political culture is resistant to providing public funds or public provision of anything at all. In addition, as argued in chapter 1, there are particular problems in the United States with child care: Our status as a middle-class nation reinforces the notion that children need parental care so they can build up the human capital they need to "succeed." These are political facts of life. This is not to say they are unchangeable—in my lifetime alone, I have seen a wide swing in U.S. politics, from a political culture far more open to government involvement to the current climate, where government has been successfully demonized. But it has been demonized. Consequently, it seems foolhardy to link hopes for feminist transformation to expansion of the government sphere for the time being.

In sharp contrast, in the formerly Communist countries today, a strong ethic of socialization remains in place, and men generally refuse to do "women's" work. Therefore, even if programs are formally designed to be gender-neutral (which they should be), the focus inevitably will be on socialization more than on redistributing work within the household. This does not mean that programs need be tied to women's biology. Even parenting leave (aside from true pregnancy disabili-

---

*Calculating the costs of child care against the *mother's* salary, of course, reflects the assumption that the costs of child care are not to be offset against the *father's* salary. This reflects the (typically unconscious) assumption that child care is the mother's responsibility. Within the frame of that assumption, the mother's only choice becomes whether to finance the child care through money or by marginalizing her own workforce participation.

ty leave) deals with issues of social role rather than biology and should be designed in a gender-neutral fashion in order to begin the process of delinking caregiving from body shape. Otherwise, programs designed to help caregivers will penalize any caregivers who are not women, and will become an integral part of the process of policing men out of caregiving roles and women into them.

Issues concerning the design of socialization strategies should be separated from issues concerning their desirability. In countries with a viable public sphere but little sense that gender equality requires men to do "women's work," socialization strategies may well work better than strategies that aim for redistribution of family work within the household.

Probably the preeminent proponent of the strategy of socializing family work in the United States is Martha Fineman. As noted above, the importance of Fineman's work can hardly be exaggerated. She has played a crucial role in placing family work at the center of feminist analysis. When most feminists still were focused on getting women into the workforce, she foregrounded the dignity and importance of family work. Fineman has also played a crucial role in family law, where her eminence has made feminism hard to ignore.[93]

Less explicitly, Fineman's work can be read as a class critique of mainstream feminism. One of her goals is to democratize domesticity by equalizing access to parental care for children of working-class and poor parents as well as the rich. From the beginning Fineman's work has reflected an edge of working-class anger against the social fact that parental care is increasingly linked to privilege. This issue deserves to be further developed; it is far more important than has been commonly recognized. As noted in chapter 6, a much lower percentage of poor than working-class mothers work full time in a social context where union polling suggests that the number one concern of union members is that both parents have to work to support a family. Fineman's proposal for socializing dependency emerges as an alternative method for defusing working-class anger against welfare, by democratizing access to domesticity.

Fineman's strategy nonetheless has important limitations. Do we want to wait until U.S. society is ready to institute a large new social program in order to achieve gender equality? In today's climate politicians typically focus on how much to cut existing social programs, not whether to implement huge new ones. Fineman realizes this and labels her proposal "utopian." But its utopian quality means that feminists also need a strategy that is politically plausible in the shorter term.[94]

Utopian strategies also raise the question of whether this is the dream we want to dream. Fineman's proposal to eliminate the legal significance of the sexual family revives a theme popular in feminism in the 1970s and still vibrant in the gay community today: that heterosexual marriage is inherently oppressive and the goal should be to abolish it. This theme lives on in feminist discourse in other countries, notably Latin America, where marriage remains so patriarchal that many women do not marry because they feel it deprives them of important weapons in bargaining with their mates. Notes one anthropologist, of Nicaragua:

[M]ost men I interviewed said that they would prefer a legal ceremony. Their reasons were straightforward enough: a legally married woman would be much less likely to leave her husband. Most women countered that legal marriage tips the balance of power in favor of men and that informal union works to the overall benefit of women. Their reasoning, too, is straightforward.... Men have a variety of threats at their disposal in the event of quarrels: they might withhold money and child support, or they might resort to violence. By contrast, the main leverage women have is that they might abandon their compañero, thus leaving him alone and humiliated. A legal marriage, then, diminishes the wife's freedom somewhat more than the husband's. Because divorce is difficult, the wife would not be at liberty to leave a bad marriage, and her main threat would be diminished. A man, however, would remain free to pursue other women outside of his marriage; convention holds that womanizing is not grounds for divorce.... And, indeed, in a legal marriage the husband would be at greater liberty to beat his wife in the event of disagreements, for she would have fewer retaliatory options.[95]

The widespread acceptance of *uniones de hecho* (free unions) and the severely patriarchal nature of marriage in Latin America has created a situation different from that predominating in the United States. Here, surveys show that the overwhelming majority of Americans, gay and straight, would like to be married. This is true even in an age of divorced and never-married motherhood, for we are talking not of realities but of aspirations. Dreams of domesticity are alive and well among the working and middle classes, as discussed in chapter 5; even impoverished single mothers in inner-city communities dream of married motherhood, according to sociologist Elijah Anderson. Fineman's proposal to eliminate marriage as a legal status altogether and define families in terms of the mother-child bond opens up important conceptual space, but her proposals are not likely to yield large popular coalitions.[96]

But Fineman's work serves as a reminder that American feminists should not forget altogether that their discourse currently operates within an intensely privatized frame. American feminists need to remind ourselves to keep checking the wind, so that we stand ready to reconsider alternative strategies when they become more feasible. We also need to remember that the peculiarities of U.S. political culture may limit the relevance of the American experience to those places—most of the world—where the public sphere is not as constricted as it is here.

Redistributing Entitlements Between Employers and Employees

The political culture in the United States makes it impractical to gain government support for family work (at least in the short term); the strong ideology of gender equality makes the strategy of involving men in family work seem feasible, if employers stop the practice of marginalizing anyone with substantial caregiving responsibilities. This is the configuration that leads to the proposal to use the language of family values to renegotiate rights between employers and employees.

Despite its promise, this strategy has two chief drawbacks. The first is the low rate of union membership, for unions are an obvious arena in which to push for a shift in employee entitlements. The second is that most unions traditionally have placed work/family issues low on their list of priorities. A rich literature exists on the ways in which U.S. unions have been focused on gaining ideal-worker status for working-class men rather than on opening it up to working-class women. The recent revival of energy and creativity in the union movement shows some glimmers of change, but they remain only glimmers. For example, in the successful 1997 Teamster strike against United Parcel Service, the focus was still on changing low-paying part-time jobs into higher-paying full-time jobs, although more recently the AFL-CIO has begun to take the position that part-time workers should get the same hourly wages as full-time workers. Unions in Europe have often played a key role in gaining entitlements related to family work for men as well as women; a re-vitalized union movement in the United States could play a similar role if it has the will to do so. An alliance with unions remains an important, and underutilized, feminist strategy, particularly in view of the fact that women and minorities currently are being organized at a faster rate than are white men.[97]

The initial instinct may be that Western Europeans do not need to restructure market work because they have made such strides in funding and providing child care through the public sphere. But, as discussed in chapter 2, in Sweden—one of the countries that has been most successful in reconfiguring the public and private spheres—mothers still are marginalized, and sex segregation is even higher than in the United States. In France, another country with strong public supports for child rearing, mothers again typically work part time in an economy where the best jobs require full-time work. This suggests, as argued in chapter 2, that the strategy of shifting family work to the public sphere will not, of itself, solve the problem of women's marginalization.[98]

The situation in East-Central Europe is more complex still. One instinct among feminists in East-Central Europe is to preserve the maternalist programs formerly financed by the government, by shifting the financial burden to employers. Employer-financed maternalist policies also exist in Latin America: Examples are laws that require employers to furnish a child-care facility if they employ some minimum number of women (five in Ecuador, twenty in Chile).[99]

Employer-financed maternalist policies have one signal limitation: Employers often respond by refusing to hire women. The problem is particularly acute, of course, in countries that lack strong antidiscrimination statutes or the will to enforce them; unfortunately, this situation is all too common. Employers in both Latin America and East-Central Europe often cite maternalist statutes as the reason they refuse to hire women; maternalist programs probably have contributed to the extremely high and disproportionate rates of female unemployment in Russia and other countries.[100]

Creating a Conversation Focused on the Three Axes
Rather than on Sameness and Difference

This section has presented a new way to frame discussions about the design of policies to restructure the relationship of market and family work. Once strategies are assessed in terms of the three potential axes of gender change—the relationship of employer and employee, of the public and private spheres, and of men and women within the household—a conversation emerges in which issues of policy design remain separate from questions about whether men and women are, and should be treated, the same or different.

CONCLUSIONS ON EQUALITY AND STRATEGY

Feminists need not to eschew equality but to redefine it. It does not mean equal opportunity to live up to norms framed around men. Women need to demand not accommodation but their due—which includes the dismantling of masculine norms.

Once feminists end their gender wars over the design of policies to restructure market work and family entitlements, special-treatment feminists and equal-treatment feminists can unite with dominance feminists on the goal they all share: creating a world that holds the promise of delivering men as well as women from the roles and gender performances currently demanded by conventional masculinity and femininity under domesticity. The new vision of equality without discrimination bridges the gap between the early legal feminists and contemporary ones. This bridging is particularly important because Ruth Bader Ginsburg is now on the Supreme Court. She appears, from *United States v. Virginia* (also known as *VMI*), still focused on the strategy of achieving a strict-scrutiny standard for categories based on sex. But *VMI* also shows her continuing commitment to requiring that masculine norms be changed if necessary to achieve true equality. She is now in a position to lead the Supreme Court to take the next important steps toward this goal.[101]

In addition to its conclusions about equality, this chapter also suggests conclusions about strategy. It is striking how the special-treatment debate deteriorated into a gender war in which two groups of committed feminists mischaracterized each other's positions in ways that veiled the broad areas of agreement between them. Here's a simple rule: Don't fight with your friends. A key characteristic of domesticity is that it protects men's privileged access to power by pitting women against each other. Feminists need to name this phenomenon and to set an example of how women can avoid it. Gender wars killed the ERA and have jeopardized access to abortion; when feminists turn their attention back to work and family issues, avoiding them is of vital importance.

While surface acceptance of feminism is the norm in most polite upper-middle-class society, once one shifts the subject away from the topic of "men behaving badly" (domestic violence, rape, sexual harassment) to a renewed critique of the organization of market and family work, solidarity becomes indispensable. Men who feel quite happy decrying those wicked men who beat their wives quickly become defensive when the subject shifts to how their own careers reflect the gender privilege of being able to perform as ideal workers. When the topic is not misbehavior but conventional gender roles, tact becomes essential in our highly gendered society, where the accepted self-description is of self-invention through unfettered choice.

This makes the reconstructive feminist seem to rain on others' parades, for the first step toward reconstruction is to show how much our lives diverge from our ideals. While this step is unavoidable, it often reopens old wounds. It requires women to remember the battles they have lost, which makes them feel ineffectual; it brings them face-to-face with the fact that their relationships are not as equal as they would have wished. It reminds them that they have given up their dreams.

The men, of course, get even madder, for feminists are reopening conflicts where men won not only the battle but the right to describe the war. For some outsider to barge in and define their hard-won career as the result of gender privilege, particularly when his own wife describes the situation as the result of her free choice, is maddening, especially in a culture where one of the key gender privileges men enjoy is the privilege of describing themselves as living in the most equal of worlds.

Why don't women challenge them? Often they do. But feminists should not forget that equality is not everything, even for feminists themselves. Most feminists I know are marginalized compared to their partners. This is not because they are hypocrites but because they didn't make the world: Their personal goals include not only achieving gender equality, but being good mothers and sustaining intimate relationships with male partners. These goals police them back into conventional gender performances, from red toenails to marginalized careers. When the topic is work and family, we are on very tricky ground. We need to stop our gender wars because we will need solidarity to pull us through.

CHAPTER EIGHT

The New Paradigm Theorized:
Domesticity in Drag

"It's all about power—getting it and keeping it."

> [Philosophy] starts not from science, not from ascertained knowledge,
> but from moral convictions, and then resorts to the best knowledge and
> the best intellectual methods available in their day to give a form of
> demonstration to what [is] essentially an attitude of will, or a moral reso-
> lution, to prize one mode of life more highly than another, and the wish to
> persuade others . . . that this is the wise way of living.
>
> —JOHN DEWEY

Reconstructive feminism stems from Dewey's vision of reconstruction in philosophy.[1] It embeds several themes from Dewey's pragmatism. The first is nonfounda-
tionalism, the decision to abandon the search for absolute truth in favor of a social
theory of meaning. This entails not relativism but the recognition that truths are
made by human hands. The second is Dewey's conviction that the philosopher's role
is not to deduce truths through logic but to tease out the "precious values embedded in our traditions." Dewey's central message is that, in a democracy, other people's
truths must be acknowledged rather than shouted over or ignored. Together these
tenets work to create a very different kind of conversation than does a feminism
based on the authoritarian vision of discovering a single truth and delivering it up.[2]

These themes have driven much of the analysis thus far. Thus I have sought to
write this book in an approachable style, in an attempt to spark a movement within feminist theory that is theoretically sophisticated, yet committed to talking in
language capable of reaching audiences outside of academics. I have focused sustained attention on the rhetoric of choice and the full-commodification model,
though neither is currently at the center of academic debate, because both exercise
tremendous influence in people's everyday lives.

In addition, this book represents a sustained attempt to respect the power of
other people's truths about gender. Thus, though I am a career woman, I have tried
to understand the logic of the lives of women at home. Though I am a white woman
and a privileged one, I have tried to understand what domesticity feels like to
working-class women and women of color. Though I have never believed that all
women share an ethic of care, I have tried to speak respectfully of those who do.

I also have been influenced by Dewey's vision of philosophy as "a powerful form
of social criticism grounded in moral imagination and disciplined by . . . knowledge." This book represents an exercise of moral imagination of what it would be
like to take equality seriously, eliminating not only formal and intentional discrimination but also the masculine norms anchoring the bonds of womanhood that still
hold women down.

Thus my goal is not to deliver the truth but to inspire social change. Because
gender divides women in ways that often track race and class, gender change typically will involve coalition politics, not transcendent bonding. The goal of reconstructive feminism is to build coalitions capable of reconstructing social life, so its
focus is more on issues of strategy than on issues of authenticity. This raises the
question of how not to lose touch with authenticity in the search for coalition.

This concern arises as well from my preoccupation with "the precious values embedded in social traditions." My goal has been to tease out the values embedded in the tradition of domesticity, separating them from the disempowerment that traditionally has accompanied them, in order to use those values through the strategy of domesticity in drag. The clearest example is the attempt in part I to transform domesticity's norm of mothercare into a norm of parental care with the potential to end the system of providing for children's care by marginalizing their caregivers. Additional examples were discussed in chapter 6, as when domesticity is used to reframe the rhetoric of the abortion rights debate. The strategy of domesticity in drag again raises the issue of where to draw the line in the search for coalition.

This chapter first considers that issue, and then considers whether feminists' current language of gender and power serves the goals of reconstructive feminism. U.S. feminists have often assumed that, if we need a language of gender and power, Catharine MacKinnon's language of gender as dominance is the one we need. I contest that assumption. MacKinnon's foot-on-the-neck model, with its claim that "it's all about power," so oversimplifies the workings of gender in the context of work and family that it makes feminists easy to caricature, as illustrated by the above cartoon. More important—for feminists will always be subject to caricature—MacKinnon's dominance feminism makes it easy for people to dismiss the notion that gender differences often involve power differentials between men and women. MacKinnon's freighted language can easily elicit the response that since it isn't all about power, in fact none of it is.

Feminists will be in a much stronger position if they develop a new language that communicates, with humor as well as anger, how men's social power is built into the fabric of everyday life. To quote bell hooks: "Men *do* oppress women"; "People *are* hurt by rigid sex roles." We need a new language of gender and power that keeps both facts in focus. This chapter begins by proposing a new language, based on the image of gender as a force field of social power. This imagery dramatizes both why gender has proved so unbending and why the strategy of domesticity in drag is an effective strategy for gender bending in the context of market work and family work.[3]

GENDER AS A FORCE FIELD:
WHY GENDER IS SO UNBENDING

We don't want so much to see a female Einstein become an assistant professor. We want a woman schlemiel to get as quickly promoted as a male schlemiel.[4]

Picture a man in a skirt. One sees them in gay rights parades but never on the bus, for a simple reason: They would stand in serious danger of getting beaten up. This is a simple but pointed example of gender pressures on men.

Gender pressures on women are often subtler, for women enjoy a much wider range of acceptable gender performances. But gender pressures on women exist nonetheless. Take Deborah Fallows' decision to abandon her career in linguistics. We know from her description the gender pressures she felt. Some stemmed from her job: She felt guilty when she failed to live up to the ideal-worker norm by working part time. Others stemmed from her husband's job, which for a time took him away from home virtually every waking minute. Still others stemmed from Fallows' notion of the support required by a loving wife. These worked in combination with the gender pressures on her husband to perform as an ideal worker and her sense that she should have all the time in the world to give to her children.

All these forces added up to a great sucking sound that pulled her home. This suggests the image of a force field exerting a steady pull in the direction of conventional behavior, enforced by sanctions less brutal than a beating but equally effective in securing conventional gender performance. "They can't do much to you," noted one astute sociologist, "but then they don't have to."[5]

Feminists sorely need a theory of conventionality. Postmodern theorists, focused on identities in flux, often ignore the profound influence of conventionality on social life. To quote Lillian Rubin once again: "[O]nly a tiny minority of us ever are involved in inventing our present, let alone our future. Ordinary men and women—which means almost all of us—struggle along with received truths as well as received ways of being and doing." Outside rarified intellectual circles, giving an unconventional gender performance means flirting with social ineptness. Though gay activists may celebrate men in skirts, most people have a different reaction. Less energy is required today than twenty years ago to sustain nontraditional gender performances, but it still takes time and commitment. All adults choose their battles, and many forces exert a strong pull toward conventional behavior. Sexual arousal is often linked with low necklines or tight clothes; being respectable is linked with "behaving like a lady"; being "classy" is linked with a specific type of feminine gender performance (think Katharine Hepburn); being rebellious can be expressed by "sleeping around" or "dressing slutty." The list goes on and on. As noted in chapter 6, gender provides rich cultural imagery that most people find a convenient metaphor, one available to carry so many different loads of social meaning that the prospect of persuading people to abandon its use altogether is slim indeed. Thus while it is true that "all cultural orders must be seen as being . . . made . . . actively and continuously," gender as a metaphorical system gives many different people many different reasons to perpetuate conventional gender symbolism by using it in their everyday lives.[6]

Gender is unbending not only because of its infinite availability as a metaphor, but also because of the way it intertwines gender roles with attractive ideals. The single most powerful weapon at domesticity's disposal is the way it links women's marginalization with their dreams for their children. Domesticity also ties women's marginalization with their aspirations for romantic love in a culture that treats love as a key source of meaning in life. Our hopes and aspirations, our rebellions and proprieties—all are linked with gendered roles and norms. From the norm of parental care to the structure of the erotic, gender exerts built-in headwinds pushing men and women back into line with conventional gender performances.

This analysis leads to a new analysis of stereotypes. Traditionally, United States feminists have faulted stereotypes as irrational. This is an important perspective; it *is* irrational to assume that a human cannot drive a backhoe because she has a vagina, or that a caregiver does not need survivor's benefits because he has a penis. Stereotypes also have been faulted because they are unfair to women who do not conform to them. This, too, is an important perspective, yet it leaves feminists open to the charge that they care only about women who do not have conventionally feminine concerns or life patterns. The more profound point is that stereotypes create power differentials between men and women in situations where no one is making a conscious attempt to dominate women. The way stereotypes create power differentials is captured brilliantly in the following chart, quoted by the eminent Latin American feminist Alda Facio in her *When Gender Rings, the Changes it Brings: A Methodology for the Analysis of Gender in Legal Phenomena.*

He Works/She Works

He Works	She Works
He has a photo of his family on his desk.	She has a photo of her family on her desk.
He's a solid family man, conscious of his responsibilities.	Her family will always come before her career.
He speaks with his colleagues. He must be discussing his latest deal.	She speaks with her colleagues. She's gossiping.
He's not in his office. He must be at an important congressional meeting.	She's not in her office. She took off to go shopping.
He lunches with the general manager. Surely he's going to get a raise.	She lunches with the general manager. They must be lovers.

This chart gives a graphic picture of gender power at work in a way that invites laughter—and gets it, even in Latin American audiences not notably receptive to gender analysis. Its approachable tone presents gender power as something that happens quite innocently in everyday ways, but which ends up making our societies into what MacKinnon has aptly called "an affirmative action plan for white men." This message—often an unwelcome one—becomes convincing to a much wider audience when linked with a description that dissects everyday life with disarming concreteness and humor.[7]

"He Works/She Works" offers a simple but powerful way of talking about how male norms create gender power. It is commonly used in Latin American "gender trainings" for audiences so nonfeminist the word *feminist* is taboo. It provides a good way to reach out to people not already convinced of the power of feminist analysis. It uses humor, yet retains the sharp critical edge necessary to achieve feminist goals.

The key is to show how power differentials are built in subtle ways into everyday life. This is particularly important when the subject is work and family. Gender power may well feel like men with their feet on our necks in the context of rape, domestic violence, and sexual harassment, but in the work/family context it more often feels like a force field pulling women into traditionally feminine roles by making them implausible in traditionally masculine ones. For example, in a recent study, a group of mid-level managers were asked to evaluate the resumes of four fictitious employees whose resumes were identical in terms of work success. The two that bore male names were consistently ranked higher than those bearing female names when the managers evaluated the resumes to evaluate each candidate for promotion and salary increase purposes. Note that one-fourth of the managers doing the evaluations were women: The force field pulling women down is created not only by men, but also by women who share conventional gendered assumptions. One liability of the common conflation of gender with women is that it sets up a situation where, if women are involved, this is cited as proof that the result is not discriminatory.[8]

The case of Nancy Ezold, who was rejected for partnership at the Philadelphia law firm of Wolf, Block, Schorr & Solis-Cohen, provides a detailed picture of the forces at work in traditionally masculine jobs. Ezold's case needs to be considered in conjunction with a study that found that while women law school graduates at the top of their class got job offers as good as or better than their male peers, women just below that level experienced far less success than did men with equivalent qualifications. Ezold was not a superstar, though the evidence suggests that many of the men who made partner at her firm had the kind of positive but mixed performance evaluations she had. Nonetheless, the firm felt differently about Ezold, for reasons that upon close examination were very gendered. The chairman of her department told her during an interview that it would not be easy for her to fit in because "she was a woman, had not attended an Ivy League school, and had not been on law review." He and a subordinate subsequently assigned her to only small matters, which gave her little opportunity to shine. When she once suggested that this was happening because she was a woman, she was told, "Nancy, don't say that around here. They don't want to hear it." When Ezold stood up for (predominantly female) paralegals, arguing that they were overworked and underpaid, her evaluations faulted her judgment, saying it was sometimes "clouded" by "oversensitivity to what she misperceives as 'wome[n's] issues.'" In addition, like Ann Hopkins before her, in the stereotyping case discussed in chapter 3, she was criticized on the grounds that she did not get along well with staff, a common allegation that merits further analysis.[9]

Note that, in a law firm context, virtually all the males are lawyers, but women are split by class, into support staff and female attorneys. Professional women often report that support staff have different expectations of them than of the men;

this may reflect class conflict. Support staff who do not question taking orders from the men may well resent taking orders from a woman, for without the protective covering of gender, the class differential between female lawyers and female support staff emerges in clear focus.[10]

Arguably, Ezold would have faced none of the difficulties named had she been a man; together, they added up to a force field that pulled her out of contention by undermining her reputation, particularly among lawyers who had not worked with her. Yet the appeals court found no discrimination.[11]

The force field imagery shows how women are disadvantaged by small incidents that might seem trivial, or not gender-related, if each was considered in isolation. It also provides a language for showing how women are disadvantaged by gender that does not deny their resistance and their agency. As discussed in chapter 1, mothers' "choice" occurs within a habitus that pulls them back toward domesticity. Linking the force field image with Bourdieu's notion of habitus reminds us that gender is a system of inherited tradition—"embodied history, internalized as second nature and so forgotten as history"—built into our peculiar organization of market work and family work; into our sense of what men are entitled to within the family and the world of work; into our sense of what is due to children; into the structure of the erotic; into our imagery of rebellion and propriety, and much more.[12]

The experience of Latin American feminists highlights how the cultural context of U.S. feminists affects their theory. Feminist jurisprudence in North America typically is written by full-time law professors who enjoy a comfortable existence as academics and who write for a specialized audience of other feminists. The signal advantage of this situation is that it gives U.S. feminists the time to work out feminist theory at a rigorous and abstract level. But this is accompanied by a signal disadvantage: Theorists often spend their lives talking to other theorists and to students who have accepted feminist ways of thinking. In a country where only about one-quarter of women self-identify as feminists, this means that we spend a disproportionate amount of time preaching to a small, elite choir and fighting among ourselves.[13]

In sharp contrast, feminist lawyers in Latin America do not have the luxury of academic positions. The institutional infrastructure of feminism in Latin America is a network of human rights nongovernmental organizations that do trainings of judges, legislators, faculties, and others in "the perspective of gender." Many feminists also do popular education stemming from the work of Paulo Freire, a Brazilian leftist who developed a method that linked literacy training with consciousness raising.[14]

Because Latin American feminists spend much of their professional lives focused outside the feminist community, they recognize the need for feminism to function not only as a language of bonding in anger against male privilege; feminists also need a language of persuasion to produce in people who do not identify with feminism the click of recognition of how women are disadvantaged in everyday life.[15]

Reconstructive feminism seeks to develop new forms of gender talk capable of reaching wide popular audiences. An important element of "He Works/She

Works" is that it substitutes humor for the anger people expect to hear. Anger remains important for consciousness raising, but anger should not be the only tone people hear when feminists speak, for people who are always angry soon lose their audience. (As has been noted, the language of anger against men also can trigger class and race solidarity against feminism.)

Facio's methodology provides an effective way to communicate the results of recent psychological research on stereotypes. In contrast to the common assumption that discrimination is the result of a conscious decision to ignore evidence, social cognition theory ties discrimination to the way people process information. In reviewing the relevant literature, Linda Hamilton Krieger notes that stereotypes form part of the "social heritage of society" that "profoundly affect how we interpret a person's subsequent behavior, what about that behavior we remember, and how we use the behavior in judging the person later." Krieger cites studies showing that behavior that is classified as "playing around" when performed by whites is often classified as "violent" or "aggressive" when done by blacks; behavior classified as "passive" when performed by a woman or an Asian may well be seen as "prudent" or "restrained" in a white man. Krieger also reports that people tend to remember stereotype-confirming behavior better than counter-stereotypical behavior, and to assume that stereotype-confirming behavior will be repeated. In-group members also are more likely to perceive ambiguous behavior as stereotyped, because in-groups perceive out-groups as being more homogeneous than themselves. Moreover, in-group individuals are more likely to perceive the behavior of themselves or their group as resulting from constraints, whereas outsiders' behavior is more likely to be attributed to personality drawbacks or lack of ability.[16]

Social cognition theory highlights the subtle ways that stereotypes make "politics as usual" different for women than for men. These subtle dynamics combine with more obvious male norms to create a force field that pulls women down. Take the example of law school teaching. Twenty years after large numbers of women entered law schools, at a time when 45 percent of law graduates are women, women still are only 20 percent of tenured law professors and only 5 percent of law school deans. Several studies have found that women still do not fare as well as men in getting jobs, nor do they fare as well at getting jobs at the most prestigious law schools. The reasons reflect both the ideal-worker norm and politics as usual.[17]

A threshold factor is that entrance into the academy typically requires relocation, available to many men but few women. A recent study showed that woman professors are significantly more likely than male professors to limit their job searches for family reasons. Another factor is that law school teaching requires high levels of effort in the years before tenure, precisely the period when many families have small children that require significant amounts of parental time (given disproportionately by women). These obvious masculine norms make it difficult for women to obtain law teaching jobs, to take up visiting offers, to "trade up"—in short, to establish themselves as "hot properties." Gender also enters in in the context of other "objective" measures.[18]

A key factor in promotion at many law schools is student evaluations (which often play a much larger role in retention of law faculty than in retention of other faculties). For a number of reasons, getting good evaluations is trickier for women as a group than for men as a group. One study reported that 18 percent of male students, 48 percent of female students, and 73 percent of minority females thought female faculty bore a heavier burden of proving themselves than did male faculty because of students' sex-based expectations of competence. Another study that examined course evaluations at one "top ten" law school found that women professors were more likely to get complaints about lack of control, unpreparedness, bias, and disrespect of students. Women professors were also considered more patient and supportive, approachable, and congenial. Male professors were considered more knowledgeable, rigorous, humorous, and to have more dynamism and tell better stories.[19]

Using the "He Works/She Works" methodology, we might construct a table:

He Teaches	She Teaches
1. He is tough and firm; you really learn a lot from him.	1. Boy, is she a b**ch.
2. He is so gentle. He really makes you want to learn from him.	2. She really needs to learn to take command of the classroom.
3. He is a really innovative teacher. He doesn't just do the same old stuff.	3. We don't learn what the other sections are learning. She clearly doesn't know how law is taught.
4. He is great because he is really available to students: He's in his office and willing to talk anytime.	4. She is so stand-offish. She is never around when you want to talk with her.
5. He is so friendly. He invites small groups of students to his house for dinner.	5. She is very unfriendly. She never socializes with students or invites them to her house.

This chart describes some of the ways gender affects law school teaching. Points 1 and 2 remind us that virtually the same behavior from men and women can be interpreted very differently, because masculinity is intertwined with messages of "natural" authority while femininity is not. The easiest way around this is for women to give a masculine gender performance. For example, in my first semester as a professor (teaching students not much younger than myself) I was severely criticized on the grounds that I should "take control" of the classroom. A year later I had some of the highest teaching evaluations in the school; one student described me as "Professor Kingsfield's younger daughter."[20]

My sense is that a study would show that woman law professors who adopt this style are much more likely to get high evaluations than any other group of woman law professors. Yet women face a tricky situation. To the extent that students expect nurturing from a woman, they may penalize her for "firm" behavior they would not question in a man. We saw this kind of catch-22 in the *Hopkins* case, discussed in chapter 3, in which Ann Hopkins was faulted for the aggressive style that is the lingua franca of her profession. This kind of double bind is a key way stereotypes disadvantage women in traditionally male jobs. A woman may be penalized for being too firm, but she may also be penalized for being too gentle. Behavior that would be admired in a man with no need to establish his authority (because the culture does it for him) may in a woman be interpreted as evidence of her inability to take command.

Point 3 highlights the fact that, in a situation where men "naturally" command authority but women do not, innovations by women may be seen as evidence that they "just don't know how law is taught" in situations where similar innovations by men are seen as—well, as innovative.

Points 4 and 5 return us to the more straightforward type of masculine norms: that the standards in a predominantly male profession are set by men with wives to take care of their children, enabling them to work long hours and provide the kind of hospitality that requires extensive time and preparation. Again, in a society where many male professionals are married to homemakers while most female professionals are married to other professionals, these patterns place women at a disadvantage. To the extent that woman professors commute, the problem of availability is exacerbated. We don't ordinarily think of "commitment" and "availability" as norms that reflect men's privileged access to family work and other gender privileges. But they do. "Commitment" often not only helps after appointment but gives men a jump-start in the profession: The strongest positive factor relating to initial rank at the time of appointment is the presence of a nonemployed spouse.[21]

Also important for promotion and tenure is one's general reputation for being a team player. Women in situations of tokenism are more likely to find themselves labeled as "difficult." For example, a woman who challenges sexism in her institution can often successfully be labeled "not a team player." To the extent that more demands are placed on women than men—and there are many reports of women being expected to teach new courses more often than men, to serve on more committees, to teach courses that are more time-intensive—a woman's refusal may again generate criticism.

Why are more intensive demands often placed on women? The motivations range from the sense that the men are already doing "important work," or that the courses the woman is being asked to teach are not so hard after all (often because, like family law or gender courses, they are conceptualized as easy because of their association with women). Another common motivation is that the decision maker wants to spend as few political points as possible achieving a given goal, and asking a woman involves spending less political capital than imposing on a man. The unconscious expectation that women will be more accommodating, whereas "a real man won't let himself be pushed around," sometimes drives this political assessment. Similar dynamics may emerge when predominantly female senior staff in charge of allocating offices or classrooms, making schedules, or ordering books feel less comfortable asking men than women to do something no one particularly wants to do. The fact that staffs are typically female means that some may well have higher expectations of women to be "reasonable." One wonders, when Nancy Ezold was labeled as "very demanding, prima donna-ish, not a team player" because she handled matters relating to office and secretarial space "too assertively," whether she was facing matters few men have to face.[22]

The result is not a glass ceiling in the sense of an impermeable barrier. Instead, it is a system of built-in headwinds where women have to work harder and be politically more astute than men in order to survive. Women often feel caught: They can stand up for themselves and get a reputation for being difficult; they can spend a huge amount of time getting their way through subtle machinations; or they can accept "without a fuss" offices, classrooms, schedules, that ultimately place them at a disadvantage—for teaching at 8:30 A.M. in a room with bad acoustics can lead to bad evaluations. Though everyone must fight their own battles, professional women often feel they are handed more battles to fight because they have to struggle to get what men are offered automatically. These complexities can be compounded if the women must deal with sexual harassment, pregnancy, or other issues men do not face.

What women face is not a foot on their neck but the trivial minipolitics of everyday life, which are gendered in many institutions in the sense that they operate differently for women than for men. And the forces that work against women often feed on each other, as when someone's political support erodes because "she is not a team player" or "her teaching is controversial." Outside of institutions where there are literally no women, the problem today is that fewer women get jobs and fewer women thrive because women are disadvantaged by the force fields created by masculine norms and politics as usual.

Hence the importance of Bella Abzug's statement, quoted earlier in this chapter, that liberation will be not achieved until a female schlemiel is promoted as fast as a male schlemiel. Gender operates not as a bar to all people of a certain body shape, but as a force field that makes it more difficult for women to survive and thrive. This analysis highlights the inadequacy of discrimination laws in the United States, in which courts often limit actionable discrimination to that which is conscious and intentional. "He Works/She Works" shows that much discrimination, far from being intentional, is not even conscious. Women are systematically disadvantaged by "shared expectations built into established patterns of behavior ... [that] become institutionalized as simply the way things are done." We need to shift from a model that depicts discrimination as caused by a bad actor who needs to be removed, to an analysis of established patterns of behavior that operate to disadvantage women in subtle but systematic ways without any one person being at fault. Linda Hamilton Krieger has delineated the changes to Title VII law that will be required to achieve this.[23]

This analysis also highlights the limitations of an affirmative action jurisprudence that assumes that its purpose is to remedy past discrimination. Affirmative action is important not in order to remedy past discrimination by people long dead, but to remedy the disadvantage created by the unselfconscious default modes in which we function day to day. Affirmative action is necessary because the gravitational pull of Venus is more than twice that of Mars. Gender, like gravity, still pulls women down.[24]

The *Ezold* case, "He Works/She Works," and the law school example all highlight the importance of what social scientists call the interactional model of gender, which stresses that gender is "heterogeneously produced in a variety of social sites, including schools, clinics, churches, courtrooms, shop floors, and social movements." Gender pressures emanate from so many sources that they feel as difficult to shift as the wind itself. This is why, after forty years of feminist activism, so much remains the same. Gendered institutions and norms exert such steady pressure that it takes a constant output of energy to resist. Women often note that battles over the distribution of family work have to be fought over and over again. The old roles and stereotypes have proved remarkably resilient because gender carries such a load of meanings that individuals change only what irks them most immediately. To use an image common in philosophy, we are in a boat, trying to rebuild it. But we have to preserve all we can because we are in the middle of the sea.[25]

Conformity to convention stems not from an imprint we carry forth from childhood but from the steady pressures that persist throughout our lives. Conventional femininity is a pull, not a mandate, but it is a strong and steady pull that can wear a girl down.

IS MACKINNON'S ANALYSIS OF GENDER AND POWER THE ONE WE NEED?

Feminist jurisprudence in the United States often elides the question of whether feminists need an analysis of gender and power with the question of whether Catharine MacKinnon's dominance feminism is the one we need. Dominance feminism analyzes gender as male dominance over women. "On the first day that matters, dominance was achieved, probably by force." "Get your foot off our neck," MacKinnon noted in her discussion of women's voice, "and you will see in what voice women speak." While dominance feminism has made many important contributions, once the focus shifts away from rape, sexual harassment, domestic violence, and pornography back onto work and family issues, three problems emerge with MacKinnon's analysis.[26]

The first is MacKinnon's conviction that gender is produced by the structure of the erotic: "Male and female are created through the erotization of dominance and submission. The man/woman difference and the dominance/submission dynamic define each other." While MacKinnon's analysis of the eroticizing of dominance is brilliant, her claim to have found the single engine of gender glosses over the long literature documenting the role of work and family in creating a gendered world.[27]

The eroticizing of dominance is an extremely important engine of gender. It plays a central role in the context of rape, domestic violence, and sexual harassment; it also plays a role in structuring work and family life. Men end up with more power within families in part because women tend to marry men who are older, richer, and taller than they. This custom creates a power differential between partners, as when a couple "naturally" moves to the city of the husband's job because he is more advanced in his career, or when a couple decides it is "only logical" that the wife should quit because, since she is younger, she earns less than her partner. Yet the eroticizing of dominance is only a small part of the dynamic that creates men's power in family life. As noted in the introduction, if we woke up tomorrow and found a society where dominance was not eroticized, people's dreams for work and family life would still lead them into gender roles that give men power over women. To understand the full dynamics of gender power in work and family life, we need not only an analysis of sexuality but also an analysis of domesticity.

A second limitation of MacKinnon's foot-on-the-neck model is that while that model often works well in context of Men Behaving Badly (where individual men sexually harass, rape, or beat women because they find it erotic), it is not equally resonant in the context of men behaving well. Few women view men consistently behaving as dutiful husbands and fathers as having their feet on our necks. This is particularly true in nonprivileged communities, as discussed in chapter 5, where MacKinnon's language of anger against men will often have the effect of creating class or racial solidarity in opposition to feminists' proposals. Another key danger of the foot-on-neck model, noted above, is that it opens up the claim that because men do not really have their feet on our necks, gender power does not exist.

The third and fourth limitations of MacKinnon's foot-on-neck model have received the most attention in feminist jurisprudence. MacKinnon's statements that the division of the sexes "underlies the totality of social relations" and that male dominance is "perhaps the most pervasive and tenacious system of power in history" make her sound less than sensitive to other systems of social power, notably race and class, than one might wish. In addition, commentators such as Kathryn Abrams have argued that MacKinnon's language sometimes appears to discount women's agency; the fact that women face important constraints does not mean that they do not exercise agency as well.[28]

The model of gender as dominance remains important for situations in which men actively oppress women. But it does not capture the workings of gender in the everyday lives of people who live the household life, trying to do the best they can. When attention turns back to the everyday contexts in which most of us live, we need an alternative to dominance feminism. We need a new way of talking about gender and power that needs to focus not on the eroticizing of dominance but on the structure of market work and family work. It needs direct attention to the subtle ways gender power is created in the context of work and family (subtlety that is often unnecessary when the subject is power and desire). It needs to capture women's agency as well as the constraints they face. It needs to recognize that the language of anger against men presents threats to feminist coalition building.

Finally, it needs to account for why gender is so unbending, so difficult to change. The notion of gender as a force field of social power is designed to meet these needs.

UNBENDING GENDER CONTINUED: HOW GENDER INTERACTS WITH OTHER FIELDS OF SOCIAL POWER

The analysis of gender as social power paves the way for integrating gender into the study of other forms of social power. By this I do not mean a grand, overarching Final Text, but an assessment of the way genderings interact with people's location in other fields of social power, notably race, class, and sexuality. (I have not focused on sexuality in this book because it is not central to an analysis of domesticity, yet sexuality plays a very important role in other contexts.)

The dominant metaphor today is of "intersectionality." Perhaps a stronger image is of force fields interacting to create different pulls and eddies at different social locations, "an analysis of locations in the space of positions of power." Thus privileged white women feel the steady downward pull of gender because class and race privilege provide them with a "natural" buoyancy, making the drag of gender disadvantage seem the key to social power.

In sharp contrast, white working-class men (and their advocates) often identify class as the one true field of social power: Advantaged as they are by race and gender, their attention is tightly focused on the hidden injuries of class. Because working-class men's expectations are set by the entitlements they enjoy as men, they overlook the social power they have and problematize the social power they lack. So many battles have been fought over whether gender or race or class constitutes the most important type of social analysis; but what we need is an analysis that focuses attention on the complex interactions between these different fields of social power.[29]

Once we look simultaneously at race, gender, and class, the interaction of the different fields of social power yields a distinctive pattern: People tend to play off their social privilege to counter their social disadvantage. Thus WASP women typically give a muted gender performance that avoids public displays of femininity while stressing their high class status; they play up their social privilege (class) to mute their social disadvantage (gender). The same phenomenon appears in other contexts as well. Privileged women of color often have sought to counter the negative messages sent by race (their social disadvantage) with positive messages that they are "high-class" (their social privilege). Thus black women in the nineteenth century tried to insist on sitting in "ladies' cars," and Anita Hill's regal bearing during the Hill-Thomas hearings distanced her from jezebel stereotypes and appropriated for her the power of injured womanhood. A third example is that white working-class men have often insisted on differentiating themselves from black men, demanding "the wages of whiteness," and are often more openly traditionalist on gender issues as well; they seek to hold on to the social power they have as men and as whites to protect them from the hidden injuries of class.[30]

Part of what makes gender so unbending is the pattern of people playing one field of social power against another. It leads nonprivileged men to insist on maintaining their gender privilege to counterbalance their class, race, or ethnic disempowerment. It gives many nonprivileged women pause before they join a feminist coalition that further undercuts "their" men. And it may tempt privileged feminists to use their class or racial privilege to overcome their gender disadvantage, as when nineteenth-century feminists argued that they should get the vote before less educated and less worthy (black or immigrant) men.[31]

This pattern has profound implications for coalition building. Feminists need to develop strategies to counteract it. No single strategy will work in every context. One useful strategy is to stress that gender involves *social location* rather than the *actual ability to dominate*. Feminist theory has often failed to sufficiently distinguish the two. This is not to minimize the extent to which men dominate women. Many do. But the existence of social power available to men is not the same as the inevitable domination by each man of all women. The relationships between men and women are complex; men's social power is only one element. To claim that "it is all about power" glosses over the fact that people are constituted not only by their social power position but also by individual psychology, level of talent, force of personality, and luck. The force field imagery reminds feminists that what they offer is an analysis of gender traditions, not a full description of individual lives.

Thus far we have explored why gender has proved so difficult to change. Yet while gender is unbending, it is not completely impervious to change. The following section explores new strategies for gender bending.

NEW STRATEGIES FOR GENDER BENDING: DOMESTICITY IN DRAG

> To the extent that gender is an assignment, it is an assignment which is never quite carried out according to expectation, whose addressee never quite inhabits the ideal s/he is compelled to approximate.[32]

Though the image of gender as a force field pulling women into conventional gender performances captures an important element of women's experience, it is important not to exaggerate gender's rigidity. Individuals often follow the path of least resistance when subjected to the steady pull toward conventional gender performances, but gender conformity is not inevitable. One need not live life in the default mode.[33]

The image of gender as a force field, which captures the profound influence of conventionality, must be complemented with imagery that stresses that gender is an assignment that is often not carried out according to expectation. This leads us to the image, common in anthropology and sociology, of gender negotiations. Yet it is important to use the imagery of negotiation with the recognition that women's gender negotiations reflect not only the relationships between isolated individuals; they reflect people's relationships to their gender traditions. People are involved in everyday negotiations both *with* and *within* their gender traditions.[34]

This imagery offers a new perspective on women's "different voice." Consider the male and female managers who each give a conventionally gendered performance in order to gain good evaluations from a traditionalist supervisor. Rather than describing this in the language of women's voice, it could be redescribed as a negotiation over gender performance. College teaching provides another example. One study found that students required different gender performances of men and women professors; the women received good evaluations if they ran relaxed classrooms with considerable student participation, while men were rewarded for skilled use of a "male expert" style that depended largely on lectures. Women were expected to be "nice," "caring," and available outside class, whereas men were not penalized for being distant. Women also handled grading differently, specifying grading criteria, writing detailed comments on papers, or requiring students to submit protests in writing, whereas men, more confident that their basic authority would not be questioned, did less to gird themselves against complaints. Women end up giving a conventionally feminine gender performance as a by-product of their negotiations with their students.[35]

These negotiations result in a wide array of masculinities and femininities, in sharp contrast to domesticity's tidy dichotomy of striving men and selfless women. The image of negotiation stresses the openness of women's gender assignment, while the image of the force field reminds us of the intense social pressures people face, day in and day out, to conform to gender conventions. Sustaining a nontraditional gender performance is possible, but it requires sustained energy and commitment: One has to get up every day and decide how to dress on the bus.[36]

We have seen many instances of gender negotiation throughout this book. Though Deborah Fallows embraced domesticity's caregiver role, for example, she did not embrace her culture's description of it. She vehemently rejected the dominant imagery of the housewife as a docile scrubber of floors. Women negotiate hard; if they are clever enough, they can make gender work *for* as well as against them. Thus Mae West made the dumb blonde into a strategy of personal empowerment.[37]

This new imagery highlights the open-ended quality and the complexity of genderings. Genderings are complex in part because women play off their unconventionality along one gender axis against their conventionality along another. They can do so because gender reflects not only one's relationships with domesticity but also one's relationships to other important axes of gender, notably the eroticizing of dominance and gender display. People taking risks along one axis tend to send reassuring messages along another. Thus though Jackie Joyner-Kersee has dedicated her life to achieving extraordinary physical prowess, she is willing to insist she's just another Avon lady.[38]

Gender is a field of social power with which people establish relationships of great complexity. In the course of their negotiations people reach very different "deals." Femmes include not only Madonna's sardonic drag but Junior League matrons in Talbots and the odd adherent of frills. The complexity of being female in the United States reflects, in part, that one of the chief accomplishments of United States feminism has been that women now fit much more loosely into their traditions than they did in 1960.

The complexity of gender also reflects the fact that gender varies in different social situations. The dress and manner of a professional woman may well be different at a business lunch than at a romantic dinner. Given the eroticizing of feminine gender display, one would be surprised if they were not. Genderings change over the life cycle as well. Many studies document the intense gendering of youth, when competent gender performance is treated as just one more task in children's command of social skills. Yet surveys of twenty-somethings document the existence of a period after childhood and before the gender roles associated with child rearing have emerged. Surveys suggest that many young women in this age cohort focus on roughly the same things as young men: making it on the job and in bed. Things change dramatically with marriage and the birth of children, when traditional gender patterns reemerge in full force.[39] A friend tells the story of a sister who married the boyfriend she had lived with for many years. On the Sunday after the wedding, her sister found herself asking, "Who's getting the cold cuts?" She didn't even like cold cuts. But their father always bought cold cuts on Sunday; it just seemed part of being married. Once children are born, women face the clash between the norms of parental care and market work discussed in part I. Some women never recover. Those who do, at age fifty, often are headed in the opposite direction than their partners, with the women gearing up their careers after time off for child rearing, while the men are gearing down after the intense ambition of their thirties and forties.[40]

Not every American follows these broadly sketched patterns; the point is that gender pressures change for people of different ages, in different places, at different times of day. Grade-school girls are concerned about cooties; women in their twenties and thirties typically focus on men's lack of emotional expressiveness (if my feminist jurisprudence classes are representative); mothers obsess about sharing of family work; retired women (assuming a decent income) may not feel that gender affects them much at all.

The image of gender negotiations in a force field captures these complexities as well as the ways gender differs in different class and racial contexts. It joins a postmodern insistence on people's potential for inventing new sexual idioms with the older project of reimagining mothering in ways that delink it from domesticity. (Perhaps the best example is Sara Ruddick's famous "Maternal Thinking," an analysis that seeks "to bring a *transformed* maternal thought into the public realm.")[41]

The question is how to use women's open-ended negotiations to reconfigure the steady pull of the force fields pulling us toward gender conventions. One answer is that when domesticity is not working for us, it is working against us. If feminists do not use the norm of parental care to deconstruct domesticity, it will serve only to fuel the force field pulling women home; to make abortion rights implausible; to target career women as selfish. The alternative is to use domesticity's rhetoric of selfless motherhood to defend abortion rights and the right of mothers both to be ideal workers and to live up to the norm of parental care.

Women do this all the time. Recall Denise, the Gilligan interviewee who described her decision to abort in the language of self-sacrifice. Self-sacrifice is an unusual choice of word in this context; why did it come to mind for Denise? She lives in a culture where women are under intense gender pressure to become mothers and to be selfless once they are. What better way to diffuse these pressures than for Denise to tell herself that abortion is the truly selfless course of action? She used domesticity's metaphors to flip domesticity's mandate that mothers be selfless, so that it supported, rather than opposed, her aspirations for autonomy. This is the strategy of using domesticity's power against itself, in the manner of a judo flip that disarms one's opponent by using his own momentum to get him off balance. My goal in using the norm of parental care is to flip and bend domesticity into new configurations, using Foucault's insight that power circulates, so that even the disempowered can sometimes make power work for them if they are persistent and clever enough.[42]

Power may circulate but it does not circulate enough. Note that Denise, in her complex negotiations with gender, avoided an all-out, head-on collision. This caution holds an important message for feminists. I have come to believe that feminists' early unswerving opposition to domesticity's description of women ultimately served to divide feminists and weaken feminism. A more effective strategy is to use domesticity's momentum to bend it into new configurations. Thus chapter 1 proposes using domesticity's norm of parental care to deconstruct the ideal-worker norm in market work, and chapter 6 proposes to use other elements of domesticity as tools in the context of abortion rights and welfare-reform debates. The strategy of domesticity in drag involves a new kind of gender bending, focused not on gender display but on changing the relationship of market work and family work.

Domesticity in drag presents important issues of authenticity. If coalition building requires strategy, not transcendent bonding, then feminism involves not the search for a shared authenticity but coalition politics; hence the focus on persuasion throughout this book. But in reaching out to others, how does one stay in touch with oneself? The remainder of this chapter addresses this important question.

PRAGMATISM AND INCOMMENSURABILITY, CERTAINTY AND TRUTH

> Certainty is *as it were* a tone of voice in which one declares how things are, but one does not infer from the tone of voice that one is justified.[43]

We have seen that, in the context of gender, people's truths often conflict. If the goal is to construct coalitions among people who do not share each other's certainties, a key issue is how to proceed effectively under conditions of incommensurability. One obvious key is mutual respect, but that raises the question of where respect for difference should end in favor of being true to ourselves. The remainder of this chapter first explores the epistemological issues related to pragmatists' social theory of truth, by asking what people's truths mean. I then turn to the question of where to draw the line in respecting others' truths, in a discussion centered on female genital cutting and the veil.

The Mormon Mother and Me

To illustrate the social and situated nature of truths and to explore what this means for feminism, let me begin with something I believe with absolute certainty: Without access to abortion, equality is impossible for women. For me, this is a truth in the sense that I cannot imagine changing my mind about it. Philosophers will note that I am conflating notions traditionally considered to be very different: I am treating "truths" as the same as "certainties." I do this because once pragmatists abandon the notion of absolutes, traditional distinctions between certainties and truths blur.

A closer examination of my truth about abortion shows that it does not reflect timeless, universal principles. Instead, it reflects who I am. Like most women of my class, I view an active sexual life as an entitlement and children in part in terms of opportunity costs.* From the time I was sexually active, I knew I had a lot to lose if I had children at the wrong time. A pregnancy could deprive me of "my future," I would have said in college. This meant that if I got pregnant too early, I would forfeit the entitlement I felt to an "interesting, successful career." As chapter 1 shows, this reflected a clash between the ideal-worker norm and the norm of parental care. As chapter 5 shows, it also represents my position as a privileged woman.

Now consider a middle-aged Mormon mother of five who believes that her purpose in life was defined by her marriage, that the purpose of marriage is procreation, that sex outside of marriage is wicked, and that the wicked shall be punished. She is unalterably opposed to abortion under any circumstances.

Am I in danger of being persuaded by the Mormon mother? No. This is merely to say I like being who I am. And as long as my life retains the shape it has today, my position on abortion will not change. My views reflect who I am, just as the opposing truth of the Mormon mother reflects the shape and tenor of her life. Our truths are a product of our social location and what we have chosen to make of it. This is the sense in which truths reflect not outside reality but the texture of given life. Truths are expressions of identity.

This linkage of truth and identity has important implications for social theory.

---

* Let me state clearly what is clear already to people of goodwill: that I view children in many other, more positive lights as well. The fact that they present opportunity costs results from the current structuring of market work and family work, not from an inadequacy in the children themselves.

Many theorists assume that rational discussion by parties acting in good faith will produce consensus on which all reasonable parties will agree. I do not. My disagreement with pro-life advocates reflects not their irrationality but the fact that they take different things as the "givens" of their lives. Truths reflect not some outside reality but the exhortation "Be like me!"

Many perfectly decent people do not want to be like me. Many less privileged women cannot be. Our goal must be to overcome that certain blindness in human beings that makes others' truths so hard to fathom. In this book I have tried to understand the diverse relationships people have to gender, because of their different social locations and the different "deals" they strike with the gender pressures upon them. This is the first step toward that reconstruction of society that Dewey sees as the goal of a reconstruction in philosophy.[44]

The second step is to seek strategies to communicate across the social gulfs created by incommensurability. This book has attempted to provide some. Its underlying message is that the social theory of truth does not undermine feminist claims, for they retain the only status any truth can claim: "a moral resolution to prize one mode of life."

Feminism does not represent a commitment to "discover" eternal truths whose blinding light will persuade everyone. It represents a commitment to negotiate with our traditions, and within them, to make arguments capable of building coalitions for gender change. Feminists need to take incommensurability as a given and construct coalitions by choosing strategies and rhetoric that appeal to people in a variety of social locations.

These coalitions will differ because gender change involves at least four agendas. This books has discussed two: challenging the eroticizing of dominance and the organization of market and family work. Two others are the goal of making conventional gender display less oppressive and working for women's right to free sexual expression. The coalitions required to make progress on each of these issues differs. For example, antipornography feminists often align with cultural conservatives, while feminists intent on defending women's right to a range of sexualities would never do so. Pro-sex feminists might well align with gay activists, while feminists intent on restructuring work could expect to find more interest among "family men" than among gay men in whose lifestyle children play no central part. (Note that this description does not include all gay men; some are fathers raising children.)

Because women strike different deals with domesticity, not all agree on the need to reconstruct the relationship of market and family work. This highlights the need for coalitions with like-minded men. While all-women groups remain ideal for consciousness raising, feminists have always worked with men. The Violence Against Women Act did not pass with female support alone. The importance of these coalitions has been erased in feminist theory. Feminists need to acknowledge their alliances with men and identify their enemy as the current construction of gender and abuses of male power, not as men.[45]

Coalition work involves trade-offs, both in terms of rhetoric and in terms of substance. For example, in writing this book, a publisher friend advised me to omit *feminism* from the title. I omitted it. Then another friend, a writer, advised me to omit the word entirely from the book, again on the grounds that it would unduly restrict my audience. There I drew the line. I have lived a life defined by domesticity; feminism has been my lifeline. I will reframe feminism so people will listen. I will link it to values people's ears are tuned to hear. But I will not abandon an analytic that has provided the central logic of my life.

Where Do You Draw the Line?
Pragmatism, Female Genital Cutting, and the Veil

The Government can cover our faces. But underneath, we still want our rights.[46]

The hard question is where should we draw the line in respecting other women's truths. Any approach based on the social theory of truth must provide a response to the question of where to draw the line in the face of incommensurability. This issue is often framed in terms of the Nazis. What does the pragmatist say when the storm trooper knocks?[47] This is a question any pragmatist must address. I will do so by beginning with the Nazis themselves.

The central tenet of Nazi ideology was that the lives of some were less valuable than the lives of others. This would have sounded plausible in the past: Romans treated death as spectacle and sport. Today, however, widespread consensus exists that it is wrong to treat some people's lives as less valuable than others'. If we interpret Nazi truths as the invitation to "be like me," I can make short work of the invitation. I have no desire to. I think that is a bad way to live.[48]

This is not a statement I make lightly. I do not, for example, condemn the Mormon mother's chosen frame. Though it does not appeal to me, I cannot say with confidence that the life I live makes me happier or contributes more than hers does. So the question becomes whether social theory should be framed around the Mormon mother or around the Nazis, around incommensurability or around evil.

In the context of feminism, disagreements are more likely to reflect incommensurability than evil. Consensus on gender issues is so hard to reach not because irrational people refuse to acknowledge irrefutable truths, but because people's truths differ. Sometimes, as in the situation of abortion, we have to do what the logic of our own lives demands—for example, defending abortion rights—while reassuring our opponents of our humanity, and our shared values, as best we can.

This leaves the question of how to balance the demands of strategy with the demands of authenticity. I conclude with a few thoughts that stem from transnational feminism, because this issue is best focused by a discussion of female genital cutting (FGC) and the veil.

FGC plays the same role in feminism that Nazis play outside it: as a close-out argument establishing the perniciousness and implausibility of the social theory of meaning. If a social theory of meaning means that we cannot judge FGC, goes the argument, then isn't it worse than useless? The situation is further complicated by the fact that the social theory of meaning has been used against feminists in this context. They have been called imperialists by Africans defending female genital mutilation as integral to their traditional culture. Who is right?[49]

It is useful to begin with a more detailed description of FGC, which is a generic name for a series of practices. The first (and rarest) is female circumcision, which involves removal of the clitoral foreskin. The second is clitoridectomy, in which a girl's clitoris and all or part of the labia minora are cut away. The third (and most common) is infibulation, which involves amputation of the clitoris, all of the labia minora, and much of the labia majora. The two sides of the vulva are then stitched together with silk, catgut, or thorns; a tiny sliver of wood or a reed is inserted to preserve a small opening, often about the size of a matchstick or fingertip, for urine and menstrual blood. The girl's legs are then bound together from ankle to knee until the wound has healed, which typically takes from a week to a month. These operations are often performed in villages without medical equipment in unhygienic conditions; common complications include uncontrolled bleeding, infection, extreme pain, urine retention, shock, damage to urethra or anus, and keloid scarring. A Kenyan study reported that more than 80 percent of infibulated women report at least one medical complication after FGC. Other reports estimate that between 15 and 30 percent of all girls and women die from bleeding or infections. Infibulation requires that a woman be cut again on her wedding night, and can lead to complications upon childbirth.[50]

A variety of rationales are given for these practices. A common one is to ensure women's virginity before marriage and chastity afterward. In cultures that practice FGC, a woman who has not undergone it often is considered unclean, licentious, unmarriageable. The procedure typically takes place as part of an initiation rite in which attention and gifts are showered on the young girl in a ceremony that marks the transition from girlhood to full womanhood.[51]

Why do these practices offend us? For simple reasons: They show a willingness to deprive women of sexual sensation in the interest of controlling their supposedly unruly sexuality, and when performed in traditional (unhygienic) conditions, they value control of women's sexuality over their health and survival. FGC violates one of the most basic principles we have been raised with, expressed in human rights discourse as the rights to survival, to equal dignity, to bodily integrity.

If we consider the cultural "truths" that motivate FGC, an invitation to "be like me" holds close to zero appeal. As Westerners and as feminists, there is no chance we will change in ways that would make FGC seem reasonable. This initial step shows why it is inevitable that we make judgments and why we need to stand by them even when not all women agree with our conclusions. We need not stop dead in the absence of a consensus among women. In fact, in this as in so much else, a consensus among women is not in the cards, for many groups of women are deeply invested in the traditional practice. The most obvious example is the women who perform the cutting, who can attain "exceptional power and influence in a culture where women are otherwise subordinated." Many ordinary women will support the practice as well, given that refusing to circumcise a daughter can make her un-marriageable in societies where women have few economic alternatives, or can cause her to be considered unclean and, in effect, a prostitute. In this cultural context, women who oppose FGC will have to be "moral entrepreneurs" willing to risk considerable social opprobrium for what they think is right. Obviously, most of us live more ordinary lives and do what is expected of us. Note, too, that if we cannot expect a consensus among women, then we surely cannot expect to develop a consensus against the practice among men.[52]

Our goal is not consensus, but solidarity among women who interpret their traditions in ways that empower women. The question is how we as Westerners can best support the efforts of such women. Given the historical relationship of Westerners to Africa, Western feminists need to proceed with extreme caution lest FGC become a rallying cry for cultural integrity against racism and imperialism.[53]

As a threshold matter, the charge that an assault on FGC is an assault on traditional culture requires a simple response. It is an assault, but only to the extent that traditional culture endorses sexual hierarchy. Feminism inevitably challenges inherited cultures, other people's as well as our own. A feminist's job is to use some aspects of a culture to provide a purchase for critiques of other aspects of it—to use cultural commitments to dignity and equality against practices that treat women as mere members in a hierarchy, as less than full people.

This does mean judging traditional African practices according to Western standards of personhood, which is what makes transnational feminism so perilous. But the only alternative is for Westerners to abandon their Western ideals of personhood in their dealings abroad. The United States and other industrialized countries often use their imperial power to express their most precious cultural values. If feminists are silenced, the only steady pressure from the West will be for values like free trade. It makes no sense for feminists to help create a world where countries in Africa and elsewhere feel the pressure to conform with Western commercial values but no pressure to conform to Western ethical values, of which equality for women is one.

This analysis highlights that human rights talk is aspirational, not declarative. The power of human rights talk (feminism as well as other varieties) is as a rallying cry to make certain practices universal. To rally effectively, we need to give persuasive reasons. Treating human rights talk as simply declarative of preexisting truths deflects our attention from the need to persuade.

This understanding helps to explain why Western feminists can legitimately use human rights talk to critique and challenge other people's cultures. It is part of their aspiration to create an international coalition to make a certain image of personhood universal: that all people should be treated as ends, not means. This is a legitimate enterprise, but much depends on the means we use to accomplish it.

Isabelle Gunning has written perceptively about the need for "appropriately toned dialogue." Westerners need rigorously to avoid a condescending and judg-mental manner. That is why I have avoided the use of the term "female genital mutilation," which is probably too accusatory to be useful. Yet Gunning's term, "fe-male genital surgery," seems to endorse the notion that the procedures have legiti-mate medical goals, which they do not. I have used an intermediate term: "female genital cutting," which seems to avoid the difficulties presented by both "female genital mutilation" and "female genital surgery."

Westerners need not only to exercise careful tone control. They need as well to recognize that the force fields that keep FGC in place are even more powerful than those that keep domesticity alive and well; after all, Western women do not face unmarriageability and a reputation for uncleanness and promiscuity for violating the mandates of domesticity, as do African women who refuse to be cut. Western-ers also need not only to respect the pressures African women are under but to act in alliance with women who want to change their traditional culture in precisely the same ways as Western feminists do. These Africans do not see the elimination of FGC as a violation of *their* traditional values. Many are health professionals who have treated women suffering from the side effects of FGC: well-known examples are Nawal El Saadawi, an Egyptian physician and feminist organizer, and Nahid Toubia, a Sudanese surgeon. These and others like them see FGC as inconsistent with the values they hold as participants in their own cultures. What is at issue in the conflict over FGC is not the preservation of traditional culture but two war-ring interpretations of traditional culture. Those defending FGC seek Western al-lies to favor one interpretation. Those opposed to it seek allies, too. Sharing a national culture does not mean sharing a consensus. This becomes more and more obvious as women seek asylum based on fear of FGC. The asylum-seekers make it crystal clear that Africans are divided over the practice. Consider the case of Fauziya, whose father had opposed FGC and prevented Fauziya's five older sisters from experiencing it; the issue of whether she would be cut arose because he had died by the time she came of age. Once feminists recognize that they are not repre-senting all women, but rather are building a coalition of like-minded people to ac-complish specific types of gender change, the fact that some women disagree with their goals will no longer be understood to undermine their legitimacy.[54]

Though the social theory of truth confirms the legitimacy of challenging FGC, it should also make us cautious about how we do so. In a world where the West has often abused its power, feminist efforts to oppose FGC can easily hurt more than help unless these efforts are conceptualized as alliances with local feminists, for women embedded in the relevant communities will often have greater insight than foreigners into what will be effective strategies. For example, the prosecution of FGC in France has led to situations where women were prosecuted while the males at whose insistence the practice took place were not. Knowledgeable observers believed that strategies other than prosecution would have been more effective and more equitable.[55]

Yet a word is in order in response to those who oppose any efforts other than educational ones—even legislation prohibiting FGC inside the United States—until cultural consensus has been reached. The crucial issue outside the United States is to find out what local feminists leading the battle against FGC see as the most effective strategy. Any international sanction or penal legislation needs to be developed in conjunction with them. One could imagine some contexts in which sanctions would be welcomed as an effective weapon by local feminists. Where they are, it would seem odd for an American feminist to oppose them: After all, if we had waited until a consensus existed on the need for Title VII, we would not have had it for the last thirty-five years, during which it has substantially changed what it means to be a woman in this country. Allowing legislation only after consensus has been achieved would mean that reformers could never use legislation as a means to spark social change.[56]

A number of African feminists have expressed interest in working with Western feminists, and have given firm guidance as to appropriate roles. The astute commentator Hope Lewis has pointed this out, quoting Assitan Diallo, a Malian activist:

> I want to collaborate with them. But I don't think I can be in the same group with them to fight something in my own country, because I will feel, "Here we go again, colonization." But I love being asked by people working on female circumcision, "What are the specifics in Mali?" And suggesting to me, "You know, people do circumcision in France, and we French people want to fight against it." I want them to allow me to say, "I'm suggesting you do it this way, because these people are from my country, and I think this will be better." Again, I'm suggesting something, not imposing it on them. That's the kind of working relationship I want.

This statement gives Western feminists opposed to FGC important guidance.[57]

Although guidance by Africans is crucial, a final note is in order on the issue of the "middle way" suggested by Amede Obiora: to move not toward outright prohibition, but toward shifting FGC to one, performed in hospitals, in which the clitoris is nicked without removing any tissue. At least in the United States, this seems to be the best approach. It leaves intact the highly freighted symbolic system surrounding FGC, which helps protect women against the charge that they are unclean and unmarriageable if they have not been cut. Yet it divorces that symbolic system from the actual cutting off of sexual organs, and from the other deleterious effects of traditional FGC.

Of course, as Obiora herself acknowledges, precisely because this middle way does not disrupt the traditional symbolic system, it does not make FGC a place where feminists draw the line against traditional conceptions of women as in need of sexual controls and "naturally" under the economic power of men. Yet we all have to choose our battles, and the question is whether FGC is the right arena in which to contest these fundamental issues. The decision, of course, is up to African women, but my sense is that FGC is not the right arena. Given the very heavy social consequences of being uncut, the solution of ritual nicking seems to protect women's physical integrity while not insisting that each individual woman become a moral entrepreneur committed to putting her social life on the line in the defense of women's ultimate liberty. This solution parallels the strategy of domesticity in drag. It preserves the symbolism embedded in entrenched customs but translates that symbolism into a ritualized gender performance no longer associated with dramatically adverse physical and social consequences for women.[58]

Turning from FGC to the veil, U.S. feminists working with Middle Eastern women face even more delicate issues of cross-cultural negotiations than do those working with Africans, given the cynical misuse of feminism for imperialist ends in the West's dealings with the Middle East. "The peculiar practices of Islam with respect to women ha[ve] always formed part of the Western narrative of the quintessential otherness and inferiority of Islam," notes Leila Ahmed. She documents the misuse of feminism for colonialist purposes in the nineteenth and twentieth centuries. "Veiling—to *Western* eyes, the most visible mark of the differentness and inferiority of Islamic societies—became the symbol now of both what was seen as 'Islam's degradation of women' and the backwardness of Islam," as well as "the spearhead of the assault on Muslim societies." Ahmed discusses how the British consul general in Egypt, vociferous in decrying Islam for its degradation of women, was a founding member and sometime president of the Men's League for Opposing Women's Suffrage back home in England. "Feminism on the home front and feminism directed at white men was to be resisted and suppressed; but taken abroad and directed against the cultures of colonial peoples, it could be promoted in ways that admirably served and furthered the project of the dominance of the white man." The veil was used as justification for colonialism and European wars against Islamic nations.[59]

This is a heritage Western feminists should not forget. In the Middle East even more than elsewhere, the most effective role for Westerners may well be in supporting local activists rather than in taking public roles themselves. This is particularly true in the Middle East, because the most effective feminist strategy appears to be to turn the debate over women's roles into a debate about the true meaning of Islam. Leila Ahmed, Anouar Majid, and others have stressed that feminism in the Middle East needs to be fought on Islamic ground, as the retrieval of an emancipatory Islamic tradition. The goal, Ahmed has argued persuasively, should be to retrieve "the ethical voice of Islam."[60].

In this context, should unveiling women be an important agenda for Western feminists? Since I have already said that Westerners need to defer to Middle Eastern feminists even more than to feminists in other parts of the world, the real question is how deeply Western feminists should regret the upsurge of veiling among Arab women in the late twentieth century.

Ahmed and others point out that veiling has some very practical advantages for women in contemporary Islamic societies. Veiling often allows women to enter into jobs and other arenas of public life that they would not feel free to enter unveiled. "[T]he ritual invocation through dress of the notion of segregation places the integrated reality in a framework that defuses it of stress and impropriety. At the same time it declares women's presence in public space to be in no way a challenge to or a violation of the Islamic sociocultural ethic," argues Ahmed. Another commentator sees veiling as a way Islamic women "carv[e] out legitimate public space for themselves," thereby redefining public space as appropriate for women. Finally, because Western ways benefited privileged classes but not poorer ones, reveiling by privileged women is sometimes seen as an act of cross-class solidarity.[61]

In the end, after all, veiling involves only dress. Many Muslim women have come to the conclusion that battles over dress simply are not that important, as did the Afghan woman in the quote with which this section begins. They may well be right. Western feminists in the last twenty years have, in effect, come to the conclusion that norms of dress are both extraordinarily difficult to change and ultimately not that important.

Western feminists opposed feminine dressing both in the nineteenth century and the twentieth. Some feminists in each century designed uniforms intended to free them from the ways conventional femininity commodified women and made them into "sex objects." Many older feminists, myself included, avoided overtly feminine dressing for a decade or more.[62]

Of all the projects of second-wave feminism, the project to eliminate femininity in dress is one of the most absolute of failures. If feminism did not kill domesticity, it has had even less effect on feminine norms of dress and carriage. Most feminists today embrace femininity and sexy dressing and offer a variety of rationales.[63]

Yet the fact remains, as Muslim feminists point out early and often, that "the West uses women and female sexuality to increase profits." Sexy dressing encourages what we used to call "being a sex object," a point not lost on Muslims. Nonetheless, traditional forms of feminine dress have experienced a resurgence in the West just as they have in the Middle East.[64]

Feminists across the globe have been willing to offer conventional gender display as a token of reassurance, in return for which they demand other forms of empowerment they consider more important. If feminists in the West have followed this strategy, it makes no sense to bemoan the fact that many Middle Eastern women have reached the same conclusion (at least for now). This is precisely the kind of negotiation, of playing off one axis of gender against another, that feminists must begin to see more clearly and to accept without recrimination. Feminists are asking women to change a symbolic system that structures their identities. This is a tall order. Women need to be free to choose those battles they are emotionally able to fight. Dress seems not to be one of them.

Backing off the agenda of eliminating femininity in dress does not mean giving up altogether. The strategy that has worked in the West can be called femininity in drag: observing the symbolism of traditional forms of dress, while disassociating them from constriction and discomfort. This strategy has proved remarkably successful. When I came of age, in the mid-1960s, norms of dress in the United States were infinitely more oppressive than they are today. First of all, my height (I was 5′9″ at age fourteen) and shoe size (9) made me feel literally deformed. It meant I "could not" wear high heels in an era when any other kind of shoes for women were still denigrated as "sensible shoes" that connoted a lack of sexual self-confidence and womanly self-respect. Thus in a mystery novel of the 1940s, a woman with a badly scarred face wears "sensible shoes" until she learns to accept herself as she is, at which point she heads for the high heels. In sharp contrast to the messages I received about height, many young women today consider being tall as no big deal: by the mid-1980s, my students were upset if they were short rather than if they were tall. Maybe the supermodels haven't been all bad.

In addition, in the mid-1960s, I wore stockings held up with a garter belt. Mine was covered in sunflowers, and I was proud of it, though it always made me feel vaguely trussed up. For that reason I—at 5′9″ and 110 pounds—preferred my girdle, which made me feel svelte, and in which I worried less about boys seeing my underpants. This was a live issue in the 1960s because we wore short, short skirts that restricted our movement and advertised sexual availability whether we meant it or not. I still recall being spirited out of a New York restaurant in 1970 by a seventeen-year-old boyfriend alarmed at the sizzle produced by the chemical reaction between my miniskirt and Puerto Rican waiters.

While it is true that women's clothing remains "marked" in ways that men's is not, it is also true that a woman today can find appropriate clothing that is comfortable and does not enact sexual availability. Wearing clothing that restricts movement and advertises sexual availability is no longer the only way to give a competent feminine gender display. Western feminists today appear to have essentially given up on the project of ending the use of women's bodies to sell products. If taking on capitalism proved too tall an order in the West, we can hardly fault Muslim feminists for not taking on Islam.[65]

Are similar strategies useful in framing ways to help transmute the veil? While Westerners cannot lead the way, the women who do will find new ways of signaling deference to Islam that are less restricting than the veil as currently practiced. I am hardly in a position to discern what those might be. What I think of are those little pink hats waitresses wear pinned to their hair, the endpoint in the West of the tradition of having women cover their hair.

Four Themes of Conclusion

WHAT DO WOMEN WANT? WHAT DO MEN NEED?

In closing, let's return to the conversation with which the book began, which took place while I was sitting side by side with a woman I had just met at Plastercraft, chatting as our daughters painted Cinderellas a gaudy pink. "I decided to quit my job and stay home," she told me. "But it was my choice; I have no regrets." I asked her whether she would not really prefer to continue working as a lawyer, with shorter hours of work. She replied wistfully: "Of course, that's what I really want."

A central goal of this book is to persuade women to think about their own lives in a different way, not as expressions of personal priorities that occur within their heads but as a clash between the way society tells women that children should be raised and the way it chooses to organize market work.

Ideal-worker analysis points out that our work ideal is not ungendered. It is framed around the traditional life patterns of men and so discriminates against women. Women who now attribute their difficulties to work/family conflict inside their heads need to begin identifying the problem as discrimination that exists in the outside world. My goal is to give women a sense of entitlement to a work world restructured to eliminate labor market hostility to working mothers.[1]

"Of course it's discrimination, but you'll never do anything about it," one federal judge told a student in a job interview. My second goal is to challenge the instinctive belief that, however much we would like to, we cannot change the way we structure market work because it would be economically unfeasible. A moment's reflection about how much employers currently spend to train employees who leave work to raise children suggests, and the massive work/family literature confirms, that restructuring work in many circumstances will lead to *greater*, rather than *less*, productivity.

Arguments about discrimination often are linked with male bashing. This is important to avoid, for strategic as well as other reasons. The ways we organize (market and family) work disadvantage men as well as women; the fact that women's disadvantage is called "discrimination" is not inconsistent with saying that men also are ill-served by current gender arrangements. Early feminist theorists were right to stress that gender roles constrict the potential of men as well as women, for if conventional femininities marginalize and disempower women, conventional masculinities make it difficult for men to engage fully in family life and trap them in a "gray life of hard labor."[2]

DO FEMINISTS REALLY NEED THIS ABRUPT
CHANGE OF DIRECTION?

You're right, something has to be done. But it's risky. The reason we have insisted that women are being integrated into the economy and performing just like the men is that, once we acknowledge that women want time off work, they'll say, "See, I told you women could never make it. Isn't that what I've been telling you all along?"

This book proposes a sharp shift in feminist strategy. Since the second wave of American feminism began in the 1960s, its central thrust has been to insist that women wanted to work and would do so if only they were given the chance, and to frame available statistics to show that women were behaving more and more like men, that ever increasing numbers were in the labor force, were working full time, were earning more than their husbands. This book, instead, acknowledges that women's load of family work often interferes with their ability to perform as ideal workers.

How can we as feminists come to terms with these statistics without undermining opportunities for women? Won't employers say "[t]hat's why I don't want to hire women. It's not sex discrimination; it's just that women aren't willing to follow through." Many feminists expressed again and again the worry conveyed in the epigraph above.

My first response, as noted in chapter 1, is that many women *do* "follow through." Discriminating against all women because some take time off for caregiving is illegal. The fact that some women leave the workforce does not prove that the women who stay there will not do as good a job as any man.

My second response is that today, after thirty years of feminist activism, it is time to acknowledge that work patterns of many women are not the same as men's. As documented in the introduction, a majority of mothers remain economically marginalized. The majority do not even work full-time; roughly 80 percent of women still work in low-paid, sex-segregated "women's work."[3]

It is time to admit that women as a group do not perform the same as men as a group when jobs are designed around an ideal worker with men's physique and/or men's access to a flow of family work most women do not enjoy. Once we invent a language that defines this situation as the result of *discrimination against women*, rather than *mothers' choice*, we can face the facts and make new demands to restructure work. The time is ripe for this interpretive shift because it represents, at core, a generational shift. What strikes me in talks with feminists from seven to seventy is that the older feminists are quite different from younger ones. Those born in the 1930s went to college in the 1950s and chose professional careers in an era when that decision took considerable moral courage. In an era when their peers were getting their "MRS.," they were getting Ph.D.'s.

These early feminists took the personal risks associated with feminism in the early years because they were moral entrepreneurs. They were courageous nonconformists; often they also were tomboys along every conceivable axis.[4]

Though I deeply admire them I am not like them. By the time I came along it took far less courage to be a feminist, with the result that far more conventional people were attracted to feminism. This process continues unabated. I recently spoke with a legal feminist who was so deeply concerned that sexual harassment claims were opening women up to ridicule that she wanted to cut back sharply on such claims. It simply never occurred to my generation that feminists could avoid ridicule. Ridicule is the first and often the most effective weapon to keep women in their place: We experienced it often and tried not to take it personally.

If this situation represents a loss it also represents a gain, for the revolutionary quality of earlier generations of feminists created some distinct failures of communication between feminism as a movement and the American people in general. Reconstructive feminism aspires to help remedy those failures. It uses tools that would be repugnant to the initial revolutionaries, many of whom would rather relegate the norm of parental care to the trash heap than to use it as a wedge for transforming market work. But the increased conventionality of contemporary feminists is not only a watering-down; it also holds the potential to diminish the gap between feminism and the American public.

Reconstructive feminism represents a gain in another way as well. While the commitment of younger feminists to caregiving roles and feminine gender display at one level represents a disappointing return to traditionalism, at another level it represents a far healthier development. For while many older feminists knew that they had to act just like the men if they were to have any glimmer of a chance to succeed in "a man's job," many younger women feel a sense of entitlement to good jobs on their own terms. People now in their twenties, men as well as women, want to put limits on work time in order to leave time for family life. Said one New York attorney:

> There is a growing problem that everyone is facing and no one talks about: that the generational values have changed. You talk to partners who are forty-five or fifty and older; they don't even have a clue how many billable hours they work, they don't care, it's part of the modus operandi. The newer generation, there is a great deal of seeking "quality of life" decisions.[5]

They see no reason why women should not be able *both* to keep on doing the work they want to do *and* to behave in other ways as women traditionally have. Translating these sentiments into the language of feminist theory, this generational shift means that the time is ripe to challenge the masculine norms that frame market work, framed as they are around a vision of masculinity that appeals to few women and ever fewer men. Younger women's sense of ownership fuels a rich reservoir of gender anger that can be combined with the fury over the treatment of women upon divorce. My goal is to channel both into the work of reconstruction, working in alliance with men.

POLICY IMPLICATIONS

Reconstructive feminism also has messages for policy makers. A central message of this book is that our current system designs market and family work *in a particular way*. This system, which I have called domesticity, arose at a particular historical period for particular reasons; the question is whether we want to preserve or change it.

Probably we want to preserve part and change part. One part worth preserving is the notion that children need parental guidance and companionship throughout their youth in order to learn the skills required to find their own way in our complex and intensely individualistic society. This does not mean that one adult need stay home with them twenty-four hours a day. Indeed, this model is not ideal, for many reasons detailed in this book. The alternative is to end the system of providing for children's care by marginalizing their caregivers. This proposal should appeal not only to feminists but also to those concerned with childhood poverty.

This book also holds messages for anyone involved in labor and employment issues. It shows the need for comprehensive legislation on contingent work, such as the 1994 Contingent Workforce Equity Act, which requires equal pay for equal work performed by full- and part-time employees. It also shows the need for legislation forbidding discrimination against parents, as proposed by President Clinton in his 1999 State of the Union Address. Legislation is also needed to end the practice of tying work benefits to the ideal worker norm in the context of Social Security, unemployment, the Family and Medical Leave Act, ERISA, and the tax system.[6]

It shows as well that the ways labor statistics are collected needs to be changed. While current wage gap data are important, they seriously underestimate the extent of women's marginalization in the workforce, because they compare the wage rates of *full-time* women with those of *full-time* men in an economy where more than half of mothers do not work full-time. Wage gap data need to be complemented with data that document the economy of mothers and others, using the "family gap" calculations developed by Jane Waldfogel and cited in the introduction to this book. For example, if the wages of part-time workers are included, the wage gap between men and women rises, with women earning only about half of men's wages.[7]

In addition to the messages for legislatures and executive agencies, this book also holds messages for courts. Courts, if they chose, could effect tomorrow the paradigm shift from attributing the economy of mothers and others to "mothers' choice," to attributing it to discrimination against women. Courts have begun to recognize such discrimination against mothers as sex discrimination in disparate treatment cases; they need to interpret the marginalization of mothers as sex discrimination as well in Equal Pay Act and Title VII's disparate impact cases. Redesigning a society with over a million workplaces will take time, effort, and struggle. But the result will be more responsible parenthood, better use of women workers' human capital, a saner life for all workers, and a society that has regained the time and energy to invest in community life.[8]

On the family side of work/family issues, family court judges need to abandon their embrace of the "he who earns it, owns it" rule. This entails rethinking who owns the ideal worker's wage, and abandoning the traditional conception of that wage as the sole property of the ideal worker. Instead, the wages of both the ideal worker and the primary caregiver should be treated as joint property, for the primary caregiver provided the flow of family work that allowed the ideal worker to meet our work ideals. The joint property theory has important implications for the "executive divorce" cases, where the principle should be that wives own half the family property whether it consists of $1000 or $1,000,000,000. The joint property theory also has implications for levels of child support and alimony in the large bulk of families where accumulated assets are few. In addition, family law courts need to end the cruel practice of pushing women into the workforce only to penalize them for being there, by depriving working mothers of custody in punishment for their failure to live up to outdated ideals of full-time motherhood.[9]

Legislation and executive action are needed as well in the arena of family law. New statutes should reconceptualize economic entitlements upon divorce. The child support guidelines need to be recalculated to reflect the joint property theory, so that the standards of living between the two postdivorce households are roughly equalized. State alimony statutes should be redrafted to link alimony statutes not to need alone, but to need linked to the caregiving role. A more sweeping legislative agenda would include ending the traditional system of separating child support and alimony, to replace it with a single calculation that reflects the impossibility of separating out the economic entitlements of children and those of their caregivers in a system that provides for children by marginalizing their caregivers.

This book also has an important message for the community of work/family consultants. That community needs to reframe its goals: The key issue is not whether employers have flexible policies on their books, but whether the policies provided break the traditional link between flexibility and marginalization. An effective test for whether a flexible policy marginalizes the workers who use it is to see whether men as well as mothers use it, for virtually no men will use policies that offer flexibility at the price of marginalization.

IMPLICATIONS FOR FEMINIST THEORY

When feminist jurisprudence turned away from work/family issues in the early 1980s, a sense of staleness hung over the sameness/difference debate. Since then, dominance feminism has changed the subject rather than solved the theoretical problems that were endlessly recycled but never resolved. What is needed to resolve them is an analysis of domesticity. This clears up first the debate over women's voice, which is extraordinarily important because, although it has died out in feminist jurisprudence, it continues in vernacular gender talk. Second, it clears up important issues, never illuminated by *CalFed* or by current debates over caregivers' entitlements, about how to design policies to change the relationship of market work and family work. Third, it proposes a truce based on domesticity in drag: a self-conscious use of domesticity that makes no claim to represent the true voice of women, but instead treats domesticity as part of women's gender traditions that can be mobilized in working for positive social change.[10]

Although dominance feminism cannot substitute for an analysis of domesticity, its explorations into the eroticizing of dominance have proved important, indeed inspirational. The approaches advocated in this book are meant to add to dominance feminism, not to replace it. Indeed, the foot-on-neck model can be viewed as the Newtonian physics of gender and power: It works to explain the obvious cases of gender subordination in the context of domestic violence, sexual harassment, and violent pornography. In other contexts, as Vicki Schultz has so clearly pointed out, dominance feminism's tight focus on the structure of sexuality can distort its vision; sometimes sexual harassment is about work, not sex. When it is, the key to understanding it is not the eroticizing of dominance but the desire to police women out of blue-collar jobs, one of the few arenas that working-class men feel give them dignity as men.[11]

In the context of work and family issues, dominance feminism has many limitations. Its foot-on-neck model does not resonate with women when they "choose" to marginalize "for the good of their children"; it makes women sound like they don't know their own minds and makes the men they often see as responsible and caring into unrecognizable demons. In the work/family context, feminists need a language that shows how both men and women are caught in force fields that suck them back toward the ideal-worker and marginalized-caregiver roles. The key point is that gender hierarchy often happens without any bad actor in the picture; these roles result from the current structure of work rather than from the systematic abuse of male power. Although both men and women get caught in conventional gender roles, this is not to equate the oppression of the master with the oppression of the slave. The two are very different, as emerges only too clearly in the context of divorce. In fact, to explain the way divorce courts systematically impoverish women in the name of preserving the sexual freedom of men requires nothing more subtle than the old-fashioned foot-on-neck model of gender and power.

If dominance feminism has created problems for feminists in the context of work and family issues, these are small compared to the problems it has created in dealing with nonessential women. Dominance feminism has never fully understood how feminism could coexist with postfoundationalism, and this is a theoretical problem that impedes feminists' ability to communicate with working-class women and women of color. This book attempts to remedy that problem by showing how the critique of absolutes leads us not to relativism but to the social theory of truth, and from there to a recognition that our goal is to persuade others in an open-minded conversation, rather than to enlighten them to some preexisting truth we have and they don't.[12]

The social theory of truth provides an important resource for feminism by defining how different groups of women can structure mutually respectful conversations in which no one feels her voice has been drowned out. This includes not just conversations that include working-class women and women of color inside the United States but conversations in a transnational context as well. The issue is not relativism versus universalism, but how to create a dialogue sensitive to the situated nature of our own certainties and those of others. For me, the key insight is that I do not know everything about what is best for women. I have a few basic commitments—to equal opportunities for meaningful (market and family) work, to equal entitlements to bodily integrity, to ending the eroticizing of dominance. Beyond that, I tack back and forth, bargaining with my traditions, much as other women do. Like them, I try to do the best I can.

NOTES

Preface: What This Book Is About

1. Lillian Rubin, Families on the Fault Line 79 (1994); Arlie Hochschild, *The Time Bind: When Home Becomes Work & Work Becomes Home* 135 (1997). Initial quote changed from present to past tense.

2. The four characters are composites; the quotes are real. *See* Lisa Belkin, *Bars to Equality of Sexes Seen as Eroding, Slowly*, N.Y. Times, Aug. 29, 1989, Sect. 1, at 1; Carol Gilligan, *In a Different Voice* (1982) (a society that defines . . .).

3. Rubin, *supra* note 1, at 81–82.

4. *See* Hochschild, *supra* note 1, at 59, 66–68.

Introduction

1. *See* Alice Kessler-Harris & Karen Sacks, *The Demise of Domesticity*, in *Women, Households, and the Economy* (Lourdes Beneria & Catharine R. Stimpson eds., 1987). *See also* Margaret F. Brinig & June Carbone, *The Reliance Interest in Marriage and Divorce*, 62 Tul. L. Rev. 855, 858–70 (1988); Frances Elisabeth Olsen, *Feminism in Central and Eastern Europe: Risks and Possibilities of American Engagement*, 106 Yale L. J. 2215, 2232 (1997); Daphne Bianchi & Suzanne M. Spain, *The Balancing Act* 81 (1996).

2. *See* Nancy Cott, *The Bonds of Womanhood* 63 (1977).

3. *See* Richard Morin & Megan Rosenfeld, *With More Equity, More Sweat; Poll Shows Sexes Agree on Pros and Cons of New Roles*, Wash. Post, Mar. 22, 1998, at A1 (two-thirds); John Gray, *Men Are from Mars, Women Are from Venus* (1992); Gilligan, *In a Different Voice* 74 (1982) (linking women with ethic of care); Robert S. Weiss, *Men and Their Wives' Work*, in *Spouse, Parent, Worker: On Gender and Multiple Roles* 110 (Faye J. Crosby ed., 1987) (men as providers); Theodore F. Cohen, *What Do Fathers Provide?*, in *Men, Work, and Family* 3 (Jane C. Hood ed., 1993) (for the quotation).

4. Statistics are based on the computations of Professor Manuelita Ureta, who used machine-readable versions of Bureau of the Census, U.S. Department of Commerce, Current Population Survey, March Supplement, Public Use Files (1996) [hereinafter Ureta Census Data]. Grateful thanks to Professor Ureta for her help. Full time full year is defined as working at least forty hours/week, at least forty-nine weeks/year. Note that school teachers are excluded, since they do not work 40 hours/week full year; this in keeping with my goal of measuring women's exclusion from traditionally male jobs. The Census Bureau classifies as "full time" any worker who works more than 35 hours/week; in my view, this underestimates the extent of mothers' marginalization. *See also* Anne L. Kalleberg, *Part-Time Work and Workers in the United States: Correlates and Policy Issues*, 52 Wash. & Lee L. Rev. 771, 780 (1996) (marginalization of part-time workers).

5. *See* Jane Waldfogel, *The Effect of Children on Women's Wages*, 92 Am. Soc. Rev. 209, 211 (1997) (never married homemakers). *See also* Jane Waldfogel, *Understanding the "Family Gap" in Pay for Women with Children*, 12 J. Econ. Persp. 137, 156 (1998) (homemakers and full-time workers) [hereinafter *Family Gap*]; Chris Tilly, *Half a Job: Bad and Good Part-Time Jobs in a Changing Labor Market* 16 tbl. 2.1 (1996) (part-time married woman workers).

6. *See* Ureta Census Data, *supra* note 4 (93 percent of mothers work 49 hours/week or less). Juliet B. Schor, *The Overworked American: The Unexpected Decline of Leisure* 5 (1991) (increase in work); Joan C. Williams, *Gender Wars: Selfless Women in the Republic of Choice*, 66 N.Y.U. L. Rev.

1559, 1598–99 (1991) (mommy-track literature). *See also* Rachel Williams Dempsey, Working on Weekends, Science Fair Project, April 1997.

7. *See* Betty Holcomb, *Not Guilty!* 131 (1998) (women better-educated). Remainder of data from Waldfogel, *Family Gap, supra* note 5, at 144, 147–48; Jane Waldfogel, *The Family Gap for Young Women in the U.S. and Britain,* 16 J. Labor Econ. 505 (1998) (60 percent); Jane Waldfogel, *Effect of Children, supra* note 5, at 209 (nearly 90 percent of working women becoming mothers in the course of their working lives). The 60 percent figure is between mothers and fathers who work full time. Recent reports note that the wage gap between men and women is narrowing. *Wage Gap Between the Sexes Is Narrowing,* N.Y. Times, June 10, 1998, at A20. Note that the standard wage gap calculation compares full-time male workers to full-time female workers. Consequently it misses most of the marginalization mothers experience, because it does not take into account either part-time workers or women staying home with children. (Of course, wage gap data is very useful for other purposes, notably for comparing ideal-worker men with ideal-worker women.)

8. *See* John P. Robinson & Geoffrey Godbey, *Time for Life* 105 tbl. 3 (1997) (thirty-one hours; distribution of family work—housework figure excludes shopping). *See also* Erik Olin Wright, Karen Shire, Shu-Ling Hwang, Maureen Dolan & Janeen Baxter, *The Non-Effects of Class on the Gender Division of Labor in the Home,* 6 Gender & Soc'y 253, 266–67 (1992). Considerable controversy exists about how much family work men do. Studies based on self-reporting are notoriously unreliable. One study found that reports by women of their husbands' contribution are generally about 75 percent of the men's reports of their own contributions. *See id.* at 260. Another also found high levels of overreporting, that high-status men exaggerate their level of contribution the most, and that the reporting gap is so high it is large enough to overshadow the small increases in husbands' housework observed in recent years. *See* Julie E. Press & Eleanor Townsley, *Wives' and Husbands' Housework Reporting,* 12 Gender & Soc'y 188, 203, 208 (1998). Studies based on self-reporting include the influential reports of the Families and Work Institute, one of them being a study that announced to much fanfare in 1998 that men are assuming a bigger share at home. *See* Tamar Lewin, *Men Assuming Bigger Share At Home, New Survey Shows,* N.Y. Times, Apr. 14, 1998, at A18. *See also* Ellen Galinsky, James T. Bond & Dana E. Friedman, *The Changing Workforce: Highlights of the National Study* (1993) 1. Note that some men do much more than other men; it is important that men who do a lot recognize that they are being penalized along with the women. It is not in their interest to overestimate the amount of household work done by the large majority of men doing very little. When Arlie Hochschild interviewed fifty men in the 1980s, she found that 80 percent did not share household work or child care at all. *See* Arlie Hochschild, *The Second Shift* 173 (1989). Fathers' family work increases most when they and their wives work split shifts, or the wives work weekends and evenings. *See* Carol S. Wharton, *Finding Time for the "Second Shift,"* 8 Gender & Soc'y 189, 190 (1994) (quoting Brayfield & Hofferth's study).

9. The notion that gender patterns tend to mutate rather than to disappear completely is developed in Reva B. Siegel, *Home as Work: The First Woman's Rights Claims Concerning Wives' Household Labor, 1850–1880,* 103 Yale L.J. 1073 (1994); Reva B. Siegel, *The Modernization of Marital Status Law: Adjudicating Wives' Rights to Earnings, 1860–1930,* 82 Geo. L.J. 2127 (1994). This book builds upon the work of many prior legal scholars, including not only Siegel's but also Mary Joe Frug, *A Postmodern Feminist Legal Manifesto,* 105 Harv. L. Rev. 1045, 1049 (1992), *reprinted in* Postmodern Legal Feminism 125, 129 (1992) (discussing labor market hostility to working mothers); Nancy Dowd, *Work and Family: Restructuring the Workplace,* 32 Ariz. L. Rev. 431 (1990); Deborah Rhode, *Justice and Gender: Sex Discrimination and the Law* (1989); Deborah Rhode, *The*

"No-Problem" Problem: Feminist Challenges and Cultural Change, 100 Yale L. J. 1731 (1991) [hereinafter Rhode, *The "No Problem" Problem*]; Deborah Rhode, *Gender and Professional Roles*, 63 Fordham L. Rev. 39 (1994); Katharine Silbaugh, *Turning Labor into Love: Housework and the Law*, 91 Nw. L. Rev. 1 (1996).

10. *See* Demie Kurtz, *For Richer or for Poorer* 3, 205–26 (1995); Barbara Bennett Woodhouse, *Towards A Revitalization of Family Law*, 69 Tex. L. Rev. 245, 268–69 (1990).

11. *See* Diane Ehrensaft, *When Women and Men Mother*, in *Mothering: Essays in Feminist Theory* 41 (Joyce Trebilcot ed., 1983) (12 minutes); Michael Lamb *et al.*, *A Biosocial Perspective on Paternal Behavior and Involvement*, in *Parenting Across the Lifespan: Biosocial Dimensions* 111, 127 (Jane B. Lancaster *et al.* eds., 1987) (three times as much).

12. *See* The 40-Hour Workweek Trends and Research 1 (Apr. 11, 1995) (unpublished Briefing Paper for the Secretary of Labor) (on file with author).

13. *See* James T. Kloppenberg, *The Virtues of Liberalism* (1998) (eighteenth-century liberalism framed by virtues); Joan Williams, *Domesticity as the Dangerous Supplement of Liberalism*, 2 J. Women's Hist. 69 (1991) (domesticity siphons off virtues of liberalism); Marlise Simon, *Child Care Sacred as France Cuts Back on Welfare State*, N.Y. Times, Dec. 31, 1997, at A1 (child care in France).

14. *See* Deborah L. Rhode, *The "No-Problem" Problem*, *supra* note 9, 1764 (1991).

15. *See, e.g.*, *Work & Family: A Retrospective* 113, 128–30 (Work & Family, Inc. ed., 1995) (discussing the results of various studies which conclude that family-friendly policies increase retention of employees and serve as "important tools for recruiting workers in the future").

16. *See* Madeline Blais, *Who's Got Time To Stay at Home?*, N.Y. Times, Apr. 5, 1998, $6 (Magazine), at 48, 50 (at-home mother; note that it is the mother at home whose picture is on the magazine cover).

17. Griggs v. Duke Power Co., 401 U.S. 424, 432 (1971).

18. *See* Ann Bookman, *Flexibility at What Price? The Costs of Part-Time Work for Women Workers*, Wash & Lee L. Rev. 799, 800 (1995).

19. *See* Judith Stacey, *Brave New Families* 17 (1991) (postmodern family).

20. *See* Barbara Vobejda, *Traditional Families Hold On*, Wash. Post, May 28, 1998, at A2; Nancy E. Dowd, *In Defense of Single-Parent Families* 6 (1997) (nearly 90 percent statistic; poverty of single-parent families).

21. *See* Waldfogel, *Effect of Children*, *supra* note 5, at 209 (nearly 90 percent statistic); Galinsky et al., *supra* note 8, at 41 (40 percent statistic; one-quarter statistic).

CHAPTER ONE: *Is Domesticity Dead?*

1. Ruth Wilsea Adkins '85, Letter to the Editor, Yale Alumni Magazine, Feb. 1992, at 4–5.

2. *See, e.g.*, Solomon W. Polacheck, *Occupational Self-Selection*, 63 Rev. Econ. & Stat. 60 (1981). For a concise introduction to the "New Home Economics" from a feminist perspective, see Katharine Silbaugh, *Turning Labor into Love: Housework and the Law*, 91 Nw. L. Rev. 1 (1996); Nadja Zalokar, *Male-Female Differences in Occupational Choice and the Demand for General and Occupation-Specific Human Capital*, 26 Econ. Inquiry 59, 71 (1988) (quote).

3. *See* Duspiva v. Duspiva, 581 N.Y.S. 2d 376, 377 (1992) (family law case); Equal Employment Opportunity Commission (EEOC) v. Sears, Roebuck & Co, 628 F. Supp. 1264 (N.D. Ill. 1986), *aff'd*, 839 F.2d 302 (7th Cir. 1988); Ruth Milkman, *Women's History and the Sears Case*, 12 Fem. Stud. 375, 382 (1986).

4. *See* Vicki Schultz, *Telling Stories About Women and Work: Judicial Interpretations of Sex Segrega-*

tion in the Workplace in Title VII Cases Raising the Lack of Interest Argument, 103 Harv. L. Rev. 1749, 1820 n. 262 (discussing impact of women's family work) (1990) [hereinafter Schultz, *Telling Stories*]; Jane Waldfogel, *The Family Gap for Young Women in the United States and Britain,* 16 J. Lab. Econ. 505, 519 (1998). Waldfogel finds that an additional 23 percent of the gap reflects differential returns to work experience, a factor that includes both women's different family roles and old-fashioned discrimination against mothers (documented in Chapter 3). For a recent study measuring the impact of discrimination, see Linda K. Stroh, *All the Right Stuff,* 77 J. Applied Psych. 215 (1992).

5. *See* Arlie Hochschild, *The Second Shift* (1989). The Schultz articles are good examples of the labor literature, as is Daphne Bianchi & Suzanne M. Spain, *Balancing Act* (1996); other examples are cited in chapter 3. Examples of the family law literature are cited in chapter 4.

6. Ureta Census Data, *see* note 4 in the introduction.

7. For other analyses of choice in feminist jurisprudence, see Kathryn Abrams, *Ideology and Women's Choices,* 24 Ga. L. Rev. 761 (1990); Lucinda M. Finley, *Choice and Freedom: Elusive Issues in the Search for Gender Justice,* 96 Yale L. J. 914, 931–40 (1987) (book review); Alice Kessler-Harris, *Equal Opportunity Employment Commission v. Sears, Roebuck and Company: A Personal Account,* 35 Radical Hist. Rev. 57, 68, 72 (1986); Robin West, *Colloquy: Submission, Choice and Ethics: A Rejoinder to Judge Posner,* 99 Harv. L. Rev. 1449, 1455–56 (1986). At the turn of the century, Charlotte Perkins Gilman warned against assumptions about men's and women's choices. *See* Charlotte Perkins Gilman, *Women and Economics* 8, 141–68 (3d ed., 1900). For a comprehensive look at the analyses developed to challenge the traditional individual choice model, *see* Deborah Rhode, *Justice and Gender* 165–67 (1989); Deborah Rhode, *Occupational Inequality,* 1988 Duke L. J. 1207, 1216–27. *See also* Deborah L. Rhode, *The "No-Problem" Problem: Feminist Challenges and Cultural Change,* 100 Yale L. J. 1731 (1991); Deborah L. Rhode, *Gender and Professional Roles,* 63 Ford. L. Rev. 39 (1994).

8. *See* Reva B. Siegel, *The Modernization of Marital Status Law: Adjudicating Wives' Rights to Earnings, 1860–1930,* 82 Geo. L. J. 2127, 2200 (1994) [hereinafter Siegel, *Modernization*]; Reva B. Siegel, *"The Rule of Love": Wife Beating as Prerogative and Privacy,* 105 Yale L. J. 2117 (1996) [hereinafter Siegel, *"Rule of Love"*]; Reva B. Siegel, *Home as Work,* 103 Yale L. J. 1073 (1994); Graham v. Graham, 33 F. Supp. 936 (E.D. Mich. 1940) (husband's right to determine place of domicile); Deborah L. Rhode, *Occupational Inequality, supra* note 7, at 1216 (men moving families).

9. Lillian Rubin, *Families on the Fault Line* 70–84 (1994) [hereinafter Rubin, *Fault Line*]; (working-class families); Roberta Sigel, *Ambition & Accommodation* 159 (1996) (same).

10. Deborah Fallows, *A Mother's Work* 22 (1985).

11. *See id.* at 11.

12. *See id.* at 43–44 (all quotes).

13. *See id.* at 45.

14. *See id.* (both quotes).

15. *See id.* (first quote); Rhona Mahony, *Kidding Ourselves* 118 (1995) (second quote); Graham v. Graham, 33 F. Supp. 936 (E.D. Mich. 1940).

16. *See* Siegel, *Modernization, supra* note 8, at 2200 (citing Blackstone), 2176 (block quote, citing In re Callister's Estate, 47 N.E. 268 (N.Y. 1897)).

17. The requirement for legal "consideration" is, in effect, a requirement that no contract is enforceable if one party gets something for nothing.

18. *See* Siegel, *Modernization, supra* note 8, at 2199 (citing Borelli v. Brusseau, 16 Cal. Rptr. 2d 16, 20 (Cal. Ct. App. 1993)).

19. *See* Betty Friedan, *The Feminine Mystique* (1962); Fallows, *supra* note 10, at 11–13, 27–28, 35.

20. *See* Fallows, *supra* note 10, at 219 (quote); chapters 4–12.

21. *See id.* at 10–11.

22. Patriarchy includes many different gender systems. I use the term to highlight the open reliance on hierarchy that characterized gender relations in eighteenth-century America. I do not mean to claim that all patriarchal systems are the same; there has always been a wide variety of patriarchal systems, and there still is today.

23. *See* Jeanne Boydston, *Home and Work* 10–20 (1990).

24. *See id.* at 11.

25. *See* Joan D. Hedrik, *Harriet Beecher Stowe* 6 (1995).

26. *See* Steven Mintz & Susan Kellogg, *Domestic Revolutions* 5 (1988).

27. *See* Stephanie Coontz, *The Social Origins of Private Life* 85 (1988).

28. *See* Mintz & Kellogg, *supra* note 26, at 14.

29. *See id.* at 54.

30. *See* Curtis J. Berger & Joan C. Williams, *Property: Land Ownership and Use* 11 (1997); Rhys Isaac, *The Transformation of Virginia, 1740–1790*, 309, 345 (1982).

31. *See* Mintz & Kellogg, *supra* note 26, at 10, 54.

32. *See* Isaac, *supra* note 30, at 20–21.

33. *See* Siegel, *"The Rule of Love,"* *supra* note 8, at 2117. Puritan husbands were legally prohibited from striking their wives; however, convicted wife-beaters typically received mild sentences. *See* Mintz & Kellogg, *supra* note 26, at 10–11.

34. *See* Boydston, *supra* note 23, at 24 (property ownership); Coontz, *supra* note 27, at 79; Mintz & Kellogg, *supra* note 26 (other data).

35. *See* Mintz & Kellogg, *supra* note 26, at 11 (reverence); Isaac, *supra* note 30, at 345 (quote).

36. *See* Larry May & Robert Strikwerda, *Rethinking Masculinity* 76 (1992) (discussing Filmer's *Patriarcha*) (political theory); Mintz & Kellogg, *supra* note 26, at 5 (quote).

37. *See* Coontz, *supra* note 27, at 86.

38. *See id.* at 87.

39. Feminists sometimes use patriarchy as a generic term for male power over women. This usage blurs important differences between domesticity and the different gender system that preceded it.

40. *See* Barbara Welter, *The Cult of True Womanhood: 1820–60*, 18 Am. Quarterly 152 (1966) (women submissive); Elaine Tyler May, *Homeward Bound* 138 (1988) (father on a higher plane).

41. *See* Coontz, *supra* note 27, at 58.

42. Michael Kimmel, *Manhood in America* 44–50 (1996).

43. Lillian Rubin, *Worlds of Pain* 124–25 (1976) [hereinafter Rubin, *Pain*].

44. Deborah Tannen, *You Just Don't Understand* 49–53 (1990).

45. Alice Kessler-Harris, *Women Have Always Worked: A Historical Overview*, 14–17, 38–39, 63 (1981); Kathy Peiss, *"Charity Girls" and City Pleasures: Historical Notes on Working-Class Sexuality, 1880–1920*, in *Powers of Desire* (A. Snitow, C. Stansell & S. Thompson eds., 1983); Molly Martin, *Introduction*, in *Hard-Hatted Women: Stories of Struggle and Success in the Trades* 8 (M. Martin ed., 1988) (two or three times the pay).

46. Ureta Census Data, *see* note 4 in the introduction (fathers of children under 18, aged 25–45).

47. Robert E. Gould, *Measuring Masculinity by the Size of a Paycheck*, in Joseph Pleck & Jack Sawyer, *Men and Masculinity* 96 (1974).

48. R. Woolfolk & F. Richardson, *Sanity, Stress, and Survival* 57 (1978), *cited in* Joseph H. Pleck, *The Myth of Masculinity* 133 (1981).

49. Coontz, *supra* note 27, at 83.

50. Robert L. Griswold, *Fatherhood in America: A History* 2 (1993).

51. *See* E. Anthony Rotundo, *American Manhood: Transformations in Masculinity from the Revolution to the Modern Era* 167 (1993) ("a man's work . . . his social identity"); id. at 175 (a law student in 1820), 168 (a woman to her suitor; a New York college student); Griswold, *supra* note 50, at 2 ("the great unifying element").

52. *See* Kimmel, *supra* note 42, at 20, 26 ("breadwinner"; "self-made man"); Rotundo, *supra* note 51, at 176 (first two quotes).

53. Boydston, *supra* note 23, at 73 (breadwinner status underlying claims to dominance); Kimmel, *supra* note 42, at 23, 43, 45 (first three quotes); Rotundo, *supra* note 51, at 169, 175 (Bailey, Webster, and Rice quotes); Berger & Williams, *supra* note 30, at 411–16 (Homestead Acts).

54. Joseph H. Pleck & Jack Sawyer, *Men and Work*, in *Men and Masculinity*, *supra* note 47, at 94, 94 (quote).

55. Peggy Orenstein, *Almost Equal*, N.Y. Times, Apr. 5, 1998, § 6 (Magazine), at 42, 43 (initial quote), Theodore F. Cohen, *What Do Fathers Provide?*, in *Men, Work, and Family* 3 (Jane C. Hood ed., 1993) (quoting L. Thompson and A. Walker, *Gender in Families: Women and Men in Marriage, Work and Parenthood*, J. Marriage & Fam. 51, 290–301 (1989)). *See also* Robert S. Weiss, *Men and Their Work*, in *Spouse, Parent, Worker: On Gender and Multiple Roles* 109 (Faye J. Crosby ed., 1987) (literature review quote); Jean L. Potuchek, *Who Supports the Family?* 4 (1997) (last quote). *See also* Joan Z. Spade, *Wives' and Husbands' Perceptions of Why Wives Work*, 8 Gender & Soc'y 170 (1994); Kathleen Gerson, *No Man's Land* (1993). Gerson's book uses very vague categories ("turning towards family") that, in my view, overestimate the extent that men have turned away from breadwinning. A careful look at the group she calls egalitarian shows that they did not participate equally in family work. *See id.* at 12 ("significantly involved"). In view of the skewed self-reporting of men's contributions, a category that lumps men who "plan to become equal" caregivers with those who actually do is too vague.

56. *See* Potuchek, *supra* note 55, at 42, 45–48, 61–63, 66–90, 7.

57. *See* Harold Benenson, *Women's Occupational and Family Achievement in the U.S. Class System: A Critique of the Dual-Career Family Analysis*, 35 Brit. J. Soc. 19, 28 (1984) (wives of high-income husbands half as likely to work outside the home than are wives of median-income men).

58. *See* Susan A. Ostrander, *Women of the Upper Class* 42, 49 (1984) (quotes); Hochschild, *Second Shift*, *supra* note 5, at 23; Devon Spurgeon, *Divorce Means an Equal Split, Judge Rules in Big-Money Case*, Wash. Post, Dec. 4, 1997, at E1 (Lorna Wendt).

59. *See* Arlie R. Hochschild, *The Time Bind: When Work Becomes Home & Home Becomes Work* 59 (1997) (bargain); *id.* at 66 (he knew little; a mild regret), 67 (missed birthdays), 68 (why should I?); Sidney M. Jourard, *Some Lethal Aspects of the Male Role*, in *Men and Masculinity*, *supra* note 47, at 21.

60. *See* Rubin, *Fault Line*, *supra* note 9, at 119 (1994).

61. *See* Elijah Anderson, *Street Wise* 114 (1990); H. Edward Ransford & Jon Miller, *Race, Sex, and Feminist Outlooks*, 48 Am. Soc. Rev. 46, 46 (1983).

62. Beth Israel Rosen, *Bitter Choices* 103–4 (1987) (all quotes).

63. Sigel, *supra* note 9, at 158.

64. *See* Michael Vermuelen, *What People Earn*, Wash. Post, June 18, 1995, Parade Magazine, at 4, 5 (hourly wages shrinking); Chapter 3 (few women in blue-collar jobs); Sue Headless & Margery Elfin, *The Cost of Being Female* 11 (1996) (39 percent of managers are women); Rubin, *Fault Line*, *supra* note 9, at 103 (jobless men); Frank Levy & Richard Michel, *The Economic Future of American Families* 4, 10, 18, 77 (1991) (salaries fallen since 1974).

65. Kevin Phillips, *The Politics of Rich and Poor* 19 (1990). *See also* Vermuelen, *supra* note 64, at

4 (wages of blue-collar males have shrunk by 14.6 percent since 1978).

66. Two years after losing his job, the average autoworker is earning 43 percent less. *See* Sarah Kuhn & Barry Bluestone, *Economic Restructuring and the Female Labor Market*, in *Women, Households, and the Economy* 3 (Lourdes Beneria & Catharine Stimpson eds., 1987) (average guy can deliver the house, the car, etc.). *See also* George Sternlieb & Carole W. Baker, *Placing Deindustrialization in Perspective*, in *Women, Households, and the Economy* 85, 99 ("[W]hen men lose their jobs, in general they suffer from lengthier layoffs than women do … [and] are far more likely than women to be laid-off or permanently separated, i.e. fired."); *id.* at 100 ("The erosion of middle-income jobs for men, particularly in the high-wage blue collar area but also in lower and middle management in the hardest-hit industries, is pointing towards the demise of the 'family wage' for all but high-income professionals"); Levy & Michel, *supra* note 64, at 4 (wives' incomes rise faster); Kuhn & Bluestone, *supra* note 66, at 22 ("The good fortune of women in the economy, it appears, is therefore good largely because the recent fortunes of men have been so bad"); Bianchi & Spain, *supra* note 5, at 95 (80 percent figure).

67. Michelle Fine, Lois Weis, Judi Addelston & Julia Marusza, *(In)Secure Times: Constructing White Working Class Masculinities in the Late 20th Century*, 11 Gender & Soc'y 52 (1997).

68. *See* Rubin, *Fault Line, supra* note 9, at 60–61, 78, 84, 87; Sigel, *supra* note 9, at 160–61.

69. Jacqueline Jones, *Labor of Love, Labor of Sorrow* (1985); Patricia Hill Collins, *Black Feminist Thought* 59 (1990) (typical pattern is higher-paying but less secure work for African-American men, contrasted with lower-paying, more plentiful work for black women); Evelyn Nakano Glenn, *Cleaning Up/Kept Down: A Historical Perspective on Racial Inequality in "Women's Work,"* 43 Stan. L. Rev. 1333, 1337 (1991) ("Because of the dual labor system, men of color rarely earned a wage sufficient to support a family. Thus, wives and mothers had to contribute economically to support their families. Where employment was available, women entered the labor market"). Black women are far more likely than white women to rate men as economically unreliable and untrustworthy. *See* Ransford & Miller, *supra* note 61, at 46.

70. Lisa Saunders, *Relative Earnings of Black Men to White Men By Region, Industry*, 118 Monthly Labor Rev. 68 (Apr. 1995).

71. A common reaction among the disenfranchised poor (sometimes called the "underclass") is to redefine masculinity in more attainable terms. *See* Anderson, *supra* note 61, at 114 (1990) (underclass males define masculinity in terms of sexual prowess rather than in terms of the good-provider role). Interestingly, the girlfriends of these men appear to retain the good-provider definition of true masculinity: They are driven, Anderson argues, by dreams that their boyfriends will marry them and support them in respectable (and middle-class) domesticity. *See also* Ransford & Miller, *supra* note 61, at 46 (poor black males have been denied the traditional avenues of masculine expression—economic success, career achievement, and upward mobility—and consequently have developed a "ghetto-specific masculinity").

72. Richard Sennett & Jonathan Cobb, *The Hidden Injuries of Class* (1973); bell hooks, *Ain't I a Woman* 178 (1981); for a study that finds that black men have far richer definitions of manhood, see Andrea G. Hunter & James Earl Davis, *Constructing Gender: An Exploration of Afro-American Men's Conceptualization of Manhood*, 6 Gender & Soc'y 464 (1992).

73. Cynthia Fuchs Epstein, Robert Saute, Bonnie Oglensky & Martha Gever, *Glass Ceilings and Open Doors: Women's Advancement in the Legal Profession: A Report to the Committee on Women in the Profession, The Association of the Bar of the City of New York*, 64 Fordham L. Rev. 291, 443 (1995) (female lawyers not urging their husbands to cut back their hours); Karen D. Pyke, *Class-Based Masculinities: The Interdependence of Gender, Class, and Interpersonal Power*, 10 Gender & Soc'y 543 (1996) (quote).

74. Beverly Sills & Lawrence Linderman, *Beverly: An Autobiography* 117 (1987).

75. Fallows, *supra* note 10, at 13; Nancy Levit, *The Gender Line* 33 (1998) (88 percent).

76. *See* James T. Kloppenberg, *The Virtues of Liberalism: Christianity, Republicanism, and Ethics in Early American Political Discourse*, 74 J. Am. Hist. 9 (1987).

77. Nancy F. Cott, *The Grounding of Modern Feminism* 64 (1987).

78. *See id.* at 68.

79. "Cockpits, Lifts and Family Values," Panel on Work/Family Conflict, American University, Washington College of Law Centennial, April 1996.

80. *See* Fallows, *supra* note 10, at 68, 73–74.

81. *See, e.g., id.*, at 68, 73–74.

82. *See* Boydston, *supra* note 23, 158.

83. Martha N. Beck, *Breaking Point* (1997) (block quote); Lorraine Dusky, *Still Unequal* 318 (1996) (data on husbands of homemakers). When wives work part or full time: *See* John P. Robinson & Geoffrey Godbey, *Time for Life* 104 (1997) (women's percent of family work); Ellen Galinsky, *The Changing Workforce* 48, 49 tbl. 24; Judith Lorber, *Paradoxes of Gender* 163 (1994) (statistics on when women stay home); Roberta Brandes Gratz & Elizabeth Pochoda, *Women's Lib: So Where Do Men Fit In*, Glamour, July 1970, at 138 (rich attention; phrase used in a different context).

84. Fallows, *supra* note 10, at 27–28 (take more responsibility).

85. *See* Ruth H. Bloch, *American Feminine Ideals in Transition: The Rise of the Moral Mother 1785–1815*, 4 Feminist Stud. 101, 113, 114 (1978) (men withdrew from family work; ceased to be primary instructor); Kimmel, *supra* note 42, at 58 (first quote); Boydston, *supra* note 23, at 103 (shopping); Ruth Schwartz Cowan, *More Work for Mother* 64 (1983).

86. Dorothy E. Smith, *The Everyday World as Problematic* (1987). The principals of both of my grade-school children have announced in parents' meetings that studies show that children whose parents volunteer do better in school. When I followed up, neither could cite me a specific source. Suffice it to say that when principals make these kind of statements, the effect is the same whether or not underlying studies exist!

87. Hochschild, *Time Bind*, *supra* note 59, at 135; interview with Mary Siegel, Washington, D.C., May 1998 ("my mom Mary").

88. Boydston, *supra* note 23, at 156.

89. Christine Stansell, *Women, Children and the Uses of the Street*, 8 Fem. Stud. 309, 310 (1982).

90. *See* Julia Wrigley, *Other People's Children* 13–17 (1995) (upper-class and child rearing before nineteenth century; middle class and child rearing); Barbara Ehrenreich, *Fear of Falling* (1989); Boydston, *supra* note 23, at 80 (same).

91. Boydston, *supra* note 23, at 42, 81–82, 145.

92. *See* Rubin, *Pain, supra* note 43, at 127–28; Ehrenreich, *supra* note 140, at 83 (block quote); Lorber, *supra* note 83, at 175 (quoting Bourdieu and Passeron). *See also* Wrigley, *supra* note 90, at 15.

93. *Cf.* Mary Ann Cantwell, *Taming Little Tyrants*, N.Y. Times, May 27, 1998, at A27.

94. *See* Betty MacDonald, *Mrs. Piggle-Wiggle* 54, 107 (appeasing husbands), 28 (baking) (1987; originally published 1947); Betty MacDonald, *Mrs. Piggle-Wiggle's Farm* 11 (Earnest Workers' Club), 56 (serving husbands meals), 57 (appeasing husbands), 7, 12, 106 (gardening), 24, 106–27 (children doing errands), 53 (children entertaining themselves) (1982; originally published 1954); Betty MacDonald, *Hello, Mrs. Piggle-Wiggle* 10 (helping with husbands' careers), 17, 32, 68, 78, 113 (baking), 75 (gardening), 18, 33, 35 (children doing errands), 18, 64, 66, 68, 96, 92 (children entertaining themselves), 67, 98 (children's clubs), 90 (music lesson) (1987; originally published 1957).

95. See Phyllis Palmer, *Domesticity and Dirt: Housewives and Domestic Servants in the United States, 1920–1945,* at 81 (1989) (first quote); Stanley Greenspan & Jacqueline Salmon, *The Challenging Child* (1995) (floor time); Natalie Wexler, *Beyond Quality Time,* Wash. Post, March 24, 1996, at W18 (block quote).

96. See Mary P. Ryan, *Cradle of the Middle Class: The Family in Oneida County, New York, 1790–1865* (1981).

97. William Steig, *The Amazing Bone* 9, 19 (1976)

98. William Faulkner, *Requiem for a Nun* 92 (1951).

99. Rubin, *Fault Line, supra* note 9, at 160.

100. *See, e.g.,* Kathryn Abrams, *Songs of Innocence and Experience,* 103 Yale L. Rev. 1533 (1994).

101. Pierre Bourdieu, *The Logic of Practice* 56, 26 (1980), *cf.* Catharine MacKinnon, *Feminism Unmodified* 16 (1987) (what we need to do to function).

102. *See id.* at 58.

CHAPTER TWO: *From Full Commodification to Reconstructive Feminism*

1. Betty Friedan, *The Feminine Mystique* (1962; 1983). Barbara Bergmann, *The Only Ticket to Equality,* 9 J. Contemp. L. Issues 75 (1998).

2. *See id.* at 392 (sex-role revolution); Julia Kirk Blackwelder, *Now Hiring* 195 (1997) (increasing labor force participation of women).

3. Friedan, *supra* note 4, at 282 *et seq.* (concentration camp).

4. Anna Quindlen, *Let's Anita Hill This,* N.Y. Times, Feb. 28, 1993, at 15 ("At a meeting I attended, one of the women said that the women's movement had been the guiding force in her life until she had children, and then she felt abandoned by feminist rhetoric and concerns").

5. Steven A. Holmes, *Is This What Women Want?,* N.Y. Times, Dec. 15, 1996, at 1 (quoting Heidi Hartman: "That may be feeding some of the backlash against feminism among some women. People are saying that all feminism ever got us was more work").

6. *See* Ginia Bellafante, *Feminism: It's All About Me!,* Time, June 29, 1998, at 54. The "feminist majority" argument is associated with the Fund for a Feminist Majority, now called the Feminist Majority Foundation. *See* <http://www.feminist.org>. *See also* Nancy Levit, *The Gender Line* 123–67 (1998).

7. Charlotte Perkins Gilman, *quoted in* Delores Hayden, *The Grand Domestic Revolution* 198 (1988).

8. Friedan, *supra* note 1, at 342.

9. Reva Siegel, *Home as Work,* 103 Yale L. J. 1073.

10. *See, e.g.,* Paolo Wright-Carozza, *Organic Goods: Legal Understandings of Work, Parenthood, and Gender Equality in Comparative Perspective,* 81 Cal. L. Rev. 531 (1993).

11. *See* Barbara L. Epstein, *The Politics of Domesticity: Women, Evangelism, and Temperance in Nineteenth Century America* (1981). *See generally* Sara Evans, *Born for Liberty: A History of Women in America* 67–143 (1989) (discussing emergence of women's associational activity); *see also* Epstein, *supra* note 10, at 115–51 (1981) (describing growth of Woman's Christian Temperance Union), Evelyn Brooks Higginbotham, *Righteous Discontent: The Women's Movement in the Black Baptist Church, 1880–1920* (1993).

12. Arlie R. Hochschild, *The Time Bind: When Work Becomes Home and Home Becomes Work* (1997).

13. Friedan, *supra* note 1, at 24 (first quote), 21 (second), 22 (third), 343–44 (fourth).

14. *See* Wini Breines, *Young, White, and Miserable: Growing Up Female in the Fifties* 28–29 (1992); *id.* at 32–33 (quoting Reisman).

15. *Id.* at 364. *See* Glenna Matthews, *"Just a Housewife"* 197–200 (1987) (misogynist stereotyping); Friedan, *supra* note 1, at 356, 364.

16. Friedan, *supra* note 1, at 384 (sex-role revolution), 349 (only two trips), 345 ("now being paid"), 349 (last quote).

17. *Id.*

18. Daniel Horowitz, *Rethinking Betty Friedan and* The Feminine Mystique: *Labor Union Radicalism and Feminism in Cold War America*, 48 Am. Q. 1, 20 (1996) (Friedan quote).

19. *See* Friedan, *supra* note 1, at 350, 354, 385; Betty Friedan, *The Second Stage* (1981).

20. Breines, *supra* note 14, at 32–33 (first quote: quoting Jessie Bernard); Rosalind C. Barnett & Carl Rivers, *She Works, He Works: How Two-Income Families Are Happier, Healthier, and Better-Off* 32 (1996) (second). *See also* Jessie Bernard, *The Future of Marriage* (1972, reprint 1973).

21. Rivvy Berkman, *The Funny, Searching, Scary, Devastatingly Honest Diary of A Young Woman's Decision to Return to Work*, Glamour, Sept. 1971, at 280 (schoolmarm clothes); Vivian Cadden, *How Women Really Feel About Working*, McCall's, June 1974, at 125 (So what!); Roberta Brandes Gratz & Elizabeth Pochoda, *Women's Lib: So Where Do Men Fit In*, Glamour, July 1970, at 138 (rich attention; not an impossible dream); Claudia Wallis, *Onward, Women: The Superwoman Is Weary, the Young Are Complacent, but Feminism Is Not Dead, and Baby, There's Still a Long Way to Go*, Time, Dec. 4, 1989, at 80, 81 ("fry it up in a pan"); Lynn Langway, *The Superwoman Squeeze*, Newsweek, May 19, 1980, at 256 (TV jingle).

22. Shirley G. Streshin, *The Guilt of the Working Mother*, Glamour, Sept. 1975, at 256 (Mrs. Chechik); Gratz & Pochoda, *supra* note 21, at 138 (not enough rights).

23. Anne Roiphe, *Loving Kindness* (1987).

24. Deborah Fallows, *A Mother's Work* 28, 214 (1985) (all three quotes).

25. *See* Joan C. Williams, *Gender Wars: Selfless Women in the Republic of Choice*, 66 N.Y.U. L. Rev. 1559, 1612 (1991).

26. *Id.*; Wendy Kaminer, *Feminism's Identity Crisis*, Atlantic Monthly, Oct. 1993, at 56 (quote and *Redbook* survey); Martha Burk & Heidi Hartman, *Beyond the Gender Gap*, The Nation, June 10, 1996, at 18 (machinist); Wallis, *supra* note 21, at 80 (*Time*/CNN poll). It appears that more recent polls did not ask the "what should be the woman's movement's most important goal" question. See Bellafante, *supra* note 12, at 3.

27. *See* Langway, *supra* note 21. Arlie Hochschild found that, after adding together the time it takes to do home and child care with the time it takes to do a paying job, women work about fifteen hours longer per week than do men. *See* Hochschild, *supra* note 12, at 3.

28. Langway, *supra* note 21, at 72 (all other quotes).

29. *See generally* Hochschild, *supra* note 12, at 110–27.

30. *See id.* at 257–78, Arlie Hochschild, Inside the Clockwork of Male Careers, in *Women and the Power to Change* (Florence Howe ed., 1971).

31. *See id.* at 266–70.

32. Lillian Rubin, *Families on the Fault Line* 79 (1994).

33. Emily Couric, *Women in Large Firms: A Higher Price of Admission?*, Nat. L. J., Dec. 11, 1989, at S2, S12.

34. Rubin, *supra* note 32, at 79 (national psyche); Peggy Orenstein, *Almost Equal*, N.Y. Times, Apr. 5, 1998, § 6 (Magazine), at 45 (Boston nanny).

35. *See* Richard Morin & Megan Rosenfeld, *With More Equity, More Sweat; Poll Shows Sexes Agree on Pros and Cons of New Roles*, Wash. Post, Mar. 22, 1998, at A1 (two-thirds).

36. *See* Joan C. Williams, *Privatization as a Gender Issue*, in *A Fourth Way? Privatization, Property, and the Emergence of the New Market Economies* 215 (Gregory S. Alexander & Grażyna Skąpka eds., 1994) (Russia and East-Central Europe); Barbara Bergmann, *Saving Our Children from*

Poverty: What the United States Can Learn from France (1996) (data on France and Belgium); Marlise Simons, *Child Care Sacred as France Cuts Back the Welfare State*, N.Y. Times, Dec. 31, 1997, at A1 (French parents fight to get children in); Marguerite G. Rosenthal, *Sweden: Promise and Paradox*, in *The Feminization of Poverty: Only in America?* (Gertrude Schaffuel Goldberg & Eleanor Kremen eds., 1990) 129, 137, 144, 147–49 (Sweden).

37. Mary Frances Berry, *The Politics of Parenthood* 137–38, 142 (1993) (Nixon quote; 1975 quote); Jane Rigler, *Analysis and Understanding of the Family and Medical Leave Act of 1993*, 45 Case W. Res. L. Rev. 457 (1995) (less governmental support in United States).

38. *See* Gina C. Adams & Nicole Oxendine Poersch, Children's Defense Fund, Key Facts About Child Care and Early Education: A Briefing Book, at B–7 (1997) (low pay and high turnover).

39. Press Release from University of Tennessee News Center, by Dr. Jan Allen, at ‹http://www.utenn.edu/uwa/vpps/ur/news/may96/kidcare.htm›.

40. *See* Amy Hauth & Jane Humble, *Family-Care Policies in the High Tech Workplace: It's a Good Business Investment*, Indus. Mgmt., Nov. 1992, at 11 (lack of good alternatives).

41. *See* Juliet B. Schor, *The Overworked American* 30 tbl. 2.2 (1992) (Hours per Week, Labor Force Participants) (only those fully employed) (workweek); Peter T. Kilborn, *The Work Week Grows; Tales from the Digital Treadmill*, N.Y. Times, June 3, 1990, § 4 (Week in Review), at 1 (24 percent; managers' hours; first quote); Peter T. Kilborn, *It's Too Much of a Good Thing, G.M. Workers Say in Protesting Overtime*, N.Y. Times, Nov. 22, 1994, at A16 (production workers); Schor, *supra*, at 41 (5:00 dad); Ureta Census Data, *see* note 4 in the introduction (one-third of fathers).

42. *See* Rosenthal, *supra* note 36, at 137, 144, 147–49; Janeen Baxter & Emily W. Kane, *Dependence and Independence: A Cross-National Analysis of Gender Inequality and Gender Attitudes*, 9 Gender & Soc'y 193, 195 (1995) (level of sex segregation).

43. For power studies, see Robert O. Blood & Donald M. Wolfe, *Husbands and Wives: The Dynamics of Married Living* (1960); Phyllis N. Hallenbeck, *An Analysis of Power Dynamic in Marriage*, 28 J. Marriage & Family 200 (1966); Gerald W. McDonald, *Family Power: The Assessment of a Decade of Theory and Research, 1970–1979*, J. Marriage & Family 841 (1980); Paula England & Barbara Stanek Kilbourne, *Markets, Marriages, and Other Mates: The Problem of Power*, in *Beyond the Market Place: Rethinking Economy and Society* (Roger Friedland & A. F. Robertson eds., 1990).

44. T. Berry Brazleton, *Infants and Mothers: Differences in Development* 59–60 (first quote), 270, 271, 273 (1983).

45. Fallows, *supra* note 24, at 30.

46. *See* S. M. Miller, *The Making of a Confused, Middle-Aged Husband*, in *Men and Masculinity* 44, 50 (Joseph H. Pleck & Jack Sawyer eds., 1974); Rosenthal, *supra* note 36, at 137, 144, 147–49.

47. Bureau of Labor Statistics, U.S. Department of Labor, Unpublished Marital and Family Tabulations from the Current Population Survey, tbl. 28A (1996) ("Unemployed Persons Not at Work and Persons at Work in Nonagricultural Industries by Actual Hours of Work at All Jobs During Reference Week, Marital Status, Sex, and Age, Annual Average 1995").

48. Interview with Martha Fineman, July 1998 (discussing her forthcoming book); Schor, *supra* note 41, at 30 tbl. 2.2 (forty-four hours). *See also* Martha Albertson Fineman, *The Neutered Mother, The Sexual Family* 131–33 (1995).

49. *See* Peter A. Morrison, *Congress and the Year 2000: Peering into the Demographic Future*, Bus. Horizons, Nov. 1, 1993, at 55.

50. *See* Linda Haas, *Equal Parenthood and Social Policy: A Study of Parental Leave in Sweden* 158–60 (1992).

51. *Work & Family: A Retrospective* 148 (Work & Family, Inc. ed., 1995) (1989 poll); *id.* at 137

(Gallup poll), 127–28 (polls reporting preference for flexible scheduling over day care), *Family Matters: A National Survey of Women and Men Conducted for the National Partnership for Women and Families*, Feb. 1998, at 9 (1995) (poll on time pressures; elder care); K. Downey & R. H. Melton, *Full-Time Moms Earn Respect, Poll Says*, Wash. Post, Mar. 22, 1998, at A9, A16 (80 percent statistic); Rosenthal, *supra* note 36, at 148.

52. *See* Wallis, *supra* note 21, at 80 (top priority of women's movement); Peter D. Hart Research Assocs. & Mellman Group, *The Economic Situation Facing Working Families* 9 (1996) (labor union surveys).

53. Nancy Dowd, *In Defense of Single-Parent Families* 5 (1997) (well over half of children spend time in single-parent families).

54. *See* studies cited *supra* note 43. For recent economic modeling, see Rhona Mahony, *Kidding Ourselves: Breadwinning, Babies, and Bargaining Power* (1995); Amy L. Wax, *Bargaining in the Shadow of the Market: Is There a Future for Egalitarian Marriage?*, 84 Va. L. Rev. 509 (1998).

55. Rubin, *supra* note 32, at 83 (Kilson); Dowd, *supra* note 53, at 57 (women are the ones who "anticipate [children's] needs, remember schedules, and so forth."); Amina Mama, *Sheroes and Villains: Conceptualizing Colonial and Contemporary Violence Against Women in Africa*, in *Feminist Genealogies, Colonial Legacies, Democratic Futures* 53 (M. Jacqui Alexander & Chandra Tulpade Mohanty eds., 1997) (quote). *See also* Martha F. Davis & Susan J. Kraham, *Protecting Women's Welfare in the Face of Violence*, 22 Ford. Urb. L. J. 1141, 1145, 1150, 1154 (1995).

56. Patricia Hersh, interviewed on the *Diane Rehm Show*, National Public Radio, Apr. 27, 1998. For two versions of the claim that women's liberation hurts children, *see* Carl N. Degler, *At Odds* (1980); Christopher Lasch, *Haven in a Heartless World* (1977).

57. Kathleen Gerson, *No Man's Land: Men's Changing Commitments to Family and Work* 44 (1993) (Edward, an unmarried physician).

58. *Id.* at 13 (13 percent). *See also* Rubin, *supra* note 32, at 91 (16 percent, mostly of split shifters).

59. Robert L. Griswold, *Fatherhood in America: A History* 199 (1993).

60. Gerson, *supra* note 57, at 12 (initial quote); Schor, *supra* note 41, at 21 (statistics on overtime); Hochschild, *supra* note 12, at 128 (hairy chests quote); Al B. Tross, *The Reality of Law School*, 10 Nova L.J. 879 (1986) (final quote).

61. Schor, *supra* note 41, at 43 ("gray life at hard labor"); Hochschild, *supra* note 12, at 132 ("family man"); Sue Shellenbarger, *Lessons from the Workplace: How Corporate Policies and Attitudes Lag Behind Workers' Changing Needs*, 31 Hum. Resource Mgmt. 157 (1992) (final quote).

62. Lorraine Dusky, *Still Unequal: The Shameful Truth About Women and Justice in America* 318 (1996) (wage gap); John P. Robinson & Geoffrey Godbey, *Time for Life: The Surprising Ways Americans Use Their Time* 105 tbl. 3 (1997) (statistics on men's family work); Paul Heald, electronic correspondence to author, Sept. 20, 1996 (on file with author) (final quote).

63. Griswold, *supra* note 59, at 224 (preference for daddy track); Berry, *supra* note 37, at 22 (1990 poll).

64. *See* Barbara Allen Babcock, et al., *Sex Discrimination and the Law: History, Practice, and Theory* 867 (2d ed., 1996); Andrew Hacker, *Two Nations: Black and White, Separate, Hostile and Unequal* 94–95 (1992).

65. E. Anthony Rotundo, *American Manhood: Transformations in Masculinity from the Revolution to the Modern Era* 166 (1993) (men's sense of self); Susan Crowley, *Men's Self-Perceived Adequacy as the Family Breadwinner*, 19 J. Fam. & Econ. Issues 7, spring 1998 (men's self-esteem); Rubin, *supra* note 32, at 119 (impotence), 121 (divorce); National Research Council, *Family and Work* 44–45 (1991) (final quote).

66. Dana Friedman, The Conference Board, *Linking Work-Family Issues to the Bottom Line* 31 (1991) (initial statistics); *id.* at 33 (National Long Term Care), 35 (quit rates).

67. *See Work & Family: A Retrospective, supra* note 51, at 114 (1995) ("Will it work?"); William A. Galston, *Divorce American Style*, 124 Pub. Interest 12 (1996).

68. Joe Dominguez & Vicky Robin, *Your Money or Your Life: Transforming Your Relationship with Money and Achieving Financial Independence* 6 (1992) (initial quote); *id.* at 5 (second quote).

69. *See* Schor, *supra* note 41, at 2 ("1948 standard of living"), 13 (second quote; 40 percent), 22 (one-third; workers' comp claims).

70. Bruce O'Hara, *Working Harder Isn't Working* 97 (1993) (initial quote); Schor, *supra* note 41, at 142–50 (proposals).

71. Josephine Marcotty, *A Nation on Overtime*, Star Trib., Sept. 5, 1994, at 1A; Paul A. Eisenstein, *Can Big Three Automakers Keep Up Profit Bonanza?*, Christian Sci. Monitor, Feb. 7, 1995, at 9; Rick Haglund, *GM, UAW Is a Matter of Survival*, Plain Dealer, Feb. 5, 1995, at 1G; Randolph Heaster, *Working Overtime, or Overworking?: America's Employees Feel the Strain of Good Economy, Less Hiring*, Kan. City Star, Nov. 15, 1994, at A1.

72. Steven Greenhouse, *Unions Unite in Campaign for Child Care*, N.Y. Times, Feb. 2, 1998.

73. Celinda Lake, Research Report to the AFL-CIO 33 (1997); Hart & Mellman, *supra* note 52, at 9; Peter D. Hart Research Assocs. & Mellman Group, Summary of Opinion Research on Living Standards, May 6, 1996.

74. Curtis J. Berger & Joan C. Williams, *Property: Land Ownership and Use* 41 (1997) (one-fifth of children poor); Joan Williams, *Notes of a Jewish Episcopalian: Gender as a Language of Class, Religion as a Dialect of Liberalism*, in *Debating Democracy's Discontent* (Anita Allen & Milton Regan eds., 1998) (nearly 80 percent).

CHAPTER THREE: *Deconstructing the Ideal-Worker Norm in Market Work*

1. *See* 490 U.S. 228, 233 (initial quote), 234 ($25 million), 235 (final quote) (1989) (citing the lower court opinion in 618 F. Supp. 1109, 1112–13 (1985)).

2. Computations of Professor Manuelita Ureta, based on machine-readable versions of Bureau of the Census, U.S. Department of Commerce, Current Population Survey, March Supplement, Public Use Files (1996). Washington: Bureau of the Census [producer and distributor], 1962–1997. Santa Monica, CA: Unicon Research Corporation [producer and distributor of CPS Utilities], 1997 [hereinafter Ureta Census Data].

3. *See* Erving Goffman, *Gender Display*, 3 Stud. in Anthropology of Visual Comm. 1976, at 69–77.

4. Nadine Taub & Wendy Williams, *Will Equality Require More Than Assimilation, Accommodation or Separation from the Existing Social Structure?*, 37 Rutgers L. Rev. 825, 839 (1985).

5. *See* Dahlia Moore, *Feminism and Occupational Sex Segregation*, 25 Int'l L. J. Soc. Fam. 99, 101 (Spring 1995) (most women work with other women); *Risks and Challenges: Women, Work, & the Future* 147 (Wider Opportunities for Women ed., 1990) (giving statistics from National Commission of Working Women for Wider Opportunities for Women). Responsible estimates range from 70 percent to 91 percent. *See* Moore, *supra* at 101 (asserting that 70 percent or more of all working women are still concentrated in very few female occupations in which at least 70 percent are women). *See* Glass Ceiling Comm'n, U.S. Dep't of Labor, *Good for Business: Making Full Use of the Nation's Human Capital* 16 (1995) [hereinafter *Good for Business*] (three-fourths of working women in predominantly female occupations).

6. *See Good for Business, supra* note 5, at 147.

7. *See* Bette Woody & Carol Weiss, *Barriers to Work Place Advancement: The Experience of the White Female Work Force* 18 (Dec. 1993) (unpublished manuscript, on file with the Federal Glass Ceiling Commission) ("a virtual closing"); Deborah L. Rhode, *The "No-Problem" Problem: Feminist Challenges and Cultural Change*, 100 Yale L. J. 1731, 1764 (1991) ("still dramatically under-represented") [hereinafter Rhode, *No-Problem*]; Work/Family Directions, *Corporate Consulting* (visited June 7, 1998) <http://www.wfd.com/corp_desc.htm> (46 percent; 5 percent); Julia Lawlor, *Cracking the Glass Ceiling: A Report on Women's Climb to the Top*, Working Mother, May 1995, at 30, 30 (from 3 percent to 7 percent).

8. *See* Cynthia Fuchs Epstein et al., *Glass Ceilings and Open Doors: Women's Advancement in the Legal Profession*, 64 Fordham L. Rev. 291, 296, 314 (1995) (law firms in NYC); American Bar Ass'n Comm'n on Women in the Profession, *Basic Facts from Women in the Law: A Look at the Numbers* 3 (1995) (87 percent)[hereinafter *Basic Facts*]; Rhode, *No-Problem, supra* note 7, at 1758 (more than twice as likely); Patricia M. Wald, *Glass Ceilings and Open Doors: A Reaction*, 65 Fordham L. Rev. 603, 604 (1996) (twice as many men).

9. *See* Joan Williams, *Gender Wars: Selfless Women in the Republic of Choice*, 66 N.Y.U. L. Rev. 1559, 1602 (1991) (women's median income 40 percent lower); American Bar Ass'n Comm'n on Women in the Profession, *Unfinished Business, Overcoming the Sisyphus Factor* 10, 11 (1995) (10 percent to 35 percent; equity partners) [hereinafter *Unfinished Business*].

10. Wald, *supra* note 8, at 604 (initial quote); Epstein, *supra* note 8, at 297 (sharp decrease).

11. *See* Rhode, *No-Problem, supra* note 7, at 1765 n.168 (99 percent; 5.6 percent; Federal Glass Ceiling Comm'n); *Good for Business, supra* note 5, at 12 (CEOs).

12. *See* Woody & Weiss, *supra* note 7, at 59–62 (fewer chances for advancement); Rhode, *No-Problem, supra* note 7, at 1764 n.165 (1990 study); Woody & Weiss, *supra* 7, at 45 (Stanford Business School), 46 (compensation for women executives); Kirstin Downey Grimley, *MBA No Ticket to Top for Women*, Wash. Post, Mar. 24, 1998, at A1 (final quote).

13. *See* Martha S. West, *Women Faculty: Frozen in Time*, Academe July–August 1995, at 26 (quote), 26–27 (statistics); Rhode, *No-Problem, supra* note 7, at 1764 (fewer than 15 percent); *Basic Facts, supra* note 8, at 5 (81 percent; 92 percent). *See also* Martha S. West, *Gender Bias in Academic Robes: The Law's Failure to Protect Women Faculty*, 67 Temple L. Rev. 67 (1994).

14. *Good for Business, supra* note 5, at 34 (Labor Dept. Report; "46-long guys").

15. *See id.* at 36 (common glass ceiling practices), 28 (first quote); 34 (lack of access to informal networks), 148 (almost 93 percent; "being a woman/sexism").

16. *See* Deborah J. Swiss & Judith P. Walker, *Women and the Work/Family Dilemma* 5 (1993) ("maternal wall"); Deborah L. Rhode, *Myths of Meritocracy, in Responses to Glass Ceilings and Open Doors: Women's Advancement in the Legal Profession*, 65 Fordham L. Rev. 585, 588 (1996) (initial quote); Betty Holcomb, *Not Guilty!* 125 (1998) (Vladek quotes); Kingson, *infra* note 26, at A15 (block quote); Sue Shellenbarger, *Lessons from the Workplace: How Corporate Policies and Attitudes Lag Behind Worker's Changing Needs*, 31 Hum. Resource Mgmt. 157, 160 (1992) (final quote).

17. Cynthia Fuchs Epstein et al., *Glass Ceilings and Open Doors: Women's Advancement in the Legal Profession*, 64 Fordham L. Rev. 291, 425 (final quote) (1995) (New York researchers); Harvard Women's Law Association, *Presumed Equal: What America's Top Women Lawyers Really Think About Their Firms* (1995) (Harvard researchers).

18. Audience member, Balancing Work & Family panel discussion at Washington College of Law (Fall 1997).

19. Arlie Russell Hochschild, *The Time Bind: When Work Becomes Home and Home Becomes Work* 106 (1997) (block quote), 106–7 (final quote).

20. Betty Holcomb, *Unequal Opportunity*, Working Mother, July/August 1998, at 42.

21. *See* Peter T. Kilborn, *Tales from the Digital Treadmill*, N.Y. Times, June 3, 1990, Sect. 4, at 1 [hereinafter Kilborn, *Tales*] (50–50 percent; 56 percent); Dupont, *infra* note 24, at 4 (Dupont); The 40-Hour Workweek Trends and Research 1 (Apr. 11, 1995) (unpublished Briefing Paper for the Secretary of Labor) (on file with author) (Americans now work longer hours).

22. *See* S. Elizabeth Foster, *The Glass Ceiling in the Legal Profession: Why Do Law Firms Still Have So Few Female Partners?* 42 U.C.L.A. L. Rev. 1631, 1652 (1995) (statistical information); Epstein, *supra* note 8, at 379 ("influential report"), 394 (block quote).

23. Grimley, *supra* note 12, at A1 (survey of executive women). *See* Lois B. Shaw et al., *The Impact of the Glass Ceiling and Structural Changes on Minorities and Women* 17 (Dec. 15, 1993) (unpublished manuscript, on file with the Federal Glass Ceiling Commission) (citing Joy A. Scheer & Frieda Rutman, *Effects of Alternative Family Structures on Managerial Career Paths*, 36 Acad. of Mgmt. J. 830 (1993)). The Family and Medical Leave Act of 1993 allows employers to exclude the top 10 percent of their employees (based on earnings) from the act's requirements. As the glass ceiling report points out, this simply reinforces the view that no one except the ideal worker married to a marginalized caregiver should be eligible for senior management and professional positions. *See id.* at 30. Deborah L. Rhode, *Perspectives on Professional Women*, 40 Stan. L. Rev. 1163, 1187 (1988) (hereinafter Rhode, *Perspectives*) (if a woman wants to obtain a top management position, she cannot be the primary caretaker of her child).

24. *Id.* (women must choose between work and family while men can have both). *See* Suzannah Bex Wilson, *Eliminating Sex Discrimination in the Legal Profession: The Key to the Widespread Social Reform*, 67 Ind. L. J. 817, 828 (1992) (nine out of ten men); *see also* Cathleen D. Zick & Jane L. McCullough, *Trends in Married Couples' Time Use: Evidence From 1977–78 and 1987–88*, 24 Sex Roles 459, 463 (1991) (noting that "an increase in husband's wage rate is translated into an increase in the amount of solitary housework done by his wife"). *See* Rhode, *Perspectives*, *supra* note 23, at 1187 (one-third of women in senior positions but only 6–8 percent of men never marry); *see also* Dana Friedman, The Conference Board, *Linking Work-Family Issues to the Bottom Line* 11 (1991) (noting the disparity in the number of men in high-level positions who have children as opposed to similarly situated women professionals); E. I. du Pont de Nemours and Company, Corporate News Release 1 (Oct. 30, 1995) [hereinafter "DuPont"] (documenting the results of a ten-year comparison of two previous studies). *See id.* at 1 (a recent DuPont study).

25. Michael Levin, *Comparable Worth: The Feminist Road to Socialism*, Commentary, Sept. 1984, at 13, 15 (citing letter from Susan Sharp, of Sharp and Co., to Fortune, September 6, 1982 in which she asks, "Did it ever occur to you that the reason [women] seem less committed to careers is that they don't have the luxury of a wife to take care of home and children while they blaze their career paths?"). The de facto definition of an ideal professional worker as a man who can delegate virtually all domestic responsibilities means not only that most women are disadvantaged, but also that men who cannot are. Some recent research indicates that the finding that married men have higher earnings than single men applies only to married men with nonemployed wives. *See* Shaw, *supra* note 23, at 18. The Institute of Women's Policy Research reports that this finding means that not only are black women placed at a disadvantage by the ideal-worker norms, but that black men are as well, since far fewer have nonworking wives. *See id.*

26. Jennifer A. Kingson, *Women in the Law Say Path Is Limited by 'Mommy Track,'* N.Y. Times, Aug. 8, 1988, at A1, A15. Kingson also notes that in contrast to a forty-hour part-time workweek, full-time status at some large firms may require being on call twenty-four hours a day.

See id. This requirement is additional proof that full time is the amount of time men work. *Id.* (quote by big-firm associate).

27. *See Women, Households, and the Economy* 226 (Lourdes Beneria & Catharine R. Stimpson eds., 1987) (restricted advancement prospects and lower pay); Anne L. Kalleberg, *Part-Time Work and Workers in the United States: Correlates and Policy Issues,* 52 Wash. & Lee L. Rev. 771, 779 (1995) ("they don't take you serious[ly]"). *See* Epstein, *supra* note 8, at 395–99 (part-timers taken off partnership track); Elizabeth Ehrlich, *Juggling Kids and Careers in Corporate America Takes a Controversial Turn,* Bus. Wk., Mar. 20, 1989, at 126 (virtually only profession where career not harmed by part-time work is nursing); *id.* (don't consider me for promotions now).

28. Shellenbarger, *supra* note 16, at 163 (part-time work viewed as occupational dead end); Kingson, *supra* note 26, at A15 (women who take part-time work are so grateful for option they don't mind facing dimmer prospects). *See* Wilson, *supra* note 24, at 843. Assuming the 55 percent figure is accurate and that the associate worked four-fifths of the time, this associate worked 80 percent of the traditional full-time load and received 55 percent of full salary, so she was being paid at 69 percent of the full salary rate—somewhat higher than the national average of 60 percent. Epstein, *supra* note 8, at 396 (only responsible way to work part-time is to work full-time); *id.* at 399 (people who work part time and who are seriously committed to their practice don't really work part time); *id.* (part-time lawyer received bonus but pay calculated at 80 percent work schedule).

29. *See* Jane Waldfogel & Marianne Ferber, *The Long-Term Consequences of Nontraditional Employment,* 121 Monthly Lab. Rev. 3 (1998).

30. Kingson, *supra* note 26, at A1, A15. For further discussion on the way that employers take advantage of part-time workers; see Wilson, *supra* note 24, at 846 (documenting that part-time attorneys tend to be billed out at a higher fraction of the average full-time rate than their part-time salary indicates). *See* Epstein, *supra* note 8, at 396–97 (low-profile assignments hurt chances for success); Kingson, *supra* note 26, at A15 (top tier is full-time partnership track lawyer, bottom tier is part-time track made up largely of women); Williams, *supra* note 9, at 1602 (mommy track a formal option). Women recognize this trend. Surveys show women in male-dominated professions expect to earn about as much as men at the beginning of their careers, but not later on. Parenting is the major reason many of these women plan to reduce their labor force participation. *See* Francine D. Blau & Marianne A. Ferber, *Career Plans and Expectations of Young Women and Men: The Earnings Gap and Labor Force Participation,* 26 J. Hum. Resources 581, 599 (1991). Women are "realistic" about the trade-offs they will be forced to make; they also express considerable anger and outrage that they are forced to marginalize in a profession many have paid nearly $100,000 to enter. Personal conversations between the author and students in Property, and Gender and the Law classes, 1993–1996.

31. *See* Hochschild, *supra* note 19, at 25 (few parents take advantage of family-friendly policies). *See id.* (parents work longer hours). *See id.* at 162 (Hochschild concludes parents prefer to work at home).

32. *See* Hochschild, *supra* note 19, at 88–100 (detailing Watson's efforts to obtain shorter hours); *id.* (suggestion that new engineer take over four hours); *id.* (40 percent payment); *id.* (worked more than agreed hours); *id.* (excelled at work but boss resisted arrangement).

33. *Id.* at 92–93 (amount of hours worked is basis for getting ahead); *id.* at 89–90 (Eileen's boss worked extremely long hours); *id.* at 135 (most managers' wives were homemakers); *id.* at 71 (balance between work and family); *id.* (the way managers managed their lives and way they were brought up challenged); DuPont, *supra* note 24, at 2 (DuPont vice president);

Debra B. Schwartz, *An Examination of the Impact of Family Friendly Policies on the Glass Ceiling* 25 (Jan. 1994) (unpublished manuscript on file with the Federal Glass Ceiling Commission). Work & Family Connection, Inc., *Work & Family: A Retrospective* 130 (1995) [hereinafter *Retrospective*] (study by Families and Work Institute).

34. Ilhardt v. Sara Lee Corp., 118 F.3d 1151, 1152 (1997) (detailing that the employee's position was eliminated despite the fact that her employer was "extremely satisfied with her performance"); Shellenbarger, *supra* note 16, at 163 (part-time workers among first released during layoff); Betty Holcomb, *Not Guilty!* 127 (1998) (recent study).

35. *See* Hochschild, *supra* note 19, at 94 (after Eileen was fired she was given two months to find a new job within the company); *id.* at 95 (two years later, Eileen working full time); *id.* at 97 (what workers like Eileen want).

36. *Id.* at 56 (how to succeed in business); *id.* at 57 (twelve top managers); *id.* (most managers had never experienced tug of family needs); Betsy Morris, *It's Her Job, Too,* Fortune, Feb. 2, 1998, at 65, 76 (quoting Linda K. Stroh, associate professor of organizational behavior at Loyola University in Chicago) (successful men tend to have gendered patterns); Hochschild, *supra* note 19, at 61 (the higher up you go, more likely to have traditional marriage).

37. *Id.* at 32 (policy on flextime is that there is no flextime); *id* ("one more headache").

38. *See id.* at 103–114 (detailing female employees' experience working in an "old boys" office); *id.* at 107 (co-workers cornered Denise with questions); *id.* (with a gender war on, shorter hours meant surrender).

39. *See* Deborah L. Rhode, *Occupational Inequality,* 1988 Duke L. J. 1207, 1214. Moreover, women are not asked to relocate as often as their male counterparts. *See Good for Business, supra* note 5, at 151.

40. *See* Rhode, *No-Problem, supra* note 7, at 1749 n.80 (1985 poll); Swiss & Walker, *supra* note 16, at 10 (one study, one-fourth of women MBAs).

41. Irene Padavic, *White-Collar Work Values and Women's Interest in Blue-Collar Jobs,* 6 Gender & Soc'y 215, 215 (1992) (best jobs available for working class people are in blue collar work); June O'Neill, *Women & Wages,* The Am. Enterprise, Nov.–Dec. 1990, at 25, 31 (only alternative is low-paying service work or pink-collar job); *id.* at 31 (women's presence in blue-collar work "miniscule"); Sharon L. Harlan & Catherine White Berheide, *Barriers to Work Place Advancement Experienced By Women in Low-Paying Occupations* 14 (Jan. 1994) (unpublished manuscript, on file with the Federal Glass Ceiling Commission) (providing that women are predominately found in these "dead-end jobs"); Barbara F. Reskin, *Bringing the Men Back In: Sex Differentiation and the Devaluation of Women's Work,* Gender & Soc'y, Mar. 1988, at 58, 69 (men and women in same job category, women get lower-paying jobs); Kemp, *infra* note 52, at 212 (best blue-collar jobs to go to white males).

42. *Hard-Hatted Women: Stories of Struggles and Success in the Trades* 29 (Molly Martin ed., 1988).

43. *See* Boyd v. Ozark Air Lines, 568 F. 2d 50, 52 n.1 (8th Cir. 1977) (cockpit case where 25.8 percent of men and 93 percent of women excluded); Ellen Shapiro, *Remedies for Sex-Discriminatory Health and Safety Conditions in Male-Dominated Industrial Jobs,* 10 Golden Gate Univ. L. Rev. 1087, 1089–92 (1980) (detailing the relationship between productivity and design of equipment).

44. Interview with Marley Weiss, Professor of Law, University of Maryland Law School, Spring 1997 (rebundling).

45. *See* Vicki Schultz, *Telling Stories About Women and Work,* 103 Harv. L. Rev. 1749, 1832–39 (1990); Vicki Schultz, *Reconceptualizing Sexual Harassment,* 107 Yale L. J. 1683, passim (1998); *see generally Hard-Hatted Women, supra* note 42 (intensely gendered job descriptions); Schultz,

supra note 45 at 1802 (discussing rule barring women from a number of jobs in a meatpacking plant); Elvia R. Arriola, *"What's the Big Deal?" Women in the New York City Construction Industry and Sexual Harassment Law, 1970–1985*, 22 Colum. Hum. Rts. L. Rev. 21, 64 (1990).

46. Schultz, *supra* note 45, at 1811 (hidden injuries of class); Richard Sennett & Jonathan Cobb, *The Hidden Injuries of Class* (1973) (masculinity often measured by size of paycheck); Karen D. Pyke, *Class-Based Masculinities*, 10 Gender & Soc'y 527, 531 (1996).

47. *Hard-Hatted Women*, *supra* note 42, at 195 (men reconstruct their position as embodying true masculinity).

48. *See* Arriola, *supra* note 45, at 63 (co-worker twice exposed his genitals to tradeswoman); *id.* (constantly dropped pants in front of female electrician); *Hard-Hatted Women*, *supra* note 42, at 115 (foreman put his hand into her underwear while she worked on window trim); *id.* at 11 (subway conductor frequently propositioned).

49. *Id.* at 74, 78 (much of harassment not sexual); Arriola, *supra* note 45, at 59 (police officer's partner aimed his gun at her); *id.* at 63 (female ironworker forced to use equipment usually operated by two); Schultz, *supra* note 45, at 1833 (woman welder's account of harassment); *Hard-Hatted Women*, *supra* note 42, at 10 (two distinct kinds of harassment); Schultz, *supra* note 45, at 1825 n. 286 ("alarmingly high"); *Hard-Hatted Women*, *supra* note 42, at 44 (male environment adds a lot of stress to job); *id.* at 146 (almost as many women leave nontraditional work as enter it); Schultz, *supra* note 45, at 1826 n. 287 (high turnover reason sex segregation decreased only slightly).

50. *Id.* at 1835 (bulk of training acquired informally on job); *Hard-Hatted Women*, *supra* note 42, at 91 (woman's ability to succeed depends on willingness of supervisors and co-workers to teach); *id.* at 147 (quote by operating engineer); *id.* (sprinkler fitter); Crutchfield v. Maverick Tube Corp., 854 F.2d 307, 307 (8th Cir. 1988), *aff'd*, 664 F. Supp. 455 (1987) (worker demoted to previous job); telephone interview by Linda Chanow with Thomas E. Bauer, counsel for plaintiff (Jan. 9, 1998) (employee locked in closet).

51. *See* Harlan & Berheide, *supra* note 41, at 17 (asserting that seniority systems account for the absence of women in the best jobs); Women's Bureau, U.S. Dep't of Labor, *Facts on Working Women* 3 (1993) (working-class women particularly vulnerable).

52. *See e.g.*, Brigid O'Farrell, *Women and Nontraditional Blue Collar Jobs in the 1980's: An Overview*, in *Women in the Workplace* 135, 154 (Phyllis A. Wallace ed., 1982) (promotion tracks tend to require a flow of family work mothers generally lack); Harlan & Berheide, *supra* note 41, at 24 (promotion depends on on-the-job training); Alice Abel Kemp, *Women's Work, Degraded and Devalued* 247 (1994) (skilled workers trained through apprenticeship). Structure of training programs presented in Jonathan R. Veum, *Training Among Young Adults: Who, What Kind, and For How Long?*, 116 Monthly Lab. Rev., Aug. 1993, at 27, 28 (analyzing the results of the National Longitudinal Survey of Youth and determining that "men spent about twice as much time in company training than did women"). Furthermore, apprenticeship programs averaged twenty-seven hours per week, as compared to business schools whose less "intense" program averaged only fifteen hours. *Id.* at 30.

53. Peter T. Kilborn, *It's Too Much of a Good Thing, G.M. Workers Say in Protesting Overtime*, N.Y. Times, Nov. 22, 1994, at A16 (in 1994 factory workers put in highest levels of overtime ever recorded).

54. *See* Jim McKay, *Working More, Liking It Less*, Pittsburgh Post-Gazette, Oct. 9, 1994, at C1 (overtime has doubled in manufacturing since 1980). In Flint, Michigan, autoworkers struck over sixty-six-hour workweeks; factory workers could be fired if they refused to work over-

time more than six times. At one steel company, one worker was required to work forty-two straight days, missing family weddings, funerals, and his daughter's college graduation. For more discussion see Kilborn, *infra* note 73, at A16, and Sandra Livingston, *Overdosing on Overtime; Workers See Companies Increase Their Hours Instead of Work Force*, Plain Dealer, Oct. 2, 1994, at 1A. *See* Juliet B. Schor, *The Overworked American* 66–67 (1991). There is also evidence that the massive amounts of overtime now being clocked has stretched even fathers' image of the amount of time it is appropriate to spend with their families. Rod Haworth, of the UAW, recognized that the desire for additional income often conflicts with other priorities: "You are caught between that desire to spend more time with your family, and at the same time to have an increased income to enable you to do other things. It's a Catch-22." Marcotty, *supra* note 116, at 1A. *See also* James Bennet, *Auto Workers Pushed to the Limit*, N.Y. Times, Sept. 24, 1994, at B1; Livingston, *supra* note 54, at 1A (commenting that a worker could afford "a house in Lakewood, $40 jeans for his two teenagers, and a video camera to record all the birthdays and school-league football games he missed along the way"). When comparing this data with a *Stanford Law Review* survey, a similarity exists between the attitudes of both white and blue collar male workers. *See Law Firms and Lawyers with Children: An Empirical Analysis of Family/ Work Conflict*, 34 Stan. L. Rev. 1263 (1982). Although a small minority of both recognize that their long hours detract from their time at home, they are not willing to trade in their breadwinner status for more quality time with their family.

55. *See* O'Farrell, *supra* note 52, at 149.

56. *Hard-Hatted Woman*, *supra* note 41, at 56 ("pure hell"), 62 ("more compatible").

57. *See* Marion Crain, *Feminizing Unions*, 89 Mich. L. Rev. 1155, 1216 (1991) (6 percent of skilled craft positions available part-time); W. Steven Barnett, *Long-Term Effects of Early Childhood Programs on Cognitive and School Outcomes, The Future of Children's Programs*, 1995, at 45 (1995 study); DuPont, *supra* note 24, at 2 (employees in manufacturing jobs found it more difficult to balance work and family lives); Schwartz, *supra* note 33, at 2, 10 (high-income employees have greater access to flexibility and non-minorities compared to minorities); *Hard-Hatted Women*, *supra* note 42, at 100 (quote by operating engineer).

58. Rhoda Mahony, *Kidding Ourselves* 16 (1995).

59. Linda Micco, *DOL Creates Clearinghouse on Gender Bias in Pay*, HR News, Jan. 1997, at 5; William Goodman, *Women and Jobs in Recessions: 1969–1992*, 116 Monthly Lab. Rev., July 1993, at 26, 27 (documenting the industry distribution of employed women in December 1969 and July 1990); Mahony, *supra* note 58, at 15 (1993 statistics); Ann Bookman, *Flexibility at What Price? The Costs of Part-Time Work for Women Workers*, 52 Wash & Lee L. Rev. 799, 804 (1995) (60 percent of women hold jobs in traditional women's work); Brigid O' Farrell and Suzanne Moore, *Unions, Hard Hats, and Women Workers*, in *Women and Unions* 69, 70 (Dorothy Sue Cobble ed., 1993); *Hard-Hatted Women*, *supra* note 42, at 8; Kemp, *supra* note 53, at 195 (documenting that women in traditional women's work earn 57 percent of the average wage of workers in traditionally male jobs).

60. *See* Daphne Spain & Suzanne M. Bianchi, *Balancing Act* 96 (1996).

61. The point is often made that women's work does not make parenting any easier, because it is so low in status that women doing it have little autonomy or flexibility. *See, e.g., id.* at 175; Donald Tomaskovic-Devey, *Gender & Racial Inequality at Work* 51 (1993). This no doubt is true, but does not obviate the points made in the text.

62. While feminists focused on women's family work tend to stress that women's family workload impedes their ability to perform as ideal workers, feminists focused on gaining ac-

cess for women to nontraditional careers tend to stress that women's family responsibilities do not affect their ability to perform as ideal workers. *Cf.* Shelley Coverman, *Gender, Domestic Labor Time, and Wage Inequality,* 48 Am. Soc. Rev. 623, 264 (1983) ("[W]omen with children tend to select jobs that have convenient hours or locations and thus can be integrated easily into their domestic responsibilities"). The two are talking about different groups of women. Those who focus on family work are focusing on the bulk of women whose workforce participation is affected by family work; those who focus on gaining access to traditionally male careers typically are focused on the barriers faced even by women who can perform as ideal workers. This issue is discussed further in the book's conclusion. T. Beechey, *A Matter of Hours: Women, Part-time Work and the Labour Market* (1987) (British study).

63. *See* Kathleen Barker, *Changing Assumptions and Contingent Solutions: The Costs and Benefits of Women Working Full- and Part-Time,* 28 Sex Roles 47, 53, 65 (1993) (confirming that almost two-thirds of part-time work is in clerical, sales, and service occupations and that subsequent earnings are not affected by part-time status); John D. Owen, *Why Part-time Workers Tend to Be in Low Wage Jobs,* Monthly Lab. Rev., June 1978, at 11, 11.

64. Harlan & Berheide, *supra* note 41, at 2 (lack of advancement opportunities).

65. *See* Jennifer Glass, *The Impact of Occupational Segregation on Working Conditions,* 68 Soc. Forces 779, 790–91 (1990) (concluding that although conflicts are lower, flexibility is minimal in traditionally female jobs and noting that most professional and skilled trades jobs are held by men); Mary Ann Mason, *Beyond Equal Opportunity: A New Vision For Women Workers,* 6 Notre Dame J. L. Ethics & Pub. Pol'y 393, 398 (1992) (recognizing that female dominated occupations, which often provide regular hours, little to no overtime, and the ability to accommodate pregnancy and childcare responsibilities, are often the only feasible occupations for women to enter); Barker, *supra* note 63, at 65 (finding that "female-dominated professionals . . . were . . . the largest group selecting work as where they were the happiest").

66. *See* Linda Micco, *DOL Creates Clearinghouse on Gender Bias in Pay,* HR News, January 1997, at 5 (reporting that according to the Labor Department, "About half of U.S. working women hold 'traditionally female' low paying jobs . . . 75 percent to 97 percent of these jobs are held by females"). *See* Harlan & Berheide, *supra* note 41, at ii (nearly 60 percent of full-time female employees are paid less than $25,000/year); Woody & Weiss, *supra* note 7, at 60 (traditionally female jobs don't offer much chance for advancement).

67. Bureau of the Census, U.S. Dep't of Commerce, *Expanding Business Opportunities for Women: The 1995 Report of the Interagency Committee on Women's Business Enterprise* 3 (1996) (sharply increasing number of women work in women-owned business); Joel L. Smith, *Women Wheel and Deal for More Federal Contracts,* Det. News, Jan. 19, 1996, at B1 (number of women-owned businesses surged); *Women-Owned Businesses: Breaking the Boundaries, The Progress and Achievement of Women-Owned Enterprises,* Fact Sheet (Nat'l Found. for Women Business Owners, Silver Spring, MD), 1994 (rate of growth four times faster than males'); Theresa J. Devine, *Characteristics of Self-Employed Women in the United States,* Monthly Lab. Rev., Mar. 1994, at 20, 20 (women-owned businesses employed 35 percent more people than Fortune 500 companies); Center for Policy Alternatives, *Women's Voices: Solutions for a New Economy, State of the States: Women & Economic Security* (visited Oct. 31, 1997) <http://www.womensvoices.org/report.html> (increasing number of self-employed workers). *See* Rebecca Freligh, *Working at Home Gains Credibility, Women like Self-Employed Environment,* Harrisburg (PA) Patriot & Evening News, July 5, 1995, at B5 (top women-owned businesses have shifted dramatically); Diane Richbourg, *Women's Work Is in the Home: Home-based Businesses Proliferate,* Corpus Christi Caller Times, Aug. 15, 1995, at 5 (many women-owned businesses structured to accommodate women's load of

work); Devine, *supra* note 67, at 23 (self-employed women more likely to be married); *id.* at 24, 25 (more likely to work part-time); Stephanie N. Mehta, *Number of Woman-Owned Business Surged 43 percent in 5 Years Through 1992*, Wall St. J., Jan. 29, 1996, at B2 (study by National Foundation of Women Business Owners); Devine, *supra* note 67, at 25 (pent-up productivity).

68. Congresswoman Diane DeGette, Address at Lawyers, Work & Family: A Forum, American University, Washington College of Law (April 2, 1998).

69. Interview with Andy Marks, March 1998.

70. *See* Lotte Bailyn, *Breaking the Mold* 85 (1993) (Arthur Andersen).

71. Work & Family Benefits Inc., *Why Invest in This Employee Benefit?* (visited Oct. 31, 1997) ⟨http://www.wfbenefits.com/WHYINVST.HTM⟩ (highly respected survey); *The Work-family Equation: More Companies Are Finding It's Good Business to Consider the Family Needs of Their Employees*, St. Paul Pioneer Press Dispatch, Nov. 26, 1990, at 1F (survey of 200 human resources managers).

72. Richard W. Judy & Carol D'Amico, Hudson Institute, *Workforce 2020*, at 112 (1997).

73. For a discussion of trade-offs that employees would make to gain access to dependent care assistance, see Ellen Galinsky, James T. Bond, Dana E. Friedman, *The Changing Workforce: Highlights of The National Study of the Changing Workforce* 88 (1993); *id.* at 80 (88 percent of workers have access to some leave, 57 percent access to part-time work, 29 percent access to flex-time); Charlene Marmer Solomon, *Job Sharing: One Job, Double Headache?*, Personnel J., Sept. 1994, at 88, 90 (1993 Catalyst study); Peter T. Kilborn, *Factories That Never Close Are Scrapping 5-Day Week*, N.Y. Times, June 4, 1996, at A1 [hereinafter Kilborn, *Factories*] (recent study by Mercer).

74. *See Retrospective, supra* note 33, at 115, 118, 120.

75. *See* Amy Saltzman, *Companies in a Family Way*, (visited Oct. 31, 1997) ⟨http://www.usnews .com/usnews/issue/970512/12comp.htm⟩ (First Tennessee Bank); *Retrospective, supra* note 33, at 121 (dawn patrols).

76. *See* Chuck Martin, *Good Day Care Seen as Bottom-Line Issue*, Milwaukee J., Dec. 4, 1991, at C10 (on-site child care important); *id.* (Marquette Electronics); Fried & Sher, Inc., *A Profile of Family-Friendly Organizations: What's Happening Around the Country?* (visited Nov. 7, 1998) ⟨http://www.friedandsher.com/corpprog.htm⟩ [hereinafter Fried & Sher, *Profile*] (mobile child-care center for construction company).

77. *See Retrospective, supra* note 33, at 113 (study of 10 large companies); Solomon, *supra* note 73, at 90 (3.5 million managers and professionals worked part-time in 1992).

78. *See* Kilborn, *Factories, supra* note 73, at D21 (new schedules); DuPont, *supra* note 24, at 2 (key is stability); *id.* (schedules that have men complaining welcome to some women). *Cf.* Kilborn, *Factories, supra* note 73, at D21 (discussing some employees concerns that the traditional weekend is being eliminated) *with* Saltzman, *supra* note 75, at 2 (stressing the advantages perceived by working mothers).

79. *See* Susan Seitel, *Update on Job-Sharing* (visited Oct. 31, 1997) ⟨http://www.workfamily .com/online/JobShare.htm⟩ (Minnesota law firm); *id.* ("job sharing means someone is always there").

80. *See Retrospective, supra* note 33, at 117 (everyone allowed flexible schedule at Xerox); Solomon, *supra* note 73, at 94 (Bank of America job share); DuPont, *supra* note 24, at 3 (20 percent of DuPont employees use flexible scheduling).

81. Work & Family Connection, Inc., *Leave Law Successful After A Year, Says Florida Business* (visited Aug. 18, 1998) ⟨http://www.workfamily.com/online/Nb5322.htm⟩ [hereinafter W&F, *Leave Law Successful*].

82. *See Retrospective, supra* note 33, at 126.

83. *See* Phyllis H. Raabe, *The Organizational Effects of Workplace Family Policies: Past Weaknesses and Recent Progress Toward Improved Research*, 11 J. Fam. Issues 477, 482 (1990) (inflexible policies generate costs); Sally Coberly & Gail G. Hunt, Washington Business Group on Health, *The Metlife Study of Employer Costs for Working Caregivers* 6–8 (1995) (report on elder care).

84. Michael Cook, chairman and CEO of Deloitte & Touche, in Lawlor, *supra* note 7, at 32.

85. Hochschild, *supra* note 19, at 31.

86. Schwartz, *supra* note 33, at 5, 18 (family-friendly policies); *Retrospective, supra* note 33, at 113 (recent survey); *id.* at 112 (report by the Conference Board).

87. *See* DuPont, *supra* note 24, at 116 (DuPont was losing people); Lawlor, *supra* note 7 (Deloitte); *id.* at 116–17 (DuPont treats part-timers identically with full-timers).

88. *See Retrospective, supra* note 33, at 128 (mothers who work for bosses who offer flexibility seven times less likely to quit); *id.* at 129 (study out of Notre Dame); *id.* at 127 (1992 survey of IBM); *id.* at 130 (First Tennessee Bank); Friedman, *supra* note 74, at 80 (Conference Board Report).

89. *See New Ways to Work, Flexibility Compelling Strategies for a Competitive Workplace* 8 (1991); *Retrospective, supra* note 33, at 126 (Aetna Life and Casualty introduced a number of flexible work options); *id.* at 118 (Helene Curtis' flextime program increased return rate of new mothers); *id.* at 122 (Nation's Bank); *id.* at 123 (Steelcase, Inc.); *id.* at 118 (survey by National Council for Jewish Women for Department of Labor); Seitel, *supra* note 79 (flexibility holds advantages in retaining and recruiting workers); *id.* at 129 (Automatic Data Processing).

90. *See* Fried & Sher Inc., *A Cost-Benefit Analysis of Family Friendly Programs* (visited May 21, 1998) ⟨http://www.friedandsher.com/bottlin.htm⟩ [hereinafter Fried & Sher, *Analysis*] (Patagonia saved money by offering on-site child care); *id.* (Virginia Mason Medical Center in Seattle, zero turnover with workers using on-site child care); *id.* (turnover rate for on-site child care center users at 53 percent of the companies studied was zero).

91. *See Retrospective, supra* note 33, at 112–30; Friedman, *supra* note 73, at 53 (decreasing turnover important because of strong link between retaining employees and retaining clients); Seitel, *supra* note 79 (Deloitte gave clients option to switch to new person when accountant's hours decreased, virtually all chose not to switch).

92. *See* Friedman, *supra* note 73, at 52 (absenteeism and tardiness dramatically reduced by flextime); *Retrospective, supra* note 33, at 123 (survey by AMA); Fried & Sher, *Analysis, supra* note 90, at 1 (on-site child care reduces absenteeism).

93. *See id.* at 1124; *New Ways to Work, supra* note 89, at 11 (Engelhard Corporation); *Retrospective, supra* note 33, at 126 (Pella Corporation); *id.* at 120 (Union County).

94. *See Retrospective, supra* note 33, at 120.

95. Hochschild, *supra* note 19, at 73.

96. *See* Friedman, *supra* note 73, at 83–84 (increased productivity major reason companies institute flexible work plans); Seitel, *supra* note 79 (more productive instead of less, smarter about the way they work); Simcha Ronen, *Alternative Work Schedules: Selecting, Implementing, And Evaluating* (1984); *see also* Diana Zuckerman & Young-hee Yoon, *Reduced-time Work Opportunities For Professionals And Managers* (summarizing ten studies).

97. *See* Saltzman, *supra* note 75 (bank with active second-generation work/family program); *id.* (Ford Foundation study of Xerox); *30 Hours Work for 40 Hours Pay May Not Be as Crazy as It Sounds*, Work & Family Newsbrief (Work & Family Connection, Inc., Minnetonka, Minn.), May 1998, at 3 (Metro Plastics).

98. *See Retrospective, supra* note 33, at 126 (Canadian autoworkers) *id.* (Pella window company); *id.* at 128 (Bank of America).

99. See Fried & Sher, Analysis, supra note 90 (City of Phoenix); Carol Hymowitz, As Aetna Adds Flextime, Bosses Learn to Cope, Wall St. J., June 18, 1990, at B1 (Aetna manager); Seitel, supra note 79 (Minneapolis law firm); Work & Family Connection, Inc., A Worker-Friendly Production Line? "That's A Doozy!" (visited Oct. 31, 1997) ‹http://www.workfamily.com/online/tr0694.htm› (Marquette Electronics); Seitel, supra note 79 (Maslon, Edelman, Barman and Brand).

100. See Retrospective, supra note 33, at 114 (more productive because workers start fresh); Seitel, supra note 79 (Schreiber Goods); Retrospective, supra note 33, at 126 (Northwestern Life Insurance Company); id. (citing Royal Bank Workers Back Flexible Hours, Daily Herald Trib., Dec. 20, 1994) (Royal Bank of Canada).

101. W&F, Leave Law Successful, supra note 81 (Southern Bell worker grateful for six months leave to care for sick child); DuPont, supra note 24, at 1 ("go the extra mile"); Retrospective, supra note 33, at 125 (citing Alaska Spark, Winter, 1991) ("go out of their way to make the job work"); id. ("more loyal"); Saltzman, supra note 75, at 2 (increases in loyalty can translate into direct increases in productivity).

102. See Renee M. Landers, James B. Rebitzer, & Lowell J. Taylor, Rat Race Redux, 86 Am. Econ. Rev. 329, 335–336 (1996).

103. Data on percentage of mothers who are homemakers: Ureta Census Data, supra note 2 (25 percent of prime-age mothers are not in labor force).

104. Schwartz, supra note 33, at 22 (employers and employees view use of family-friendly policies and the desire for career advancement as mutually exclusive choices); Hochschild, supra note 19, at 27 ("so small, it's shocking"); Deborah L. Rhode, Fleeing Home for the Comforts of an Office, Nat'l L. J., Oct. 6, 1997, at A23 (88 percent of manufacturing firms offered part-time work, only 3–5 percent took advantage).

105. Saltzman, supra note 75, at 1 (levels of retention); Schwartz, supra note 33, at 28 (quote about redefining the nature of work itself).

106. A 1989 report by Catalyst found that flexibility plans that prorate employee benefits for part-time employees and use a full-time equivalency system rather than head counts impose minimal costs for most companies. New Ways to Work, supra note 89, at 18 (head-counting system); Retrospective, supra note 33, at 114 (Department of Labor study).

107. Ellen Ernst Kossek, et al., Using Flexible Schedules in the Managerial World: The Power of Peers, 38 Human Resource Management J. 33 (1999), cited in Martin H. Malin, Fathers and Parental Leave Revisited, 19 N. Ill. U. L. Rev __ (forthcoming 1999) (manuscript at 23, on file with author) (hereinafter Revisited); Work and Family: Juggling Both Is an Endless Struggle—and Companies Aren't Helping Much, Bus. Wk., Sept. 17, 1997 at 86, 98 (employees more likely to use flexible policies when managers use them); Retrospective, supra note 33, at 116 (work/family program should be introduced by the CEO of the company).

108. See Schwartz, supra note 33, at 30–31.

109. See, e.g., Hochschild, supra note 19, at 92–93 (quoting one manager's response to an employee's request for alternative scheduling, "Everyone here has a large volume of work. That's all I know how to understand as a basis for getting ahead"); Solomon, supra note 73, at 96 (presenting one human resources director's view, "[managers] need to alter the concept that people need to be available the minute you need them or that people need to be at their desks in order to be doing a good job"); Saltzman, supra note 75 (managers played a board game).

110. See Retrospective, supra note 33, at 116 (DuPont is a leader in the field); id. at 117 (takes time to shift company culture); Bailyn, supra note 70, at 92, 94 (new style of management that focuses on results).

111. See Retrospective, supra note 33, at 117, 122.

112. Institute for Women's Policy Research, Research-In-Brief, *The Economic Impact of Contingent Work on Women and their Families* (1995) ("contingent" work); Judith Evans & Beth Berselli, *UPS, Union Fail to Agree on Contract*, Wash. Post, Aug. 2, 1997, at F1 (major issue of UPS strike was that 57 percent of employees were part-time workers); Marianne Ferber & Jane Waldfogel, Radcliffe Pub. Pol'y Inst., *Contingent Work* 4, 5 (1996) (structural change, rather than merely a cyclical phenomenon).

113. Schwartz, *supra* note 33, at 28.

114. *See* Chris Tilly, *Reasons for the Continuing Growth of Part-Time Employment*, 114 Monthly Lab. Rev., Mar. 1991, at 10, 12 (employers typically exact a price for part-time work). The average hourly wage in 1990 was $5.06 for part-time workers and $8.09 for full-time workers. Anne L. Kalleberg, *Part-Time Work and Workers in the United States: Correlates and Policy Issues*, 52 Wash. & Lee L. Rev. 771, 780 (1995) (citing Polly Callaghan & Heidi Hartmann, Economic Pol'y Institute, *Contingent Work: A Chart Book on Part-Time and Temporary Employment* (1991)). *See* Tilly, *supra* note 114, at 12 (noting that almost two-thirds of part-time work is in clerical, service occupations, and sales, occupations that are low-paid even for full-time workers, who earn 83 percent and 64 percent of the median full-time weekly wage, respectively, for clerical and service, while salesworkers earn the median wage). Additionally, there is evidence that part-time salesworkers are concentrated in the lower-paying sectors. *Id.* at 17, n. 6. Kalleberg, *supra* note 114, at 780 (only about half of the differential between pay rates of full- and part-time can be explained by "objective factors").

115. International Labor Organization, Part-Time Work Convention, 1994 (visited July 1, 1997) ⟨http://www.ilolex.ilo.ch:1567/public/5...3DC175&highlight=on&querytype=bool⟩ (hereinafter ILO) (ILO proposed a convention that would end discrimination against part-time work); Josephine Marcotty, *A Nation on Overtime*, Star Trib., Sept. 5, 1994, at 1A; Paul A. Eisenstein, *Can Big Three Automakers Keep Up Profit Bonanza?*, Christian Sci. Monitor, Feb. 7, 1995, at 9; Rick Haglund, *GM, UAW is a Matter of Survival*, Plain Dealer, Feb. 5, 1995, at 1G; Randolph Heaster, *Working Overtime, or Overworking? America's Employees Feel the Strain of Good Economy, Less Hiring*, Kan. City Star, Nov. 15, 1994, at A1.

116. Conversation with the author at Turtle Park, Van Ness and 45th Streets NW, Washington D.C., summer 1988.

117. Bureau of Labor Statistics, U.S. Dep't of Labor, Unpublished Marital and Family Tabulations from the Current Population Survey, tbl. A ("Work Experience of Wives by Husbands' Annual Earnings in 1994, Presence and Age of Children, Educational Attainment of Wives, and Race and Hispanic Origin, Primary Families"), March 1995.

118. Jennifer Tucker & Leslie R. Wolfe, Center for Women's Policy Studies, *Defining Work and Family Issues: Listening to the Voices of Women of Color* 1 (1994) (high-status workers are more likely to be offered flexible policies). *See* Shellenbarger, *supra* note 16, at 157 (report).

119. Audience comment, author's presentation for the Harvard Divinity School Women's Studies in Religion Leadership Committee, Jan. 31–Feb. 1, 1998.

120. *See Retrospective, supra* note 33, at 114–15, 118, 120, 123. Furthermore, a 1989 report by Catalyst found that flexibility plans that pro-rate employee benefits for part-time employees and use a full-time equivalency system rather than head counts impose minimal costs for most companies. *See id.* at 123.

121. *See* Mary Frances Berry, *The Politics of Parenthood* 22 (1993).

122. Posting, Starbucks, 5345 Wisconsin Avenue, Washington, D.C. (Aug. 1998).

123. Martin H. Malin, *Fathers and Parental Leave*, 72 Tex. L. Rev. 1047, 1089 (1994) (men who already have significant caregiving responsibilities would benefit from restructuring more

than women); *id.* at 1078 (study found that 63 percent of large employers considered it unreasonable for a man to take any parental leave).

124. *See id.* at 1055–57 (studies in Sweden); *id.* at 1057 (children turn to mothers when the chips are down).

125. Mary Anne C. Case, *Disaggregating Gender from Sex and Sexual Orientation: The Effeminate Man in the Law and Feminist Jurisprudence,* 105 Yale L. J. 1, 81–82 (1995).

126. For patient assistance in helping me frame these lawsuits and proposals, thanks to Martha Chamallas, Stanford Ross, Susan Ross, Michael Selmi, and Marley Weiss. The mistakes that remain, of course, are mine. Though I have focused on litigation in the text, litigation, to be effective, must be part of an integrated approach that includes community-based programs such as that described in Sylvia Law, *Girls Can't Be Plumbers—Affirmative Action for Women in Construction: Beyond Goals and Quotas,* 24 Harv. Civ. Rts.-Civ. Lib. 45 (1989).

127. For a thorough discussion of disparate treatment law, see Michael J. Zimmer et al., *Cases and Materials on Employment Discrimination* 93–398 (4th ed., 1997); 42 U.S.C. § 2000e (1998) (sexual harassment violates Title VII).

128. Trezza v. The Hartford Inc., 1998 U.S. Dist. LEXIS 20206; 78 Fair Empl. Prac. Cas. (BNA) 1826.

129. Phillips v. Martin Marietta, 400 U.S. 542 (1971).

130. *See, e.g.,* Piantanida v. Wyman Center, Inc., 927 F. Supp. 1226 (E.D. Mo. 1996), *aff'd* 116 F. 3d 340 (8th Cir. 1997). *See also* Martha Chamallas, *Motherhood and Disparate Treatment,* __ Villanova L. Rev. __ (forthcoming 1999) (draft in possession of the author) (citing other cases).

131. Equal Pay Act of 1963 (EPA), 29 U.S.C. § 206 (1) (1963).

132. *See* Bookman, *supra* note 59, at 805. These "new" part-time employees were mostly women and received no health care benefits, pensions, vacation or sick leave. *See id. See e.g.,* Judith Evans, *Teamsters, UPS Agree to Resume Talks at Federal Mediator's Behest,* Wash. Post, Aug. 7, 1997, at E7 ("I'm a part-timer, but work 50 to 60 hours a week, receive part-time pay, while the person standing next to me does the same job and earns more"); 29 U.S.C. § 206 (1) (1963) (equal skill, effort, and responsibility).

133. *See* Joan Acker, *Doing Comparable Worth* 99 (1989).

134. 417 U.S. 188 (1974) (Corning Glass Works v. Brennan), *id.* at 191 (part-time work is not a factor other than sex); *id.* at 202 ("work hazards"). For a discussion of the treatment of the relationship between temporary/part-time employees and the EPA, see Zimmer, *supra* note 127, at 1018; Martha Chamallas, *Women and Part-Time Work: The Case for Pay Equity and Equal Access,* 64 N.C. L. Rev. 709 (1986).

135. Title VII challenges to unequal pay may also be available; suits contesting unequal benefits would have to be filed under Title VII, because the EPA covers only wages. Because of the legal complexity of such suits, they will be described in depth in a forthcoming law review article (which also will spell out the lawsuits discussed here in more detail).

136. The basic format for disparate-impact suits involving financial issues, as when paying women in a predominantly female part-time track a lower wage rate for part-time work, combine requirements from the EPA and from Title VII, as well as complex threshold issues. For that reason, they will not be discussed separately, although they are discussed in a law review article on litigating work/family conflict (forthcoming); the article also discusses the EPA suit and disparate impact promotion suits in much greater depth.

137. 42 U.S.C. § 2000e(2)(k)(1) (1991).

138. *See* 42 U.S.C. § 2000e–2(k)(1) (1998).

139. The Civil Rights Act of 1991 added the requirement that "the complaining party . . .

demonstrate that each particular challenged employment practice causes a disparate impact...."
42 U.S.C. § 2000e2(k)(1)(1991); *id.* ("[I]f the complaining party can demonstrate to the court
that the elements of a respondent's decisionmaking process are not capable of separation for
analysis, the decisionmaking process may be analyzed as one employment practice"); Zimmer,
supra note 127, at 456–59 (discussing methods for challenging multiple component systems).

140. See Griggs v. Duke Power Co., 401 U.S. 424, 429–31 (1971) (finding that the high-
school completion requirement and general intelligence test "do not bear a demonstrable relationship to successful performance of the jobs" where the employer adopted them
"without meaningful study" and employees hired prior to their adoption "who ha[d] not
completed high school or taken the tests . . . perform[ed] satisfactorily"); 490 U.S. 642 (1989)
(employer must be able to articulate a reasonable "justification for his use of the challenged
practice"); *id.* at 659 ("there is no requirement that the challenged practice be 'essential' or
'indispensable' to the employer's business for it to pass muster").

141. See Bailyn, *supra* note 71, and 77 (quoting Virginia E. Schein) (corporate convenient);
see also Deborah J. Vagins, *Occupational Segregation and the Male WorkerNorm: Challenging Objective
Work Requirements under Title VII*, 18 Women's Rts. L. Rep. 79 (1996) (student paper written at
the suggestion of the author).

142. For a discussion of the role of costs, see Barbara Allen Babcock et al., *Sex Discrimination and the Law* 871–72 (1996).

143. See S. 14247 Cong. Rec. S14247 (daily ed., Oct. 5, 1994) (statement of Sen. Metzenbaum) (Contingent Workforce Equity Act); ILO, *supra* note 115 (proposed ILO convention
similar to CWEA).

144. See Boyd v. Ozark Air Lines, 568 F.2d 50, 52 (8th Cir. 1977) (only men were employed
as pilots); *id.* at 54 (fifteen women applied and were denied employment); *id.* at 52 n.1 (company maintained height rule that excluded 93 percent of the women but only 25.8 percent of
men); *id.* at 53 (trial court held that rule had disparate impact on women).

145. See *id.* at 53 (airline claimed business necessity); *id.* at 54; Boyd v. Ozark, 419 F. Supp.
1061, 1064 (E.D. Mo. 1976) (Eighth Circuit found that an individual's ability to operate all the
instruments in the cockpit dependent upon height); *Boyd*, 568 F. 2d, at 54; *Boyd*, 419 F. Supp.
at 1064 (trial court found height requirement to be two inches shorter).

146. See, e.g., Blake v. City of Los Angeles, 595 F.2d 1367, 1371, 1374 (tracing the substitution of
height and weight requirements for male-only hiring policies); *Boyd*, 419 F. Supp. at 1064 ("The
evidence established, however, that a requirement of 5'5", which would lessen the disparate
impact upon women, would be sufficient to insure the requisite mobility and vision").

147. EEOC Decision par. 6223, 1971 WL 3968 (E.E.O.C.), at *3 (rejecting employer's argument that a general height requirement was necessary to preserve the "routine assignability
of employees . . . from job to job").

148. See Ellen Shapiro, *Remedies for Sex Discriminatory Health and Safety Conditions in Male Dominated Industrial Jobs*, 10 Golden Gate Univ. L. Rev. 1087, 1089–92 (1980) (4 percent of airline
pilots are women); Laura J. Geissler, Note and Comment, *Unfinished Business: Intermediate
Scrutiny, "Real Differences" and "Separate-but-Equal"* in United States v. Virginia, 116 S. Ct. 2264
(1996), 20 Hamline L. Rev. 471, 506 n.255 (1996) (issue is whether the exclusion of women
will be built into the design specifications for generations to come).

149. 42 U.S.C.A. §§ 12111–12117, 12131–12134 (Supp. 1993) (Americans with Disabilities Act);
interview with Randy Rabinowitz, Professor of Law, American University, Washington
College of Law, Washington, D.C. (spring 1998) (post-ADA back injuries).

150. See, e.g., Industrial Union Dep't, AFL-CIO v. Hodgson, 499 F. 2d 467 (1974) (disparate

impact cases); *id.* (recognizing "a four year delay is not irrational with regard to those industries that require that long to meet the standard"); Edward J. McCaffrey, *Taxing Women* 99–100 (1997) (working women deliberately excluded).

151. *See* S. 2504 § 103, 104, 105, 106, 201, 204, 103d Cong. § 204 (1994) (CWEA); 140 Cong. Rec. S14248–53 (daily ed., Oct. 5, 1994) (statement of Sen. Metzenbaum); McCaffrey, *supra* note 150, at 99–100; Nancy C. Straudt, *Taxing Housework*, 84 Georgetown L. J. 1571 (1996); Marjorie E. Kornhauser, *Love, Money, and the IRS*, 45 Hastings L. J. 63 (1993).

152. *See* Mark A. Rothstein et al., *Cases and Materials on Employment Law* 352–359 (2d ed., 1991).

153. *See* Bookman, *supra* note 59, at 810 (National Employment Law Project); Malin, *Revisited, supra* note 107, at 30–33 (when employee discharged due to failure to show up); S. 2504 § 401, 103d Cong. § 204 (1994); 141 Cong. Rec. S14252 (daily ed., Oct. 5, 1994) (statement of Sen. Metzenbaum) (CWEA proposed changes).

154. *See* Bookman, *supra* note 59, at 812 (Family and Medical Leave Act does not cover workers who work less than twenty-five hours per week); S. 2504 § 201, 141 Cong Rec. S14249 (daily ed., Oct. 5, 1994) (statement of Sen. Metzenbaum) (CWEA proposed changing FMLA).

155. *See* Bookman, *supra* note 59, at 813 (Employee Retirement Income Security Act of 1974 governs private sector employee benefits); S.2504 §202, 141 Cong. Rec. S14253 (daily ed., Oct. 5, 1994 (statement of Sen. Metzenbaum) (15 percent of part-time workers had pensions, CWEA proposed to lower the threshold of hours).

156. *See* Edward J. McCaffery, *Taxation and the Family*, 40 U.C.L.A. L. Rev. 983, 1000 (1993).

157. *See* Mary E. Becker, *Obscuring the Struggle*, 89 Colum. L. Rev. 264, 282 (1989) (divorced husband gets twice what his ex-wife gets in Social Security benefits, and three times as much upon remarriage); *id.* (divorced wife's claim may terminate upon remarriage).

158. *See* Katharine T. Bartlett & Angela P. Harris, *Gender and Law: Theory, Doctrine, Commentary* 339–40 (1998).

CHAPTER FOUR: *Deconstructing the Ideal-Worker Norm in Family Entitlements*

1. *See* Arlie Hochschild, *The Second Shift* (1989).

2. *See* Peter A. Morrison, *Congress and the Year 2000: Peering into the Demographic Future*, Bus. Horizons, Nov. 1, 1993, at 55.

3. Reva B. Siegel, *Home As Work: The First Woman's Rights Claims Concerning Wives' Household Labor, 1850–1880*, 103 Yale L. J. 1073, 1102 (1994) [hereinafter Siegel, *Home As Work*] (quoting Letter from Frances Gage to Gerrit Smith (Dec. 24, 1855), in 1 *History of Woman Suffrage*, 842–43 (Elizabeth C. Stanton et al. eds., reprint ed., 1985)).

4. *See* Stephen Rose, *On Shaky Ground: Rising Fears About Incomes and Earning* (National Comm'n for Employment Policy Research Report No. 94–02, 1994) (70 percent); Demie Kurz, *For Richer or for Poorer* 3 (1995) (nearly 40 percent).

5. *See* Joan Williams, *Is Coverture Dead? Beyond a New Theory of Alimony*, 82 Geo. L. Rev. 2227, 2227 n. 1 (1994) (detailing the literature on postdivorce impoverishment); Jay D. Teachman & Kathleen M. Paasch, *Financial Impact of Divorce on Children and Their Families*, in *The Future of Children: Children & Divorce*, Spring 1994, at 63; Kathleen R. Funder, Margaret Harrison & Peter McDonald, *Principles, Practices and Problems in Property and Income Transfers*, in Kathleen Funder, Margaret Harrison, & Ruth Weston, *Settling Down: Pathways of Parents After Divorce* 656–57 (1993) (affluent families).

6. *See* Marion Crain, *Where Have All The Cowboys Gone? Marriage and Breadwinning in Postindus-*

trial Society __ Rutgers L. Rev. __ (1999) (twenty-two states; no-fault reform proposals; final quote, from Joseph Guttman, *Divorce in Psychosocial Perspective: Theory and Research* 1, 4 (1993)); Katharine T. Bartlett & Angela P. Harris, *Gender and Law* 421–22 (1998) (other commentators on no-fault). *See generally* Laura Bradford, *The Counterrevolution: A Critique of Recent Proposals to Reform No-Fault Divorce Laws*, 49 Stan. L. Rev. 607 (1997).

7. *See* Crain, *supra* note 6, at 17.

8. Matilda Hindman, *Who Will Support You?*, New Northwest, Oct. 10, 1878, at 4, *quoted in* Siegel, *Home as Work, supra* note 3, at 1156–57. Note the striking similarity of the language used in one of the relatively few cases I have found that grants a homemaker an entitlement based solely on domestic work:

Here, plaintiff bore the children, was the principal in providing child care and maintaining the domestic setting, and was also employed part-time for several years while defendant attended medical school. To hold that plaintiff's only value is the income she generates ignores the value of her contributions in every other aspect of family life. The logical conclusion is that motherhood and nurturing of children are valueless; that preserving and maintaining a home is worthless; and that the functions of mother, homemaker, and helpmate contribute nothing of value to a family. We refuse to so limit our definition of support.

Martinez v. Martinez, 754 P.2d 69, 77 (Utah Ct. App. 1988), *rev'd*, 818 P. 2d 538 (Utah 1991).

9. *See generally* Norma Basch, *In the Eyes of the Law: Women, Marriage, and Property in Nineteenth-Century New York* (1982); Peggy A. Rabkin, *Fathers to Daughters: The Legal Foundations of Female Emancipation* (1980).

10. *See* Robin West, *Jurisprudence and Gender*, 55 U. Chi. L. Rev. 1, 15 (1988) (official story); Siegel, *Home as Work, supra* note 3, at 1135–46, 1179–89; Siegel, *The Modernization of Marital Status Law: Adjudicating Wives' Rights to Earnings*, 82 Geo. L.J. 2127, 2134 (1997) [hereinafter Siegel, *Modernization*].

11. Siegel, *Home as Work, supra* note 3, at 1101 ("wife owes service"); 1126 ("in a true marriage"); 1102 ("Do not the majority?"); 1115 (resolution of 1851).

12. *Id.* at 1180–81 (MWPA coverage); 1093 (block quote); 1096 (Siegel quote); Jeanne Boydston, *Home and Work* (1990) (pastoralization).

13. DeWitt v. DeWitt, 296 N.W.2d 761, 767 (Wis. Ct. App. 1980) ("so coldly undertaken"); Hoak v. Hoak, 370 S.E.2d 473, 478 (W.Va. 1988) ("not a business arrangement"); 476 ("demeans the concept"); Ann E. Weiss, Note, *Property Distribution in Domestic Relations Law: A Proposal for Excluding Educational Degrees and Professional Licenses from the Marital Estate*, 11 Hofstra L. Rev. 1327, 1345–46 nn.131–36 (1983) ("commercial investment loss"); 1335 n. 57 ("arm's length").

14. Margaret Jane Radin, *Market-Inalienability*, 100 Harv. L. Rev. 1849, 1905–6 (1987), as quoted in Katharine Silbaugh, *Commodification and Women's Household Labor*, 9 Yale J. of Law & Feminism 81, 84.

15. *Accord* Silbaugh, *supra* note 14, *passim.*

16. *See* Reva B. Siegel, *Modernization, supra* note 10; In re Callister's Estate, 47 N.E. 268, 270 (N.Y. 1897) (quote).

17. Borelli v. Brusseau, 16 Cal. Rptr. 2d 16 (Cal. Ct. App. 1993).

18. Woody Allen, quoted in Eric Lax, *Woody and Mia: A New York Story*, N.Y. Times, Feb. 24, 1991, Sect. 6 (Magazine), 31, 31.

19. For a discussion of discretion in family law, see Mary Ann Glendon, *Fixed Rules and Discretion in Contemporary Family Law and Succession Law*, 60 Tul. L. Rev. 1165, 1167–68 (1986) [hereinafter Glendon, *Fixed Rules*]; Cynthia Starnes, *Divorce and the Displaced Homemaker*, 60 U. Chi. L. Rev. 67, 92–96 (1993); Jane Murphy, *Eroding the Myth of Discretionary Justice in Family Law*, 70 N.

C. L. Rev. 209 (1991). For the estimated ratio of unpaid family work to GDP, see Katharine Silbaugh, *Turning Labor into Love: Housework and the Law*, 91 Nw. L. Rev. 1 (1996).

20. Ralph T. King, *A Phone Fortune Is at Stake as McCaws Wrangle over Divorce*, Wall St. J., Aug. 7, 1996, at 1.

21. *See Big Divorce, Big Fees*, 19 Nat'l L.J. A7 (col. 2) (McCaw divorce); *see* Marcia Garrison, *How Do Judges Decide Divorce Cases? An Empirical Analysis of Discretionary Decisionmaking*, 74 N. C. L. Rev. 401, 457 (1996) (U.S.) [hereinafter Garrison, *How Do Judges*]; Funder *et al.*, *supra* note 5, at 656 (Australia).

22. *See* Carol S. Bruch & Norma J. Winkler, *The Economic Consequence*, 36 Juv. & Fam. Ct. J. 5, 20 (1985).

23. *See* Lorraine Dusky, *Still Unequal: The Shameful Truth About Women and Justice in America* 322 (1996) (wealthy wives fare worst); Garrison, *How Do Judges*, *supra* note 21, at 457 (three-quarters of wives); Commission on Gender Fairness in the Courts, *A Difference in Perceptions: The Final Report of the North Dakota Commission on Gender Fairness in the Courts*, 72 N.D. L. Rev. 1115, 1192 (tbl. 22) (1996).

24. *See* Starnes, *supra* note 19, at 95; Ann Lacquer Estin, *Maintenance, Alimony, and the Rehabilitation of Family Care*, 71 N.C. L. Rev. 721, 748 n.93, 749–54 (1993); Silbaugh, *supra* note 19, at 56–62.

25. *See* Linda D. Elrod & Robert G. Spector, *A Review of the Year in Family Law*, 30 Fam. L. Q. 765, 777 (1997) (courts place primary emphasis on need and ability to pay); Lynn A. Baker & Robert E. Emery, *When Every Relationship Is Above Average: Perceptions and Expectations of Divorce at the Time of Marriage*, 17 Law & Hum. Behav. 349, 443 (1993) (women's expectations); Lee E. Teitelbaum, *Divorce, Custody, Gender, and the Limits of Law On Dividing the Child*, 92 Mich. L. Rev. 1808, 1823 (1994) (8 percent); Deborah L. Rhode & Martha Minow, *Reforming the Questions, Questioning the Reforms: Feminist Perspectives on Divorce Law*, in *Divorce Reform at the Crossroads* 191, 202 (Stephen D. Sugarman & Herma Hill Kay eds., 1990) (two-thirds of awards are temporary); Mary E. O'Connell, *Alimony After No-Fault: A Practice in Search of a Theory*, 23 New Eng. L. Rev. 437, 437 (1988) (few women have ever gotten alimony); Bureau of the Census, U.S. Dep't. of Commerce, Current Population Reports Series P-60-200: Money Income in the U.S. (Sept. 1998) 42 Table 11.

26. *See* Maryland Gender Bias Report, Maryland Special Joint Comm., *Gender Bias in the Courts* 59–62 (1989) ("without diminishing current lifestyle").

27. *See* Oldham, *Feminization of Poverty*, *supra* note 28, at 843, 868–69, 843 (feminization of poverty; procedural rules, including rule that child support obligees do not have the right to information about increases in income of child support obligors and that obligees bear full costs of finding this information out through costly litigation); Uniform Marriage & Divorce Act Sect. 316 (a), 9A U.L.A. 147, 489–90; Marsha Garrison, *Child Support and Children's Poverty*, 28 Fam. L.Q. 475, 482 (1994) (erosion of value of awards over time); Joel F. Handler, *Symposium: Institutional Barriers to Women in the Workplace: Women, Families, Work, and Poverty*, 6 U.C.L.A. L. Rev. 375, 421 (1996) (same).

28. *See* June Carbone, *Redefining Family as Community*, 31 Hous. L. Rev. 359, 385 n. 135 (1994) (90 percent of divorced mothers remain primary caregivers); Child Support Enforcement Amendments of 1984 (42 U.S.C. 651). *See* J. Thomas Oldham, *Abating the Feminization of Poverty: Changing the Rules Governing Post-Decree Modification of Child Support Obligations*, 1994 B.Y.U. L. Rev. 841, 858 (in theory child support guidelines move away from need) [hereinafter Oldham, *Feminization of Poverty*]; Nancy D. Polikoff, *Looking for the Policy Choices Within an Economic Methodology*, 1986 Women's Legal Def. Fund's Nat'l Conf. on the Dev. of Child Support Guidelines 27, 33; Robert H. Mnookin & D. Kelly Weisberg, *Child, Family & State* 269–70 (1995) (majority of states' models described); Bartlett & Harris, *supra* note 8, at 429–40 (quoting

Marianne Takas, *Improving Child Support Guidelines: Can Simple Formulas Address Complex Families,* 26 Fam. L.Q. 171 (1992)); Teitelbaum, *supra* note 25, at 1825.

29. *See* Bartlett & Harris, *supra* note 6, at 430 (caps are common); Minn. Stat. Ann. Section 518.551, subd. 5 (b) (West Supp. 1997) (Minnesota); Sharon J. Badertscher, *Note: Ohio's Mandatory Child Support Guidelines: Child Support or Spousal Maintenance?* 42 Case W. Res. L. Rev. 297, 301, 316 (1992) (Ohio).

30. *See* Lenore Weitzman, *The Divorce Revolution* 30–31 (1985) (most homes sold); Starnes, *supra* note 19, at 80 n.52 (children move to cheaper housing); Mary A. Glendon, *The New Family and the New Property* 94 (1981) [hereinafter Glendon, New Family] (same); Marsha Garrison, *The Economics of Divorce, Changing Rules, Changing Results,* in *Divorce Reform at the Crossroads* 75, 82, 88 (Stephen D. Sugarman & Herma Hill Kay eds., 1990) (same) [hereinafter Crossroads]; Jonathan Kozol, *Savage Inequalities* 54–55 (1991) (quality of schools linked with housing).

31. *See* Frank Levy & Richard C. Michel, *The Economic Future of American Families: Income and Wealth Trends* 19–21 (1991) (importance of college to earnings); Mnookin & Weisberg, *supra* note 28, at 271 (eleven states; California study, *quoting* Judith S. Wallerstein & Shauna B. Corbin, *Father-Child Relationships After Divorce: Child Support and Educational Opportunity,* 20 Fam. L.Q. (No. 2) 109 (1986)); Barbara Ehrenreich, *Fear of Falling* (1989) ("fear of falling"); Barbara Bennett Woodhouse, *Towards a Revitalization of Family Law,* 69 Texas L. Rev. 245, 268–70 (1990) (final quote).

32. *See* John H. Langbein, *The Twentieth Century Revolution in Family Wealth Transmission,* 86 Mich. L. Rev. 722, 734–36 (1988).

33. The average American commutes twenty minutes each way, so a worker working eight hours a day would typically be away from home slightly less than nine hours. Joan Williams, *Gender Wars: Selfless Women in the Republic of Choice,* 66 N.Y.U. L. Rev. 1559, 1597 (1991).

34. Amy Wax, *Bargaining in the Shadow of the Market,* 84 Va. L. Rev. 509, 585 (1998) ("powerful cultural expectations"). *See* Diane Ehrensaft, *When Women and Men Mother,* in *Mothering: Essays in Feminist Theory* 41 (Joyce Trebilcot ed., 1983) (twelve minutes); Graeme Russell & Norma Radin, *Increased Paternal Participation,* in *Fatherhood and Family Policy* 139, 142 (Michael Lamb & Abraham Sagi eds., 1983) (twelve to twenty-four minutes); Michael Lamb et al., *A Biosocial Perspective on Paternal Behavior and Involvement,* in *Parenting Across the Lifespan: Biosocial Dimensions* 111, 127 (Jane B. Lancaster et al. eds., 1987) (three times as much).

35. Jane Waldfogel, *Understanding the "Family Gap" in Pay for Women with Children,* 12 J. Econ. Persp. 143 (10–15 percent); Victor R. Fuchs, *Women's Quest for Economic Equality* 52 (1988) (3:4, 3:1).

36. For "courts and commentators acknowledge," see Elizabeth Smith Beninger & Jeanne Wielage Smith, *Career Opportunity Cost,* 16 Fam. Legal Q. 201, 203 (1982); Carol S. Bruch, *Property Rights of De Facto Spouses Including Thoughts on the Value of Homemakers' Services,* 10 Fam. L. Q. 101, 110–14 (1974); B. F. Kiker, *Divorce Litigation: Valuing the Spouses' Contributions to the Marriage,* 16 Trial 48, 48 (Dec. 1980). *See also* Dusky, *supra* note 23, at 318 (higher raises for men with wives at home); Sally F. Goldfarb, *Marital Partnership and the Case for Permanent Alimony,* in *Alimony: New Strategies for Pursuit and Defense* 45 (American Bar Ass'n, 1988) (single fathers).

37. Since the entitlement proposed stems from the dominant family ecology, it is limited to families with children. This does not mean that sharing is never justified in families without children. For arguments that marriages involving children should be treated differently than marriages without children, see Mary Ann Glendon, *Family Law,* 44 La. L. Rev. 1553, 1560 (1984); J. Thomas Oldham, *Putting Asunder in the 1990s,* 80 Cal. L. Rev. 1091, 1129 (1992) [Oldham, *Putting Asunder*]; *Fixed Rules, supra* note 19, at 1167, 1169–78, 1182–83; Susan M. Okin, *Justice,*

Gender, and the Family 183 (1989); Judith Younger, *Light Thoughts and Night Thoughts on the American Family*, 76 Minn. L. Rev. 891, 900–7 (1992).

38. *See, e.g.,* Joan M. Krauskopf, *Theories of Property Division/Spousal Support: Searching for Solutions to the Mystery,* 23 Fam. L. Q. 253 (1989); Cynthia Starnes, *supra* note 19, at 124.

39. Ira M. Ellman, *Should the "Theory of Alimony" Include Nonfinancial Losses and Motivations,* 1991 B.Y.U. L. Rev. 259, 274 (1991) (first quote); Dusky, *supra* note 23, at 320 (second).

40. *See* Mary Becker, *Barriers Facing Women in the Wage-Labor Market,* 53 U. Chi. L. Rev. 934, 948 (1986); Eleanor Maccoby & Robert Mnookin, *Dividing the Child* 112, 116 (1992).

41. *See* Jacob Mincer & Solomon Polachek, *Family Investments in Human Capital,* in *Economics of the Family* 397 (Theodore W. Schultz, ed., 1974) (1.5 percent); college-educated wives can lose as much as 4.3 percent).

42. For a judicial expression of this position, see Lesman v. Lesman, 88 A.D.2d 153, 159 (N.Y. App. Div. 1982) ("Every unsuccessful marriage results in the disappointment of expectations, financial as well as non-financial, but it does not result in a financial loss in a commercial sense").

43. In Re Ramer, 231 Cal. Rptr. 647, 652 (Cal. Ct. App. 1986).

44. My proposal is similar to others that propose to place the needs of children over the right of the noncustodial parent. *See Family Law, supra* note 37, at 1558–60; Weitzman, *supra* note 30, at 266–67; Rutherford, *Duty in Divorce: Shared Income as a Path to Equality,* 58 Fordham L. Rev. 539, 585–88 (1990). But *see* Oldham, *Putting Asunder, supra* note 37, 1125 ("Many, myself included, would find it unfair to burden unduly the noncustodial parent's ability to remarry"). It depends, of course, on what one means by "unduly," but I suspect my definition would diverge from Sugarman's.

45. *See* Milton C. Regan, Jr., *Spouses and Strangers,* 82 Geo. L. J. 2303, 2395 (1994) [hereinafter Regan, *Spouses and Strangers*].

46. *See* Peggy A. Thoits, *Negotiating Roles,* in *Spouse, Parent, Worker: On Gender and Multiple Roles* 11, 19 (Faye J. Crosby ed., 1987) (the more affluent, the less likely); Susan A. Ostrander, *Women of the Upper Class* 42, 49 (1984) (quote).

47. *See* Lixandra Uresta, *It's Her Job Too,* Fortune, Feb. 2, 1998, at 64.

48. *See* Lloyd Cohen, *Marriage, Divorce, and Quasi Rents,* 41 J. Legal Stud. 267, 279, 286 (1987) (quote; remarriage rates); Zoe Moss, *It Hurts to Be Alive and Obsolete,* in *Sisterhood Is Powerful* 188 (Robin Morgan ed., 1970) (youth and looks eroticized in women); Robert E. Gould, *Measuring Masculinity By the Size of a Paycheck,* in *Men and Masculinity* 96 (Joseph Pleck & Jack Sawyer eds., 1974) ("success" eroticized in men); Wax, *supra* note 34, at 547.

49. The argument made here may be contrasted with the argument that family claims should be recognized to achieve an equitable result. *See, e.g.,* Inman v. Inman, 578 S.W.2d 266, 268 (Ky. Ct. App. 1979) ("[T]here are certain instances in which treating a professional license as marital property is the only way in which a court can achieve an equitable result"). This formulation leaves husbands' claim in the realm of entitlement, and family claims in the discretionary realm of equity, and therefore reproduces rather than solves the problems underlying the current system.

50. *See* Marsha Garrison, *Good Intentions Gone Awry: How New York's Equitable Distribution Law Affected Divorce Outcomes,* 57 Brook. L. Rev. 619, 621 (1991).

51. For other proposals to equalize standard of living, see Okin, *supra* note 37, at 179, 183; Milton C. Regan, Jr., *Family Law and the Pursuit of Intimacy* 148 (1993); Weitzman, *supra* note 30, at 337–43; Goldfarb, *supra* note 36, at 50–53; Deborah Rhode & Martha Minow, *Reforming the Questions, Questioning the Reforms,* in *Crossroads, supra* note 30, at 201, 203.

52. Thomas C. Grey, *The Disintegration of Property*, in *Property: Nomos XXII* 69 (J. Roland Pennock & John W. Chapman eds., 1980). This assumption that calling something "property" necessarily entails a permanent entitlement emerges clearly in degree cases. *See, e.g.*, Stevens v. Stevens, 492 N.E.2d 131, 134 (Ohio 1986) (stating that to consider degree as property would be unfair to professional because husband would be prevented from ever changing careers); In re Marriage of Olar, 747 P.2d 676, 680 (Colo. 1987) (holding that degree is not property because it represents opportunity to make money based on future events too indefinite to calculate); Mahoney v. Mahoney, 453 A.2d 527, 532 (N.J. 1982) (stating that degree cannot be property because of potential for inequity to failed professional, or one who chooses to change careers); DeWitt v. DeWitt, 296 N.W. 2d 761, 768 (Wis. 1980) (holding that degree is not property because person could generate less than average income but still be compelled to share something that does not exist; as property, division could not be adjusted to reflect long-term change in circumstances).

53. I would not limit the period of dependence to the age of majority. For a discussion of the central role of college in contemporary wealth transmission, see John H. Langbein, *The Twentieth Century Revolution in Family Wealth Transmission*, 86 Mich. L. Rev. 722, 734–36 (1988). For a discussion of the impact of this trend on the children of divorced parents, see Weitzman, *supra* note 30, at 278–81 (discussing impact of decreasing age of majority from twenty-one to eighteen); Woodhouse, *supra* note 31, at 269 (noting that children of divorce are less likely to obtain a college education). My proposal also differs from Okin's, in that she would equalize "for at least as long as the traditional division of labor in the marriage did and, in the case of short-term marriages that produced children, until the youngest child enters first grade and the custodial parent has a real chance of making his or her own living." *See* Okin, *supra* note 37, at 183. My approach would not be tied to proof of traditional roles; such proof would introduce too much discretion. Nor would it assume that mothers could perform as ideal workers once their children reached first grade, both because mothers' workforce participation still would be affected by the children's need for after-school care, their illnesses, and other child-care-related circumstances, and because of the long-term impact of mothers' inability to perform as an ideal worker. Note that my proposal assumes that mothers will reenter the workforce as soon as their caregiving responsibilities allow them to do so—typically by the time their youngest child reaches first grade—but it recognizes that their incomes will suffer as a result of both past and ongoing caretaking responsibilities.

54. I sometimes refer to caregivers as "mothers" because the overwhelming number are mothers. However, the entitlement I propose is triggered by caregiving, not by sex. Thus, caregivers in same-sex couples would receive it, as would caregivers who are fathers in heterosexual couples, or who become custodial parents after divorce. The entitlements typically would not be affected by joint custody arrangements, since studies have found that in most families where the parents have joint custody, the mother remains the primary caregiver. *See* Carbone, *supra* note 28, at 385 n.135 (stating that when joint custody is awarded, mothers remain responsible for more than half of child care). As Estin points out, courts have long been in the business of figuring out who the primary caregiver is. *See* Estin, *supra* note 24, at 726. To the extent that feminists are apprehensive about granting the entitlement to custodial fathers, note that the income transfer will be minimal except in cases where the noncustodial mother is earning a lot more than the custodial father.

55. Income equalization should apply in situations involving marriage because of the expectations of mutual dependence that marriage brings. However, the proposal, to be effective, would have to apply not only to formal but also to de facto marriages. Otherwise fathers could evade income equalization by refusing to marry. Some precedent exists for

treating de facto marriage the same as legal marriage. See Connell v. Francisco, 898 P.2d 831 (Wash. 1995). The 2:1 ratio is from Jana Singer, who proposes it in a somewhat different context. See Singer, *Divorce Reform and Gender Justice*, 67 N.C. L. Rev. 1103, 1117 (1989). This proposed entitlement would bring many long-married homemakers close to her husband's retirement age, during which she should be (and often is) entitled to share in his pension. See Ira Mark Ellman, *Family Law: Cases and Materials* 261–62 (3d. ed., 1992). A woman who married at age twenty, raised children the youngest of whom ceased to be dependent when she was forty, and divorced after twenty years of marriage in the same year, would receive income sharing until she reached fifty, giving her ten years to save and/or retrain for self-support. This represents the young end of the long-married homemaker scenario.

56. See Carbone, *supra* note 28, at 383 (recounting Mary Ann Glendon's description of the prototypical marriage as one that ends after four years and two children).

57. For example, if he earned $80,000 and she earned $20,000, equalizing the standards of living of the two households would give 40 percent of the combined incomes to him and 60 percent to her and the children, then income equalization would require him to pay $40,000 ($80,000 + $20,000 = $100,000; $100,000 x 0.4 = $40,000; $80,000 − $40,000 = $40,000). If her salary rose to $40,000, the amount he owed her would fall to $32,000 ($80,000 + $40,000 = $120,000 x 0.4 = $48,000; $80,000 − $48,000 = $32,000).

58. Various commentators have discussed what Jane Rutherford calls "the problem of the loafer," Rutherford, *supra* note 44, at 588–89, which occurs when the wife does all, or virtually all, of both the market and the household work; these situations may also involve domestic violence. Because my proposal is designed to award property rights to the spouse performing nonmarket labor in the dominant family ecology, it would not award income sharing to the "loafer." June Carbone raises the question of what would happen in a truly egalitarian marriage with no children, or where the parents have contributed equally to family work. See Carbone, *supra* note 28, at 407–9. This proposal would not mandate income sharing in those situations. (Note that it is important to avoid the *Doonesbury* syndrome, where the father is treated as a hero despite the fact he has contributed far less than half of family work.)

59. See Aviva Breen, *How Child Support Guidelines Address the Special Concerns of Low Income Families*, in *Critical Issues, Critical Choices: Special Topics in Child Support Guidelines Development* 155 (Women's Legal Defense Fund ed., 1987) (describing self-support set-asides); Stephen D. Sugarman, *Reforming Welfare Through Social Security*, 26 U. Mich. L. Ref. 1 (1993).

60. See Martinez v. Martinez, 754 P.2d 69, 78 (Utah Ct. App. 1988), rev'd, 818 P.2d 538 (Utah 1991).

61. Thomas v. Thomas, 346 N.W.2d 595 (Mich. Ct. App. 1984).

62. See Glendon, New Family, *supra* note 30 (some early support); Weitzman, *supra* note 30, at 110–42 (same). For courts, see Archer v. Archer, 493 A.2d 1074, 1076 (Md. 1985); for commentators, see Eric Julian Mayer, Comment, *For Richer or Poorer—Equities in the Career Threshold, No-Asset Divorce*, 58 Tul. L. Rev. 791 nn.12–13 (1984) (many family law scholars argue that property concepts do not work in degree cases); Regan, *Spouses and Strangers*, *supra* note 45 (same); Singer, *supra* note 55, at 1116–17 (same); Rutherford, *supra* note 44, at 575–77 (same).

63. See William Blackstone, 2 *Commentaries* *2; Forrest McDonald, *Novus Ordo Seclorum* 13 (1985) (not an accurate description); Restatement of Property §§ 1–4 (1936).

64. In re Graham, 574 P.2d 75 (Colo. 1978) (en banc).

65. See Hodge v. Hodge, 520 A.2d 15, 16–17 (Pa. 1986).

66. For examples, see Gardner v. Gardner, 748 P.2d 1076, 1080 (Utah 1988) ("An educational degree, such as an M.B.A., is simply not encompassed even by the broad views of the concept

of "property"); Hodge v. Hodge, 520 A.2d 15, 17 (Pa. Super. 1986) ("Since a professional license does not have the attributes of property, it cannot be deemed 'property' in the classical sense"). For a description and critique of this type of legal thought, see Felix Cohen, *Transcendental Nonsense and the Functional Approach*, 35 Colum. L. Rev. 809, 820–821 (1935); Duncan Kennedy, *Toward an Historical Understanding of Legal Consciousness*, 3 Res. In L. & Soc. 3 (1980).

67. DeWitt v. DeWitt, 296 N.W.2d 761, 768 (Wis. Ct. App. 1980) (1908 Wisconsin court); Muckelroy v. Muckelroy, 498 P.2d 1357, 1358 (1972). *See also* In re Aufmuth, 152 Cal. Rptr. 668, 667–78 (Cal. Ct. App. 1979); Todd v. Todd, 78 Cal. Rptr. 131, 135 (Cal. Ct. App. 1969). Some courts sweep away these metaphysical arguments with the impatience they deserve. *See, e.g.*, Woodworth v. Woodworth, 337 N.W.2d 332, 335 (Mich. App. 1983).

68. *See* In re Graham, 574 P.2d 75, 76–77 (Colo. 1978) (en banc) (not alienable, etc.); Curtis J. Berger & Joan C. Williams, *Property: Land Ownership and Use* 120–31 (Aspen Law and Business 4th ed., 1997) (life estates and fees tail); Robert C. Shuman, Note, *Equitable Distribution of Degrees and Licenses*, 49 Brook. L. Rev. 301 (1983) (spendthrift trusts).

69. *See* Julian Mayer, *For Richer or Poorer—Equities in the Career Threshold, No-Asset Divorce*, 58 Tul. L. Rev. 791 nn.12–13 (1984) (pensions and goodwill); Bishop v. Wood, 426 U.S. 341, 344–46 (1976) (property right in a job).

70. Todd v. Todd, 78 Cal. Rptr. 131, 135 (1969) (first quote); Kenneth J. Vandervelde, *The New Property of the Nineteenth Century*, 29 Buff. L. Rev. 325, 341–54 (1980) (dephysicalization).

71. *See* Joan Williams, *The Rhetoric of Property*, 84 Iowa L. Rev. 277, 282–289 (1998); Lucas v. South Carolina Coastal Council, 112 S. Ct. 2886, 2899–902 (1992) (court refusing to redistribute); Keystone Bituminous Coal Ass'n v. DeBenedictus, 480 U.S. 470, 493–502 (1987) (court redistributes).

72. *See* Murphy, *supra* note 19, at 219 n.49 (most judges are male); chapter 3 (successful lawyers work long hours); Hochschild, *supra* note 1, at 189–93 (ideology of gender equality); Lawrence Friedman, *The Republic of Choice* 27–38 (1990).

73. *See, e.g.*, In re Graham, 574 P.2d 75, 77 (Colo. 1978) (en banc) ("An advanced degree is a cumulative product of many years of previous education, combined with diligence and hard work."); O'Brien v. O'Brien, 66 N.Y.2d 576, 581 (Ct. App. 1985) (wife worked several jobs simultaneously and passed up an opportunity to get a teaching certificate that would have qualified her for a higher salary).

74. *See* Bureau of Census, U.S. Dep't of Commerce, *Current Population Survey* (1993) (11.4 percent of U.S. population has professional degrees). For a discussion of the class bias involved in awarding family claims only for professional degrees, see Lesli F. Burns & Gregg A. Grauer, *Human Capital as Marital Property*, 19 Hofstra L. Rev. 499, 537–40 (1990).

75. A third important drawback was that the entitlement proposed required complex calculations that necessitate expensive expert witness testimony that many wives cannot afford. *See* Burns & Grauer, *supra* note 74, at 515.

76. *See* Joan M. Krauskopf, *Theories of Property Division/Spousal Support: Searching for Solutions to the Mystery*, 23 Fam. L. Q. 253, 280 (1989) (first quote); Ellman, *supra* note 55, at 42, 67, 44, 58; Starnes, *supra* note 19, at 125, 124.

77. For protests, see Carl E. Schneider, *Rethinking Alimony*, 1991 B.Y.U. L. Rev. 197, 241–42; Robert J. Levy, *A Reminiscence About the Uniform Marriage and Divorce Act—and Some Reflections About Its Critics and Its Policies*, 1991 B.Y.U. L. Rev. 43, 64–65.

78. *See* Scott E. Willoughby, Note, *Professional Licenses as Marital Property: Responses to Some of O'Brien's Unanswered Questions*, 73 Cornell L. Rev. 133, 139 n.32 (1987) ("too speculative"); Mahoney v. Mahoney, 453 A.2d 527, 531 (N.J. 1982) (guesswork); Washburn v. Washburn, 677

P.2d 152, 162–63 (Wash. 1984) (no more speculative than wrongful death and other cases); William A. Callison, Comment, *Professional Licenses and Marital Dissolution in O'Brien v. O'Brien*, 72 Iowa L. Rev. 445, 459 (1987) (same); DeWitt v. DeWitt, 296 N.W.2d 761, 770–71 (Wis. Ct. App. 1980) (Pykman, J., concurring) (no more speculative than unvested pension claims).

79. For cases that express concern for husbands' freedom, see Mahoney v. Mahoney, 453 A.2d 527, 532 (N.J. 1982); In Re Olar, 747 P.2d 676, 678–79 (Colo. 1987); DeWitt, 296 N.W.2d at 767–68; Stevens v. Stevens, 492 N.E.2d 131, 133–34 (Ohio 1986) (servitude; final quote); Severs v. Severs, 426 So.2d 992, 994 (Fla. Dist. Ct. App. 1983) (constitutional argument); DeWitt v. DeWitt, 296 N.W.2d 761, 767 (Wisc. Ct. App. 1980) (Pykman, J., concurring); Hoak v. Hoak, 370 S.E. 2d 473, 476 (W.Va. 1988); In re Olar, 747 P.2d 676, 678 (Colo. 1987).

80. *See* Ellman, *supra* note 55, at 330–31, 451 (expressing concerns about modifications); Sugarman, *supra* note 59, at 152 ("lifetime provider").

81. The exception would be in very long-term marriages. For example, if a wife was divorced at age fifty after thirty years of marriage, using Jana Singer's 2:1 ratio, she would share income with her husband for fifteen years, until age 65 (whereupon, she would presumably receive a share of her former husband's pension). Note, as always, that the closer the wife's income is to the husband's, the less impact income sharing will have on the husband. Thus, the income transfer will typically be least where the couple has relatively egalitarian roles, and will become greater the more marginalized the wife has become.

82. A medical student with a $90,000 debt would repay a total of $260,698 for a thirty-year loan at 9 percent interest. The student would repay a total of $136,810 if the same loan was repaid within ten years. *See* Law Access, Inc., *Federal Consolidation Loans* (1994).

83. Sugarman, *supra* note 59, at 152.

84. Karen Pyke, *Women's Employment as a Gift or Burden?: Marital Power Across Marriage, Divorce, and Remarriage*, 8 Gender & Soc'y 73, 77 (1994) (first quote); Karen Dugger, *Social Location and Gender-Attitudes: A Comparison of Black and White Women*, in *The Social Construction of Gender* 46 (J. Lorber & S. A. Farrell eds., 1991) (second quote); Weitzman, *supra* note 30.

85. *See* Betty Holcomb, *Not Guilty!* 95 (*quoting* Marney Rich Keenan, *Like All Moms, Marcia Clark Can't Have It All*, March 4, 1995); Prost v. Greene, 652 A.2d 621, 624 (D.C. 1995) ("devotion to her job"); Nancy Dowd, *In Defense of Single Parent Families* 6–7 (1992) (discussing *Prost v. Greene*); Dusky, *supra* note 23, at 340–41; Margaret A. Jacobs, *Court Custody Rulings Favor At-Home Dads*, Wall St. J., July 17, 1998, at B1, B6 ("leave work by 3:00 p.m.").

86. *See* Ireland v. Smith, 542 N.W.2d 344 (Mich. Ct. App. 1995), *aff'd as modified*, 547 N.W.2d 686 (Mich. 1996) (student mother); Parris v. Parris, 460 S.E.2d 571, 573 (S.C. 1995) ("aggressive real estate agent"); Dowd, *supra* note 85, at 7–8 (discussing *Ireland* and *Parris*); Dusky, *supra* note 23, at 343–45.

87. Young v. Hector, 1998 23 Fla. App. LEXIS 7517. *See* Melody Petersen, *The Short End of Long Hours*, N.Y. Times, July 18, 1998, at B1; Jacobs, *supra* note 85, at B1, B6.

88. *See* Burchard v. Garay, 42 Cal. 3d 531, 229 Cal. Rptr. 800, 724 P. 2d 486 (1986); Peterson, *supra* note 87, at B1; Jacobs, *supra* note 85, at B1, B6.

89. 490 U.S. 228 (1989).

90. *See* Petersen, *supra* note 87, at B1; Jacobs, *supra* note 85, at B1, B6.

91. *See* Martha Ertman, *Commercializing Marriage: A Proposal for Valuing Women's Work Through Premarital Security Agreements*, 77 Tex. L. Rev. 17, 72 (cultural feminist); Martin Malin, *Fathers and Parental Leave*, 72 Tex. L. Rev. 1047 (1994) (radical feminist). In response to my 1989 article "Deconstructing Gender," I was often called a sameness feminist, up to the publication of "Is Coverture Dead?," after which I was more often associated with difference feminism.

PART II

1. Karl Kraus, *Beim Wort Genommen* 326 (1955), *quoted in* G.P. Baker & P.M.S. Hacker, 1 *Wittgenstein: Understanding and Meaning* 528 (1980).

2. *See* Joan Williams, *Privatization as a Gender Issue*, in *A Fourth Way?: Property, Privatization, and The New Democracies* 215 (Gregory S. Alexander & Grażyna Skąpska, 1993).

3. Cecilia Medina, *Toward a More Effective Guarantee of the Enjoyment of Human Rights by Women in the Inter-American System*, in Rebecca J. Cook, *Human Rights of Women: National and International Perspectives* 263 (1994).

4. *Id.* at 257.

5. Ludwig Wittgenstein, *Philosophical Investigations*, ¶109 (G.E.M Anscombe trans. 1958).

CHAPTER FIVE: *How Domesticity's Gender Wars Take on Elements of Class and Race Conflict*

1. *Ann Landers*, Wash. Post, June 17, 1996.

2. Robert L. Griswold, *Fatherhood in America: A History* 2 (1993) (gender unites men; class and ethnicity pull them apart).

3. *See* Nina Darnton, *Mommy v. Mommy*, Newsweek, June 4, 1990, at 64, 65.

4. *See* Editorial, *The Half-Baked Response to Hillary Clinton*, Wash. Post, Apr. 4, 1992, at A21; Editorial, *Deciding to Stay Home—No Piece of Cake*, Wash. Post, Mar. 28, 1992, at A19; Gwen Ifill, *The 1992 Campaign: Hillary Clinton Defends Her Conduct in Law Firm*, N.Y. Times, Mar. 17, 1992, at A20. Clinton quickly adjusted her rhetoric to signal respect for homemaking. *See* Christopher B. Daly, *Hillary Clinton Faults Washington's Values*, Wash. Post, May 30, 1992, at A10.

5. *See* Darnton, *supra* note 3, at 65; Peggy Orenstein, *The Working Mother: Almost Equal*, N.Y. Times, Sect. 6 (Magazine), Apr. 5, 1998, at 42, 47.

6. Jane J. Mansbridge, *Why We Lost the ERA* 110 (1986).

7. Donald G. Mathews & Jane Sherron De Hart, *Sex, Gender and the Politics of ERA* 160 (1990) ("libbers"), 161 (housewives no less likely support ERA), 160 (block quote), 162 ("subvert behavior"), 168 ("You Olympic swimmers").

8. Rebecca E. Klatch, *Women of the New Right* 376, 377 (1987).

9. *See* Rosalind P. Petchesky, *Abortion and Woman's Choice: The State, Sexuality, and Reproductive Freedom* (1984) (men's attempt to control women); Joan Williams, *Gender Wars: Selfless Women in the Republic of Choice*, 66 N.Y.U. L. Rev. 1559, 1573–74 (1991) (activists on both sides women).

10. Faye Ginsburg, *Contested Lives* 185 (1989).

11. Linda Gordon, *Why Nineteenth Century Feminists Did Not Support "Birth Control" and Twentieth-Century Feminists Do: Feminism, Reproduction, and the Family*, in *Rethinking the Family: Some Feminist Questions* 40, 51 (Barrie Thorne & Marilyn Yablom eds., 1982).

12. Kristin Luker, *Abortion and the Politics of Motherhood* 163 (1984).

13. Ellen Israel Rosen, *Bitter Choices: Blue-Collar Women in and Out of Work* 172 (1987).

14. The reader will note that, although this chapter discusses patterns that affect a wide range of women from the working class to the very rich, it does not address the distinct experience of poor women. As will be discussed in greater depth in chapter 6, no strategy for gender change will solve the difficulties faced by women whose poverty results not from a maldistribution of resources within the family but from a lack of resources overall. Indeed, poverty is the only context in which men and women have relatively equal labor market positions (aside from the drug trade, which is gendered male). *See generally* Elizabeth M.

Almquist, *Labor Market Gendered Inequality in Minority Groups*, 1 Gender & Soc'y 400 (1987). Yet this is not the kind of equality feminists can celebrate. Strategies for gender change must be accompanied by antipoverty strategies if feminists' goal is to help all women (as it should be).

15. Luker, *supra* note 12, at 194–95 (pro-choice women work), 195 (pro-life women less likely to work).

16. Linda Blum, *Between Feminism and Labor: The Significance of the Comparable Worth Movement* 192 (1991).

17. Arlie Hochschild, *The Time Bind: When Work Becomes Home and Home Becomes Work* 88 (1997).

18. Personal communication, James X. Dempsey, December 1980 ("that's why they pay you"); Studs Terkel, *Working: People Talk About What They Do All Day and How They Feel About What They Do* (1972); Lillian Rubin, *Worlds of Pain* 158–59 (1976) [hereinafter Rubin, *Pain*] (all quotes).

19. *See generally* Karl Marx, *Writings of the Young Marx on Philosophy and Society* (Lloyd D. Easton & Kurt H. Guddat eds., 1967); Rubin, *Pain, supra* note 18, at 159 (first block quote); personal communication, Waterbury, Connecticut, Dec. 1991 (discomfort); Mary Anna Madison, "*I Can Handle Black Men; What I Can't Handle Is This Prejudice*", in *Drylongso: A Self-portrait of Black America* 170, 173–74 (John Langston Gwaltney ed., 1980) (1993); Myra Marx Ferree, *Family and Job for Working-Class Women: Gender and Class Systems Seen from Below*, in *Families and Work* 289, 291 (Naomi Gerstel & Harriet Engel Gross eds., 1987) ("achievement in a specialized vocation"); Lillian Rubin, *Families on the Fault Line* 104 (1994) [hereinafter Rubin, *Fault Line*] ("multifaceted"); Glass Ceiling Comm'n, U.S. Dep't of Labor, *Good For Business: Making Full Use of the Nation's Human Capital* 16 (1995) (three-fourths).

20. *See* Rosen, *supra* note 13, at 171 ("a bunch of middle-class women"); Catharine A. MacKinnon, *Reflections on Sex Equality Under Law*, 100 Yale L. J. 1281 (1990) (even privileged women are oppressed by gender).

21. *See* Rubin, *Pain, supra* note 18 (58 percent of the women Rubin interviewed in the 1970s were working, mostly part time); Rubin, *Fault Line, supra* note 19, at 72 (final quote).

22. bell hooks, *Feminist Theory: From Margin to Center* (1984).

23. *See* Sarah Kuhn & Barry Bluestone, *Economic Restructuring and the Female Labor Market: The Impact of Industrial Change on Women*, in *Women, Households, and the Economy* 3, 12–13 (Lourdes Beneria & Catharine B. Stimpson eds., 1987) (prerogative of middle class); Martha May, *The Historical Problem of the Family Wage: The Ford Motor Company and the Five Dollar Day*, in *Unequal Sisters* 275 (Ellen C. Dubois & Vicki L. Ruiz eds., 1990) (family wage); Rubin, *Fault Line, supra* note 19, at 81–82 (Doug).

24. Rubin, *Fault Line, supra* note 19, at 82–83.

25. *See id.* at 93 (quotes); Majorie E. Starrels, *The Evolution of Workplace Family Policy Research*, 13 J. Fam. Issues 259, 265 (1992) (day-care data).

26. Rubin, *Fault Line, supra* note 19, at 96, 98, 99.

27. *See id.* 96–97 (split shift); Martin H. Malin, Fathers and Parental Leave 14 (1998) (draft for publication in the Northern Illinois University Law Review; on file with the author) (split shift); Rubin, *Fault Line, supra* note 19, at 94, 96–97 (quotes).

28. Rubin, *Fault Line, supra* note 19, at 75.

29. *See, e.g., id.*

30. Terkel, *supra* note 18, at 401 (Carter quote); Rosen, *supra* note 13, at 8 ("intimacy, pride and autonomy"). The view of family work as political among African-Americans is discussed below. *Cf.* James R. Green, *The World of the Worker: Labor in Twentieth-century America* 217

(1980) (working-class people living in middle-class suburbs "stay close to home and make the house a haven against a hostile, outside world"); Gita Sen, *The Sexual Division of Labor and the Working-class Family: Towards a Conceptual Synthesis of Class Relations and the Subordination of Women*, 12 Rev. Radical Pol. Econ. 76 (1980) ("almost the only institution in capitalist society"); Richard Sennett & Jonathan Cobb, *The Hidden Injuries of Class* (1973).

31. *See* Mary P. Ryan, *Cradle of the Middle Class: The Family in Oneida County, New York, 1790–1865*, at 145–85 (1986) (invented as a strategy to differentiate); Nancy F. Cott, *The Bonds of Womanhood*; Barbara Welter, *The Cult of True Womanhood: 1820–1860*, 17 Am. Q. 151 (1966); Bonnie Thornton Dill, *Our Mothers' Grief: Racial Ethnic Women and the Maintenance of Families*, 13 J. Fam. Hist. 414 (1988) (having a wife at home).

32. *See* Rodgers & Assocs., DuPont Work Life Study: Summary 2 (E.I. du Pont de Nemours & Co., Corporate News Release, Oct. 30, 1995).

33. Rubin, *Fault Line*, *supra* note 19, at 94.

34. *See* Rosen, *supra* note 13, at 119, 173.

35. Erik Olin Wright, Karen Shire, Shu-Ling Hwang, Maureen Dolan & Janeen Baxter, *The Non-Effects Class on the Gender Division of Labor in the House: A Comparative Study of Sweden and the United States*, 6 Gender and Soc'y 252, 276 (1993) (class location not a powerful determinant); Jane Riblett Wilkie, *Changes in U.S. Men's Attitudes toward the Family Provider Role, 1972–1989*, 7 Gender and Soc'y 261, 273 (1994) ("research suggests").

36. Rosen, *supra* note 13, at 169 ("not seek an egalitarian division"), 8 ("integral part"), 102–3 ("He doesn't really mind"), 103 ("source of self-esteem").

37. *See* Kuhn & Bluestone, *supra* note 23, at 22 (skidding incomes); H. Edward Ransford & Jon Miller, *Race, Sex, and Feminist Outlooks*, 48 Am. Soc. Rev. 46, 46 (1983).

38. Rosen, *supra* note 13, at 104 ("welfare," "obligation and willingness," "help," "Fairness"), 171 ("right to be taken care of," "women drive the bus").

39. Roberta Sigel, *Ambition & Accommodation* 116 (1996) (traditionalism); Rubin, *Fault Line*, *supra* note 19.

40. Sigel, *supra* note 39, at 159 (block quote); Rosen, *supra* note 13, at 159 (other quote). *See also* Ransford & Miller, *supra* note 37, at 46 (working-class males both black and white "very traditional"). As Deborah Tannen has astutely noted, one reason men who expressed less traditional views in phone interviews expressed more traditional ones in focus groups may be their concern with the impressions made on other men in the group. E-mail from Deborah Tannen to Joan Williams on June 22, 1999.

41. Sigel, *supra* note 39, at 161 (more willing to acknowledge needs for self-fulfillment); Rubin, *Fault Line*, *supra* note 19, at 89 (willing to concede).

42. Rubin, *Fault Line*, *supra* note 19, at 86.

43. Judith Stacey, *Brave New Families: Stories of Domestic Upheaval in Late Twentieth-Century America* 253 (1991).

44. *Id.* at 25 ("vehemently reject": quoting Hossfeld), 177–92 ("returned to him and his pension"), 41–89 (Pamela Gama).

45. Karen D. Pyke, *Class-Based Masculinities: The Interdependence of Gender, Class, and Interpersonal Power*, 10 Gender & Soc'y 527, 531, 538, 539, 541, 545 (1996).

46. Audre Lorde, *Who Said it was Simple* in *Chosen Poems: Old and New* 7 (1982).

47. bell hooks, *Talking Back* 42 (1989) (quoting one of her students).

48. Mary Romero, *Maid in the U.S.A.* 98 (1992) (quoting Martin & Seagrave). *See also* Karen Sacks, *Towards a Unified Theory of Class, Race, and Gender*, 16 Am. Ethnologist 534 (1989).

49. *See* Deborah K. King, *Multiple Jeopardy, Multiple Consciousness: The Context of a Black Feminist*

Ideology, 14 Signs 42, 60 (1988) (first quote) ; Paula Giddings, *When and Where I Enter: The Impact of Black Women on Race and Sex in America* (1984); Angela Y. Davis, *Women, Race, and Class* 145–46 (1981).

50. See Maxine Baca Zinn, *Feminist Rethinking from Racial-Ethnic Families,* in *Women of Color in U.S. Society* 303 (Maxine Baca Zinn & Bonnie Thornton Dill, eds., 1994) [hereinafter *Women of Color*] (divides along ethnic lines). On the Irish, see Hasia R. Diner, *Erin's Daughters in America: Irish Immigrant Women in the Nineteenth Century* (1983); Noel Ignatiev, *How the Irish Became White* (1995). See Tera W. Hunter, *To 'Joy My Freedom': Southern Black Women's Lives and Labors After the Civil War* 228–29 (1997) (black women coerced); Leith Mullings, *Images, Ideology and Women of Color,* in *Women of Color, supra* note 50, at 273 (statistics).

51. Julia Wrigley, *Other People's Children: An Intimate Account of the Dilemma Facing Middle-class Parents and the Women They Hire to Raise Their Children* 11 (1995) (first quote); Sharon Hartley, *For the Good of Family and Race: Gender, Work, and Domestic Roles in the Black Community, 1880–1930,* in *Black Women in America: Social Science Perspectives* 159, 171 (Micheline R. Malson et al. eds., 1990) ("I get full"); Teresa Amott & Julie Matthaei, *Race, Gender, and Work: A Multi-Cultural Economic History of Women in the United States* 324 tbl. 10–3 (1996) (more likely to work in domestic service).

52. See Romero, *supra* note 48, at 71, 98; Wrigley, *supra* note 51, at xi.

53. See Evelyn Nakano Glenn, *Cleaning Up/Kept Down: A Historical Perspective on Racial Inequality in "Women's Work",* 43 Stan L. Rev. 1333, 1341 (1991) (long hours in the nineteenth century); Pierrette Hondagneu-Sotelo, *Gendered Transitions: Mexican Experiences of Immigration* 555 (1994) (long hours today); Elizabeth Clark-Lewis, From Servant to Day Worker (1983) (unpublished Ph.D. dissertation, University of Maryland) (on file with the University of Maryland Library). Commentators note the irony: Evelyn Nakano Glenn, *Issei, Nisei, War Bride: Three Generations of Japanese American Women in Domestic Service* (1986); Judith Rollins, *Between Women: Domestics and Their Employers* (1985); Romero, *supra* note 48.

54. See Gina C. Adams & Nicole Oxendine Poersch, Children's Defense Fund, Key Facts about Child Care and Early Education: A Briefing Book, at B-7 (1997) (low wages paid to child-care workers).

55. Highly exploitative relationships: See Bonnie Thornton Dill, *"The Means to Put My Children Through": Child-Rearing Goals and Strategies among Black Female Domestic Servants,* in *The Black Woman* 107 (La Frances Rodgers-Rose ed., 1979); Rollins, *supra* note 53, at 153; Bonnie Thornton Dill, *"Making You Job Good Yourself": Domestic Service and the Construction of Personal Dignity,* in *Women and the Politics of Empowerment* (Ann Bookman & Sandra Morgen eds., 1988); Phyllis Palmer, *Domesticity And Dirt: Housewives and Domestic Servants in The United States, 1920–1945* (1989); Evelyn Nakano Glenn, *From Servitude to Service Work: Historical Continuities in the Racial Division of Paid Reproductive Labor,* 18 Signs 1 (1992); Romero, *supra* note 48; Glenn, *Cleaning Up/Kept Down, supra* note 53. Quote: Glenn, *Issei, Nisei, War Bride, supra* note 53, at 1337; Peggie R. Smith, *Separate Identities: Black Women, Work, and Title VII,* 14 Harv. Women's L. J. 21, 74 n. 176 (1991).

56. Peggy Cooper Davis, *Neglected Stories: The Constitution and Family Values* 12 (1997).

57. See John W. Blassingame Jr., *The Slave Community: Plantation Life in the Antebellum South* (2d. ed., 1979) (basic perquisites of masculinity); Hazel Carby, *Reconstructing Womanhood* (1987) (mammies and jezebels); Brenda E. Stevenson, *Gender Convention, Ideals, and Identity Among Antebellum Virginia Slave Women,* in *More than Chattel: Black Women and Slavery in the Americas* 169, 180 (David Gary Gaspar & Darlene Clark Hine eds., 1996) (final quote).

58. Peggy Davis, *supra* note 56, at 32, 103, 29, 35.

59. Susan A. Mann, *Slavery, Sharecropping, and Sexual Inequality,* in *Black Women in America, supra*

note 51, at 133, 139.

60. *Id.* at 139 ("Dey done it 'cause dey wanted to"); transposed into standard English, 140 (block quote: quoting Blassingame); Peggy Davis, *supra* note 56, at 93.

61. *See* hooks, *Feminist Theory, supra* note 22, at 37 (political goal); Peggy Davis, *supra* note 56, at 213–49.

62. *See* Bonnie Thornton Dill, *Fictive Kin, Paper Sons, and* Compadrazgo: *Women of Color and the Struggle for Family Survival,* in *Women of Color, supra* note 50, at 149, 155 (withdrawing wives from field work); Peggy Davis, *supra* note 56, at 24; *id.* at 143, 153 ("it is nonsense"); Jacqueline Jones, *Labor of Love, Labor of Sorrow* 147–51 (1985) (whites saw true womanhood as inappropriate for blacks); Mann, *supra* note 59, at 141 (final quote).

63. *See* Jennifer Tucker & Leslie R. Wolfe, *Defining Work and Family Issues: Listening to the Voices of Women of Color* 4 (1994) (black mothers' workforce participation); Sharon Harley, *When Your Work Is Not Who You Are: The Development of a Working-Class Consciousness Among Afro-American Women,* in *Gender, Class, Race, and Reform in the Progressive Era* 42 (Noralee Frankel & Nancy S. Dye eds., 1991) (first quote); Harley, *supra,* at 170 ("For a . . . people one generation out of slavery"), 164 ("the race needs": quoting Giles B. Jackson and D. Webster Davis), 46 (the ideal role); Patricia Hill Collins, *Black Feminist Thought: Knowledge, Consciousness, and the Politics of Empowerment* 54 (1991) ("black women wanted to withdraw"), 44 (unpaid domestic work); Sarah Fenstermaker Berk, *The Gender Factory: The Apportionment of Work in American Households* (1985) ("gender factory"); Elsa Barkley Brown, Hearing Our Mothers' Lives 11 (1986) (unpublished paper written for Fifteenth Anniversary of African-American and African Studies, Emory University).

64. Cheryl Townsend Gilkes, *"If It Wasn't for the Women . . .": African American Women, Community Work, and Social Change,* in *Women of Color, supra* note 50, at 229, 235–37 ("betterment"); personal communication, Adrienne Davis, April 1998.

65. Richard Morin, *"A Crisis": Among Blacks, Major Changes in Family Structure,* Wash. Post, Mar. 3, 1998, A5 (statistics; a man's responsibility to provide). "Significantly more traditional": *see* Ransford & Miller, *supra* note 37, at 51, 56 (middle-class black males are far more traditional than white males); 58 (for black males and females, the higher the person's social class identification, the greater the traditional outlook). The Ransford & Miller study measured both attitudes toward market work for women and attitudes toward women's suitability for political roles. It found that middle-class black males are more traditional than any other subgroup. *See id.,* at 56; Beth Willinger, *College Men's Attitudes Towards Family and Work,* in *Men, Work, and Family* 124 (Jane C. Hood, ed., 1993).

66. Zinn, *Feminist Rethinking, supra* note 50, at 304 (quoting Rapp); hooks, *Feminist Theory, supra* note 22, at 37; King, *supra* note 49, at 71 ("many . . . conditions . . . perceived as privileges"); Diane K. Lewis, *A Response to Inequality: Black Women, Racism and Sexism,* in *Black Women in America, supra* note 51, at 41, 48 ("privileges of the dominant group").

67. *See* Laura Marie Padilla, draft of a work in progress 36 (on file with author); Louise Lamphere, Patricia Zavella, Felipe Gonzales & Peter B. Evans, *Sunbelt Working Mothers: Reconciling Family and Factory* 225 (1993).

68. *See* Hondagneu-Sotelo, *supra* note 53, at 551, 559 (reluctance to delegate child care); Scott Coltrane, *Family Man: Fatherhood, Housework, and Gender Equity* 86 (1996) (average birth rates); Lamphere et al., *supra* note 67, at 226 tbl. 23 (70 percent); Wilkie, *supra* note 35, at 273–74 (Latin men express disapproval); Denise A. Segura, *Working at Motherhood: Chicana and Mexican Immigrant Mothers and Employment,* in *Mothering: Ideology, Experience, and Agency* 211, 227 (Evelyn Nakano Glenn, Grace Chang, Linda Rennie Forcey eds., 1994) (strong support for

domestic mothers and provider fathers); Mary Frances Berry, *The Politics of Parenthood* 8 (1993) (fewer Latina mothers in labor force); Amott & Matthaei, *supra* note 51, at 305 tbl. 9–4 (labor force participation differs); Villa Ortiz, *Women of Color: A Demographic Overview*, in *Women of Color*, *supra* note 50, at 13, 26–28; Patricia Zavella, *Women's Work and Chicano Families: Cannery Workers of the Santa Clara Valley* (1987).

69. *See* Esther Ngan-Ling Chow, *The Development of Feminist Consciousness Among Asian American Women*, in *The Social Construction of Gender* 256 (Judith Lorber & Susan A. Farrell eds., 1991) ("hierarchy of authority"); Rubin, *Fault Line*, *supra* note 19, at 91 (generally participate least; men in ethnic neighborhoods); In-Sook Lim, *Korean Immigrant Women's Challenge to Gender Inequality at Home: The Interplay of Economic Resources, Gender and Family*, 11 Gender & Soc'y 31 (1997) (data on Koreans).

70. Glenn, *Cleaning Up/Kept Down*, *supra* note 53, at 1343.

71. *Redstockings Manifesto*, in *Sisterhood Is Powerful* 598, 599 (Robin Morgan ed., 1970).

72. bell hooks, *Feminist Theory*, *supra* note 22, at 68.

73. *See* Rubin, *Fault Line*, *supra* note 19, at 72 (what working-class women say and do about feminism). "General agreement": *See* Rosen, *supra* note 13; Rubin, *Fault Line*, *supra* note 19, at 132; Rubin, *Pain*, *supra* note 18; Stacey, *supra* note 43, at 25; Willa Mae Hemmons, *The Women's Liberation Movement: Understanding Black Women's Attitudes*, in *The Black Woman*, *supra* note 55, at 285, 289–90 (73 percent); *Time/CNN Poll*, Time, June 29, 1998, at 58, 58 fig. (28 percent); Ginia Bellafante, *Feminism: It's All About Me!*, Time, June 29, 1998, at 54, 57 (53 percent).

74. Rubin, *Fault Line*, *supra* note 19, at 74, 76. Rubin notes that Acosta says she does not want "to be like my mom. . . . [My father] never does anything for her." *Id.* at 74. The language of reciprocity traditionally used to defend separate spheres is what Acosta uses to formulate demands on her husband: "I don't mind making him feel important; I like it sometimes. But I want him to take care of me and make me feel important, too." *Id.*

75. *See* Rubin, *Fault Line*, *supra* note 19, at 76 (pain at acknowledging the distance); Sigel, *supra* note 39, at 191 (too much invested); Rosen, *supra* note 13, at 104.

76. Rubin, *Fault Line*, *supra* note 19, at 77; Stacey, *supra* note 43, at 41–60, 64–67, 78–82.

77. Rosen, *supra* note 13, at 104 (contingent manhood); Rubin, *Pain*, *supra* note 18, at 179; 113 ("On the surface, working-class women generally seem to accept and grant legitimacy to their husbands' authority, largely because they understand his need for it. If not at home, where is a man who works on an assembly line, in a warehouse, or a refinery to experience himself as a person whose words have weight, who is 'worth' listening to?"). Working-class men's need to assert masculinity in a society where male gender performance is so closely linked to work success helps explain one pervasive feature of blue-collar jobs: the way men bond together to harass women out. *See* Barbara R. Bergmann, *Economic Emergence of Women* (1986); Vicki Schultz, *Reconceptualizing Sexual Harassment*, 107 Yale L. J. 1683 (1998). For a particularly insightful study, see Michael Yarrow, *The Gender-Specific Class Consciousness of Appalachian Coal Miners: Structure and Change*, in *Bringing Class Back In: Contemporary and Historical Perspectives* 285 (Scott G. McNall, Rhonda F. Levine & Rick Fantasia eds., 1991).

78. *See* Mullings, *supra* note 50, at 281 (full rights of manhood); Angela Davis, *supra* note 49, at 153 ("white men institutionalized slavery, white women were its most immediate beneficiaries"), 124–37 (white women are racist); Giddings, *supra* note 49, at 307–11 (fight that left them out).

79. bell hooks, *Ain't I a Woman?* 124 (1981) [hereinafter hooks, *Ain't I a Woman*] (initial quote), 18 (exaggerated expressions of chauvinism), 73 (he is hurt), 69 (compassion); Mullings, *supra* note 50, at 281 (women of color are caught). On black men's labor market position, see Jacqueline

Jones, *supra* note 62, at 147–51; Collins, *supra* note 63, at 59; Glenn, *Cleaning Up/Kept Down, supra* note 53, at 1337. Black women are far more likely than white women to rate men as economically unreliable and untrustworthy. *See* Ransford & Miller, *supra* note 37, at 58.

80. Cheryl Townsend Gilkes, *"Together and in Harness": Women's Traditions in the Sanctified Church*, in *Black Women in America, supra* note 51, at 223, 243 (initial quote). For "a strong and articulate movement," see, e.g., Lewis, *supra* note 66, at 50–51; Kimberlé Crenshaw, *Mapping the Margins: Intersectionality, Identity Politics, and Violence Against Women of Color*, in *Critical Race Theory: The Key Writings that Formed the Movement* 357 (Kimberlé Crenshaw, Neil Gotanda, Gary Peller & Kendall Thomas eds., 1995); hooks, *Feminist Theory, supra* note 22, at 73 (these two realities). *See also* Glenn, *Cleaning Up/Kept Down, supra* note 53, at 1355 (arguing for the need to keep race and class as well as gender in focus when devising and implementing feminist strategies).

81. *See* King, *supra* note 49, at 57 (initial quote), 55 (discussing criticism of black feminists "over their supposed collusion with whites in the oppression of black men"); bell hooks, *Ain't I a Woman, supra* note 79, at 5 ("What had begun as a movement to free all black people from racist oppression became a movement with its primary goal the establishment of black male patriarchy."). Recent news article: Donna Britt, *What About the Sisters? With All the Focus on the Problems of Black Men, Someone Got Left Out*, Wash. Post, Feb. 2, 1992, at F1 (black liberation must be re-visioned). *See also* Angela Davis, supra note 49, at 59–60.

82. Mullings, *supra* note 50, at 281 (Asian-American feminists criticized for weakening solidarity); Denise A. Segura, *Chicanas in White Collar Occupations: Work and the Gendered Construction of Race-Ethnicity*, in *Color, Class, and Country: Experiences of Gender* 36, 39 (Gay Young & Bette J. Dickerson eds., 1994) (betrayal of *la cultura*); Alma M. Garcia, *The Development of Chicana Feminist Discourse, 1970–1980*, in *Social Construction of Gender, supra* note 69, at 276 ("divisive ideology"); 279 (block quote). *See also* Yen Le Espiritu, *Asian American Women and Men: Labor, Laws and Love* (1997).

83. Karen Dugger, *Social Location and Gender-Role Attitudes: A Comparison of Black and White Women*, in *Social Construction of Gender, supra* note 69, at 38, 40.

84. MacKinnon, *supra* note 20, 1291–97; Robin West, *Caring For Justice* (1997); Martha A. Fineman, *Challenging Law, Establishing Differences: The Future of Feminist Legal Scholarship*, 42 Fla. L. Rev. 25, 38 (1991) ("different perspectives"); Martha Fineman, *The Neutered Mother, The Sexual Family* 48 (1995) ("gendered-life reference point"); Christine Littleton, *Does it Still Make Sense to Talk about Women?*, 1 U.C.L.A. Women's L. J. 15 (1991).

85. *See* Angela Harris, *Race and Essentialism in Feminist Legal Theory*, 42 Stan. L. Rev. 581 (1990).

86. *See* Dugger, *supra* note 83, at 38.

87. *See* Patricia Hill Collins, *Shifting the Center: Race, Class, and Feminist Theorizing about Motherhood*, in *Mothering: Ideology, Experience, and Agency, supra* note 68, at 45, 55 (Afrocentric tradition); Pierrette Hondagneu-Sotelo & Ernestine Avila, *I'm Here, But I'm There: The Meanings of Latina Transnational Motherhood*, 11 Gender & Soc'y 458, 551 (1997) (quoting Carol B. Stack & Linda M. Burton, *Kinscripts: Reflections on Family, Generation, and Culture*, in *Mothering: Ideology, Experience, and Agency, supra* note 68, at 33) (kinscription); Sylvia Ann Hewlett & Cornel West, *The War Against Parents* (1998); Marian Wright Edelman, *The Measure of Our Success* (1992).

88. Bonnie Thornton Dill, *The Dialectics of Black Womanhood*, in *Black Women in America, supra* note 51, at 65, 77. *See also* Hondagneu-Sotelo, *supra* note 53, at 563 (Chicano women have "an elastic definition of motherhood, one that included both meeting financial obligations and spending time with the children").

89. Stephen J. Rose, *Rising Fears About Incomes and Earnings* 24 (National Comm'n for Em-

ployment Policy Research Paper No. 94–02, 1994) (70 percent); Andrew Hacker, *Two Nations: Black and White, Separated, Hostile, Unequal* 94–95 & tbl. (incomes and earnings) (60 percent); Philip N. Cohen, *Replacing Housework in the Service Economy: Gender, Class, and Race-Ethnicity in Service Spending*, 12 Gender & Soc'y 219, 222 (1998) (black fathers contribute more); Beth Anne Shelton & Daphne John, *White, Black, and Hispanic Men's Household Labor*, in *Men, Work, and Family*, *supra* note 65, at 133–34 (reviewing the literature on whether black fathers contribute more, noting inconsistent conclusions). The relative earnings patterns places black women with good jobs—particularly those of working-class origins who have achieved middle-class status—in an uncomfortable position with respect to work and family. *See, e.g.*, Rhetaugh Graves Dumas, *Dilemmas of Black Females in Leadership*, in *The Black Woman*, *supra* note 55, at 203. Latinas earn 88 percent of what Latinos earn. These figures represent a slight rise for white women and Latinas and a slight fall for black women: for earlier figures, see Glenn, *Cleaning Up/Kept Down*, *supra* note 53, at 1347.

90. Carolyn Heilbrun, *Toward a Recognition of Androgyny* x (block quote); xviii, xv (1982).

91. Richard Wasserstrom, *Racism, Sexism and Preferential Treatment: An Approach to the Topics*, 24 U.C.L.A. L. Rev. 581, 604 (1977).

CHAPTER SIX: *Do Women Share an Ethic of Care?*
Domesticity's Descriptions of Men and Women

1. Christine A. Littleton, *Does It Still Make Sense To Talk About "Women"?*, 1 UCLA Women's L. J. 15, 31–32 (1991) [hereinafter Littleton, *Talk about "Women"*].

2. Pierre Bourdieu, *In Other Words: Essays towards a Reflexive Sociology* 130 (Matthew Adamson trans., 1990) ("system of perception").

3. Carol Gilligan, *In a Different Voice: Psychological Theory and Women's Development* (1982); Ellen Carol Dubois, Mary C. Dunlap, Carol J. Gilligan, Catharine A. MacKinnon, Carrie J. Menkel-Meadow, Isabel Marcus & Paul J. Spiegelman, *Feminist Discourse, Moral Values, and the Law—A Conversation*, 34 Buff. L. Rev. 11, 49–54 (1985); Joan C. Williams, *Deconstructing Gender*, 87 Mich. L. Rev. 797 (1989).

4. 479 U.S. 272 (1987) (*CalFed*). *See* Linda J. Krieger & Patricia N. Cooney, *The Miller-Wohl Controversy: Equal Treatment, Positive Action and the Meaning of Women's Equality*, in *Feminist Legal Theory: Foundations* 156 (D. Kelly Weisberg ed., 1993) [hereinafter *Foundations*]; Wendy W. Williams, *Equality's Riddle: Pregnancy and the Equal Treatment/Special Treatment Debate*, in *Foundations*, *supra*, at 128; Martha L. Fineman, *Implementing Equality: Ideology, Contradiction and Social Change*, 1983 Wis. L. Rev. 789 ; Mary Becker, *Maternal Feelings: Myth, Taboo, and Child Custody*, 1 Rev. L. & Women's Stud. 133 (1992); Lucinda M. Finley, *Transcending Equality Theory: A Way Out of the Maternity and the Workplace Debate*, 86 Colum. L. Rev. 1118 (1986); Christine A. Littleton, *Reconstructing Sexual Equality*, in *Foundations*, *supra*, at 248.

5. Ann C. Scales, *The Emergence of Feminist Jurisprudence: An Essay*, 95 Yale L. J. 1373 (1986), *reprinted in Foundations*, *supra* note 4, at 40–57; Finley, *supra* note 4, at 1160–62; Littleton, *Talk about "Women," supra* note 1, at 31–32. *See also* MacKinnon, *Difference and Dominance: On Sex Discrimination*, in *Feminism Unmodified* 32, 33–34 (1987).

6. Herma Hill Kay, *Equality and Difference: The Case of Pregnancy*, in *Foundations*, *supra* note 4, at 180, 181–82; Sylvia A. Law, *Rethinking Sex and the Constitution*, 13 U. Pa. L. Rev. 952, 963–69 (1984).

7. *See* MacKinnon, *supra* note 5, at 33–36 (only one way of framing the issues); Catharine A. MacKinnon, *Desire and Power*, in *Feminism Unmodified*, *supra* note 5, at 46, 50–51, 53–54 (the eroticizing of dominance).

8. Terri Apter, *Working Women Don't Have Wives* 26 (1993).

9. Michele Ingrassia & Pat Wingert with Karen Springen & Debra Rosenberg, *The New Providers*, Newsweek, May 22, 1995, at 36, 36.

10. Stephanie Coontz, *Social Origins of Private Life* 58 (1988) (quote).

11. Gilligan, *supra* note 3, at 66 ("moral person"), 54 ("endlessly giving"), 136 ("selfless"), 93 ("example of hard work"), 70 ("interpersonal, empathetic": *quoting* Norma Haan, *Hypothetical and Actual Moral Reasoning in a Situation of Civil Disobedience*, 32 Personality & Soc. Psychol. 255–70 (1975)), 69 ("empathy and compassion"), 62 ("ideal of care"), 28 ("not a math problem"), 169 ("women's sense of self").

12. *See* Robin West, *Jurisprudence and Gender*, 55 U. Chi. L. Rev. 1, 20 (1988); Carol Gilligan, *supra* note 3, at 69 ("seeking to reinterpret").

13. *See* Gilligan, *supra* note 3, at 80–82 (Denise).

14. *See* Celeste Michelle Condit, *Decoding Abortion Rhetoric* 135–36 (1990).

15. *See* Gilligan, *supra* note 3, at 71 (initial quote; dialectical mixture). Commentators: Leslie Bender, *A Lawyer's Primer on Feminist Theory and Tort*, 38 J. Legal Educ. 3 (1988); Carrie Menkle-Meadow, *Portia in a Different Voice*, 1 Berkeley Women's L. J. 39 (1985); Hilary Charlesworth, Christine Chinkin & Shelley Wright, *Feminist Approaches to International Law*, 85 Am. U. Int'l. L. Rev. 615 (1991); Marjorie Kornhauser, *The Rhetoric of the Anti-Progressive Tax Movement*, 86 Mich. L. Rev. 465 (1987); Kit Kinports, *Evidence Engendered*, 1991 U. Ill. L. Rev. 413.

16. Betty Holcomb, *Not Guilty!* 100 (1998) (block quote).

17. *Id.* at 89 (*Newsweek*: quoting Ingrassia et. al., *supra* note 9); John Gray, *Men Are from Mars, Women Are from Venus* 18 (1992) (first advice); *id.* at 19 ("a woman's sense of self"), 22 (men focus on achievement); Gilligan, *supra* note 3, at 162–63, 170.

18. Deborah Tannen, *You Just Don't Understand: Women and Men in Conversation* (1990).

19. *See, e.g.,* Deborah Tannen, *Talking from 9 to 5: Women and Men in the Workplace* 14–17 (1994) (disclaimer).

20. Deborah Tannen, *The Relativity of Linguistic Strategies: Rethinking Power and Solidarity in Gender and Dominance*, in *Gender and Conversational Interaction* 165, 165–66 (Deborah Tannen ed., 1993); Deborah Tannen, *Gender and Discourse* 8 (1994).

21. Jeanne L. Schroeder, *Feminism Historicized: Medieval Misogynist Stereotypes in Contemporary Feminist Jurisprudence*, 75 Iowa L. Rev. 1135, 1143 n.12 (1990).

22. Earlier strategy of embracing domesticity: *See* Sara Evans, *Born for Liberty: A History of Women in America* 67–143 (1989) (discussing emergence of women's associational activity). *See also* Barbara Leslie Epstein, *The Politics of Domesticity: Woman, Evangelism, and Temperance in Nineteenth-Century America*, 115–151 (1981) (describing growth of Woman's Christian Temperance Union), Evelyn Brooks Higgenbotham, *Righteous Discontent: The Women's Movement in the Black Baptist Church, 1880–1920* (1993).

23. *See* Offer of Proof Concerning the Testimony of Dr. Rosalind Rosenberg, ¶¶ 1, 11, 16–22, EEOC v. Sears, Roebuck & Co., 628 F. Supp. 1264 (N.D. Ill. 1986) (No. 79-C-4373), *aff'd*, 839 F.2d 302 (7th Cir. 1988).

24. *See* Gilligan, *supra* note 3, at 33–37. This leaves out a third group of women, who found Gilligan's description unconvincing. *Cf.* Joan Nestle, *The Persistent Desire: A Femme-Butch Reader* (1992).

25. Many thanks to the patience with which friends and colleagues have helped me toward this formulation: Adrienne Davis, Suzanne Lebsock, Jana Singer, and Robin West.

26. Richard Wasserstrom, *Racism, Sexism and Preferential Treatment: An Approach to the Topics*, 24 U.C.L.A. L. Rev. 581, 604 (initial quote), 606 ("the assimilationist ideal"), 615 ("strong pre-

sumptive case") (1977). Wasserstrom calls it an assimilative ideal and the idea itself assimilation; I have avoided this terminology since it has come to mean something different in feminist jurisprudence. This strategy is related in important ways to what one prominent analyst of race has called the dominant language of color evasiveness in the United States. See Ruth Frankenberg, *White Women, Race Matters: The Social Construction of Whiteness* 145 (1993).

27. Finley, *supra* note 4, at 1139.

28. Gender display: See Erving Goffman, *The Presentation of Self in Everyday Life* (1959); Erving Goffman, *Gender Advertisements* (1988). Women as sex objects: See Alice Echols, *Daring to Be Bad: Radical Feminism in America* (1989).

29. Group Rights, Victim Status, and the Law: The Eighth Annual Federalist Society Lawyers Convention (1996).

30. See Katherine M. Franke, *The Central Mistake of Sex Discrimination Law: The Disaggregation of Sex from Gender*, 144 U. Pa. L. Rev. 1 (1995); Mary Anne Case, *Disaggregating Gender from Sex and Sexual Orientation: The Effeminate Man in the Law and Feminist Jurisprudence*, 105 Yale L. J. 1 (1995); Francisco Valdez, *Queer Margins, Queer Ethics: A Call to Account for Race and Ethnicity in the Law, Theory, and Politics of "Sexual Orientation,"* 48 Hastings L. J. 1293 (1997).

31. This example comes from a sociology article I have been unable to relocate, despite sustained effort.

32. *The American Heritage Dictionary of the English Language* (3d ed., 1992) (definition of nurture).

33. See, e.g., Barbara J. Risman, *Intimate Relationships from a Microstructural Perspective: Men Who Mother*, 1 Gender & Soc. 6 (1987).

34. See Barrie Thorne, *Gender Play* 44–45 (1993) (gendered playground); id. at 49–50 (neighborhood groups), 5, 158–59 (situations where gender does not play an important role).

35. Id. at 97–100 (exaggerated masculinity).

36. See, e.g., Jeffrey Z. Rubin, Frank J. Provenzano & Zella Luria, *The Eye of the Beholder*, in *Beyond Sex-role Stereotypes* 179 (Alexandra G. Kaplan & Joan P. Bean 1976).

37. See Monci Jo Williams, *Women Beat the Corporate Game*, Fortune, Sept. 12, 1988, at 128; Leila Ahmed, *Women and Gender in Islam* 223–24 (1992); Statham et al., *Gender And University Teaching: A Negotiated Difference* 65–86 (1991).

38. *The African Queen* (Horizon Enterprises, 1951).

39. See Robin West, *Caring for Justice* 13 (1997).

40. See Judith Lorber, *Paradoxes of Gender* 207 (1994) (secretarial role); William R. Beer, *Househusbands: Men and Housework in American Families* xxi (1983) (block quote).

41. Nancy F. Cott, *The Bonds of Womanhood* 67 (initial quote), 68 ("embodied a protest"), 71 (women's self-renunciation") (1977). See Joan C. Williams, *Domesticity as the Dangerous Supplement of Liberalism*, 2 J. Women's Hist. 69 (1991) [hereinafter Williams, *Domesticity*] (Marxism you can bring home to mother).

42. West, *Jurisprudence and Gender, supra* note 12, at 1 (separation thesis; claims trivially true of men), 7 ("essentially connected"), 3 ("material consequences").

43. Id. at 3 (masculine jurisprudence).

44. See James Kloppenberg, *The Virtues of Liberalism* (1998).

45. See generally Williams, *Domesticity, supra* note 41.

46. Charles Taylor used the phrase, "fit loosely into our traditions," in a George Washington University symposium in 1994. Neither he nor I can recall where it appears in published work.

47. See Joan C. Tronto, *Moral Boundaries: A Political Argument for an Ethic of Care* 109 (Scottish

Enlightenment), 107 (set her hair, piano tuning), 112 (caregiving jobs) (1993).

48. Carrie Menkle-Meadow, *What's Gender Got to Do with It?: The Politics and Morality of an Ethic of Care*, 12 N.Y. U. Rev. L. & Soc. Change, 265, 287 (1998).

49. *See* Judith Butler, *Bodies that Matter* 231 (1993) (not carried out according to expectation).

50. West, *Jurisprudence and Gender, supra* note 12, at 7.

51. Thanks to Liam Murphy and Amy Adler for helping me think through these issues. *Cf.* Ludwig Wittgenstein, *Philosophical Investigations* ¶79 (G. E. M. Anscombe trans. 1970).

52. *See* Bureau of Labor Statistics, U.S. Department of Labor, Unpublished Marital and Family Tabulations from the Current Population Survey, tbl. A (1995) ("Work Experience of Wives by Husbands' Annual Earnings in 1994, by Presence and Age of Children, Educational Attainment of Wives, and Race and Hispanic Origin, Primary Families, March 1995"). In analyzing this data, I have used husband's income as a proxy for class.

53. *See* Sylvia Ann Hewlett & Cornel West, *The War against Parents* (1998).

54. *See* Nancy Dowd, *In Defense of Single-Parent Families* 55–102 (1997).

55. *But see* Audre Lorde, *The Master's Tools Will Never Dismantle the Master's House*, in *Sister Outsider: Essays and Speeches by Audre Lorde* 110 (1984).

56. Evidence of the speed-up: *See* Anne E. Tergensen, *Survivors of Corporate Layoffs Bear Heavy Burden*, Record, July 5, 1996, at A1; Stephen S. Roach, *A Battle over Fruit from Productivity*, Buffalo News, Apr. 2, 1995, at 7; Paul Weinberg, *Canada—Labor: Auto Workers Take on General Motors and Win*, Inter Press Serv., Oct. 25, 1996; Paul Casciato, *GM Striking Workers Dig In, City Braces*, Reuters, Oct. 3, 1996. Their needs as mothers: *See* Sue Myrick, *GOP Response to President Clinton's Weekly Radio Address*, Fed. News Serv. Mar. 15, 1997; Linda Feldmann, *How Congress Wants to Balance Work and Family*, Christian Sci. Monitor, Feb. 25, 1997, at 1. A larger role for government: *See* Albert R. Hunt, *Clinton's Edge with Women Goes Far Beyond Abortion Issue*, Wall St. J., Sept. 20, 1996, at R1 (final quote); *Why Women Like Big Government: Explaining the Gender Gap*, Christianity Today, Nov. 11, 1996, at 112; Robin Toner, *With GOP Congress the Issue, "Gender Gap" Is Growing Wider*, N.Y. Times, Apr. 12, 1996, at A1.

57. *See* Peter D. Hart Research Assocs. & Mellman Group, The Economic Situation Facing Working Families (1996); Peter D. Hart Research Assoc's & Mellman Group, Summary of Opinion Research on Living Standards (May 6, 1996).

58. Poster published by Working Women's Department of the AFL-CIO in 1997.

59. Judith Butler, *Gender Trouble: Feminism and the Subversion of Identity* 34 (1990).

60. Carol Tavris, *Mismeasure of Women* 247 (1992).

61. *Id.* at 263 (quote); Lillian Rubin, *Worlds of Pain* 125 (1976) (second quote).

62. *See* Katherine Dennehy & Jeylan T. Mortimer, *Work and Family Orientations of Contemporary Adolescent Boys and Girls*, in *Men, Work, and Family* 89–90 (Jane C. Hood ed., 1993).

63. *See* Jane Waldfogel, *Understanding the "Family Gap" in Pay for Women with Children*, 12 J. Econ. Persp. 137, 156 (1998).

64. *See The New Jewish Encyclopedia, Hillel* (1962).

65. *See* Menkle-Meadow, *What's Gender Got to Do with It?, supra* note 48, at 293.

CHAPTER SEVEN: *Do Women Need Special Treatment? Do Feminists Need Equality?*

1. *Introduction* to Aristotle, *Politics*, Book III, Chapter 8, p. 593 (Richard McKeon ed., 1947).

2. Pablo Perez Tremps, IV Curso "Mujer v Derechos Humanos," Movimiento Manuela Ramos, December 1998 (presentation on equality and difference).

3. Orr v. Orr, 440 U.S. 268 (1979).

4. On "tender years" and its demise, see Rena K. Uviller, *Father's Rights and Feminism: The Maternal Presumption Revisited*, 1 Harv. Women's L. J. 107 (1978); on the impact of eliminating the maternal presumption see Martha Albertson Fineman, *Feminist Theory in Law: The Difference It Makes*, 2 Colum. J. Gender & L. 1, 10 (1992); Mary Becker, *Prince Charming: Abstract Equality*, in *Feminist Legal Theory: Foundations* 225 (D. Kelly Weisberg ed., 1993).

5. See Martha Albertson Fineman, *The Illusion of Equality: The Rhetoric and Reality of Divorce Reform* 46–52 (1991).

6. Karl Marx, *Critique of the Gotha Program*, in *The Marx-Engels Reader* 531 (Robert C. Tucker, ed., 2d ed. 1978). For a similar argument, see Patricia A. Cain, *In Search of a Normative Principle for Property Division at Divorce*, 1 Tex. J. Women & L. 249 (1992) (book review). An exception is for children's needs; hence the importance of framing post-divorce obligations in terms of children's needs where women's dependence stems from children's needs. See Barbara Bennett Woodhouse, *Hatching the Egg: A Child-Centered Perspective on Parents' Rights*, 14 Cardozo L. Rev. 1747 (1993); letter from Barbara Bennett Woodhouse to Joan C. Williams (Aug. 24, 1992) (on file with author).

7. See, e.g., Suzanne Duyea and Miguel Székely, *The Haves and the Have-Nots*, Inter-American Development Bank, Office of the Chief Economist, Latin American Economic Policies, No. 5, 4th quarter, 1998, at 1 (income distribution in Latin America the most unequal in the world).

8. See, e.g., Thomas L. Haskell, *The Curious Persistence of Rights Talk in the "Age of Interpretation*," in *The Constitution and American Life* 324 (David Thelen ed., 1988); *The Constitution and American Life*, *supra*, *passim*. See International Covenant on Economic, Social and Cultural Rights, *reprinted in A Compilation of International Instruments*, vol. 1: *Universal Instruments* (1994); International Covenant on Civil and Political Rights, *id.* at 20; Declaration on the Elimination of Discrimination against Women, *id.* at 145; Annual Report of the Inter-American Commission on Human Rights 519–39 (1993).

9. MacKinnon, *Difference and Dominance*, in *Feminism Unmodified* 32, 37 (1987). See Katharine Bartlett & Angela Harris, *Gender and Law: Theory, Doctrine, Commentary* 64 (1998) (dividing feminist theory into small arena of formal equality and large arena of substantive equality).

10. Ludwig Wittgenstein, *Philosophical Investigations* ¶38 (G.E.M. Amscombe trans., 3d ed., 1958) (language on holiday).

11. Reed v. Reed, 404 U.S. 71 (1971).

12. Frontiero v. Richardson, 411 U.S. 677 (1973); Weinberger v. Wiesenfeld, 420 U.S. 636 (1975); Califano v. Goldfarb, 430 U.S. 199 (1977); Healy v. Edwards, 363 F. Supp. 1110 (E.D. La. 1973), *vacated and remanded for consideration of mootness*, 421 U.S. 772 (1975); Duren v. Missouri, 439 U.S. 357 (1979); Linda K. Kerber, *No Constitutional Right to Be Ladies* 124–220 (1998) (jury rules linked with women's domestic roles).

13. See David Cole, *Strategies of Difference*, 2 J. L. & Ineq. 33, 53–58 (1984). Ginsberg's understanding of Social Security probably stemmed in part from her stint as a secretary in a Social Security office when she followed her husband during his military service. See Jay Matthews, *The Spouse of Ruth: Marty Ginsburg, The Pre-Feminist Feminist*, Wash. Post, June 19, 1993, at B1 (worked in Social Security office).

14. See Wendy W. Williams, *Equality's Riddle: Pregnancy and the Equal Treatment/Special Treatment Debate*, in *Foundations*, *supra* note 4, at 144; Wendy W. Williams, *Notes From A First Generation*, 1989 U. Chi. Legal F. 99

15. Código Civil de Guatemala, Art. 114, Párrafo IV. This section of the code was upheld against a constitutional challenge in the Corte de Constitucionalidad, República de Guatemala, C.A. Expediente 84–92, and has been filed in the Inter-American Commis-

sion. The Commission has decided that the petition is admissible. Morales de Sierra v. Guatemala, Case 11.625, Report # 28/98. Inter-Am. C. H. R., OEA/Ser.L/V/II.98, Doc. 6 rev, (1998) at 148.

16. Código Civil de Peru, Art. 293, Título II in Collection Jurídica Inkari, analizado y comentado por Dr. Hernan Figueroa Estremadoyro (1998) (author's translation).

17. *See* Jean L. Potuchek, *Who Supports the Family? Gender and Breadwinning in Dual-Earner Marriages* (1997).

18. Men in the United States earn, on average, 70 percent of the household income. Stephen Rose, *On Shaky Ground: Rising Fears about Incomes and Earning*, National Commission for Employment Policy Research Report no. 94–02 (1994).

19. Alda Facio, *Cuando El Género Suena, Cambios Trae* 73–86 (1996).

20. *See, e.g.*, Ex Parte Devine, 398 So.2d 686 (Ala. 1981) (best interests of the child standard).

21. *See, e.g.*, 23 Pa. Cons. Stat. Ann. $3701(a) (West 1991) (alimony available to either party).

22. *See, e.g.*, N.J. Stat. Ann. 9:2–4(c) (West 1993) (extent and quality of time spent with child relevant to custody).

23. *See* Harry D. Krause, et al., *Family Law: Cases, Comments, and Questions* 793 (4th ed., 1998) (downward shift in duration of typical alimony award).

24. *See* Katharine Bartlett & Angela Harris, *Gender and Law: Theory, Doctrine, Commentary* 457–64 (1998) (information on the impacts of joint custody).

25. *See* Martha L. Fineman, *Challenging Law, Establishing Differences: The Future of Feminist Legal Scholarship*, 42 Fla. L. Rev. 25 (1990)[hereinafter Fineman, *Challenging Law*].

26. *See, e.g.*, Lawrence Friedman, *Rights of Passage: Divorce Law in Historical Perspective*, 63 Or. L. Rev. 649, 652 (1984); Capps v. Capps, 216 Va. 382 (1975) (physical cruelty).

27. *See., e.g.*, Uniform Marriage & Divorce Act Sect. 308.

28. *See* Convention on the Rights of the Child, 28 I.L.M. 1457 art. VII (1989) (United States and Somalia are the two countries who have not signed).

29. *See* Bartlett & Harris, *supra* note 24, at 457–64.

30. *See* Mary Kate Kearney, *Symposium: Children and the Law. The New Paradigm in Custody Law: Looking at Parents with a Loving Eye*, 28 Ariz. St. L. J. 543, 553 (1996)(summarizing critiques of best interest standard: it "too easily can become a summary of an individual's prejudices.")

31. *See* Karen Syma Czapanskiy, Santa Clara L. Rev. (1999) (forthcoming). Czapanskiy builds upon Elizabeth Scott's suggestion that custody should track the proportions of caregiving performed by the parents before divorce. *See* Elizabeth S. Scott, *Pluralism, Parental Preference, and Child Custody*, 80 Cal. L. Rev. 615 (1992). Note that the Czapanskiy model would give equal rights to primary-caregiver fathers and primary-caregiver mothers. It would also give fathers who had participated more in caregiving during the marriage greater rights upon divorce, thereby building into marriage an incentive for fathers to move toward equal parenting.

32. MacKinnon, *supra* note 9, at 36.

33. *See* Jane Waldfogel, *Understanding the "Family Gap" in Pay for Women with Children*, 12 J. Econ. Persp. 137 (1998).

34. *See* Jane Waldfogel, *The Effect of Children on Women's Wages*, 62 Am. Soc. Rev. 202, 209 (1997).

35. *See* Elizabeth M. Schneider, *Describing and Changing: Women's Self-Defense Work and the Problem of Expert Testimony on Battering*, 14 Women's Rts. L. Rep. 213, 218–30 (1992).

36. *See* Susan Estrich, *Rape*, 95 Yale L.J. 1087 (1986).

37. Joshua Dressler, *Understanding Criminal Law* 524 (1987) (resistance typically increases likelihood that a woman will suffer bodily harm).

38. *See* Roger Atwood, *Peru Strikes Law that Allowed Marriage After Rape*, Reuters North Amer-

ican Wire, April 4, 1997, Friday, BC cycle, LEXIS/NEXIS (about fifteen Latin American countries have rape laws that exonerate the rapist if he marries his victim).

39. *See* ‹http://www.whitehouse.gov›.

40. Hewlett, *infra* note 87, at 174.

41. *See Challenging Law, supra* note 25 (minimize or deny); Fineman, *Illusion, supra* note 5, *passim* (illusion of equality). *See also* Martha L. Fineman, *The Politics of Custody and the Transformation of American Custody Decision Making,* 22 U.C. Davis L. Rev. 829 (1989); Martha Fineman, *Implementing Equality: Ideology, Contradiction and Social Change,* 1983 Wisc. L. Rev. 789 [hereinafter Fineman, *Implementing Equality*]. *See* Mary Becker, *supra* note 4, at 229 (at the expense of women who are caregivers); Fineman, *Challenging Law, supra,* at 25 (same); Hewlett, *infra* note 87, at 143 (final quote).

42. *See* Linda J. Krieger & Patricia N. Cooney, *The Miller-Wohl Controversy: Equal Treatment, Positive Action and the Meaning of Women's Equality,* in *Foundations, supra* note 4, at 128.

43. *See* Christine A. Littleton, *Reconstructing Sexual Equality,* in *Foundations, supra* note 4, at 253–255 (assimilation), 254 (social males); Fineman, *Implementing Equality, supra* note 41, at 813 (description of liberal feminists); Fineman, *Challenging Law, supra* note 25, at 36 (feminism has hurt poor women); Lucinda L. Finley, *Transcending Equality Theory: A Way Out of the Maternity and the Workplace Debate,* in *Foundations, supra* note 4, at 197 (ideal of homogeneous assimilation); Mary E. Becker, *supra* note 4, at 221 (final quote).

44. *See* Wendy W. Williams, *Equality's Riddle: Pregnancy and the Equal Treatment/Special Treatment Debate,* in *Foundations, supra* note 4 at 144; Wendy W. Williams, *Notes From A First Generation,* 1989 U. Chi. Legal F. 99 (later article; quote).

45. *See* Ruth Bader Ginsburg, *Gender and the Constitution,* 44 U. Cin. L. Rev. 1, 28–30 (1975) (initial quote); *id.* at 30 (Ginsburg in 1975), 31 ("extended study programs"), 40 (final quote).

46. *See* Fineman, *Illusion, supra* note 5, at 57 (reformers), 18–20 (custodial mothers need more); 70 (one third to 50 percent).

47. *See* Krieger & Cooney, *supra* note 42, at 159–65; Becker, *supra* note 4, at 229.

48. *See* David Von Drehle, *Redefining Fair with a Simple Careful Assault: Step-by-Step Strategy Produced Strides for Equal Protection,* Wash. Post, July 19, 1993, at A1.

49. *See* Candace Kovacic-Fleischer, United States v. Virginia's *New Gender Equal Protection Analysis with Ramifications for Pregnancy, Parenting and Title VII,* 50 Vand. L. Rev. 845, 869–70 (1997). (Ginsburg's goal even today is to establish strict scrutiny for gender); Ginsburg, *supra* note 45, at 27.

50. *See* Tony Mauro, *Ginsburg Nominated,* USA Today, June 15, 1993, at 1A (personal prudishness; all-male courtrooms); *The Supreme Court: Excerpts from Senate Hearing on the Ginsburg Nomination,* N.Y. Times, July 22, 1993, at A20 ("distracting associations").

51. Though some feminists have become dissatisfied with the distinction between sex and gender, it remains indispensable when examining work and family issues, as discussed in chapter 6 (endnote 30).

52. Herma Hill Kay, *Equality and Difference: A Perspective on No-Fault Divorce and Its Aftermath,* 56 U. Cin. L. Rev. 1, 80 (1987) (block quote). *See also* Barbara Stark, *Burning Down the House: Toward a Theory of More Equitable Distribution,* 40 Rutgers L. Rev. 1173, 1179 (1988).

53. Herma Hill Kay, *Commentary: Toward a Theory of Fair Distribution,* 57 Brook. L. Rev. 755, 763 (1991) (block quote). *See, e.g.,* June Carbone & Margaret Brinig, *Rethinking Marriage: Feminist Ideology, Economic Change, and Divorce Reform,* 65 Tul. L. Rev. 953 (1991) (Kay under fire).

54. Instead, commentators define their goal as a "new theory of alimony." For a list of scholars working in the area, *see* Joan Williams, *Is Coverture Dead, Beyond a New Theory of Alimo-*

ny, 82 Geo. L. Rev. 2227, 2227–28 & n. 2.

55. *See* Katherine T. Bartlett & Carol B. Stack, *Joint Custody, Feminism and the Dependency Dilemma*, 2 Berkeley Women's L. J. 9 (1986).

56. *See* Bartlett & Stack, *supra* note 51, at 37 (actual or threatened abuse); Eleanor MacCoby & Robert Mnookin, *Dividing the Child* (1993) (substantial majority).

57. Bartlett & Stack, *supra* note 51, at 30, 34.

58. Conversations with Katherine T. Bartlett, spring 1998. Bartlett now advocates a standard proposed by Elizabeth Scott, which bases custody on who did what during the marriage, in sharp contrast to the earlier proposal to make the division of labor during the marriage irrelevant. *See* Elizabeth S. Scott, *Pluralism, Parental Preference, and Child Custody*, 80 Cal. L. Rev. 615, 617 (1992). Bartlett also proposes abandoning custody altogether in favor of parenting plans. Nonetheless, for purposes of the text, the important point is that Bartlett, like Kay, quickly abandoned her proposal to eliminate an entitlement designed to help caregivers. My thanks to Professor Jana Singer for sharing her encyclopedic knowledge on these issues.

59. *See* Lynn A. Baker & Robert E. Emery, *When Every Relationship Is Above Average: Perceptions and Expectations of Divorce at the Time of Marriage*, 17 L. & Hum. Behav. 439 (1993).

60. *See* Brief Amici Curiae of the National Organization for Women; NOW Legal Defense and Education Fund; Nat'l Bar Ass'n, Women Lawyers' Division, Washington Area Chapter; National Women's Law Center; Women's Law Project; and Women's Legal Defense Fund in Support of Neither Party, *CalFed*, 479 U.S. 272 (1987) (No. 85–494) (*passim*).

61. *See* BMW v. Gore, 517 U.S. 559 (1996); Honda Motor Co. v. Oberg, 512 U.S. 415 (1994); TXO Production Corp. v. Alliance Resources, 509 U.S. 443 (1993); Pacific Mutual Life Insurance v. Haslip, 499 U.S. 1 (1991); Browning-Ferris Indus. v. Kelco Disposal, Inc., 492 U.S. 257 (1989) (O'Connor often sides with business interests). My thanks to my colleague Andrew Popper for his help in identifying these cases.

62. *See, e.g.*, Hawaii Hous. Auth. v. Midkiff, 467 U.S. 229 (1984) (O'Connor's commitment to an unfettered market).

63. *See* Ann E. Freedman, *Sex Equality, Sex Differences, and the Supreme Court*, 92 Yale L. J. 913 (1983).

64. *See* Martin Malin, *Fathers and Parental Leave*, 72 Tex. L. Rev. 1047 (1994) (critics argue); 29 U.S.C. § 2612(a)(1)(B) (1994) (paid twelve-week leave for adoption); 29 U.S.C. § 2612 (a)(1)(A) (1994) (same for birth).

65. Sheila M. Smith, Comment, *Justice Ruth Bader Ginsburg and Sexual Harrassment Law* 63 U. Cin. L. Rev. 1893, 1905 (1995).

66. Sylvia Ann Hewlett, *A Lesser Life: The Myth of Women's Liberation in America* 147 (1987).

67. MacKinnon, *supra* note 9, at 36–37 (men's bodies and biographies).

68. Littleton, *Reconstructing Sexual Equality, supra* note 43, at 251 ("Acceptance does not"), 250–53 (symmetry and asymmetry); Christine A. Littleton, *Equality and Feminist Legal Theory*, 48 U. Pitt. L. Rev. 1043 (1987) (earlier on).

69. W. W. Williams, *Equality's Riddle, supra* note 44, at 143.

70. Samuel Issacharoff & Elyse Rosenblum, *Women and the Workplace: Accommodating the Demands of Pregnancy*, 94 Colum. L. Rev. 2154, 2158 (1994). *See, e.g.*, Hewlett, *A Lesser Life, supra* note 66, at 87 (discussions often blur).

71. *See* Martha Fineman, *The Neutered Mother, The Sexual Family and Other Twentieth Century Tragedies* 48 (1995).

72. *Id.* at 232.

73. *See* Littleton, *Reconstructing Sexual Equality, supra* note 43.

74. *See* Malin, *supra* note 64 (split shift data); Kathleen Gerson, *No Man's Land* 8, 319 tbl. 4. Kathleen Gerson's 1993 study found that 13 percent of her sample of fathers "had become, or planned to become equal or primary caretakers"; *id.* at 12. A figure documenting how many men actually carried out their plans would be more useful, since this is an arena full of good intentions unfulfilled.

75. *See* Mona L. Schuchmann, *The Family and Medical Leave Act of 1993: A Comparative Analysis with Germany*, 20 J. Corp. L. 331, 339, 341–42 (1995) (business interests).

76. *See* Christine A. Littleton, *Does It Still Make Sense to Talk About "Women"?*, 1 U.C.L.A. Women's L. J. 15, 49 (1991)[hereinafter Littleton, *Talk About "Women"*].

77. *See* Becker, *supra* note 4, at 233.

78. Lorraine Dusky, *Still Unequal: The Shameful Truth About Women and Justice in America* 314 (1996).

79. *See* Mary Jo Bane, *Household Composition and Poverty: Which Comes First?* in *Fighting Poverty: What Works and What Doesn't* 209, 227–28 (Sheldon H. Danziger & Daniel H. Weinberg eds., 1986).

80. *See* John P. Robinson & Geoffrey Godbey, *Time for Life: The Surprising Ways Americans Use Their Time* 105 tbl. 3 (1997).

81. *See* Janet Taber, Margurite T. Grant, Mary P. Huser, Rise B. Norman, James R. Sutton, Clarence C. Wong, Louise E. Parker & Claire Picard, *Gender, Legal Education, and the Legal Profession: An Empirical Study of Stanford Law Students and Graduates*, 40 Stan L. Rev. 1209 (1988).

82. *See* Kathleen Gerson, *No Man's Land* 8, 319 tbl. 4 (1993) (some men do a little, some a lot).

83. *See* Arlie Hochschild, *The Second Shift: Working Parents and the Revolution at Home* (1989); Lilian B. Rubin, *Families on the Fault Line* (1994); interview, Cambridge, Massachusetts, November 1993 (upper-middle class party); personal observation, Waterbury, Connecticut, Dec. 1997 ("Mom, not maid").

84. *See* Rubin, *supra* note 81, at 91–92 (quotes); Erle Stanley Gardner, *A Perry Mason Mystery: The Case of the Half-Wakened Wife* 131(1945); The Status of Latina Women (Films in the Humanities 1993) (Colombian executive).

85. Mary Jordan, *Japanese Court Rules for Wife in Housework Suit; Husband Had Demanded Cooking, Cleaning*, Wash. Post, Aug. 2, 1997, at A1.

86. The statement that men cannot afford, emotionally and economically, to share equally in family work is not to deny the existence of a leisure gap between men and women. *See* Sue Headlee & Margery Elfin, *The Cost of Being Female* 51 (1996) (men in dual-career families have more leisure than women).

87. Hochschild, *supra* note 81.

88. *See* Judith Lorber, *Paradoxes of Gender* 164 (1994) (Sweden); *Parental Leave in Europe*, 262 European Indus. Rel. Rev. 14, 14–23 (1995) (Norway); Barbara Bergmann, *Saving Our Children from Poverty* 287–88 (1996) (France).

89. *See* Hewlett, *supra* note 68, at 142–148 (some feminists); Fineman, *Neutered Mother, supra* note 69, at 230–32; Interview with Martha Fineman, July 1998. *See also* Sylvia Ann Hewlett & Cornel West, *The War Against Parents* (1998).

90. *See* Bergmann, *supra* note 86, 287–88 (France); Linda Haas, *Equal Parenthood and Social Policy: A Study of Parental Leave in Sweden* 158–60 (1992) (Sweden).

91. *See* Gina C. Adams & Nicole Oxendine Poersch, Children's Defense Fund, *Key Facts About Child Care and Early Education: A Briefing Book* A-1–A-5 (1997).

92. Family and Medical Leave Act of 1993, 29 U.S.C.§ 2601 *et seq.* (1994).

93. *See* Fineman, *The Neutered Mother, supra* note 69, at 161–64 (1995) (inevitable dependen-

cy); *id.* at 230–36 (public support).

94. *See id.* at 230–33.

95. *See* Nancy Polikoff, *We Will Get What We Ask For: Why Legalizing Gay and Lesbian Marriage Will Not "Dismantle the Legal Structure of Gender in Every Marriage,"* 79 Va. L. Rev. 1535 (1993); Roger N. Lancaster, *Life Is Hard: Machismo, Danger, and the Intimacy of Power in Nicaragua* 46 (1992) (block quote).

96. *See* William N. Eskridge Jr., *The Case for Same-Sex Marriage: From Sexual Liberty to Civilized Commitment* (1996) (popularity of marriage): Elijah Anderson, *Street Wise: Race, Class, and Change in an Urban Community* 113 (1990).

97. Rich literature, discussed in Marion Crain, *Feminism, Labor, and Power,* 65 S. Cal. L. Rev. 1819 (1992); Marion Crain, *Feminizing Unions: Challenging the Gendered Structure of Wage Labor,* 89 Mich. L. Rev. 1155, 1157 (women and minorities being organized faster) (1991); Marion Crain, *Images of Power in Labor Law: A Feminist Deconstruction,* 33 B.C. L. Rev. 481 (1992). *See* John Schmeltzer, *UPS Shapes Up to Ship Out,* Chi. Trib., Nov. 10, 1997, at C3 (shift at AFL-CIO).

98. This is not to say that good public policy has no effect. The level of household work in Sweden by husbands in dual-earner households is a little higher than in the United States (25 percent as opposed to 20 percent). Erik Olin Wright et al., *The Non-Effects of Class on the Gender Division of Labor in the Home: A Comparative Study of Sweden and the United States,* 6 Gender & Soc'y 252, 267.

99. The statements in this paragraph stem from conversations and public statements by Csilla Kollonay Lehoczky and other feminists from the former Communist bloc at a conference jointly sponsored by the University of Connecticut and the Network for East/West Women: The Workshop on the Status of Women in New Market Economies, April 13–14, 1996. *See* Mala N. Htun, *Women, the Law and the Judiciary in Latin America: Issue Brief,* in Women's Leadership Conference of the Americas (Washington, D.C., forthcoming 1999) (manuscript at 10, on file with author, cited with permission); Nuevo Código del Trabajo de Chile d. fl. num. 1 art. 203 (employer must provide day-care center if more than twenty workers are employed).

100. Interview with Lidia Casas-Becerra, Facultad de Derecho, Universidad Diego Portales, Santiago, June 1998. *See* Htun, *supra* note 97, at 10; Joan Williams, *Privatization as a Gender Issue,* in *A Fourth Way?: Privatization, Property, and the Emergence of New Market Economies* 218 (1994) (unemployment in Russia).

101. United States v. Virginia, 518 U.S. 735 (1996). *See* Candace Kovacic-Fleischer, United States v. Virginia's *New Gender Equal Protection Analysis with Ramifications for Pregnancy, Parenting and Title VII,* 50 Vand. L. Rev. 845 (1997).

CHAPTER EIGHT: *The New Paradigm Theorized: Domesticity as Drag*

1. John Dewey, *Philosophy and Democracy* (1918), *reprinted in* John Dewey, 11 *The Middle Works, 1899–1924,* 43–44 (Jo Ann Boydston ed., 1982). For a related vision of reconstruction in jurisprudence, see Angela P. Harris, *Foreword: The Jurisprudence of Reconstruction,* 82 Cal. L. Rev. 741 (1994).

2. *See* John Dewey, *Reconstruction in Philosophy* 26 (1948, originally published 1920) (precious values). *See generally* Robert B. Westbrook, *John Dewey and American Democracy* (1991) (democracy).

3. bell hooks, *Feminist Theory: From Margin to Center* 73 (1984).

4. *Carter's Score on Minority Hiring,* U.S. News & World Rep., Apr. 25, 1977, at 59 (quoting Bella Abzug).

5. I came across this statement when I was reading the work of Lewis and Rose Lamb Coser in connection with a case for which I was an expert witness. Despite extensive effort

I have not been able to locate its source.

6. See *Uncertain Terms: Negotiating Gender in American Culture* 7–8 (Faye Ginsburg & Anna Lowenhaupt Tsing eds., 1990) (fragmented selves); Judith Butler, *Gender Trouble* 140–41 (1990) (gender is not a stable identity); Lillian B. Rubin, *Worlds of Pain: Life in the Working-Class Family* 160 (1976); Raymond Williams, *Culture 201* (1981), *quoted in* Alan Sinfield, *The Wilde Century* 17 (1994) (quote).

7. See Weinberger v. Weisenfeld, 420 U.S. 636 (1975) (survivors' benefits); Catharine A. MacKinnon, *Difference and Dominance*, in Catharine A. MacKinnon, *Feminism Unmodified: Discourses on Life and Law* 36 (1987) (affirmative action for white men); Alda Facio, *Cuando El Género Suena Cambios Trae* 104 (1996), *translated, with minor changes by author*, in 1 Pan-American Conference on Transforming Women's Legal Status, Washington, D.C., November 3–6, 1997: *Pre-Conference Reader on Gender and the Law*, at 1.

8. See Asya Pazy, *The Persistence of Pro-Male Bias Despite Identical Information Regarding Causes of Success*, 38 Organizational Behavior & Human Decision Processes 366, 369 (1986), *cited in* Katherine T. Bartlett & Angela P. Harris, *Gender and Law* 288 (1989).

9. See also Neuren v. Adduci, Matriani, Meeks & Schill, 43 F.3d 1507 (D.C.Cir. 1995) (written evaluation of attorney noted, "Extremely difficult on staff. A bitch!").

10. Some women professionals, no doubt, do treat staff in inappropriate ways. The argument is that expectations placed on women professionals often make it more difficult for women professionals than for men to maintain good working relationships.

11. See Emily Campbell & Alan J. Tompkins, *Gender, Race, Grades, and Law Review Membership as Factors in Law Firm Hiring Decisions: An Empirical Study*, 18 J. Contemp. L. 211, 241–242 (1992); Ezold v. Wolf, Block, Schorr & Solis-Cohen, 938 F.2d 509 (3d Cir. 1992), *cert. denied*, 510 U.S. 826 (1993).

12. Pierre Bourdieu, *The Logic of Practice* 56 (Richard Nice trans., 1990; originally published in French 1980).

13. See Ginia Bellafante, *Feminism: It's All About Me!*, Time, June 29, 1998, at 54.

14. See, *e.g.*, Paolo Freire, *The Pedagogy of the Oppressed* (1993).

15. I take the "click" metaphor from the Costa Rican human rights psychologist Gilda Pacheco Oreamuno.

16. See Linda Hamilton Krieger, *The Content of Our Categories: A Cognitive Bias Approach to Discrimination and Equal Employment Opportunity*, 47 Stan. L. Rev. 1161, 1190, 1197, 1202, 1204 (1995). See also Charles R. Lawrence, *The Id, the Ego, and Equal Protection: Reckoning with Unconscious Racism*, 39 Stan. L. Rev. 317, 381–84 (1987) (discrimination often unconscious; default modes).

17. See Deborah L. Rhode, *Equal Rights*, Nat'l L. J., Feb. 2, 1998, at A19; Richard H. Chused, *The Hiring and Retention of Minorities and Women on American Law School Faculties*, 137 U. Pa. L. Rev. 537 (1988); Deborah J. Merritt & Barbara F. Reskin, *The Double Minority: Empirical Evidence of a Double Standard in Law School Hiring of Minority Women*, 65 S. Cal. L. Rev. 2299 (1992); Robert J. Borthwick & Jordan Schau, Note, *Gatekeepers of the Profession: An Empirical Profile of the Nation's Law Professors*, 25 U. Mich. J. L. Ref. 191 (1991).

18. See Deborah J. Merritt, Barbara F. Reskin & Michelle Fondell, *Family, Place, and Career: The Gender Paradox in Law School Teaching*, 1993 Wisc. L. Rev. 395. The study found the presence of children was not the determining factor. The sense that the family should move to follow the breadwinner's job, and that more men than women were considered breadwinners, probably was the determining factor in many cases. Other relevant data was that partnered women were less likely than partnered men to get teaching jobs; presumably many partnered women did not look for them because they knew they could not relocate. *Id.* at 438.

19. See Joan M. Krauskopf, *Touching the Elephant: Perceptions of Gender Issues in Nine Law Schools*,

44 Legal Educ. 311, 327 (1994); Christine Haight Farley, *Confronting Expectations: Women in the Legal Academy*, 8 Yale J. L. & Feminism 333 (1996), *cited in* Katherine T. Bartlett & Angela P. Harris, *Gender and Law* 288 (1989).

20. *See* Krieger, *supra* note 16, at 1193.

21. *See* Suzannah Bex Wilson, *Eliminating Sex Discrimination in the Legal Profession: The Key to the Widespread Social Reform*, 67 Ind. L. J. 817, 828 (1992) (male lawyers likely to be married to homemakers but female lawyers are not); Deborah Jones Merritt & Barbara F. Reskin, *Sex, Race & Credentials: The Truth about Affirmative Action in Law Faculty Hiring*, 97 Colum. L. Rev. 199, 256 (1997) (strongest positive factor).

22. *See* Ezold v. Wolf, Block, Schorr & Solis-Cohen, 983 F.2d 509, cert. denied, 510 U.S. 826 (1993).

23. *See, e.g.*, Washington v. Davis, 426 U.S. 229 (1976) (to be actionable under the constitution, discrimination must be intentional); Myra Ferree & Julia McQillan, *Gender-Based Pay Gaps: Methodological and Policy Issues in University Salary Studies*, 12 Gender & Soc'y 7, 8 (1998) (quote); Krieger, *supra* note 16, at 1239–46.

24. The gravity of Venus is .903 that of earth; Mars' is .380. *See* U.S. Geological Survey, *The Planet Venus* (last modified May 1, 1997) ⟨http://wwwflag.wr.usgs.gov/USGSflag/Space/wall /venus.html⟩; U.S. Geological Survey, *The Planet Mars* (last modified May 1, 1997) ⟨http:// wwwflag.wr.usgs.gov/USGSflag/Space/wall/mars.html⟩.

25. Karen D. Pyke, *Class-Based Masculinities: The Interdependence of Gender, Class, and Interpersonal Power*, 10 Gender & Soc'y 527, 528 (1996) (initial quote). Feminist jurisprudence would benefit from increased exposure to the work of linguists and sociologists exploring the production of gender through social interaction. *See* Deborah Tannen, *Gender and Discourse* 10 (1994); Scott Coltrane, *Household Labor and the Routine Production of Gender*, 36 Soc. Probs. 473 (1989); Candace West & Sarah Fenstermaker, *Power, Inequality, and the Accomplishment of Gender: An Ethnomethodological View*, in *Theory on Gender/Feminism on Theory* 151 (Paula England ed., 1993); Candace West & Don H. Zimmerman, *Doing Gender*, in *The Social Construction of Gender* 13 (Judith Lorber & Susan A. Farrell eds., 1991); Faye Ginsburg & Anna Lowenhaupt Tsing, *Introduction*, in *Uncertain Terms: Negotiating Gender in American Culture* 1, 5 (Faye Ginsburg & Anna Lowenhaupt Tsing eds., 1991) (discussing complexities and heterogeneity of gender) [hereinafter *Uncertain Terms*].

26. *See* Catharine A. MacKinnon, *Difference and Dominance: On Sex Discrimination*, in *Feminism Unmodified: Discourse on Life and Law* 32, 40 (1987) [hereinafter MacKinnon, *Difference and Dominance*] ("on the first day"); Ellen Dubois, Mary Dunlap, Carol Gilligan, Catharine MacKinnon & Carrie Menkel-Meadow, *Feminist Discourse, Moral Values, and the Law: A Conversation*, 34 Buffalo L. Rev. 11, 49–54 (1985) ("in what voice women speak").

27. *See* Catharine A. MacKinnon, *Feminism, Marxism, Method, and the State: Toward Feminist Jurisprudence*, 8 Signs 635 (1983) (initial quote). Long literature on work and family: *See, e.g.*, Sarah F. Berk, *The Gender Factory* (1985); Marion Crain, *Between Feminism and Unionism: Working Class Women, Sex Equality, and Labor Speech*, 82 Geo. L. J. 1903 (1994) (reviewing literature on socialist feminism). Women tend to marry older and wealthier men: *See* Leah Guhhenheimer, *A Modest Proposal: The Feminomics of Drafting Premarital Agreements*, 17 Women's Rts. L. Rep. 147, 148–51 (1996).

28. *See* MacKinnon, *Feminism Unmodified*, *supra* note 26, at 3, 2; Kathryn Abrams, *Sex Wars Redux: Agency and Coercion in Feminist Legal Theory*, 95 Colum. L. Rev. 304 (1995).

29. *See* Kimberlé Crenshaw, *Mapping the Margins: Intersectionality, Identity Politics, and Violence against Women of Color*, in *Critical Race Theory: The Key Writings that Formed the Movement* 357 (Kim-

berlé Crenshaw, Neil Gotanda, Gary Peller, & Kendall Thomas eds., 1995) (intersectionality); Pierre Bourdieu, *In Other Words* 126 (Matthew Adamson trans., 1990) (quote); *The Social Location of Gender* 38 (Judith Lorber & Susan A. Farrell eds., 1991) (social location).

30. *See* Barbara Y. Welke, *When All the Women Were White, and All the Blacks Were Men: Gender, Class, Race, and the Road to Plessy, 1855–1914*, 13 Law & Hist. Rev. 261, 277 (1995) (ladies' cars); David Roediger, *The Wages of Whiteness* (1991).

31. bell hooks, *Ain't I a Woman?* 127 (1981) (feminists and racism).

32. *See* Judith Butler, *Bodies that Matter* 231 (1993) [hereinafter Butler, *Bodies that Matter*].

33. On the gendering of institutions, *see* Joan Acker, *Hierarchies, Jobs, Bodies: A Theory of Gendered Organizations*, 4 Gender & Soc'y 139 (1990).

34. For examples of the negotiation metaphor in anthropology, see *Uncertain Terms, supra* note 25, *passim*. Many examples from sociology can be found in the journal *Gender & Society*.

35. *See* Anne Statham, *Gender and University Teaching: A Negotiated Difference* 65–86 (1991).

36. I take the image of a range of masculinities and femininities from the poet Joan Retallack. She and I use it to refer to opening up possibilities. Sociologists also use the term "masculinities" to stress the different experience of masculinities of different social classes. *See* sources cited in Pyke, *supra* note 25, at 528.

37. *See* Deborah Fallows, *A Mother's Work* 27–32 (1985).

38. *See* West & Zimmerman, *supra* note 25, at 17 (discussing E. Goffman's concept of "gender display").

39. *See Life Course Dynamics: 1960s–1980s* (Glen H. Elder Jr. ed., 1985) (defining study of the life cycle); Nancy Levit, *The Gender Line* 37–42 (1998) (gendering of children); presentation by Elizabeth Crow, Editor-in-Chief of *Mademoiselle*, to the National Leadership Council of the Harvard Divinity School, Jan. 28, 1996 (citing surveys of twenty-somethings); H. Wesley Perkins & Deborah K. DeMeis, *Gender and Family Effects on the "Second Shift": Domestic Activity of College-Educated Adults*, 10 Gender & Soc'y 78 (1996) (after children).

40. Louis Uchitelle, *Women in Their Fifties Follow Many Paths into Workplace*, N.Y. Times, Nov. 28, 1994, at B8 (women in their 50s). *But see* Ruth Sidel, *Women & Children Last* 158 (1986) (higher rates of poverty among elderly women than among elderly men).

41. New sexual idioms: *See, e.g.*, Butler, *Gender Trouble, supra* note 6; Butler, *Bodies that Matter, supra* note 32. *See* Sara Ruddick, *Maternal Thinking*, in *Mothering: Essays in Feminist Theory* 213, 226 (Joyce Trebilcot ed., 1983) (quote).

42. *See* Carol Gilligan, *In a Different Voice: Psychological Theory and Women's Development* 81–82 (1982) (Denise); Carin Rubenstein, *The Sacrificial Mother* 15–23 (1998) (selfless motherhood); Celeste Michelle Condit, *Decoding Abortion Rhetoric* 135–36 (1990) (selflessness rhetoric in abortion context); Michel Foucault, *Power/Knowledge* 98–99 (1972).

43. Ludwig Wittgenstein, *On Certainty* 6e (G.E.M. Anscombe & G.H. von Wright trans., 1969).

44. William James, *On a Certain Blindness in Human Beings*, reprinted in *Talk to Teachers on Psychology: And to Students on Some of Life's Ideals* (1958) (1907).

45. *See* Violence Against Women Act, 42 U.S.C. §§ 14031–14040 (1995).

46. Barbara Crosette, *Afghan Women Demanding End to Their Repression by Militants*, N.Y. Times, Apr. 6, 1998, A1 (quoting an Afghan woman, once a schoolteacher).

47. *Cf.* Richard Rorty, *The Consequences of Pragmatism* xlii (1982).

48. To say that widespread agreement exists is not to say that these principles are always *observed*, only that breaches of them are considered shocking and indefensible by broad sectors of the world community. A recent example is the reaction to the murder of Bishop Juan

Gerardi in Guatemala.

49. Existing terms are Female Genital Mutilation (FGM), Female Genital Cutting (FGC), and Female Genital Surgery (FGS). FGM seems so judgemental that it is bound to precipitate defensiveness. On the other hand, FGS is problematic because we associate surgeries with therapeutic value, which this procedure most certainly does not have. FGC avoids both of these pitfalls. Perhaps the best-known defender of "Irua" is Jomo Kenyatta. Jomo Kenytta, *Facing Mount Kenya: The Traditional Life of the Gikuyu* 130–54 (1938) (African Writer Series 1979). *See also* Robyn Cerny Smith, *Female Circumcision: Bringing Women's Perspectives into the International Debate*, 65 S. Cal. L. Rev. 2449, 2460 (1992) (presentation of arguments in favor of FGC).

50. *See* Hope Lewis, *Between Irua and "Female Genital Mutilation": Feminist Human Rights Discourse and the Cultural Divide*, 8 Harv. Hum. Rts. J. 1 (1995); Daliah Setareh, *Women Escaping Genital Mutilation: Seeking Asylum in the United States*, 6 U.C.L.A. Women's L. J. 123 (1995); Isabelle R. Gunning, *Arrogant Perception, World-Travelling, and Multicultural Feminism: The Use of Female Genital Surgeries*, 23 Col. Hum. Rts. L. Rev. 189, 195 (1991–92); Smith, *supra* note 49. *See also* Anouar Majid, *The Politics of Feminism in Islam*, 23 Signs 321, 323 (1988).

51. *See* sources cited in note 50.

52. *But see* Gunning, *supra* note 50, at 222 (midwives); 193 (arguing against any penal measures in the absence of consensus). *See* Richard Posner, *The Problematics of Moral and Legal Theory*, 111 Harv. L. Rev. 1637, 1664 (1998).

53. *See* Bronwyn Winter, *Women, the Law and Cultural Relativism in France: The Case of Excision*, 19 Signs 943 (1994).

54. *See* Joan C. Williams, *Culture and Certainty*, 76 Va. L. Rev. 713 (1990) (sharing a culture); Layli Miller Bashir, *Female Genital Mutilation in the United States: An Examination of Criminal and Asylum Law*, 4 Am. U. J. of Gender & Law 415, 435 (1996) (story of Fauziya). *See also* Lewis, *supra* note 50, at 24–27.

55. *See* Winter, *supra* note 53.

56. *See* Isabel R. Gunning, *Female Genital Surgeries and Multicultural Feminism: The Ties that Bind; The Differences that Distance*, in Women's Rts. & Trad. Law: A Conflict, Third World Legal Studies—1994–95.

57. Lewis, *supra* note 50, at 54.

58. *See* L. Amede Obiora, *Bridges and Barricades: Rethinking Polemics and Intransigence in the Campaign Against Female Circumcision*, 47 Case W. Res. L. Rev. 275 (1997). Various commentators have noted the danger that Western feminists might place excessive emphasis on FGC to the exclusion of economic issues that are "even more important to most African women, such as poverty or maternal mortality rates." But feminists should not allow others to set up a zero-sum game in which different feminist agendas are played off against each other. Both FGC and maternal mortality are important. The zero-sum game mentality often arises in contexts where the implicit assumption is that only one program will be targeted to helping women. This is unacceptable. Women are half the world. *See, e.g.,* Frances Elizabeth Olsen, *Feminism in Central and Eastern Europe*, 106 Yale L. J. 2215, 2224 (1997); Gunning, *supra* note 50, at 225.

59. *See* Majid, *supra* note 50, at 321 (veil used as a justification for wars and colonialism). *See* Leila Ahmed, *Women and Gender in Islam* 149, 152, 153 (1992) (remainder of information).

60. Ahmed, *supra* note 59, at 88.

61. *See id.* at 224 (both quotes); Lama Abu-odeh, *Post-Colonialism and the Veil*, 26 New Eng. L. Rev. 1509 (1992) (cross-class solidarity).

62. *See* Amy Kesselman, *The "Freedom Suit": Feminism and Dress Reform in the United States*,

1848–1875, 5 Gender & Soc'y 495 (1991) (nineteenth century); Alice Echols, *Daring to Be Bad: Radical Feminism in America, 1967–1975*, at 92–101 (1989) (twentieth century).

63. *See, e.g.,* Butler, *Gender Trouble, supra* note 6, at 134–140; Duncan Kennedy, *Sexy Dressing Etc.: Essays on the Power and Politics of Cultural Identity* 163–70 (1993).

64. Ahmed, *supra* note 59, at 194 (initial quote).

65. *See* Deborah Tannen, *Talking from 9 to 5: Women and Men in the Workplace—Language, Sex and Power* 112–13 (dress is marked).

FOUR THEMES OF CONCLUSION

1. Mary Joe Frug, *Securing Job Equality for Women: Labor Market Hostility to Working Mothers,* 59 B.U.L. Rev. 55, 98-99 (1979).

2. Juliet Schor, *The Overworked American* 43 (1992).

3. *Accord* June O'Neill, *Women & Wages,* The Am. Enterprise, Nov.–Dec. 1990, at 25, 31; Sharon L. Harlan & Catherine White Berheide, Barriers to Work Place Advancement Experienced By Women in Low-Paying Occupations 14 (January 1994) (unpublished manuscript, on file with the *Federal Glass Ceiling Commission*) (providing that women are predominantly found in these "dead-end jobs").

4. Richard Posner, *The Problematics of Moral and Legal Theory,* 111 Harv. L. Rev. 1637, 1667 (1998) ("moral entrepreneurship").

5. Cynthia Fuchs Epstein, Robert Saute, Bonnie Oglensky & Martha Gever, *Glass Ceilings and Open Doors: Women's Advancement in the Legal Profession,* A Report to the Committee on Women in the Profession, The Association of the Bar of the City of New York, 1995 Fordham L. Rev. 291, 388 (quote). *See also* Elizabeth McGuire, *Still Seeking Perfect Balance,* N.Y. Times, August 11, 1998, at A23.

6. *See* President's State of the Union Address to Congress, ___ Weekly Comp. Pres. Doc. ___ (Jan. 19, 1999) *available in* Federal News Serv. (Jan. 20, 1999) at A12 (full text); S14247 Cong. Rec. S14247 (daily ed. Cot. 5, 1994) (CEWA); 29 U.S.C. $1001 et seq. (ERISA); 26 U.S.C.A. $3304 (approval by IRC of state unemployment benefits laws); 29 U.S.C. $2601 et seq. (FMLA).

7. *See* Jane Waldfogel, *Understanding the "Family Gap" in Pay for Women with Children,* 12 J. Econ. Persp. 137 (1998); Katharine T. Bartlett & Angela P. Harris, *Gender and Law: Theory, Doctrine, Commentary* 157 (1998).

8. Phone interview with Ron Hetrick, Bureau of Labor Statistics, August, 1997 (over a million workplaces).

9. Burchard v. Garay, 42 Cal. 3d 531, 229 Cal. Rptr. 800, 724 P. 2d 486 (1986)("cruel practice").

10. California Federal Savings & Loan Ass'n v. Guerra, 479 U.S. 272 (1987).

11. *See* Vicki Schultz, *Reconceptualizing Sexual Harrassment,* 107 Yale L. J. 1683, 1755–96 (1998).

12. For an insightful treatment of this topic, see Tracy E. Higgins, *Anti-Essentialism, Relativism, and Human Rights,* 19 Harv. Women's L. J. 89 (1996).

INDEX